Post-Fascist Japan

Post-Fascist Japan

Political Culture in Kamakura after the Second World War

Laura Hein

BLOOMSBURY ACADEMIC
LONDON · NEW YORK · OXFORD · NEW DELHI · SYDNEY

BLOOMSBURY ACADEMIC
Bloomsbury Publishing Plc
50 Bedford Square, London, WC1B 3DP, UK
1385 Broadway, New York, NY 10018, USA

BLOOMSBURY, BLOOMSBURY ACADEMIC and the Diana logo
are trademarks of Bloomsbury Publishing Plc

First published 2018
Paperback edition first published 2020

A catalogue record for this book is available from the British Library.

Library of Congress Cataloging-in-Publication Data
Names: Hein, Laura Elizabeth, author.
Title: Post-Fascist Japan : political culture in Kamakuraafter the Second
World War /Laura Hein.
Description: London ; New York : Bloomsbury Academic,2018. | Series: SOAS
Studies inModern and Contemporary Japan | Includes bibliographical
references andindex.
Identifiers: LCCN 2017043750 (print) | LCCN 2018015807(ebook) | ISBN
9781350025790(PDF eBook) | ISBN 9781350025813 (EPUB eBook) | ISBN
9781350025806(hardback : alk. paper)
Subjects: LCSH: Kamakura-shi (Japan)–Politics andgovernment. |
Japan--Politicsand government–1945-1989.
Classification: LCC DS897.K3 (ebook) | LCC DS897.K3 H452018 (print) | DDC
306.20952/136–dc23
LC record available at https://lccn.loc.gov/2017043750

ISBN: HB: 978-1-3500-2580-6
PB: 978-1-3501-2650-3
ePDF: 978-1-3500-2579-0
eBook: 978-1-3500-2581-3

Series: SOAS Studies in Modern and Contemporary Japan

Typeset by Integra Software Services Pvt. Ltd.

To find out more about our authors and books visit
www.bloomsbury.com and sign up for our newsletters.

*For Vinca and Cora and their generation—with apologies from mine.
Try to fight less with the people who share your values.*

Contents

List of Figures

Acknowledgments

Writing these acknowledgments brings home how deeply embedded I am in my transnational scholarly community. The list of people who have expanded my thinking, enriched my knowledge, and corrected my errors reads very much like a comprehensive roster of the Japan Studies field. I name here only some of the many individuals to whom I owe gratitude.

In Kamakura, Emi Hirata at the Kamakura City Central Public Library, and Yoshino Miyako both shared their deep knowledge of the city and their extensive human networks. Hashizume Yukiome, Hattori Hiroaki, Hijikata Yukue, Hori Takahiko, Katō Shigeo, Koizumi Chikataka, Mizusawa Tsutomu at the Museum of Modern Art, Kamakura & Hayama, Nakamura Teruko, Watanabe Akira, and Yamanouchi Shizuo at the Kamakura Museum of Literature shared their memories and clear-eyed analyses. Kazu Mori always welcomed me home.

In Tokyo, I benefited from the indispensable advice of Amakawa Akira, Aoki Shigeru, Mark Caprio, Katalin Ferber, Fujiwara Kiichi, Katō Tetsurō, Jeff Kingston, Koseki Shōichi, Nicola Liscutin, Moriguchi Chiaki, Nishizawa Tamotsu, Odaka Konosuke, Okuda Hiroko, the late Ōuchi Tsutomu, Lawrence Repeta, Sakai Kunihide, Makiko, and Yū, Sakai Tadayasu at the Setagaya Museum of Art, Sasamoto Yukue, Shibata Tokue, Shimizu Hiroshi, the late Takemae Eiji, Tanaka Atsushi at the Tokyo Bunka Zaidan Kenkyūjo, Tsuru Tsuyoshi, Wakimura Tarō, Emiko Yamanashi, Yoshimi Shunya, Yoshimi Yoshiaki, and Yui Daizaburō. Narita Ryūichi and Osawa Machiko graciously hosted me in 2009 as a Visiting Researcher at Japan Women's University, while Nakamura Naofumi, Gregory Noble, and Uno Shigeki offered a collegial home at the University of Tokyo Institute for Social Science in Fall 2011. In Yokohama, Fukagai Yasunori, Kagesato Tetsurō, Koizumi Chikataka, Kamibayashi Tokurō at the Institute for Public Policy in Kanagawa Prefecture, Yokohama, and Kubo Takao were all compelling interviewees. Tanabe Kōtarō generously shared his work on Masaki Chifuyu. The authors of *Shōnan no Tanjō* introduced me to their world. In Kansai, Fujiwara Tetsuya, Julie Higashi, Hosoya Masahiro, Iguchi Kazuki at the Kyoto Prefectural Archive, Rebecca Jennison, Kurihara Nanako, both Matsuda Takeshi and Matsuda Ken Takeshi, Miyamoto Ken'ichi, and Murakami Mitsuhiko provided sage advice, as did Mitani Wataru of the Tanabe City Art Museum. At Osaka University, Sugita

Yoneyuki and Nakano Kōtarō, aka Rocky, each in his distinctive way, made every trip there a professional pleasure, particularly the three years I spent as Sugita's guest as a Specially Appointed Professor of Research.

In London, I very much enjoyed a stint as a 2015–2016 Centenary Fellow at SOAS, University of London, and the stimulating colleagues there: my host, Christopher Gerteis, and also Stephen Dodd, Janet Hunter, Alejandra Irigoin, Griseldis Kirsch, Angus Lockyer, Helen Macnaughtan, Timon Screech, Naoko Shimazu, and Sarah Teasley. Mark Pendleton at Sheffield University and Mami Mizutori at the Sainsbury Institute for the Study of Japanese Arts and Cultures introduced me to their lively circles of colleagues. I spent April 2007 at the University of Leiden, Modern East Asia Research Center, as a Visiting Professor. Thanks go to Katarzyna Cwiertka, Curtis Gayle, Naomi Goto, Christopher Goto-Jones, and Rikki Kersten for enlivening that opportunity.

Closer to home, Andrew Barshay, Peter Carroll, Annika Culver, Timothy S. George, Christopher Gerteis, James Huffman, Ann Sherif, and Peter Siegenthaler read complete drafts of the manuscript. Lonny Carlile, John W. Dower, Andrew Gordon, Hiromi Mizuno, Tessa Morris-Suzuki, Patrick Noonan, Mark Selden, Franziska Seraphim, and Amy Stanley each read parts of it. I know how much work that is. Thank you.

Among others, E. Taylor Atkins, Beth Berry, Daniel Botsman, Jan Bardsley, Rebecca Copeland, Kevin Doak, Alexis Dudden, Steven Ericson, Norma Field, Sabine Früstück, Glen Fukushima, Sheldon Garon, Carol Gluck, Jeffrey Hanes, Ellen Hammond, Akiko Hashimoto, David Howell, Ted Hughes, Edward Lincoln, Vera Mackie, Michele Mason, Masuda Hajimu, Laura Miller, Mark Metzler, Hiromi Mizuno, Tessa Morris - Suzuki, Jordan Sand, Mark Ravina, Franziska Seraphim, Julia Adeney Thomas, Mark Tilton, Hitomi Tonomura, Stephen Vlastos, Samuel Yamashita, and Louise Young have all been great colleagues whose ideas enrich my own. Audiences at University of Washington, Seattle, SOAS, Osaka University, University of Tokyo, Yokohama National University, the Social Science History Association, and the Association for Asian Studies have allowed me to test my ideas.

Northwestern provides an intellectually stimulating *moriawase* of relevant scholarship, including by Michael J. Allen, Kevin Boyle, Peter Carroll, Haydon Cherry, Alexa Deleon, Ben Frommer, Jon Glassman, Daniel Immerwahr, Tessie Liu, Melissa Macauley, Sarah Maza, Austin Parks, Michael Sherry, Lauren Stokes, Emilie Takeyama, and Helen Tilley. My Japan Studies colleagues, especially Andrew Leong, Patrick Noonan, and Amy Stanley, add a whole new exciting dimension to my intellectual life. One of the side benefits of this project was the opportunity to work with art historians. In addition to the people mentioned above, special thanks to Kendall Brown, S. Hollis Clayson, Huey Copeland, the late Brian A. Curran, Christine Guth, Asato Ikeda, Justin Jesty, Maki Kaneko, Aya Louisa McDonald, Christopher Reed, Ming Tiampo, Yasuko Tsuchikane, Toshio Watanabe, Gennifer Weisenfeld, Bert Winther-Tamaki, and Alicia Volk.

The Fulbright organization offered its amazing support with a 2008–2009 Fulbright Senior Research Award to Japan. May it long survive. Daniel Zellner and Dru Parrish at Academic Technologies digitized some of the images and Timothy S. George provided the gorgeous photographs of Kamakura. Vinca Merriman copy-edited and proof-read the manuscript.

Introduction: Post-Fascist Political Culture

Failed wars can lead to either intense polarization with recurrent violence or a new direction. Japan after the Second World War exemplifies the latter path. To an impressive degree, in late 1945 many Japanese people turned their energies toward creating a new political culture, that is, new social and political behaviors, policies, and institutions that would give young people skills—ones they themselves had not possessed—to prevent an erosion of civil liberties at home and coercive policies abroad. Many Japanese concluded that the Asia-Pacific War had been not only stupid and shameful but also unnecessary, and their regret at their own complicity in that disaster fueled a tremendous sense of purpose for them. For that reason, more than is commonly realized, they took responsibility for transforming their national political culture. The result was a far more equitable, democratic, and peaceful society than before surrender. The failed states and endemic violence around the world today make clear the rarity of this achievement.

In stark contrast to the presurrender years, by the 1960s Japan achieved a high standard of living for essentially all citizens, a widely accepted system to provide opportunity for young people, and flawed but functional democratic governance. Japan also managed to avoid armed conflict with other nations. These are no small things. On the other hand, in the twenty-first century, Japan seems stuck in neutral, with institutions that work fairly well for older people but are failing young adults. Japan today features growing economic inequality, heightened insularity, and startlingly dysfunctional political leadership.[1] Most of all, the optimism and energy displayed by so many Japanese in the first postwar decades have dwindled away, making Japan a sadder place than its postwar self.

What caused these outcomes? The central argument of this book is that the seismic shift of the first few postwar years and the dynamism of the next two decades were due in significant part to the actions of elite professional left-wing Japanese working through a variety of organizations, often at the local level, and their long-term engagements with more conservative leaders, the general public, and the American occupiers. The individuals highlighted here formed a particularly cohesive internal community that sustained and propelled them. They also framed nearly all their professional and public actions in political terms, leading to new narratives of historical change and national identity and—even more crucially— new institutional structures, all designed to forestall what they saw as the return of fascism. Much of this work was done from 1945 to about 1980, the timeframe of this book, but their activities infused a broad variety of institutions with democratic practices that were visible everywhere into the twenty-first century, but are now being dismantled.

My primary example is the overlapping sets of individuals who built local institutions in the small city of Kamakura, an hour's train ride south of Tokyo. Some of my protagonists were long-time Kamakura residents while others were relative newcomers, but when they sought to create new intellectual spaces, they did so in a real geographic space, one that—as they understood—imposed its own specific opportunities and challenges to people seeking change. Kamakura has been a religious, artistic, and intellectual center for nearly a millennium. Modern Kamakura, with a population of 173,331 at its postwar peak, has long been in Tokyo's powerful orbit, but is also distant enough to forge its own political and cultural identity.

Kamakura was also one of the first places in Japan to be re-imagined as modern in the nineteenth century. While Kamakura's boosters celebrated the city's rich cultural past, they did so in a thoroughly contemporary manner. Like all modern places, as both Edward Soja and Prasenjit Duara have argued, Kamakura is socially constructed from within and without and, as Soja stresses for cities in general, its urban character not only shaped the lives of its inhabitants but also contributed to their effectiveness and creativity.[2] Kamakura's distinctiveness as a place that encouraged cultural, artistic, and intellectual innovation was one of the perennial resources available for mobilization, both during and after the war. The city became a site where ideas about postwar Japanese national culture were worked out together with local culture, in part because many of the individuals most closely associated with Kamakura also operated on the national and even international stages. To put the point another way, Kamakura's local modernity simultaneously challenged and reaffirmed generalizations about what it meant to be Japanese.[3] Kamakura was by no means the only locality where more democratic institutions developed, but it was an important one.

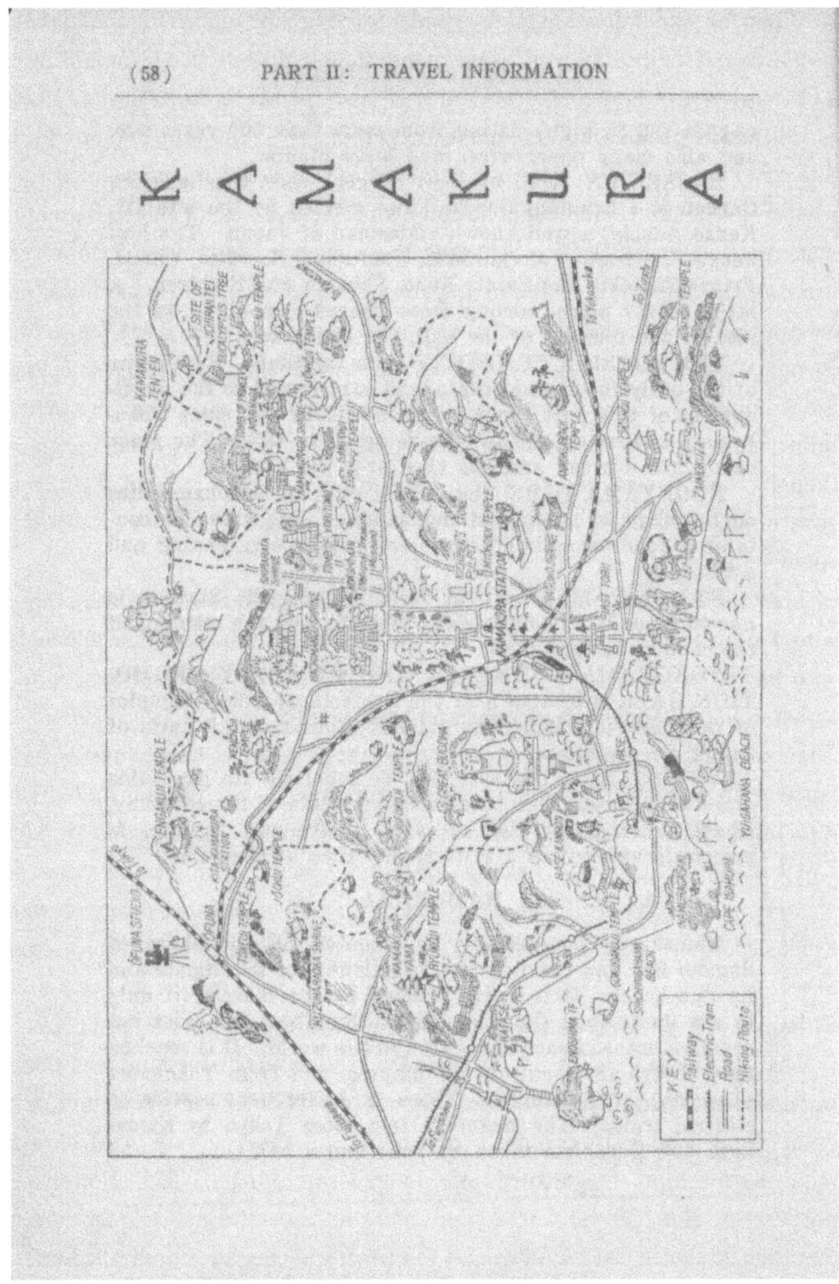

Figure I.1 Map of Kamakura, showing the train lines, main roads, the most famous religious sites, the beach, and several walking paths. 1953. Used by permission of JTB Publishing.

When the war ended, Kamakura residents took many actions to rebuild their own lives and their social world. One manifestation, discussed in Chapter 2, was a new university, the Kamakura Akademia, that opened its doors in May 1946, established by people who were not teachers themselves but wanted to provide a different kind of education to their youth. They believed that local identity was itself an important resource that helped people feel secure and able to trust and constructively engage each other. After the war, they consciously remobilized these local ties for new ends and anchored them to new local institutions. As Saigusa Hiroto, the president of that university, explained in 1951, engaging "people who get their energy from places such as Kamakura and Yokohama, that is, the political potency (*yūryoku*) of local places" was key to his vision of a better future.[4] Like the other cultural and civic leaders discussed in this book, Saigusa thought the Japanese people should have more forcefully resisted their own government's acts of repression at home and war abroad and that local identity could help them do so.

Many of the most motivated people in Kamakura and elsewhere were those who had turned a critical eye on society long before the shock of defeat, people who had been jailed, lost their jobs, or watched as friends were silenced for activities that had only a few years earlier been both legal and socially acceptable. Their own experience also often sensitized them to social inequalities within Japan, such as the fact that Okinawans were required to sacrifice far more than were others. They strove to both heal the damage done during the war and chart a new direction for postwar society—and they expended astonishing amounts of energy in the service of these goals at a time when many other Japanese were exhausted. Their labors established a set of practices that justified and protected peace, democracy, and fairness in Japan. They also accomplished a great deal without ever capturing control of the national government—the biggest prize.

The vast literature on historical memory can help us understand why these wartime critics had such an outsized postwar impact. Wars—and remembrance of them—always involve contests over meaning, because war's aftermath always requires some kind of reconciliation. And the terms of that reconciliation shape postwar societies.[5] Bigger wars require more retrospective management given that they disrupt social arrangements to a greater degree than do limited ones, for example by sending most young men overseas for lengthy tours of duty. Since the 1931–1945 Asia-Pacific War mobilized all of Japan's resources, it forced changes in every social institution. Moreover, military defeat complicated remembrance of the domestic as well as the international dimensions of that conflict. As Akiko Hashimoto has cogently argued, in defeated nations, war remembrance is "ultimately irreconcilable and incapable of engendering a coherent, unified account for the nation." That conflict over the war's meaning created obstacles to "memory work," in which Japanese people "reformulated narratives that make … self-knowledge coherent and emotionally resonant."[6] This as-yet-unresolved desire for coherence and emotional resonance has meant that Japanese people have continued to revise the narrative of the war to this day.

To be clear, I am not arguing that the wartime critics made postwar Japan alone. On the contrary, the force of their arguments was enhanced by the actions of others—especially the new power of working-class people to collectively chart their own futures through labor unions, the ballot box, and the practices of everyday life. Likewise, women took advantage of the new legal structure to simply stop accepting many of the sacrifices formerly assigned to them by their male relatives. The men—and they were all men—profiled here also benefited from the backing of the Occupation forces in the early years. Considerable reform would have happened without them. Nonetheless, as long as they were at the heart of Japanese political culture, these individuals consistently mobilized public opinion against remilitarization, social inequities, and cultural essentialism, while simultaneously reshaping most of the institutions they touched. Even today, their inventiveness, boldness, and generosity are striking. So are their snobbery, their pride, and their sexism.

Forestalling the return of fascism

From 1945, the attention of my protagonists was riveted on their conviction that they personally had survived a fascist era and also had a responsibility to destroy it—a stance I call "post-fascism" rather than anti-fascism because their response focused on the processes revealed by direct experience as much as on abstract theory. (I reserve the term for people who opposed fascism, unlike Gaspar Miklos Tamas, who uses it to mean something closer to neofascism, that is, a new expression of fascist ideas.[7]) As the Kyoto-based literature scholar Mashita Shin'ichi explained, "we learned from our double dose of tragedy—fascism and war," stressing that these were two distinct calamities.[8] When he spoke of fascism, Mashita meant the justifications for imprisoning him which included "spiritual renovation" of the nation. He was engaging directly with fascist ideas and social mobilization strategies themselves. After 1945, many thoughtful Japanese continued to take fascism seriously as an ideology that had succeeded because it had addressed real problems.

Just as in Europe, fascism had developed from the common view that democracy had failed, politically, economically, and culturally, and, furthermore, that fascism was the only viable alternative to colonial and working-class radicalism. As Reto Hofmann's recent book shows, many Japanese were interested in fascism in the 1920s and 1930s, attracted to the dynamic persona of Benito Mussolini, the economic successes of both Italy and Germany, and the ways that fascist ideology promised to energize and reunite a divided people.[9] And, while this ideology stressed Japanese uniqueness, the anxiety that powered it was both transnational and generic, since fascist regimes everywhere proclaimed their uniqueness in essentially the same ways. Interwar fascism was a fundamentally modern nationalist movement, hostile to both liberal democracy and communism, and, in Japan, as elsewhere, fascists championed violence in order to create a hierarchical community without visible dissent. Maggie Clinton has recently made a similar argument for China in the same period, although Chinese fascists foregrounded anti-imperialism more than did Japanese ones.[10] In Japan, even before the war, men such as economists Ōuchi Hyōe, Arisawa Hiromi, Ōmori Yoshitarō, Wakimura Yoshitarō, and Masaki Chifuyu had already explained the rise of fascist ideology and policies as the result of the modern processes of capitalism. In their view Japan was part of a common global experience, and they had a very large readership for their comparative analyses, both in the early 1930s and again after 1945.[11] Unfortunately, the argument that Japan's war was the result of its stunted and failed attempts to properly modernize is today all too often treated as if it was once universally accepted but this was never true.

The reasoning of the leftists who saw Japan as a modern society—and one dangerously flirting with fascism—was typified by a September 1937 essay on food shortages in Germany by Kamakura resident Ōmori Yoshitarō. Ōmori, an economist, argued that military spending was causing inflation, which reduced civilian purchasing power, meaning that Germans "are eating potatoes instead of meat and making their bread with corn." He went on to warn that Japan was in danger of triggering the same unwelcome substitutions, explicitly predicting that this scenario would become "the economic base of Japanese fascism."[12] Decades later, the official postwar history of Kamakura City opened its chapter on the war years with an analysis that echoed Ōmori's. When in the 1930s the Japanese government expanded military, rather than domestic, spending, it explained, "as one would expect, the ensuing chronic economic hard times led to a collapse in the standard of living for farmers and workers, intensifying class conflict and sparking recurring waves of repression, as well as the advance of the 'monopoly stage' of capitalism. This led to the march down the path of fascism."[13]

Nor were the economists alone. Tosaka Jun, another widely read intellectual, argued along similar lines in the early 1930s. Historians Harry Harootunian, Naoki Sakai, and their students have brought Tosaka's work to the forefront of Japanese studies in recent years precisely because he developed a sophisticated critique of Japanese fascism in the 1930s, treated Japan as part of the modern world, and identified the weaknesses in liberal thought that made it an inadequate barrier to fascism's spread. They concur with Tosaka that the rapid pace of change that characterizes modern life and the intrinsic unevenness of capitalist development acted to generate anxiety about contemporary society.[14] Fascism, or "reactionary modernism," as Jeffrey Herf usefully termed it, was the panicked response.[15] Indeed, right-wing nationalists in 1930s Japan themselves were torn between claiming fascism as a satisfyingly modern form of nationalism and rejecting it as intrinsically Italian and therefore inappropriate for domestic consumption, meaning that Japan still had to invent its own modern path. In Reto Hofmann's words, not only did fascism and nationalism operate as "two ideologies that were at the same time conflicting and overlapping," but this internal incoherence over national uniqueness was part of the logic of fascism itself.[16] In short, the modern nature of fascism was obvious to many Japanese themselves at the time.

More precisely, the people who saw fascism as the outcome of capitalism conceived of it fundamentally as ruling-class backlash motivated by fear of revolt. While the larger population was mobilized through celebrations of nativism and fear of foreigners, the true benefits were enjoyed elsewhere. Visual and performance artist Murayama Tomoyoshi, who was more interested in cultural than economic trends, thought fascism sprang from elites' unwillingness to provide social support to their compatriots in interwar Germany, Italy, and Japan, indeed, from their total lack of empathy for them. He had visited Weimar Germany where he was much influenced by visual artists George Grosz and Otto Dix, enjoying both their pointed social commentary and their eye-catching imagery.[17] Ōmori, Tosaka, and Murayama all believed that fascism was produced by and benefited elites at the expense of others, making its promises of national unity a cruel hoax.

They also saw the problem as *both* an institutional *and* an emotional and cultural one. The intervening step in Ōmori's 1937 economic analysis, for example, was that working-class desperation would trigger elite anxiety, leading to repression. While capitalist instability was rooted in massive global political-economic institutions, Ōmori believed the real damage was done by the desire to allay anxiety. Ōmori's 1937 analysis meshes well with two different streams

Figure I.2 Ōmori Yoshitarō was among the many writers and artists who moved to Kamakura in late 1920s. They patronized Kamakura's growing number of bookstores and coffee shops, such as this one. Ōmori published on a broad range of topics from fiscal policy to film criticism, and warned against fascism until his arrest in late 1937. Ca. 1931. Used by permission of Ei Masako. Photograph courtesy of Kamakura City Central Public Library.

of today's scholarship, which typically focus on either the institutional or the cultural-intellectual nature of fascism. Michael Mann, in the institutional camp, has recently found that European fascists gained power in places where elites most over-reacted to the twinned threats of social disorder and leftist political muscle.[18] Mann rests his sociological analysis on Jeffrey Herf's older scholarship mentioned above that demolished the arguments that fascism most attracted shopkeepers and rural small-holders and that it was a manifestation of underdeveloped modernity in Germany. Herf showed that rather than a movement of the nostalgic petit bourgeoisie, as famously argued by Marxists, "fascism was a movement of the lesser intelligentsia," that is, the educated elite. Peter Hayes makes a similar point for the smaller group who actively directed the slaughter of Europe's Jews. Indeed, three decades ago Yoshimi Yoshiaki found that precisely the same kind of people were the most enthusiastic mobilizers of their compatriots in Japan, since they already played an outsized role in shaping Japan's political culture.[19]

Michael Mann has shown that, cross-culturally, fascist movements' core constituencies everywhere are young men in higher-educational, military, and—especially—paramilitary organizations, including veterans' associations, in part because young men are far more likely to think they will prevail using violence than are other groups.[20] While Mann himself concludes that Japan was not fascist because paramilitary gangs never overwhelmed the official armed forces, it seems to me that the Japanese Imperial Army in the 1930s was both so independent of civilian control and so faction-ridden that it functioned much like the bands of paramilitary thugs of southern and central Europe.[21] Moreover, given that the Army High Command very nearly succeeded in carrying out its plan to lead the entire Japanese population—men, women, and children—into "glorious self-destruction," the nihilism and "pursuit of a transcendent and cleansing nation-statism" that Mann locates in the paramilitary surely characterized the Imperial Japanese Army itself by 1945. When units of the formal military system no longer fear being disciplined, they have no reason to create an ostensibly separate organization, another argument Yoshimi Yoshiaki made long ago in *Grass Roots Fascism*. This logic is also similar to Kenneth Ruoff's in *Japan's Imperial Zenith*, who argues that Japan fit the fascist condition of a charismatic leader because the *cult of the emperor* functioned much as did celebrations of charismatic leaders in Italy and Germany, even though the emperor as an individual did not.[22]

After the war, this elite and military over-reaction had intense personal meaning for its survivors. When Ōmori was imprisoned for the publication described above, it marked a grim "signpost on the road to fascism" for his friends.[23] Neither Ōmori nor Tosaka lived past 1945, both dying of medical neglect, Tosaka in prison and Ōmori shortly after early release due to the gravity of his illness. Later, when their colleagues focused on the attitudes of elite Japanese, they did so not because other people seemed less important but because they thought this group had caused their friends' deaths. Their Herculean efforts to democratize the institutions through which all Japanese interacted was a form of commemoration for their fallen comrades.[24]

Meanwhile, precisely because they were painfully aware that fascism had been popular, these individuals focused on precisely how all kinds of people had been mobilized to support it. They recognized that, as Mark Mazower stressed for Europe, "Capitalism does not create feelings of belonging," while fascism did, explaining why so many Japanese had thought accepting it would lead to a better society.[25] Mazower's focus on emotion meshes closely with Alan Tansman's recent argument that fascist aesthetics drove changes in political and economic institutions rather than the other way around in Japan. Tansman suggests that it is more useful to think of fascism "as an ideology that sought to intervene in culture" than as "an established political system."[26] He drew on several studies to demonstrate "the government's efforts to instill daily life with an ideology of beauty and purity," creating aesthetic pressure to acquiesce in war and repression. The liveliest example, in a chapter by Aaron Skabelund, shows how "the symbol of a loyal dog [Hachiko] acquired pedagogic force for promulgating values of racial purity and national essence."[27] This emotionally driven aesthetics is how the general population learned to like fascism, despite the obvious harm to them of fascist political and economic policies. As do Mann, Hofmann, and Yoshimi, Mazower and Tansman reject the argument that fascism was insufficiently modern but they foreground affective, discursive, and cultural processes rather than political-economic ones. Affection for animals, rather than either mass rallies or an embrace of "potatoes instead of meat," was a typical pathway by which a broader group of Japanese first accepted fascist priorities in this stream of analysis. Decades earlier my protagonists also paid close attention to this emotional dimension because they thought fascism had assuaged fears among Japanese that were understandable although overblown.

In retrospect, postwar Japanese people often felt most ashamed of having gloried in the emotional fantasy that violence and death in service to a community were beautiful. Kamakura-based novelist and popular historian Osaragi Jirō later recognized that he had indulged in what Tansman, following Susan Sontag, has identified as the core fascist aesthetic, one that "glorifies [personal] surrender, exalts mindlessness, and glamorizes death."[28] In 1939 Osaragi was awed by the demeanor of a group of Hitler Youth members who visited Tokyo, Kamakura, and Kyoto. He was most impressed by their handsome healthy bodies, "like saplings in the forest," and by the degree to which the 14- to 18-year-olds were physically attuned to each other on the sports field. As he wrote, "they have had flawless training so they move in total concert with each other." At other moments during the war, he celebrated the physicality and manliness of soldiers deployed in Manchuria and the "admirable deportment" of kamikaze pilots, sounding much like the Europeans of the same era described by George Mosse in *The Image of Man: The Creation of Modern Masculinity*.[29]

At the time Osaragi and other Japanese hoped that the sincerity and selflessness implied by serving up these handsome young men as battlefield sacrifices would guarantee victory. Afterward these community leaders felt less that they had been tricked than forced to acknowledge a more painful reality: they had lost their sense of moral proportion. Precisely because all aspects of society had been mobilized for war and subsumed into fascist culture, everything was already tangled together in a highly politicized way. Unraveling those knots became an obligation for postwar Japanese like Osaragi. We know that he personally felt compelled to do so because he served as a councilor in the first postwar Cabinet, headed by Prince Higashikuni Naruhiko, for two months in early autumn 1945. Osaragi spent most of his energy on repealing the Peace Preservation Laws, which had legalized the persecution of leftists.[30] His regret at having supported a wanton waste of human life served to retrospectively mark the war years as fascist.

When Japanese people who lived through those years remembered their dead, that commemorative act also rekindled the memory of how easily those warped priorities had prevailed. Today, attention to the ways that Japanese national subjects were abused by the wartime government is dismissed as self-exculpatory "victim consciousness." But such comments functioned for decades primarily to remind other Japanese that the war years had also been an era of fascism, particularly when the dead being remembered were in prison rather than in uniform.[31] And, as long as this context remained dominant, the topic of domestic repression opened an avenue to enable, rather than block, self-criticism about Japanese aggression in Asia.

The post-fascist "community of contrition"

When the war ended, Japan's small educated elite continued to play a central role in political culture, with the exception of career military men.[32] The wartime

Figure I.3 Osaragi Jirō (the pen name of Nojiri Haruhiko) and Ōmori Yoshitarō shared an interest in photography and this snapshot of Osaragi is by Ōmori. Ca. 1931. Used by permission of Ei Masako. Photograph courtesy of Kamakura City Central Public Library.

dissidents in these pages were among the tiny fraction of men—and handful of women—who had risen through the prewar educational ranks, generally emerging with degrees from Japan's best universities. Sociologist Takeuchi Yō reports that the premier gateway of educational achievement, the First Higher School, educated only about 300 students at any one time in the 1920s. As a consequence, left-wingers whose politics were far out of the mainstream frequently had slept and studied next to the men who later persecuted them.[33] While the architects of the war and their critics later came to think of each other as dangerous fanatics, these shared teen-aged experiences meant they also had a great deal in common. Masaki Chifuyu, for example, wrote that one of the most painful features of incarceration for him was that several of his jailors had been his middle school classmates. In intimate ways, they knew a great deal about the people who ran Japan during the war.[34]

Somehow, beginning in late 1945, the members of this generation had to rebuild their deeply damaged relationships along lines radically different from those dominant just a few months earlier. Mashita Shin'ichi, who was arrested in 1937 for leftist activity, remained under police surveillance until the last day of the war. He later explained how traumatic that experience had been and why he thought of it as surviving fascism. During the conflict, he had avoided thinking about Japan's impending defeat because he was afraid he would be murdered by the police. "At that critical point I didn't know what was likely to happen to people such as myself who were on a list to be taken into 'protective custody.' I was not sure I would have survived that moment." Given that the military police, working with Tokyo officers, had used the opportunity of the 1923 earthquake to detain and kill Ōsugi Sakae, Itō Noe, their preschooler American nephew, and ten labor organizers—and had evaded punishment—his fears that the police would respond violently to defeat were hardly paranoid.[35]

Mashita spent the day before the surrender at the Kyoto headquarters of the Special Higher Police, summoned to "help them with their enquiries." Increasingly anxious as the conflict drew to an end, the police had seized books and papers from Westerners living in the region and required Mashita to search for signs of Jewish Freemasonry, even though they were under no illusions that he shared their political views. On this occasion, probably with advance knowledge of the surrender, the Section Chief, a tall, painfully thin man of about Mashita's age, walked close to him and murmured quietly, "So in the end, we've lost to you people," stressing the political antagonism that accompanied the external war.[36]

These personal experiences explain the postwar priorities chosen by men such as Mashita. As Jay Winter and Emmanuel Sivan argued, collective remembrance always results from concrete actions taken by social groups who compete with each other to publicly represent the past. Winter and Sivan borrow a term from anthropology to explain that these sets of individuals "constitute 'networks of complimentarity'" that provide a sense of internal community, which, in turn, becomes the basis for a new narrative, one that, if successful, is adopted more widely. The Japanese individuals highlighted here formed a particularly cohesive internal community soldered together by their collective outrage at their own treatment mingled with acknowledgment of two uncomfortable facts: others had fared far worse, and they too all had in some ways supported fascism and war. As Winter and Sivan conclude, "Each group highlights elements close to its own traumatized members," and the journey from star student to jailbird was the exact center of trauma for them.[37]

Given the strong evidence that their experiences had indeed been traumatic, it is noteworthy that these people typically faulted themselves as well as others for having permitted fascism's rise. As Murayama explained in 1975, individuals who had been persecuted felt liberated by defeat but also "to a greater or lesser degree, I think they all felt that they too bore some responsibility for the war, through their own cowardice or mistakes or weaknesses. So to make amends for that responsibility, they felt even more strongly the need to take action and join together to create a future. I am certainly one such person."[38] Mashita too lingered on the unsettling fact that he could not be sure any real differences between himself and his jailers existed. In 1975, Mashita commented that during the darkest years he spent in prison and police interrogation rooms, he retained the belief that "people cannot live without freedom and love…The people who have it snatched from them sooner or later always get it back." When "the fifteen years of fascism and war" were happening, "it was nothing to laugh about but in the end the ones who can laugh are those of us who did not hold a blackness deep in our hearts. Or maybe it was because we could perceive that inner blackness."[39] The sting in the tail of his remarks seems designed to remind himself as well as others that he had not been immune to fascism's appeal, despite having been persecuted in its name.

Their sense of themselves as simultaneously victims and perpetrators is central to the story of this particular "network of complimentarity," and is accurately captured by Andrew Barshay and J. Victor Koschmann's characterization of leftist intellectuals as comprising a postwar "community of contrition." As Koschmann's foremost example, political philosopher Maruyama Masao, explained, the key problem impelling him and "most of my intellectually active colleagues" was a desire to understand why Japanese people, especially intellectuals, had been so willing to accept "the onrush of a blindly nationalistic militarism inspired by the crudest beliefs."[40] Truly understanding those motivations and creating better responses seemed the central postwar—and post-fascist—task to all these men.

The willingness to include themselves in their mental lists of fascist enablers demands our attention for several reasons. One is the impressive confidence and the even more impressive sense of social responsibility revealed by doing so. Those qualities fundamentally flowed from these individuals' educational experience, professional training, and social status, all of which inclined them toward such a stance. While their elitism often grated on others, it fueled their energy and honesty. Another is the rarity of this response. Tony Judt finds little to match it in postwar Europe, arguing that the "distrust of short-term memory, the search for serviceable myths of anti-Fascism—for a Germany of anti-Nazis, a France of Resisters or a Poland of victims—was the most important invisible legacy of World War Two in Europe."[41] A third reason was that it felt true; it was easier to face the fact that everyone was a perpetrator at a moment when most Japanese also were absorbing the painful fact that the fascist promise of community had been built on a savage lie. By late 1944, military leaders had begun exhorting the entire population to engage in "glorious self-destruction" rather than surrender. This was the logical endpoint of fascist culture, and essentially every adult in the postwar years had to come to terms with their own participation—often enthusiastic—in attitudes and actions that had led so insistently to that undesirable end.

Interestingly, Czechoslovak President Vaclav Havel framed the task of his new government in very similar terms in 1990 when his country broke free from the Soviet bloc. After beginning his first speech by promising not to lie to his compatriots, as his predecessors routinely had, Havel said about their task, "The worst thing is that we live in a contaminated moral environment ... we are all—though naturally to differing extents—responsible for the operation of the totalitarian machinery. None of us is just its victim. We are all also its co-creator." But, Havel continued, acknowledging this responsibility was actually empowering. "If we realize this, then all the horrors that the new Czechoslovak democracy inherited will cease to appear so terrible. If we realize this, hope will return to our hearts."[42] In postwar Japan too, refusing to lie and acknowledging one's own complicity also meant recognizing one's own power.

When these individuals expressed discomfort at their own attraction to fascism's emotional and aesthetic pull, as they often did, they were crafting a new narrative and writing a new social contract that called on their compatriots to democratize every aspect of life. A central component of that new narrative was accepting the fact that identifying morally correct behavior—even retrospectively—is not just a difficult but is sometimes an impossible task. As Arisawa commented in 1958, "Young people often argue that the old liberals were inattentive and without a clear analysis, and so bear some of the blame for being overwhelmed by the militarists." But, he continued, "when I look from the perspective of my own life, I don't see any place where we could have had the decisive battle to protect liberalism. Things just gradually got worse. The postwar system built on respect for human rights will be harder to topple but we must be watchful. That, to me, is the lesson of our experience."[43] Moral righteousness was not only unattainable; searching for it was counter-productive.

Ienaga Saburō, another famously energetic member of the intellectual "community of contrition," also zeroed in on the difficulty he personally had in identifying when and how he should have behaved differently. Including himself in his critique, Ienaga explained that he wrote *The Pacific War* (pub. 1968, English 1978) because he had not known precisely when he should have refused to cooperate. As he explained in the preface,

> no one could live through those years without being directly involved in the war. Choices had to be made: To cooperate with the authorities? Opportunistically to make the best deal possible for oneself? To feign obedience and comply? To watch the war from the sidelines? To resist? Everyone confronted these choices in their daily thoughts and actions. Unless we look back at the decisions we made and consider whether we acted properly or not, we cannot lead a serious existence in the postwar world.[44]

Neither ideology nor morality offered a reliable compass out of the fascist swamp.

Masaki Chifuyu, who later became mayor of Kamakura as covered in Chapter 4, similarly recognized that his actions had supported the war effort and he too stressed his own postwar inability to find a clear line between cooperation and resistance, given the moral murkiness of the era. Even though Masaki's four-year stint in prison was traumatic, he described his war experience up until the moment of his arrest as much like that of other Japanese. While he had expected Japan's defeat as early as mid-1939, based on the grim economic statistics he faced every day at work, Masaki set himself apart from his countrymen in no other way. The implication from his memoirs is that if the war had gone on longer, all Japanese would have come to the same conclusion—and might have found themselves imprisoned too—and thus his quandary was much like theirs. Without minimizing his role in the war effort, Masaki wrote,

> My group in the research bureau [of the Cabinet Planning Agency] was not
> involved in activism at all. Rather, we felt a sense of crisis about Japanese civilian
> standards of living if the war was to continue. So we studied the Nazi socio-
> economic structure, proposed strengthening economic controls and so forth.
> Looking at it now, I cannot honestly say whether we truly were criticizing the
> war from a left-wing stance or were saying that a wartime economy that was
> half-heartedly capitalist wouldn't work out, and so we should intensify wartime
> controls.[45]

The police, however, read their ambivalence as treason, which was why they
were arrested in January 1941.

Arisawa, Ienaga, and Masaki's wartime dilemma was very like the one
identified by Timothy Brook for people ruled by foreign occupiers, and this
makes sense if we recognize the ways in which—for them—the Japanese conflict
was a civil war. With or without a violated national border, inhabitants faced "a
tangle of compromises" and retrospective difficulty with identifying "a middle
range between innocuity and damnation."[46] The problem, of course, was not just
that they were unsure when brave defiance would actually help their cause, but
also had trouble identifying the form that such defiance could even take. This
confusion too was what they meant by having survived fascism: they understood
that no one, no matter how committed an anti-fascist at the time, could have
lived through the 1930s and early 1940s in Japan without being "a co-creator" of
"a morally contaminated environment," to use Havel's phrase.

Perhaps the most constructive consequence of their stance that, in a complex
world, both moral murkiness and ideological inconsistency were inescapable
was that it made hypocrisy and inconsistency lesser issues. Ōuchi Hyōe made
this point in a famous essay when he described his guiding philosophy as
"watching how the wind blows before crossing a bridge," which, he explained,
meant that he surrounded himself with friends whose values and judgment he
trusted and he consulted them before taking important actions. As he wrote in
1951, "my younger friends see me as dishonest and shabby when they see me
check the weather… And they often quote Lenin at me." But "skillful weather
watching" is appropriate, given that "I don't know if the bridge is stone or wood
or whether the path across it heads straight or not. This is why my goal is to
become a consummate watcher of the weather." While Ōuchi thought Lenin's
moral and theoretical certainty had given Lenin the courage to reshape history,
he rejected such certainty for himself and for postwar Japan, instead relying on
advice from his "network of complimentarity."[47]

These insights had pragmatic implications. If surviving fascism meant recognizing that it was impossible to always discern the "right" course of action, then it made sense to work with anyone willing to accept some broad priorities: build a peaceful polity that provided adequately for all citizens without imposing means tests, morality tests, or loyalty tests. Moreover, these individuals—for good reason—feared that Japan would return to the intense polarization that had so recently led to repression at home and endless warfare abroad. If anxious recoil had been the original problem, then emotional reassurance to their former adversaries was a crucial part of the solution. This was one reason why so many of the men presented here valued practical solutions and open-ended dialogue above theoretical consistency.

In her study of Spanish attempts to come to terms with their own fascist past, Paloma Aguilar reports that Spanish Civil War (1936–1939) veterans not only expressed the same concern after Franco died in 1975 but also resolved it by offering the same kind of invitation. The people who had to live with their former enemies—that is, the Republican veterans who still resided in Spain—sought reconciliation with the ruling Nationalists. By contrast the ones in exile wanted the record to show that "the Francoists alone must bear all responsibility for the war." In Aguilar's analysis,

> The exiles appear to be obsessed by the fear of being forgotten, and the demand that the authorities should pay public homage to their fallen. They themselves acknowledge that…they are very reluctant to forgive and forget. In striking contrast, the [organization for Republican veterans within Spain] speaks in terms of reconciliation and forgiveness, the need to recognize that both sides must accept their share of the blame for the atrocities committed during the war… They insisted that the war was a fratricidal conflict, and that the time had come to transcend the trauma it had left.

The outcome of the post-fascist negotiations between the two sides still living in Spain was that "the political lesson drawn from the Civil War by nearly all Spaniards, whether of Republican or Nationalist extraction, is 'never again.'" Moreover, "during this same transition period, both Right and Left agreed that the bitterest aspects of the past should not be aired in public debate." The exiles, however, rejected every aspect of this compromise.[48] They were proud of their greater militancy, misreading the Spanish residents' careful community-building as cowardice. The Kamakura activists in these pages resembled the Republicans who still lived with Franco's fascist supporters more than they did the exiles.

The obliquely stated bargain

Like their Spanish counterparts and like Vaclav Havel, elite leftists in Japan struck a similar bargain: in exchange for cooperation in their post-fascist political project, they set aside their public claims to moral superiority. They framed this arrangement as redress: to younger generations of Japanese, to the Japanese population in general from educated elites as a class, and to the wider world. Their efforts explicitly included acknowledging the harm Japan did to Asians through empire and war, as discussed below. Of course, despite their polite public stance that they shared responsibility equally, when they asked for cooperation, they also perceived—and felt—it as redress to themselves personally. To caricaturize this project as "masochism," as do right-wing nationalist groups in Japan today, is to fundamentally misunderstand it psychologically as well as politically.[49] The postwar Japanese leftists were not rejecting their true identity as Japanese individuals in harmony with their nation-state. Rather, they were redrawing the boundaries of their community in ways that invited everyone to participate in reorienting the nation—and all modern societies—around their values.

This invitation solved a huge personal and ethical problem for the people they most pointedly addressed, individuals like Osaragi who had enthusiastically mobilized their compatriots in ways that later caused them considerable shame. Because intensive mobilization had required a vast amount of work, many jobs had opened up on the continent, where the repression was particularly cruel. Most people had enjoyed the adventure, making use of their professional training, feeling a heightened sense of collective purpose, and feeling appreciated. These psychic rewards—often accompanied by fat paychecks—were extremely seductive. As Louise Young, Janis Mimura, and Annika Culver have shown in the case of Manchuria, while people across the entire social spectrum responded to such inducements, Japan's leaders in the 1930s and 1940s worked particularly hard to enlist educated individuals, whose skills they most needed.[50]

Hijikata Teiichi, whose postwar career can be summarized as a thirty-year repudiation of his wartime actions, is one such person. Hijikata spent the war in Beijing, as discussed in Chapter 3, where he ran a government research center focused on Chinese Buddhist art, immersing himself in a subject that he found intellectually fascinating. Hijikata stressed the gloriousness of Asian art and the contributions he was making by bringing it to the world's attention. He was proud that his employers treated his labor as a significant contribution to empire-building. At the time, he told himself that his work benefited China and Japan alike, even though the evidence around him made that assertion less credible every day. Hijikata's job involved travel to remote Buddhist temples to catalog and photograph the art and he soon needed army protection from an increasingly hostile Chinese population. By the time he returned to Japan in December 1945, moreover, Hijikata had had a small taste of the hardships and terrors Chinese people faced. Like many others, the experiences of becoming a refugee and repatriate in the fall of 1945 showed him how quickly a secure middle-class existence could evaporate, destroying some of his confidence in his earlier judgments and causing him to rethink his attitudes about modern China as well as Japan. From that moment on, Hijikata dedicated his enormous intellectual creativity to re-narrating the modern global experience in ways that excised both fascist aesthetics and state authority from the stories of Japanese and global art history.

This postwar bargain within the "community of contrition" was continually re-invoked, but the negotiations can be hard to see today because one of the key mechanisms was oblique cues. Such obliqueness is nearly second nature to people accustomed to censorship and had been an intrinsic element of public life for decades in Japan. Both as writers and as readers, these individuals easily translated from innocuous terms to forbidden ones in their heads; "scientific" and "historical" were two common markers signaling to readers that a Marxist analysis followed, for example. Hatenaka Shigeo, editor of the general-interest magazine *Chūō Kōron,* noted that "Our readers during the war were far more progressive than we were. They understood even without our saying it. If we just suggested something, they grasped our liberal intentions. We could substitute empty circles for the dangerous words—words like *Communism*—and our readers were able to fill them in for themselves."[51] Hatenaka may have been overstating the liberalism his colleagues were projecting but he was certainly right that his readers were skilled at recognizing disguised heretical political commentary in an environment in which frankness would have resulted in the journal's ban.

For that matter, Japan boasts an exceptionally rich history of print culture that has long taught the reading public to search for meaning expressed via synonyms, homonyms, pictorial puns, or coded historical referents. These people were fully aware that censorship, as Rachel Hutchinson has recently framed it, necessarily involves creating relationships between the artist/author, the state and the audience. Popular publications as far back as Tokugawa Japan reveled in sarcastic commentary conveyed in indirect ways as part of this triangular relationship.[52] This history is one reason why such mental adjustments were often fun for twentieth-century Japanese, as was skirmishing with the censors. They chose aliases that their friends would appreciate and took pleasure in knowing who had really written something daring under a pen name. Wakimura Yoshitarō showed his amusement when he signed some of his columns for *Sekai* in the 1950s as UU, signaling "double U/W" to his bilingual peers. By then he could have used his own initials. In fact, since he also edited the column, he could have changed the policy of running essays without the by-line of contributors and signed his full name.[53] Instead, he enjoyed the elegant allusions, now that expressing oneself freely no longer risked jail time. While such intertextual commentary was by no means unique to Japan, postwar writers there enjoyed some particularly well-honed tools for their purposes.

Their history of living with censorship also helps explain why these individuals were comfortable with the polite fiction that neither they nor the people they interacted with had been enthusiastic about the war. They were all practiced in keeping track of when people were sidestepping the truth, and often noted such evasions in published conversations (*zadankai*) and other public spaces marked informal. Indeed, such border-patrolling commentary was part of the appeal of the *zadankai* genre, which typically functioned (and still functions) not just to remind readers that such things as an author's "complete works" or the official history of an organization were carefully curated cultural productions but also that an informed circle of readers was well aware of any self-flattering omissions. While all communities have mechanisms for such self-regulation—although not all to the same degree—in the distinctive political environment of postwar Japan, the juiciest gossip was not only about universal favorites such as love affairs and shady business dealings but also about the ways in which people had supported the war and the empire. When Wakimura conducted a long series of interviews with Yonekura Mamoru in 1991, he pointed out that Hashimoto Jin, an important Tokyo art dealer, elided his intimacy with notorious total-war theorist Ishihara Kanji in his history of the fine art business, despite otherwise boasting of his closeness with famous individuals.[54] Wakimura was highlighting the extent to which, in Leith Morton's words, "self-censorship is also a form of self-invention," and making it clear that, while Hashimoto was a personal friend of many decades, Wakimura was well aware of the artifice.[55] Theirs was a culture of oblique references and constant monitoring, but also expectations of moral ambiguity.

This system of oblique reminders—a central aspect of postwar public discourse—was generated by Japanese themselves as a way to acknowledge ambivalence and emotional overload, and to recognize that both speaker/writer and listener/reader shared a complex mix of shame and sorrow. Kamakura-based literary critic Etō Jun's contention long ago, echoed in much new work today, that Occupation censorship silenced Japanese expression to the point of warping it, recognizes the existence of Japanese reticence but incorrectly insists that it derived from subservience to American sensibilities and American military rules.[56] (Etō was of course right that the Occupationaires were hypocritical when they championed free speech but practiced censorship.) As the Japanese commentary on Occupation "swaggering" discussed in Chapter 1 shows, people found many ways to convey their irritation in print despite official censorship. Indeed, they used postwar publications to communicate with each other quite freely. When they were reticent, something far more complex than American-triggered "self-censorship" was going on.

Unlike Etō Jun, the men highlighted here rarely lingered on their resentment at American hypocrisy. One reason was that the same anger at Western arrogance and double standards had served as major tinder fueling the disastrous Japanese war effort and they did not wish to rekindle that blaze. But another was that their chosen responses to surviving a "contaminated moral environment" included not just honest talk and respect for dissent, but also recognition that they too had been arrogant and hypocritical. Furthermore, if everyone "harbors a blackness deep in our hearts," as Mashita put it, it simply did not matter that the American proponents of equality, peace, and democracy failed to even notice their own egregious lapses in all three departments. Given universal human frailty, these men much preferred to adopt the ideals of democracy and equality than to declare them discredited because Americans failed to live up to them. It also helped that most of them had direct experience interacting with Americans and Europeans, including during the Occupation years, and saw them as a collection of highly diverse individuals, a point to which I will return.

Building democratic institutions

Crucially, while leftists made active use of these discursive post-fascist strategies, they never trusted such etiquette alone. Far from it. It was extremely important to them to establish formal legal protections for freedoms of speech, publication, assembly, and organization. The men profiled here collectively established at least three publishing houses and five new journals in the first postwar years—all dedicated to expanding civil society—and all were active PEN Club members.[57] They regularly organized and spoke at events designed to build support for the new constitution, particularly its protections of civil rights. They were also all committed pacifists. They opposed Japan's assistance to the U.S. war in Vietnam as well as U.S. military bases. When he was mayor of Kamakura, Masaki Chifuyu often made City Hall his platform for these messages, as discussed in Chapter 4.

More expansively, they worked to entrench post-fascist strategies by creating new institutions of many different kinds, not just ones dedicated to freedom of expression and peace. Indeed, this focus on institutions was the biggest difference from their activities before 1945, and they established an astonishing range of them, including schools, libraries, social-welfare systems, industrial policies, publishing houses, tax structures, environmental monitoring systems, and museums. They sought to weave their core beliefs into these new institutional structures to make it as difficult as possible to reconnect them to the nationalist juggernaut that had overwhelmed them and everyone they knew. When they founded or joined any organization, they paid great attention to rule-making, fully aware that earlier rules had been a primary way that all aspects of society had been mobilized for their "double dose of tragedy—fascism and war." Social scientists today refer to this process as "capacity building" or strengthening institutional "resilience." While no one in the 1940s used these terms, they capture their efforts to intensify the ways that institutions themselves nudge behavior into democratic channels or, in an even more recent idiom, make democratic practice their default setting.

This attempt to embed transparency and democracy in the institutions of everyday life was shrewd. Mann argues that, historically, fascist movements were able to seize control when the major institutions of society were configured in ways that prevented political contestation. "What mattered was less liberal ideology than institutions whose everyday practices embodied liberalism," Mann concludes.[58] Although he does not name it as fascism, Frederick R. Dickinson made the same point when he argued that Japan's war owed more to "a concerted campaign of violence that began with the assassination of [Prime Minister Osachi] Hamaguchi in August 1931" and systematically undermined governing institutions than to either the introduction of new ideologies or global economic depression.[59] The intellectuals in Kamakura similarly drew the lesson that Japanese—being human—had responded badly to anxiety generated by acts such as assassinations and colonial protests, so they needed strong social institutions to protect them from panicked fascist overreaction.

These men focused on institutions out of a pained awareness that many of the reigning ideas during the war had begun life as idealistic, cosmopolitan concepts, some of which they personally had introduced to Japan. As Hiromi Mizuno and Aaron S. Moore have noted for science and technology, and other people, including myself, have shown for economics, some of the core ideas championed by the wartime state were first articulated by Marxists in the 1920s and then were subsumed into a statist agenda in the 1930s.[60] Men such as Saigusa Hiroto and Ōuchi Hyōe had watched this transformation from close-in. Their shock at seeing the social trajectory of their own ideas as they were hijacked by their intellectual opponents was another central part of what they meant by "fascism." Realizing that they could not produce reliably impervious ideas, they concluded that a solution could come only through protecting "the postwar system built on respect for human rights." Democratic political cultures without strong institutional supports, they had concluded, had been too fragile to protect them from their peers' anxiety-driven turn toward fascism.

Some of the tools that proved most helpful in these tasks emerged from collaboration within their "networks of complimentarity," including their shared sense of belonging to a modern local community. In Kamakura, the local society the leftists invoked was neither rural nor traditional, although Kamakurans regularly borrowed from the Japanese past as well as from places such as London and Detroit when they needed inspiration, as Carola Hein argues for urban planners.[61] In particular Kamakura residents developed the ideas of cosmopolitanism and civic responsibility as ways to define their city against both the political hegemony of the central government and the cultural domination of the national capital. By cosmopolitanism, they meant an easy familiarity with the international world, especially Europe and Asia. If the war had been driven by gnawing anxiety, then true self-confidence was demonstrated through participation in global culture without attempts to dominate it. This assumption was at the core of "Shōnan stylishness," identified in Chapter 1, the curriculum at the Kamakura Akademia, as laid out in Chapter 2, the exhibits at the Kamakura Museum of Modern Art, the subject of Chapter 3, and the policy recommendations of the Mikkakai and Masaki's City Hall, as discussed in Chapter 4. Nor did Kamakurans limit their message to each other: one way they conveyed it was through the tourist industry, discussed in Chapter 1, essentially giving people advice on how to incorporate a visit to Kamakura into their status as citizens. In this scenario, visiting Kamakura was a sophisticated cultural experience that taught Japanese individuals how to be comfortable in their skins, without the angst that had herded them along the path to fascism.

Another major "community of complimentarity" for elite Kamakurans was their various circles of professional colleagues and their fidelity to the standards and values of their professions. Professional training was one of the tools they had found most useful for understanding the changes taking place around them before 1945. Put most simply, their advanced education often provided a path through moral murkiness when nothing else did. Nor was it necessary for these individuals to share the same form of expertise in order to appreciate such mastery in each other. For example, when Yasui Sotarō painted Ōuchi Hyōe's portrait in 1948, Ōuchi was so fascinated by Yasui's work process, such as preparatory sketching, choosing the pose, and managing the lighting, that he published an essay on the experience.[62] Ōuchi recognized that Yasui was drawing on modern theories, agreed-on standards of practice, and years of experience, giving the painter and the economist fundamentally the same tools for seeing beyond ideological claims and choosing among possible actions. Even though they were well aware that many modern professionals had also embraced fascism, their personal experience was that professional standards had provided more reliable reality checks than had almost anything else.

Importantly, their professional communities were international ones, including many Occupation officials. One of Masaki's postwar projects, his 1950 translation of the U.S. Strategic Bombing Survey's assessment of the American assault on Japan's wartime economy, provides an instructive example of why these people at times felt they had more in common with the Americans than with wartime leaders.[63] Arisawa Hiromi was particularly blunt in the book's preface, arguing that publishing the report was a way to repudiate the wartime—and postwar—governments' "unscalable fortress of state secrets." He recommended the book to his readers as an "autopsy of the pathology (*byōri kaibu*) of Japanese imperialism," and told them to prepare for a strong emotional impact. Arisawa went on to say that "we must absorb this information fully because if we do not, we Japanese have no hope for the future."[64] Like Masaki, Arisawa had conducted economic analyses in the early 1940s for the government, had quite bravely warned that the war would cause domestic standards of living to collapse, and had been imprisoned for his pessimism. The heart of the emotional impact of the Strategic Bombing report for them was the discovery that the American government *wanted* the honest analysis that they had tried so desperately to convey to their own leaders a decade earlier.

Given that the topic was the U.S. firebombing of sixty Japanese cities—including their own homes—it is striking that Arisawa and Masaki also treated the subject as an opportunity to emphasize their trust in the professionalism of the Americans. Both men explained that the surveyors had interviewed about 700 Japanese when preparing the report, so that, although the research project was primarily designed to "ascertain the results of the strategic bombing of Japan and to assist the defense of the United States in future wars," it rested on a broad transnational research base. They assured readers that the interviewees, many of whom they knew personally, had expressed their true opinions, and that the findings served Japanese as well as American goals.[65] Their close colleague, Takahashi Masao, similarly went out of his way in a 1947 book to praise American insistence that Japan pass legal limits on work hours in order to give every adult time for democratic political expression and for continuing education opportunities.[66] The high level of comfort all three men felt with their American counterparts—and vice versa—derived from their shared culture of modern expertise. The Bombing Survey example also shows one of the ironic, rather than direct, ways the war effort contributed to postwar economic growth.

Humanists, historians, and social scientists in postwar Kamakura drew on their expertise in somewhat different ways, however. The humanists associated with the Akademia, discussed in Chapter 2, focused on enlarging their "community of complimentarity" by making higher education available to a much wider range of people, starting immediately in the first postwar months. Their university and the great postwar expansion of higher education it contributed to were explicitly designed to encourage social mobility; while this pathway had been available before 1945 for a lucky few, after the war it became the main route upward for a vastly larger group. It was also designed to develop in young Japanese the capacity to understand complex technical problems. Japan's global excellence in educational achievement in the ensuing decades undergirded postwar prosperity because of its broad base as well as its greater accessibility to the very top universities. By the turn of the twenty-first century, not only did 95 percent of Japanese high school students graduate, they also did so with the educational equivalent of two years of an American college education, for example, typically including calculus. As Thomas P. Rohlen put it in 1988, "Today, Japan sets the world standards in mass education."[67]

At the same time, the educators at the Akademia tried to establish a new emotional and aesthetic environment for young people, one grounded in both "global culture" and the resources of "eastern Japan's cultural city of Kamakura," to counterbalance nationalism.[68] They taught young adults to both trust each other and value dissent. They did so by championing both empathy and the scientific method, particularly the principle that attaining new knowledge requires sharply questioning received authority, while still maintaining rigorous standards of proof. As Saigusa Hiroto and the others at the Akademia understood it, Japanese people had accepted inhumane policies because they had had insufficient opportunity to express their doubts or hear those of others. Thus they celebrated individual curiosity and rich sub-cultures as ways to spark emotionally sustaining and heterodox social change. This stance, that education should empower individuals, rather than inculcate reverence for the state, was their primary response to the appeal of fascism.

The Kamakura Museum of Modern Art, created in 1951 and discussed in Chapter 3, was one of the many new institutions that presented alternative and diverse narratives of local, national, and global modern history. They were characterized by the argument that creativity was the result of individuals interacting in diverse ways across social classes, with the past, and between artisans and artists. In their narratives over the next three decades, culture and aesthetics sometimes drove scientific discoveries rather than the other way around. These stories treated culture itself as continually changing rather than containing a sacred "essence" that definitively separated one national—or any other kind of—group from another. Finally, this view of culture rested less on an ethnic identity than a cosmopolitan one that constantly moved across the globe. The museum builders were well aware that writing history was a knowledge-making exercise, and they consistently sought to wield that power at the museum in ways that "rescued history from the nation," to anticipate Prasenjit Duara's project of 1997.[69] Like Duara's, their narrative rejected the ethnic nation as well as the formal state, celebrating the emotional satisfactions derived from appreciating regional and class diversity within Japan and from making transnational connections. This vision was in striking contrast to the contemporary efforts of other intellectuals to create a post-colonial mythology of an ethnically homogenous nation-state, as argued by Oguma Eiji.[70] The battle between these world views was unobtrusively visible everywhere in postwar Japan.

All these narratives were unabashed "inventions of tradition" in the sense that the people articulating them understood that, while good histories must plausibly account for the known facts, those facts always can be interpreted in a variety of ways. Many of the people mentioned throughout this book were experts on the late Tokugawa and early Meiji periods, among the most fertile locations for wholesale "invention of tradition" in global history. Their nineteenth-century subjects had boldly reimagined their own past, providing a model to do so again in postwar Kamakura in the 1950s and 1960s. The postwar experts also unearthed many parallel examples of early-modern and modern Europeans and Asians deliberately—but not cynically—reinterpreting their pasts for new ends, showing the malleability of all global backstories. Like many other postwar Japanese, the historians at places such as the modern art museum and the Kamakura city library responded to the cynical habitual lying common to fascists by stressing documentary evidence, but rather than seeing their research as "objective proof," they combined high standards with interpretive purpose. At the risk of oversimplifying, their efforts can be summarized as scouring local, national, Asian, and global histories to create indigenous post-fascist narratives for Japan.

The Kamakura city government, together with the political pressure groups designed to influence it, comprised another local post-fascist site, although the key actors there were social science experts, rather than humanists or historians. As discussed in Chapter 4, these economists, public administration specialists, and policy analysts attended most carefully to the rule-making aspects of institutions because they were convinced that social change is most effective when embedded in institutional structures. This conclusion derived from their commitment to solving real-world problems, such as controlling land development and environmental degradation, which frequently proved stubborn in unanticipated ways. They had to grapple with actual substantive conflicts of interest, ones that often failed to align with political ideologies or alliances. Empowering people required both educating and being schooled by them, heightening the need for fair and effective institutions even more. In Kamakura the policy activists succeeded in protecting environmental and historical heritage sites more effectively than in most Japanese communities. Yet, since national policymakers were hostile to these goals, doing so required constant vigilance, vigilance that extracted its own costs.

In the end, the Kamakura leftists combined appeals to reason and to emotion in individualized ways tailored to their time and place. Their bravery and commitment to improving the lives of others set them apart from most elite Japanese but arose from that social status. They typically pursued strategies based on both systemic, rational plans and emotionally satisfying interactions within their creatively imagined urban communities. While they championed scientific rigor as a strategy to prevent a slide back into fascism, they also tried to strengthen the confidence felt by all citizens and their sense of trust in each other by reworking the institutions of political culture. As they knew better than most, science, local identity, cosmopolitanism, and civic responsibility had all been harnessed to empire, fascism, and war *together with* romantic mysticism, national identity, racism, xenophobia, and coercive ideas about the inherent duties of imperial subjects. They chose to fight for the first principles anyhow, despite knowing that they could not guarantee a better future—and despite recognizing that as a set they were theoretically incoherent. Their choices epitomize the post-fascist condition.

1

Kamakura: The Place

In January 2016, a newspaper survey found that over half of the people who worked in central Tokyo wanted to live in Kamakura or its neighboring towns. In a finding that held true across all age groups, 52 percent of respondents chose "Shōnan and Kamakura" because of its "proximity to the ocean," the fact that "the area matches my hobbies and lifestyle," and "because the names of the area have high brand value."[1] This result undoubtedly satisfied Kamakura's residents since they have spent over a century of concerted efforts to create this "high brand value." The components of that "brand" were the imaginative resources that postwar Kamakurans drew on to reconstruct their society along new lines. So what were they and what was the process that led to this perception?

Kamakura is like Kyoto in that its image is both cosmopolitan and culturally national, modern and steeped in the past. Again like Kyoto, it is also fundamentally elite, setting it apart from big industrial cities like Yokohama on one hand and most rural communities on the other. While Kamakura housing prices are now quite high, it was a relatively affordable community until the late 1960s, so its elite nature was centered more on its inhabitants' education level and cultural prominence than their wealth. Louise Young has pointed out that such highly educated people shaped modern local identities in provincial cities throughout Japan in the 1920s, but Kamakura was particularly well known for its large population of writers, visual artists, and film and theater people. Other people lived there because of their engagement with its past, especially the era when Kamakura was the political capital of Japan from 1185 to 1333. While "cultural heritage" is a politicized concept everywhere, postwar Japan in general and Kamakura in particular enjoy a particularly rich array of natural and historical amenities available for this purpose. As Cox and Brumann note, much is at stake when localities make claims about their identities. Ideas about the "signifiers of the traditional and the 'Japanese' and the policies that are based on them for the promotion of heritage have a special significance, since the self-definition of the nation rests critically on them. It is the integrity of the nation as tradition that is therefore threatened by the playful borrowing and remaking of elements of the foreign and the native, the old and new."[2] None of this was obscure to the locals, who thought they should have a say in what "the integrity of the nation" meant.

In the nineteenth century, Kamakura quickly became home to a variety of new services that drew people to the region. One was education: by 1900, Kamakura hosted several specialized middle schools for boys, while the Kamakura Higher Girls' School (now Kamakura Jogakuin High School) opened its doors in 1904. The main normal school for the prefecture also relocated from Yokohama to Kamakura in 1893. In addition to schools that led to universities for elite members of society, prewar Kamakura offered space to purveyors of more specialized learning. For example, Elena Pavlova (1899–1941), a Russian émigré and ballerina, launched Japan's first classical ballet school there in the 1920s, while a large orphanage opened its doors in 1918.[3] The Shōnan coast, moreover, became known for its healthcare facilities early in the twentieth century, particularly tuberculosis sanatoria and outpatient facilities, since the sea air was considered beneficial for TB sufferers. Kamakura also offers more traditional professional services: the city is home to 41 Shintō shrines and 121 Buddhist temples, many of which date back to the city's fifteen decades as the Shoguns' capital. The Buddhist temples, like Kamakura's newer Christian churches, provide burial and memorial ceremonies for their members, another significant economic activity.[4]

This stress on lifestyle amenities such as education and healthcare was in part a pragmatic response to geography. Kamakura's location on the Shōnan peninsula—behind the hills that line the Tokaidō road-and-rail throughway from Tokyo to Osaka—sharply limits its range of economic possibilities. Since it is literally off the beaten track, the Shōnan region has never been a manufacturing center and must attract service industries rather than factories. These concentrations of schools, hospitals, and places of worship also mean that Kamakura has long enjoyed a wealthy and highly literate population. None of these developments went unnoticed by other Japanese; as historian Oya Ayumi put it regarding the schools and hospitals, "these amenities gave the area an upper-class feel and provided little Shōnan, from Hayama and Zushi to Oiso and Kōtsu, with a large reputation. The name Shōnan became entwined with a feeling of longing or aspiration and an image that evolved with the times."[5]

This evolution was a deliberately shaped process, one that first defined elite modern culture, and then continued to redefine it over the next century while making it increasingly accessible to all Japanese. Kamakura's community leaders and educators acted on the assumption that Kamakura as a place mattered—and so did others. Aoki Shigeru (b. 1933), an arts bureaucrat at the Tokyo National Museum of Modern Art, cited this local cultural environment as an important cause of the creativity that allowed the Kamakura museum to successfully compete with his employer.[6] The setting provided its own contributions to the idea of modern cosmopolitanism, despite being a small outlying city. At the same time, as is frequently the case, the people most engaged in celebrating local identity also actively participated in the transnational world of ideas and enjoyed national reputations.

Modern Kamakura itself has long been marked as an internationally inflected space, in part because one of the most economically significant service industries is tourism. While Shōnan has long been a popular destination for religious pilgrims, modern tourism at first meant foreigners. An early tourist destination for overseas travelers, in the 1850s and 1860s Kamakura appealed to Westerners because it was close enough to the foreign settlement in Yokohama that they could proceed by horseback or rickshaw and still return before dark the same day. As British diplomat Ernest Satow (1843–1929) explained, even when taking this precaution, the trip did not always go well. Japan's resident foreigners

> received a rude shock on the night of the 20th November [1864] when the governor of Kanagawa came to Mr Winchester, the British Consul, and informed him that Major Baldwin and Lieutenant Bird ... had been barbarously murdered at Kamakura, a well-known resort twelve miles from Yokohama... The two officers had visited the famous colossal Buddha, and riding along the road towards the temple of Hachiman, were just about to turn the corner into the avenue when a couple of men sprang out upon them with their keen-edged swords and inflicted such ghastly wounds as brought them to the ground almost unresistingly.[7]

But, luckily for the locals, although Kamakura was the site of this attack, the perpetrators hailed from other places and Westerners associated the danger with the disaffected samurai class, not Kamakura itself.

Indeed, just a decade later, foreigners began adopting Kamakura as a healthful summer retreat. Europeans brought the custom of sea bathing to Japan and made Kamakura's sandy beach its hottest tourist amenity for the first time.[8] They built or rented homes for the summer season, escaping the oppressive humidity of Tokyo and Yokohama. A cholera outbreak in the 1880s spurred the departure of individuals such as physician Erwin Baelz, who had already scouted the Shōnan coast in 1878 at the request of government officials, who wanted his help in choosing the best site for a seaside resort. Baelz rejected

Enoshima as too rocky but thought the beach at Shichirihama was perfect.[9] When Baelz's most famous patient, the crown prince (later the Taishō emperor), heeded his doctor's recommendation and built a house in Hayama in 1893, the area's reputation as an elite enclave was assured.[10] Following this example, high-ranking military officers, former hereditary lords, government officials, and business leaders also built vacation homes nearby, and by 1912 Shōnan boasted 454 such households.[11]

Transportation to and around the Shōnan area became increasingly convenient in the twentieth century when the Japan National Railway (JNR) began making it both financially and logistically easier for Tokyoites to get there. In 1903 JNR began offering 30–40 percent discounts on a package of day-tripper tickets that included an express train from Shinagawa to Kamakura, separate rides to Enoshima and then Fujisawa without extra charges, and an express-train return from Fujisawa the same evening. In 1925 the JNR electrified the Tokaidō line and then the Yokosuka line the following year, and in 1927 added Kita Kamakura station. The travel time from Tokyo station to Kamakura dropped to less than an hour, making day trips from the capital even easier.[12] Then when Odakyū opened a longer line from Shinjuku to Hakone in 1929, Shōnan became more accessible from Tokyo's wealthy western precincts. In the same decade, visitors also began arriving by car, particularly after a gas station opened 16 kilometers away in Chigasaki in 1931.

Soon only a small proportion of tourists came from overseas. As was true throughout the Japanese empire, railroads and national and local newspaper companies, often working closely together, were important forces in creating a domestic tourist industry in Shōnan, developing tactics such as the pricing system described above. The *Yokohama Bōeki* newspaper entered this business in 1910 when it formed a "sightseeing association" (*yūrankai*) that organized group excursions, such as a two-day tour of Kamakura and Enoshima with an all-inclusive price of 2.5 yen.[13] They did so just as the Ōdakyū company completed the 10-kilometer Enoshima Electric Rail line, consisting of fifteen Enoden stations, all launched between 1900 and 1910. The new line not only transported more travelers around the Shōnan peninsula but also spurred entrepreneurs to transform it into a series of linked beaches and tourist destinations. Local officials worked with the railroad companies to build walking routes along the ocean from each of the stations, while from 1903, hotels joined in to create attractive travel-food-lodging packages to encourage longer stays. The closely spaced series of train stops really unified the villages along the Enoden route into a single region and created a standardized tourist space that not only integrated shopping, dining, and relaxing but also established new ways to admire the specific amenities at each station.[14]

The Yokohama newspaper advertised this opportunity as a cosmopolitan experience, emphasizing the glamorous possibilities of mixing with foreign residents in neighborhoods like Kamakura's Zaimokuza—"it feels just like being at a foreign beach resort!"[15] Kamakura's encouragement of domestic tourism was a deliberate contrast to other posh vacation spots such as Karuizawa, which avoided expanding its appeal to a broader range of Japanese visitors, preferring to retain its status as an exclusive commodity available only to the select few. The contrasting stances extended to enjoying the cachet of the imperial family, which maintained vacation homes in both Karuizawa and Kamakura. The newspaper, for example, also encouraged visitors to drive past the closed gates of the crown prince's villa in Hayama, presumably to soak up the Imperial aura from afar.

Local businesses emphasized Kamakura's association with foreign customs most directly through its edible delicacies. One Kamakura specialty became bao/manju, because Kamakura claims to be one of the two places in Japan that first made the Chinese steamed buns in the thirteenth century. The Kamakura recipe, unlike that of its Kyoto rival, includes sake. Ham is another treat, dating back to the arrival of an Englishman, William Curtis, who started as a cook on an English ship, becoming a chef in a Yokohama hotel in 1874. Curtis cured his own ham and bacon, using pork imported from mainland Asia, eventually leading to Kamakura-brand ham and "Japan's first sandwich-style train-station box-lunch."[16] In the 1920s, Morinaga and Meiji Seika, both famous Western-style candy makers, opened their Shōnan factories to "campus tours" by interested vacationers.

But while foreigners—and their food—provided the promise of exotic adventure, Kamakura's image soon rested far more solidly on local Japanese who themselves embodied transnational modern culture. Angela Yiu has elegantly demonstrated that Japan's modern spaces were formed through literary imagination as well as by railroads and tourist bureaus. Much like the suburban Tokyo settings that she discusses, the Shōnan region developed a growing reputation as a place that nurtured artistic creativity starting in the 1910s, often through its association with exactly the same people who made their mark farther north. Fiction writer Tokutomi Rōka (1868–1972) was the first to popularize the term Shōnan—which originally referred to a reed-filled lake near Suzhou, China. At the same time that Tokutomi linguistically anchored the region in classical Chinese literature, he also portrayed it as a modern fashionable retreat for artistic and literary people in his publications. As Yiu shows, Tokutomi's ideas about landscape were deeply informed by Tolstoy, whom he visited in 1906. Tokutomi also went farther than most Japanese of his day to encourage the creation of new "garden cities" populated by "aesthetic farmers" who tilled the soil in order to create beauty, not food. The natural milieu of these aesthetic farmers, the suburb, ever more comfortably extended to Kamakura when it became a realistic commuting distance from Tokyo. Kamakura provided Tokutomi with an additional solution to the problem posed by the disappointment felt by provincial youth when their actual urban experience did not live up to their expectations but, as Stephen Dodd has phrased it, accommodated their "reluctant acknowledgment that any ambitious person who has tasted urban life can never again seriously contemplate returning to the native place."[17] Thus it should not be surprising that Tokutomi was by no means alone in incorporating the Shōnan region into his creative work. Japan's most famous novelist of his day, Natsume Soseki, set the key opening scene of his 1914 novel, *Kokoro*, at the Shōnan seaside. Other novels incorporated characters who moved there to recover from a serious illness. A decade after *Kokoro*, Tanizaki Junichiro's protagonist Naomi entertained her lovers at the Sanbashi and Kaiei hotels and danced "On the Beach at Waikiki" in Kamakura.[18] It is hard to know whether those particular fictional encounters enticed or terrified potential guests but certainly they brought the setting to readers' attention.

Another highly influential set of individuals who grace Yiu's pages are the White Birch (*Shirakaba*) literary and artistic group, which began publishing in 1910. They too drew from international literary traditions as well as their own experience. They liked to spend time in Shōnan, even though most of them maintained primary residences in the Tokyo suburbs. Shiga Naoya (1883–1971) wrote the introduction for the first issue of the journal at one such retreat in Kugenuma, while other members of the group lived in Shōnan at various points in their lives, including the brothers Arishima Ikuma (1882–1974) and Satomi Ton (1888–1983), painter Kishida Ryūsei, (who moved there in 1917 because he suffered from tuberculosis), Nagayo Yoshirō (1888–1961), Mushanokōji Saneatsu (1885–1976), Yanagi Soetsu (1889–1961), and the journal's editor from November 1914 to November 1916, Koizumi Magane (1886–1954). They too incorporated the location into their literary and visual art productions, usually representing the landscape and its inhabitants as combining the best of urban and rural life in a thoroughly modern melding.[19]

All these trends intensified after September 1, 1923. Shōnan's population surged when a wave of urban refugees from Yokohama and Tokyo relocated there after their homes collapsed or burned during the Great Kantō Earthquake.

Even though Kamakura was also hard-hit, suffering damage to over 80 percent of its housing, it rebuilt much faster than did Tokyo. In particular, many scholars, journalists, visual artists, and theater people moved to Kamakura then, giving the city a livelier, more energetic quality, although perhaps never quite achieving its aspirational nickname of "Ginza by the sea."[20] Their presence generated much new cultural activity, soon available to both tourists and residents. They contributed to Kamakura's image as a sophisticated center of *modern* cultural production, not just a site for Zen Buddhist temples, exceptional cabinetry, archeological ruins, and other features derived from Kamakura's status as the Shogun's "historic capital city," on the one hand, or Shōnan's cachet as a private playground for the very rich on the other. As such, Kamakura in the 1920s presaged the deliberate economic development strategy espoused by Richard Florida of relying on "the creative class."[21]

As increasing numbers of "cultural producers" lived nearby, Shōnan locations often began appearing not just in novels and short stories but also in films. The Shochiku company built a movie studio with a soundstage to produce "talkies" in Ōfuna in 1931, and film directors there and at other studios often chose Shōnan locations for their productions, extending and deepening knowledge about the area across the country. Over the next decades, the depictions of sailing, swimming, and the romantic possibilities of parasols did much to transmit the idea of a beach vacation to a wide range of Japanese. Films from the 1920s and 1930s also introduced viewers to more refined cultural venues nearby, just as did contemporary novels. Indeed, many script writers were also novelists. Satomi Ton and Osaragi Jirō, for example, both made much of their income from writing for films.[22] Ozu Yasujirō's (1903–1963) postwar movies would have an enormous influence on the international image of Kamakura as an elegant modern place but already in *Tokyo Chorus* of 1931 he portrayed the small city as a setting that nurtured considerate people who said little but felt deeply. In that silent film, an engaging scamp of a hero moved to Kamakura when he married.[23] The protagonist's status and personality were established during a scene in higher school when it was revealed that he wore no shirt beneath his jacket. Smart enough to pass the entrance exams but too poor to afford the full uniform, he shrugged off the embarrassment. But years later when his young daughter needed medical care, money meant much more; desperate, he sold off all of his wife's kimonos without consulting her to pay the Kamakura hospital bills. Ozu's film succinctly showed the ways that Kamakura became home for educated "salarimen" at a time when class difference derived more from cultural style and education than from wealth, since salary incomes were only slightly higher than those of manual workers in the 1920s. The family was just barely able to afford lifesaving modern medical care but they could give their children educational and cultural advantages by living in Shōnan. When his daughter recovered, the hero's wife forgave him and the decision to make their home in Kamakura was vindicated.[24]

The individual most responsible for integrating modern literati cultural style into Kamakura's civic image was Kume Masao (1891–1952), who enlisted other "men of culture" in the tasks of burnishing Kamakura's image and enticing visitors to the region for a quarter-century. Kume was one of Kamakura's new residents, migrating there from Tokyo in 1925. A playwright, poet, essayist, and short-story writer, Kume had attended the First Higher School and Tokyo Imperial University, where he studied under Natsume Soseki. Kume quickly made his mark, staging his first play in 1914 and publishing his first novel in 1916, when he was twenty-five years old. With other young writers Kume published a small literary magazine, *Ningen*, between 1919 and 1922. He met Akutagawa Ryūnosuke (1892–1927) as a higher school student and they maintained a close friendship until Akutagawa's death; in later years, Kume was one of the judges for the Akutagawa literary prize. Kume is in part known for a famous 1925 essay that laid out the difference between popular fiction and the highly artistic "I-novel," arguing for the elevated status of "pure literature" and "true self-expression" over mere attempts to amuse readers.[25] Kume, in other words, was at the heart of national Japanese literary culture.

Yet Kume is only the clearest example of an individual who simultaneously shaped the images of Japan, of Tokyo, and of Kamakura. Kume, Takami Jun, Osaragi Jirō, Satomi Ton, Fukada Kyūya (1903–1971), Kobayashi Hideo (1902–1983), and other members of their circle had gone to university and, often, higher school in Tokyo. They began socializing in the lively atmosphere of prewar Asakusa, where students, culture mavens, salarymen, manual laborers, and visitors from the countryside all mingled in the many tiny bars and noodle shops. One of Kume's most famous short stories, "Tiger," centers on an acutely self-conscious Asakusa-based actor who veers between pride and shame at his middling career, including portraying animals. Never sure whether to approach his life with sincerity or by laughing at himself, in a few short pages, the main character second-guesses every glance and comment in an exhausting stream of self-absorption. The male social world of Asakusa is as much a character in the story as is the protagonist. Even after they had moved to Kamakura and visited Asakusa much less often, Kume and his friends continued to celebrate it in their fiction, while simultaneously—and equally publicly—exploring the implications of Kamakura's very different cultural cachet.[26]

A gregarious man, Kume loved to organize activities, and in 1932 he took the unusual—indeed, unprecedented—step for a Tokyo Imperial University Literature Department graduate of running for Kamakura city assembly, beginning a long dual career as a politician and an intellectual. When he stood for election, he filled the local primary school auditorium—itself a highly unusual act—with his supporters, including his close friends and fellow literati.[27] An early enthusiast for large-scale tourism, Kume energetically worked with other Kamakura boosters in the 1930s to entice more visitors. His contribution was to systematically market the image of the "Kamakura men of culture" as a tourist attraction and harness their cachet to the "Kamakura brand." He cheered his friends on when they wrote Kamakura into their novels and films, welcoming the notoriety such exposure would bring. This was unusual at a time when most literati were made uneasy by merging elite and popular culture: Osaragi Jirō was at first taken aback when Kume introduced him around town as "the secret author of [swashbuckling cinematic samurai] Kurama Tengu." Later in life he appreciated as very wise Kume's stance that writers should be grateful for any popular recognition of their literary work.[28] Kume was in this way ahead of his time, even though, as noted above, he too valued difficult "pure literature" above crowd pleasers. What was unusual was his defense of both. In the twenty-first century, this has completely changed: it is now not only unremarkable but also official national Japanese policy to encourage tourism on the basis of widely read novels, films, and other forms of popular culture.[29]

Kamakura's civic leaders, including Kume, applied themselves to two problems limiting Kamakura's ability to prosper through tourism. First, relying on the beach as an engine of tourism meant that the summer season of about forty days was a very short money-making window of opportunity, so they needed to create amenities for other seasons too. Second, even in the summer, Kamakura had little evening entertainment that kept visitors there overnight. While the advances in rail transportation made it easier for Tokyoites to visit, problematically, they also whisked them home again without spending much money within the city limits.[30] Kume's solution was to make literati culture fun and far more accessible to outsiders, as part of the larger strategy to modernize and democratize traditional elite culture. One long-standing cultural activity that Kamakura's leaders updated was to emphasize the distinctive and famous gardens in Kamakura's temples, particularly in seasons other than summer. From the 1930s, the rail companies ran special seasonal "Cherry Blossom" and "Fall Foliage" trains to Kamakura to speed as many people as possible to these elegant destinations, while a Kamakura youth group installed stones with calligraphy by Kamakura poets carved by nearby stonemasons. Other local organizations published guides to the seasonal displays, while still other entrepreneurs opened branches of Tokyo bars and cafes to encourage blossom-themed feasting and drinking.[31] Flower-viewing at Kamakura temples and shrines is still a popular activity today and, as in Kyoto, each place is known for its seasonal dramatic crescendo: Spring spectacles include Jochiji for witch-hazel, Kaizoji for spirea, Sugimoto-dera for kerria, and Anjo-in for wisteria. Hasedera and Meigetsuin are both known for their hydrangeas, while Kōmyōji is famous for late-spring rhododendrons (and a pet cemetery). Kinbyōzan has both a beautiful rock garden and a multi-season show of mixed flowers. In summer, the Sasuke Inari shrine boasts spider lilies (*Lycoris*) and Myōhonji offers bush clover (*Lespedeza*), while the Engakuji maple trees are among the many lovely autumn spaces.[32] These efforts paid off. In 1934, about ten million people visited Shōnan's high-culture "great sites," mostly in Kamakura, about the same number as went to Kyoto for similar purposes. Far more people visited Kamakura than went to the other top tourist destinations of Kanagawa: Kawasaki (two million visitors), Yokohama (five million), Hakone (six million), or the Miura peninsula (one million).[33]

Nonetheless, from the 1920s the beach was perennially more popular than any other tourist attraction in Kamakura. This fact provoked considerable ambivalence among Kamakura residents because beach-going was enthusiastically adopted by people with little interest in Kamakura's other charms. And people did arrive in force. In July and August 1924, 40,000 people visited Chigasaki and Fujisawa beaches. A few years later, these numbers would come to seem small. On one day alone—August 1, 1926—35,000 people alighted at Kamakura station and 25,000 at Zushi station, nearly all of them headed for the seashore, while on a summer Sunday two years later—July 29, 1928—over 33,000 travelers went to just Zushi's beach.[34] The local towns hastily built facilities for these visitors. Using funds from both the national and prefectural government, Zushi led the way in 1929 by constructing "sea houses" (*umi no ka*) where visitors could change clothes, leave their belongings, shower off the saltwater, and purchase snacks. Each town tried to find tourist activities that distinguished it from its neighbors. Entrepreneurs in Oiso built a billiards-hall and an archery range, as well as a fancy Japanese restaurant and a geisha house, while Chigasaki aimed for more family-friendly visitors by adding fireworks, swimming lessons for children, and a photo studio. Kamakura tried hard to elevate the tone, adding billiards and table tennis, and later Go clubs and spaces for poetic recitation (*ginei*), traditionally elegant pastimes from both Europe and Japan.[35] The narrator of Soseki's *Kokoro* first met

Figure 1.1 "A view of Zushi Beach, made famous by Roka Tokutomi…It is a favorite resort for the upper and middle class, and is also well known to foreigners." (Original caption.) In later decades, it became much more crowded. 1900. George Rinhart/ Corbis Historical. Courtesy of Getty Images.

the man whose influence on him is the dramatic heart of the novel at one such "sea house" in Kamakura, where he also indulged in "such fashionable pursuits as playing billiards and eating ice cream."[36]

Yet the highlight of the festival year soon became a new tradition, the Kamakura Carnival, created by Kume Masao and launched in July 1934. Famous throughout Japan, it was celebrated annually through 1938 and then again from 1947 to 1963. The Carnival began with a parade through town, starting at the train station, winding past Tsurugaoka Hachiman Shrine, down Wakamiyaōji Avenue, through Hase, and ending at Yuiga beach, where the Carnival dance took place under the stars. The parade featured local young people dressed as famous Kamakura-period warriors, city officials, also in costume, the winner of a newly created beauty contest, Miss Carnival, and the patron deities of several local temples and shrines. Neighborhoods created competing dance squads. Kume bedecked himself as a Kamakura-era court noble, and so drew on the Japanese past while anticipating twenty-first-century interest in historically themed cosplay.[37] But, as the name Carnival suggests, this event was modeled more on European celebrations than on traditional Shintō-shrine-centered street parties, although both involved parading through town carrying religious images, open-air dancing, and consuming plenty of food and strong drink. Kume conceived of the event after spending a year in Europe in 1928 although he ignored his model's Christian context of preparation for Lent.

Starting early in the morning, participants sang and danced their way through town. This too was a modern twist on an old tradition; rather than using folksongs, Kume wrote the lyrics and Machida Yoshika the music for a new composition whose refrain was: "Summer has come to Kamakura where the women have all gone to Yuiga beach in kimono, and if you cross the dunes, you too can see the dew scattered on the moonlit grasses." Another Carnival ditty promised that "although it is near Tokyo, it looks like summer by the sea in France." Kume organized a gang of young boys on bicycles, instructing them to ride up and down the parade route, leading the marchers in song, making it easy for visitors to fully participate.[38] As David Hughes has argued, by this point all Japanese folk songs, indeed the entire genre of *min'yo*, were shot through with modern elements, although some of its practitioners thought of it as traditional. Kume's personal contribution was thus not creating a deliberately modern embellishment so much as inviting everyone else to join him in belting it out.[39]

Each year a different Supreme Being presided: on July 15, 1934, the first God of the Carnival was the Dragon King, ruler of the mythical realm below the sea thought to be accessible through a cave on Enoshima. After a committee chose the honoree, Kume had an Asakusa dollmaker's shop construct each year's deity. At the end of the night, the Carnival god was floated out to sea, evoking summer Obon festivals as well as a Roman Bacchanalia. Two years later, in 1936, the well-known American movie actress Betty Boop presided over her kingdom while straddling a giant prawn. Other film characters licensed by the Glico caramel company, such as Mickey Mouse, Popeye, and Felix the Cat, participated in other years, as did a fleet of Datsuns sponsored by Morinaga Candy Company. One year the Kamakura Pen Club paid for the fireworks. Betty Boop's Carnival was a roaring success: according to the Japan National Railroad, 580,000 people passed through Kamakura station to honor her that day. Some of the enthusiasm may have been due to Kirin Beer's sponsorship—aided by ten booths dispensing their beverage.[40] This event was the most visible way Kume popularized the "Kamakura literati" label, integrated it with tourist culture, and marketed it nationally in the 1930s. Garbed as a court noble while boogieing to jazz tunes, Kume personally embodied the ways that Kamakura proposed to interpret and celebrate modern culture while also saluting the past.

Figure 1.2 Betty Boop, Goddess of the 1936 Kamakura Carnival, the biggest party of the year. Jiji Shinpō photograph, used by permission of © *Sankei Shimbun*.

But the event also shifted its focus when full-scale war began in Japan. While Carnival proceeded much as before, the change was apparent in 1937. Rather than Betty Boop, that year's God of Carnival, whose brief reign exactly coincided with the July start of the Sino-Japanese War, was a young Japanese Everyman, Kintarō, who rode a pillbox concrete bunker—understood to be located in China—and not a juicy shrimp.[41] It is hard to imagine a more concise statement of adjusted priorities. In 1937 Kintarō and his pillbox joined other new forms of patriotic tourism, another national trend that was well represented in Shōnan. As Kenneth Ruoff has recently shown, heritage tourism not only boomed in the late 1930s, but also became tightly centered on veneration of the imperial dynasty. This imperial tourism reached its peak in 1940 with the celebration of the mythical first emperor Jimmu's ascension to the throne in 660 BCE.[42]

In Shōnan, celebrating the imperium above all meant expanding the activities performed by ordinary individuals at Shintō shrines, some of which had been created only a few decades earlier explicitly in order to buttress imperial rule. While Japanese continued to visit Shintō shrines for a variety of long-standing reasons, such as presenting their newborn children to the gods, in the 1930s and 1940s the government and shrine officials also created a set of new rituals, designed to bind national subjects in both the home islands and the empire through modernized mass forms of Emperor worship. As Hyung-il Pai reports, in Korea all guests of the Japanese military government and most private travelers were brought to "the nearby Chōsen Jingū built on the slopes of Namsan or South Mountain where they were expected to pay respects to the Goddess Amaterasu and the deceased Meiji emperor (1852–1912), the two sacred guardians and protectors of the Chōsen colony."[43] These shrine visits were mandatory for local Koreans as well and the obligation that they worship at a Shintō shrine on each national holiday was one of the regulations Koreans, especially Christian Koreans, found most odious.[44]

In an irony that goes to the heart of Kamakura's self-image, these efforts to involve all Japanese and colonial subjects in standardized expressions of patriotic zeal and heritage tourism went hand in hand with continued attempts to update and maintain Kamakura's aura of specialness, now in ways that celebrated both war and empire. Kamakura is home to three major Shintō sites: the Kamakura-gu, Kuzuharaoka, and Tsurugaoka Hachiman shrines. Tsurugaoka Hachiman shrine is by far the oldest and most centrally located of the big three, with a corresponding lion's share of visitors. Hachiman was already the protective deity for the Minamoto clan in the 1180s when the shrine was established to invoke divine protection for the new Kamakura shogunate. In fact, the city itself is organized as a sacred site around the shrine; the main boulevard through Kamakura, Wakamiyaōji Avenue, was laid out in 1182 in honor of the birth of Minamoto Yoritomo's first son and runs from Hachiman straight to the sea, punctuated now by three enormous concrete torii gates.[45]

In the 1930s, new rituals of imperial belonging at that shrine made direct use of Kamakura's warrior past. The first of these rituals occurred on November 11, 1932, when the Hachiman shrine celebrated the ancient founding of Japan by assembling 4,000 local schoolchildren, members of military associations, and a brass band to sing *Kimigayo*, read inspiring proclamations, invoke the Shintō gods, and shout *Banzai!* In April 1933, local residents—not the shrine or national officials—organized a festival featuring young people in Kamakura-period samurai costumes and folk dancing, which became an annual event that has survived into the twenty-first century.[46] This party, created by Kamakura's original local elite—people who had lived there long before the 1920s—probably inspired Kume's bigger and more commercial summer beach bash.

Soon Hachiman added more new rituals, as did other shrines across the country. As Ruoff explains "between 1937 and 1945, the Japanese government regularly called upon all imperial subjects to observe, en masse, precisely timed rituals celebrating the nation." While the cleverest and most modern aspect of this form of mobilization was that national subjects could precisely coordinate their actions from anywhere with either a clock or a radio, many people chose to do so in groups at Shintō shrines. Later celebrations of the imperial reign in Kamakura were more elaborate; by 1939 they lasted an entire week, still centered on the Hachiman shrine. In 1940 when representatives of the Meiji Shrine in Tokyo visited Kamakura to prepare for both the culminating celebration of the 2600th anniversary of Emperor Jimmu's reign and the upcoming Olympics, they were welcomed with a ceremony at Yuiga beach that was broadcast by radio to the entire nation.[47]

Tsurugaoka Hachiman was also where war victories were celebrated and failures mediated. When Singapore fell to Japanese forces on February 15, 1942, the government handed out sake and sweets there. Since Lieutenant-General Yamashita Tomoyuki, who led the Japanese forces against the British stronghold at Singapore, maintained a house in Kamakura, the locals took special pride in his achievements. (In general, however, Kamakura was more a navy than an army town.[48]) At news of Nanjing's surrender—although not of the massacre— Kamakura officials responded with a nighttime lantern procession. They raised money for munitions this way: each one-yen donation entitled the donor to one character written on a lantern. When the story of the massacre broke after the war, the official Kamakura historian wrote, "I thought back to that patriotic spectacle." He did not need to tell his readers that he did so with shame and regret.[49] Hachiman was also the primary Kamakura location at which wartime privation was recast as a sacred contribution to the military effort. From August 1942, in response to a government decree, on the first day of each month schoolchildren gathered there to pray for the success of Japan's campaigns in Asia, followed by a plain rice lunch with a single pickled plum (*hinomaru bentō*), then visits to the graves of fallen soldiers and the homes of families who were grieving for them. These were also typical activities for civic groups, and, as Sheldon Garon argues, were one of the few opportunities for "middle-class women's organizations … to exercise influence in the public sphere."[50]

These new shrine-centered activities, together with another trend that Ruoff discusses, a flourish of new work by both professional and amateur historians, validated imperial rule and codified an Emperor-centric narrative of the Japanese past. For Kamakura, this burst of interest in imperial history was an opportunity to revisit a complicated issue. The era when Kamakura hosted the shogun's government, from 1185 to 1333, unquestionably was its most famous hour but posed problems because the Minamoto had actually been rebels who defied the aristocratic court. In fact, early Meiji accounts emphasized the defeat of the Kamakura shoguns, not their rule. As the Kamakura section of Felix Beato's widely reproduced 1868 photograph album explained,

> In the year (A.D.) 1333 a powerful Daimio and great general Nita-Yoshi-sada at the head of twenty thousand cavalry, made a descent on Kamakura …

Thwarted by formidable defenses,

> he dismounted from his charger, and taking off his helmet, prayed to Ryu-jin the God of the Ocean (who corresponds to Neptune in Western mythology): and at the same time, drawing his sword, richly ornamented with gold, he threw it into the waves—Then wonderful to relate—the waves receded, and it became dry land to the distance of about two thousand yards! Whereupon his army, each desiring to be first, marched without further impediment into the town of Kamakura, captured it and put the inhabitants to the sword.[51]

Beato's account conformed to the national Meiji story—of imperial unity and legitimacy gained by defeating the Kamakura shogun and killing all the residents—just then under active construction.

The problem of Kamakura's independence from imperial rule was dealt with ritually in the nineteenth century when the Kuzuharaoka and Kamakura-gu shrines were created specifically to venerate the imperial family. The two shrines, which flank Tsurugaoka Hachiman Shrine to the east and the west, essentially confine the older deity spatially within the watchful framework created by State Shintō. Kuzuharaoka, built in 1887, celebrates the life of Hino Toshimoto (d. 1332), who was executed by the Kamakura shogunate for plotting to restore power to emperor Go-Daigo. Hino was arrested for raising funds for Go-Daigo and sent to Kamakura for trial, where he was convicted of conspiring to overthrow the Shogun, a capital offense. Kamakura-gu, erected in 1869, enshrines the spirit of Prince Morinaga, who suffered the same fate for the same reason three years later. Go-Daigo's son, Morinaga was held for months at a Zen temple where Kamakura-gu now stands, until he was executed by his captors. In 1873 the Meiji Emperor visited the site, and Morinaga's tomb, also in Kamakura, is now graced with a plaque bearing his calligraphy. These two institutions symbolically recast Hino and Morinaga into martyrs for the imperial cause and Kamakura as the site of two brave attempts to restore imperial rule, even though the men who executed Hino and Morinaga were far more closely connected to the Kamakura seat of power.[52]

In the 1930s these narratives were disseminated widely, particularly on such auspicious dates as June 3, 1932, and August 18–20, 1935, the 600th anniversaries of the men's executions. Local citizens organized lecture and film series that focused on these tales and their geographical settings, especially the visually evocative site of Morinaga's imprisonment. Perhaps still a bit anxious about his city's position, the Kamakura mayor used the anniversary in 1935 to lecture on the theme that Kamakura had also contributed much to the nation during the 1904–1905 Russo-Japanese War, when residents had raised funds to rebuild many smaller shrines.[53] Kamakura also benefited from growing interest in Japan's most nationalist Buddhist luminary, Nichiren, and in folklore's Urashima Tarō as a symbol of Japanese love of native place.[54] Ironically, after the war, scholars of the period of Kamakura rule would find it highly refreshing to shed the awkward need to rework their topic into a tale of joyful subordination to the emperor.

Kamakura—like Japan as a whole—continued to vie for the attention of foreign visitors, even in the midst of war. When a diplomatic mission from the Italian Fascist government, led by Ambassador Baron Giacomo Paolucci di Calboli, visited Japan in March 1943, city officials proudly showed off their defense plans as well as the Great Buddha and the Hachiman Shrine, and arranged for schoolchildren to line the streets waving Italian and Japanese flags as they passed by. The next month when the Hitler youth group who so moved Osaragi spent a week at a Kamakura higher school, over 2,000 people were on the streets to greet them.[55] Andrea Germer explains that these diplomatic visits and other international propaganda efforts, such as *NIPPON* Magazine, comprised an official attempt "to present Japan as a country that …excelled as a modern nation-state… Rather than deconstructing the stereotypes of 'oriental' Japan, *NIPPON* reconfirmed other established tropes such as its unique family system, the high value of tradition and the unbroken line of emperors, and simply added another technically advanced and modern image to it."[56] Kamakura thus enthusiastically participated in the core message that Japan's amazing ancient tradition was crucial to the nation's extraordinary modernity.

But gradually the war in China claimed everyone's attention. The first major wave of conscription was in 1937 when almost 200 young men left for Central China and Manchukuo, the destinations for most draftees from Kamakura in the late 1930s.[57] Kume Masao put his distinctive stamp on this ritual as well, continuing to integrate the literary elite into Kamakura's civic life by mobilizing them for the war effort. On September 11, 1938, he created a literary campaign (*bunpitsu jūgun*) to give soldiers heading to China a uniquely Kamakura-esque sendoff at the train station. As the *Tokyo Nichinichi* explained at the time, his handpicked group of extravagantly educated friends assembled to celebrate the patriotism of the mothers of the departing soldiers. They called themselves the "organization to thank the mothers of the martial nation" and found stirring words to cheer the soldiers on their journey to the battlefront.[58] Shortly afterward, Kume became one of the first Kamakura authors to join the military "pen brigades" charged with stoking the enthusiasm of Asian cultural leaders for the Japanese cause and writing favorably about the war for readers back home. Later he encouraged his friends to make similar trips.[59] When he served on the Akutagawa Prize committee during the war, he cabled his 1941 vote from Sakhalin. By 1942 Kume was absorbed enough in the war effort to ask that year's prizewinner to modify her work by removing criticism of the government's price control system.[60] Clearly people found it hard to say no to Kume.

But, despite his enthusiasm for the war, life grew grim in Kamakura as throughout the empire. In August 1944 the government banned all swimming, recreational fishing, and boat rental in Zushi and Enoshima, on the grounds that such activities were frivolous and contributed nothing to the national welfare. Some Kamakura residents, however, successfully petitioned the local police for special permission to engage in these activities, suggesting that not everyone agreed. First young women and then schoolchildren were assigned labor service on farms and nearby factories. Some of these factories had relocated from Tokyo, like the optics plant featured in Kurosawa Akira's 1944 film, *The Most Beautiful*. Although the film's setting is never stated, judging by the view of Mt. Fuji from the factory roof, it probably was on the Shōnan peninsula. In real life, over 500 women worked at nearby naval installations, either in Yokosuka or the Ōfuna Storehouse, a site used for brutal interrogation of prisoners of war.[61] Meanwhile Japan's economy was slowly collapsing. In 1944, the ancient pine trees on the edges of Wakamiyaōji Avenue, which had long served to enhance the main approach to Hachiman shrine, were hacked down to make airplane fuel from pine root oil. The protective iron railing that had once surrounded the trees was long gone, donated to the war effort in 1941.[62] These trees, once symbols of Kamakura's cultural and religious heritage, like Japan's human inhabitants, were consumed by the war that had been started in their names.

Kamakura was relatively lucky in that, unlike nearly all of Japan's sixty largest cities, it was never the target of a bombing raid, although this did not mean it escaped completely unscathed. Residents experienced fifty-nine direct hits in 1944, usually caused by a stray bombshell dropped from a plane on its way to flatten the industrial population centers of Yokohama, Kawasaki, and Tokyo. About

Figure 1.3 Wakamiyaōji Avenue is both the widest street in Kamakura and the ceremonial approach to Tsurugaoka Hachiman Shrine, linking it to the sea. Until they were chopped down for fuel in the Second World War, an outer row of pines flanked these cherry trees. 2013. Photograph courtesy of Timothy George.

2,700 Kamakura residents underwent a four-day air-raid training course just after the first B-29 air raids on Kokura on June 15, 1944.[63] They also shared one of the most nerve-wracking aspects of the late war years with all Japan's urban residents: no way to know whether Kamakura would be targeted. This tension was implied by a single sentence in the city's official history: "After 70 planes bombed Tokyo on November 24, 1944, Kamakura went on high alert for the rest of the war."[64] More surprisingly, nearby Yokosuka, home to a major dockyard, ship repair station, ammunition depot, and other navy installations, was not bombed either.[65] Yokohama and Kawasaki were not so lucky. Both cities housed major manufacturing facilities and Yokohama was eastern Japan's biggest port. These qualities made them "high-value targets" for American bombing raids and both urban centers were devastated in the last year of the war. While in 1944 the prefectural population was 2.4 million people, it had dropped to 1.86 million in late 1945; 40,000 of the missing 540,000 people had died while the rest had fled. Yokohama alone dwindled from 1 million to 610,000 people in that year.[66]

Reinventing local cosmopolitanism

Because it was spared aerial bombardment, Kamakura's population surged in 1945, giving the town an unusual combination of dynamism and stability. Urban refugee Wakimura Yoshitarō was one of many people who moved to Shōnan when his Tokyo home went up in flames on April 13, 1945. He decided he liked the area and stayed for the rest of his life. Other visitors were more short-term. Beginning on July 20, 1944, hundreds of primary-school children relocated to Kamakura with their teachers, and "the temples and shrines were all full of these kids." Some Kamakura buildings served as barracks for Japanese soldiers "and we came to know the trampling storm of their booted feet inside the temples." Despite the defilement of booted feet, the soldiers were easier to manage because, unlike either the evacuated children or military units on the Asian continent, they brought their own food rations. Nonetheless, as was typical by 1944, although the city was required to feed its inhabitants, "there never was enough for everyone."[67]

When the war ended Kamakura's residents had to adjust. The food crisis actually worsened after surrender as even more displaced people moved to Kamakura, such as repatriate Hijikata Teiichi, who imposed on his relatives for a year after his return—homeless and jobless—from China in December 1945. On May 17, 1946, the head of the Kamakura city assembly petitioned everyone who might have access to food—the prefectural governor, the Agriculture Ministry, the U.S. Eighth Army based in Yokohama, and the Allied Occupation headquarters in Tokyo—requesting emergency nutrition aid on the grounds that there simply was not enough to eat available at any price. The petition explained that, because of the refugee influx, on twelve days since August 22 city officials had had nothing at all to distribute even to people with ration cards. Moreover, the city reported that 3,076 adults and 1,021 children were severely malnourished, while 1,124 additional people were bedridden due to food inadequacy, and twenty-two people had starved to death after the war ended in August. The prefectural Governor, Uchiyama Iwatarō (1890–1971), eventually joined the battle to bring food to his constituents. Uchiyama intensively lobbied both the U.S. Army and the Supreme Command for the Allied Powers (SCAP) for 7,500 tons of food aid, which he finally secured by bringing the blackened, shriveled vegetables that were all that was for sale into the American offices and *showing* them the problem. But, Uchiyama later complained, his work was still only half completed because the national government tried to divert the rations to Tokyo rather than Kanagawa. When Kimura Hikosaburō invoked these post-defeat deprivations in the city history, he framed them as having stemmed directly from the official wartime policies that were the root cause of these assaults on Japanese bodies and souls. In contrast, Uchiyama focused less on the past than on the ignorance of the Americans and the selfishness of the postwar national government, saving his most intense ire for the latter body. Either way, their direct experiences reinforced the sense among Kamakurans that they could not leave their problems in the hands of others, either American or Japanese.[68]

As this example shows, Kamakura had considerable direct engagement with Occupation forces because the Eighth Army was stationed nearby and 220 foreigners were actually billeted in the city.[69] In fact, the range and variety of interactions between individual Japanese and Americans are hard to summarize; while this was particularly true in Kamakura, it is an under-recognized point for postwar Japan generally. The Americans employed 100,000 Japanese in Kanagawa prefecture alone, meaning that there were a great many opportunities for face-to-face exchange. The occupation is generally treated as an American versus Japanese story, sometimes in ways that praise American largesse and sometimes as a critique of neocolonialism. Yet neither narrative captures the frequent occasions when Japanese and American individuals interacted, often cooperating quite amicably. Both American and Japanese nationals report many uncontroversial exchanges over topics as diverse as telecommunications, tax policy, welfare programs, art appreciation, school reform, and interior design. Mire Koikare's recent study of occupied Okinawa tells a similar tale within the context of a generally much harsher occupation experience. Koikare's main objective is to debunk the "triumphal narrative of the occupation" but, rather than a clear-cut alternative, she finds that Okinawan-American interactions defy easy summarization. Focusing on gender reform she notes "the heterogeneous—and often disruptive, contradictory and uneven—nature of the occupation."[70] Confusingly, by "disruptive" she means moments when Japanese and Americans worked well together. Things went particularly smoothly when people had similar educational or professional experiences, and even more for the surprisingly large number of individuals who had originally met each other before the war. Others found common cause in business deals, such as the black marketeers depicted in Osaragi Jirō's two novels of the Occupation era: *Homecoming* and *The Journey*.[71] In both Okinawa and mainland Japan, the Occupation forces functioned less as either a benefactor or an oppressor than as access to the outside world. To be clear, there were many sources of tension during the Occupation years, but much of the time they flared up between one group of Japanese working with Americans against another mixed group rather than breaking down along national lines. The Japanese individuals in these pages certainly were irritated when Americans were racist, overbearing, irrelevantly anti-communist, or simply stupid, but they generally chose to focus on other issues, believing that doing so would make Japan a better place to live.[72] When they did, they had many American collaborators.

In one Kamakura example, after the war ended, tourism once again quickly became an economic and cultural mainstay of the Kamakura economy. The locals, Japanese visitors, and foreign tourists—at first mainly Americans attached to the occupation forces—shaped each other's experience of Kamakura in various ways. City leaders sought to attract individuals who were interested in the city's historic past rather than rowdy young soldiers and sailors. Many of the Occupationaires were adults with established careers, particularly people whose work involved technical skills. Frank A. Polkinghorn, who served for two years as Director of the Research and Development Division of the Civil Communication Section of SCAP, was one such person. Already married with four children when he joined the occupation forces, Polkinghorn was an electrical engineer by training. He visited many telecommunications facilities and universities around the country for his job, but was also eager to meet Japanese people and learn about their culture and society. Polkinghorn spent his first weekend in Japan on an organized tour of Kamakura, "one of the ancient capitals of Japan and the site of the famous great bronze Buddha which had been cast in sections about 1252 AD and then welded together." The following week he visited the atelier of a woodblock-print artist and, the week after that, a crystal glass manufacturing plant, before returning to Shōnan the following Sunday to photograph the seaside towns, particularly Hayashi, where "the cliffs and hills and clouds made for charming pictures." On that jaunt, Polkinghorn was particularly interested in the monument at Kurihama "erected where Commodore Mathew O. Perry turned over his letter to what he thought were the representatives of the Emperor in 1853," a comment that reveals his background reading of Japanese history. When his family arrived several months later, they visited Kamakura again several times.[73]

Kamakura town notables far preferred catering to this sort of visitor than encouraging activities typically associated with military-base towns, particularly prostitution. While Oiso had built a geisha house before the war to attract visitors, this strategy for keeping them overnight had never been a favorite in Kamakura and surely was one reason the local elites emphasized Kamakura's highbrow culture. The proximity of the Eighth Army, like the Japanese Imperial Navy before it, simply added another reason to cede such activities to Yokohama and Oiso after the war. Nonetheless, in the hard, early postwar years, as a student in Kamakura put it, one "could find black markets and pan pan girls even on Wakamiyaōji Avenue." Local policemen discouraged both by routinely directing servicemen to red light districts outside the city limits.[74]

But even the sober history buffs among the foreigners changed Kamakura tourism. The favorite Kamakura destination for Occupationaire visitors, as had been true for Westerners since the 1850s, was the Great Buddha statue. Indeed, *Life Magazine* on October 8, 1945, ran a cover photograph of Lieutenant General Robert L. Eichelberger, head of the American Eighth Army, in front of the Great Buddha.[75] By contrast, Japanese tourists traditionally were more attracted to the pilgrimage site of Enoshima and lively Zeni-arai Benten shrine, where folk gods, rather than a serene Buddha, preside. Both are fun, typically crowded spaces. The narrow steep steps up Enoshima island are lined with stalls selling trinkets; no trip there is complete without a snack of octopus tentacles-on-a-stick and a pause at the mouth of the cave rumored to be the entrance to the Dragon King's undersea realm. Zeni-arai Benten feels as though it is deep in the mountains despite being less than 2 kilometers from Kamakura train station. After passing through a solid rock tunnel, worshippers empty their pockets of coins and banknotes, and wash them in the little stream running through the shrine, in hopes of magically increasing their value. However, this hierarchy of tourist sites shifted after the war. As one postwar guidebook, which used an image of the statue for its frontispiece, explained, "the Great Buddha is now high on everyone's list," while another mused over the observation that foreigners "really seem to find the Great Buddha fascinating."[76] Kamakura's boosters also slipped new references to the storied past into unexpected places, sometimes literally underfoot. For example, the iron manhole covers installed in the streets of Shōnan towns in 1952 are unexpectedly lovely. Central Kamakura's lids sport a modern clock tower and bellflowers from the Minamoto family crest, Fujisawa's are cast in the shape of wisteria blossoms (*fuji*), and other images related to local history grace different parts of town.[77]

Kamakura's postwar attempts to encourage tourism based on high-cultural amenities fit well with the priorities of the national government of the day. One key figure aligning them was the Minister of Education from May 1947 to October 1948, Morito Tatsuo (1888–1984), an economist who in 1920 had lost his job at Tokyo Imperial University and had been imprisoned for translating and publishing an anarchist text. He knew many of the Kamakura literati well, through either his activities at the Ōhara Institute for Social Research or his interest in Weimar culture. After the war he set out to democratize and diversify

Figure 1.4 The Great Buddha of Kamakura is one of the main tourist destinations in Kamakura and defines the city for international visitors. 2013. Photograph courtesy of Timothy S. George.

the ways that Japanese history was celebrated and make it more accessible to contemporary mass audiences, eventually leading to the 1950 Cultural Properties Protection Act (*Bunkazai Hogohō*) and the 1951 Museums Law (*Hakubutsukan Hō*). These new laws built on prewar precedents but expanded heritage protection to cover "intangible cultural properties" such as performing and applied arts, "folk cultural properties," and "buried cultural properties." All three categories were represented in Kamakura, and these laws unlocked significant extra revenue from Tokyo over the next decades. For example, in 1960 Mayor Yamamoto Seiichi used national funds to reinforce buildings near both the Tsurugaoka Hachiman shrine and the Great Buddha, making them strong enough to withstand the rattling of busses passing by while "also retaining the harmony and the beauty of those places."[78]

Morito, who in 1946 had participated in drafting a constitution that drastically reduced the emperor's political authority, wanted to shift national culture away from aristocratic to popular heritage, and so both expanded and redefined culturally significant sites. According to Enders and Gutschow, the Cultural Properties Protection Act covered a very broad spectrum by international standards.[79] Morito encouraged people such as the denizens of the Takayama/Hida farm village studied by Peter Siegenthaler, who also celebrated local heritage as a tourist draw. Their message was that visitors stood on ground that nurtured a significant source of grass-roots postwar democracy, while emphasizing the diversity of democracy's sites. Like Kamakura, Hida's claims were made partially on aesthetic grounds, highlighting art objects, particularly pottery. Hida's community leaders made this case most forcefully from 1959 through the 1970s, suggesting that this approach lasted much longer in communities distant from Tokyo, where Morito was soon replaced by more conservative Education Ministers. As Siegenthaler argues, heritage worked in this context simultaneously to incorporate local into national identity and to "facilitate the assertion of particular local identities in opposition to a homogenized nationhood." His point—"the cultural forms of the Hida region stand apart from all other Japanese folk traditions, but that same uniqueness reinforces the region's capacity to reflect an authentic Japanese cultural center"—holds true for urban places as well, although Kamakura's claim is to a sophisticated transnational elite heritage rather than a plebian one.[80] Kamakura residents also pursued additional strategies unavailable to places like Hida. In 1966, after much effort by locals, including the Mikkakai pressure group discussed in Chapter 4, the Ancient Capital Preservation Law (*Koto Hozaihō*) passed the Diet. This law designated four areas of Kamakura as historic landscape preservation districts. In more recent years, the Mikkakai has focused on getting Kamakura locations registered as UNESCO World Heritage Sites.[81]

In addition to the Great Buddha's new prominence, while postwar Japanese-language guidebooks emphasized many of the same religious, architectural, literary, and political sites as had been popular before 1945, they often reframed them in ways that explicitly opened a different dialogue with modern Kamakura. Hachiman Shrine remained central to Kamakura tourism, but the two nineteenth-century Shintō shrines lost most of their popularity after the war. A 1953 booklet issued by Kanagawa prefecture included neither one in its recommended sights, for example.[82] Volume 12 of Iwanami's photobook series, *Kamakura*, published in 1950, mentioned all three Shintō shrines but in ways that shifted their meaning toward problematic morality tales rather than sites of veneration. It included a photograph of Prince Morinaga's tomb but the accompanying caption pointed out that the site was rarely visited by anyone other than children on official school trips, almost certainly a veiled critique of the post-Morito Ministry of Education's priorities. The book also included a photograph of a cave with a barred mouth near Kuzuharaoka Shrine, an image that in 1950 would have instantly evoked the grotto where Morinaga was held prisoner, but the caption used that resonance to attack State Shintō and the wartime government, explaining: "At Kuzuharaoka there are many quiet and desolate little caves. During the Pacific War the local people used the mountain paths to create shelters here but were driven out of them like game birds into the open air. Since then, the diggings have been used as graves." The author used the verb *karitaterareta* which means both being driven into the open, as with game birds, and also being incited into going to war. While these two meanings are generally written with different Chinese characters, in a deliberate ambiguity, the author chose *hiragana*.[83]

Similarly, the Iwanami author wrote of Tsurugaoka Hachiman shrine that "while no one is sure where the name Tsurugaoka comes from, probably cranes (*tsuru*) once nested there." Then he bitterly commented,

> Beginning in the Meiji era, the Japanese were thoroughly inculcated in martial values very much including homage at this shrine, something that became even more pronounced during the war. The place where many cranes danced—a bird that symbolizes peace—was hawked as a spot to 'loose an arrow.' But, despite that past, the rows of stately cedars and red shrine walls are beautiful. When the war ended, such deranged temple visitors disappeared and the shrine is now enjoyably lively.

Captions on other pages also evoke the conflict as a disastrous folly, explaining that the sand on the beach below Inamuragasaki is black because it contains iron ore, "which people during the war earnestly (*shikiri ni*) collected." Similarly, the trees along Wakamiyaōji Avenue "used to be lovely but during the war, saying that they were too obvious a target, the authorities chopped them down, including digging out the roots." Both examples evoke warped values as well as pointless effort.[84]

Postwar guidebooks also portrayed Kamakura "as a place where the soil exudes modern culture," as one 1975 book phrased it.[85] And, while celebration of Kamakura's historic past remained important to opinion leaders, modern Kamakura was the more reliable source of tourist revenue. As a photography magazine explained in 1950, "Today's Kamakura seems to attract attention not because of its historical value as one of the three major historic capital sites. Rather the city is supported by its character as a suburban center which swarms with cultural figures and intellectuals and by the popularity of the coastline as a summer retreat such as the Yuiga and Zaimokuza beaches."[86] The Iwanami book straightforwardly admired the cosmopolitan-ness of Kamakura residents, captioning one image, "Kamakura ladies are modern and effortlessly stylish." The guidebooks also glamorized Kamakura by offering readers the chance to glimpse a cinematic or literary celebrity, such as film actress Hara Setsuko or Nobel-winning novelist Kawabata Yasunari.[87]

Japan has a long history of literary travelers who leave home to enjoy the beauty of the changing seasons, get new ideas for their creative work, and invite their readers to metaphorically share their journey. As Sylvie Guichard-Anguis and Okpyo Moon note in a recent book, "the huge volume of travel diaries written about experiences abroad tell how much writing while travelling is still taken for granted."[88] The organizations that created the modern tourist industry in early twentieth-century Japan—railroads, hotels, and the national tourist bureau—built on this tradition when they invited famous writers and artists to enjoy their amenities and then publish an account of their experiences. The Japan Travel Bureau not only provided free transportation and hotel stays, but also published their impressions in its flagship journal, *Tabi*. Natsume Soseki was one of the first culture mavens to enjoy such a lavish junket, traveling to Korea and Manchuria in 1909.[89] Such travel—and travel writing—continued both during and after the war, still often commissioned by governments or transportation and hospitality firms.

What was new in Kamakura, however, was that much of the postwar tourist material featured noted intellectuals inviting visitors to join them not on the road but in their own backyards. After Kume Masao died in 1952, Osaragi Jirō inherited the mantle of "Mr Kamakura," and the self-imposed task of marketing the city as a preeminent site of tasteful Japanese modernity. Publishing houses paid for these essays, as they did for travel writing, meaning that Osaragi earned a substantial sum for essays in this vein. In a 1961 travel guide that also included articles by several other local literati, he began by saying that he loved Kyoto and Nara and visited there three or four times a year, but was always happy "to open my eyes the next morning and realize that I am at home." Why? "The vista of the mountains complete with their ranks of fast-growing red pines looks to me like something composed as an impossibly beautiful painting." Dropping in a gratuitous reference to an American walking companion, presumably to advertise his urbane sophistication, Osaragi explained that he particularly liked to visit the little temples along the back streets of the city. Then, tying Kamakura spatially to his creative practices, he explained, "This is the first time I've written a travel book [although it was not] but my work does not happen only when I am seated at my desk, it also is something I do as I walk and look at my surroundings." The "Kamakura I admire" is not just connected to the old temples and shrines, he continued:

> It is in the emotion-laden little streets....and the many peaceful hidden valleys with their villages that brim over with rustic beauty. Most tourists visit Tsurugaoka Hachiman, the Great Buddha, and Hase Kannon, and just rush through the main streets so they miss Kamakura's true beauty and so return home without experiencing its charm. I think that is a bit pathetic (*ki no doku*). People like to say that Kamakura's main avenue is just like Ginza. But today one can see big streets like that in any region of Japan. This book is not about such central arteries. Rather it is a guide to the little lanes and byways, and I hope that readers will use it to change their perspective on the central streets of Kamakura and to recognize the ways this place differs from Kyoto and Nara. That would make me happy.[90]

When Kamakura writers invited visitors to join them, they often stressed the natural beauty of the region as well. The Iwanami photo booklet, which engaged to "capture contemporary Kamakura as it is," was typical in its commentary about the glories of Kamakura's natural setting as akin to being invited to join a special club. The Iwanami editor adopted a confiding tone as he told his readers that "The best way to approach Kamakura is through the mountains … and the place names reflect the varied topography. There are temples and houses, both Western-style villas and older *kayabuki* thatched farmhouses." Then, switching to the topic of Kamakura people, he commented that "I would guess that people who have moved here from more polluted places mainly did so to be able to walk along these little mountain paths." Returning to the landscape, he explained,

> Inamuragasaki and Iijimasaki connect to the coastal road while historically Yamauchi, Mutsuura, Inamura, and Kotsuba were the four mountain passes into the city. Other than arriving by sea, there was no additional way to get to

Kamakura. There are fifty little valleys and the only way to reach them was to walk along a hilly trail, through fallen leaves or mountain grasses.

The author recommended this activity so warmly because

> this is what makes traversing the ridgetops such an emotionally satisfying invitation. If you follow one or two of the paths down and stop in a village from time to time, and then continue on, you can make a full circuit around Kamakura. The route will take you via clusters of houses and through tunnels and railway cuts (*kiritoshi*). Some valleys are separated by dense forest, which suddenly reveal a completely different place with a lovely vista of another valley. These dramatic surprises are what people who truly appreciate Kamakura's natural beauty like best.[91]

That pastoral charm was exactly what Tokutomi Rōka had most enjoyed six decades earlier.

And yet the leisure imaginary of modern Kamakura also was distinctly modern in both highbrow and popular ways. The indispensable 1950 Iwanami photo booklet captured a characteristic mixture of attraction and disaffection about this fact. The captions lavished admiration on Japanese who deployed foreign culture expertly, especially ones who had mastered leisure activities such as sailing and tennis, and on the international flavor of Kamakura. One image of people playing tennis noted that "many people who gather here are sporty and 'high collar.'" After several photos of shop signs in both English and Japanese, a composite caption commented that "it seems appropriate in a place that has moved with the times that, when you walk through the area, you can see these new elements unfold like a scroll in front of you."[92] English-language signage gave the spectacle an elegant flourish that seamlessly meshed with traditional habits of reading a long scroll.

But the booklet was far more caustic about foreign visitors themselves, treating them as a nuisance for causing traffic jams near the Great Buddha because they arrived by taxi rather than bus and bridling at their sense of entitlement. One photo of a row of old-fashioned buildings explains that "these houses were requisitioned in August 1945 and they haven't changed at all since then. That kind of person still swaggers around Kamakura too."[93] The insinuation was that Japanese owners would have improved the streetscape out of consideration for their neighbors and pride in their town. In 1950, this book still had to be approved by the Occupation censors, and it contained no photographs of Occupation forces or direct references to them. It was not necessary, however, to specify the nationality of "travelers from afar" who "swaggered" while heading "in the direction of Camp McGill."

On the other hand, while both the Iwanami editor and the photographer approved of Japanese who played tennis and read English, they were distinctly critical of other Japanese for failing to care for the historical riches of Kamakura—and tended to blame visitors more than residents. This book devotes a large fraction of its pages to photos of dilapidated temples and their unprotected contents, many of them designated Important National Cultural Properties. One image of an isolated temple showed washing on the veranda, suggesting that someone was clandestinely living there. The accompanying text hectored its readers for failing to value this heritage, commenting that few visitors entered the Kamakura Treasure Hall (*Kamakura Kokuhōkan*) despite its convenient location on the Hachiman Shrine grounds and its hoard of a thousand-year-old priceless art. "Despite the fact that Kamakura expressly assembled these important cultural treasures in one place it really isn't appreciated enough."[94] The invitation was genuine but served up with a large portion of Kamakura's intense snobbery.

Yasuda Saburō (b. 1919), a professional photographer who also worked as the archivist at the Kamakura Treasure Hall from 1950 to 1980, wrote guidebooks in his spare time. He too set out to educate visitors, although in a gentler tone. Yasuda's *Kamakura Rekishi Sansaku*, or *A Long Walk through Kamakura's Past*, 1976, is a pocket-sized book that functions as a portable visual reference work to Kamakura's historic sites. The book offers four walking routes: one through the mountains, one heading east from the station, a westerly path, and a final one straight north. It also included information on political efforts by local residents to protect green space and historically significant sites, as discussed in Chapter 4. Yasuda, who was active in both movements, explained to his readers that local civic energy protected the vistas they were presumably enjoying at that moment, explaining that "In 1964, a plan was floated to turn the hills in this area (*Kobukurozaka*) into a housing development but a protest movement succeeded in protecting 90 percent of the area. The spark that ignited that movement was the law to protect heritage in the old capitals of Kyoto, Nara, and Kamakura."[95] Yasuda thus invited visitors to join forces with residents to preserve Kamakura traditions. The actions he urged were rooted in transnational professional standards of historical analysis, museum conservation and exhibition, community-based urban planning, and environmental protection. Yasuda and Osaragi, like Education Minister Morito and the potters in Hida, were deliberately trying to create a more diverse and flexible culture that welcomed visitor and resident alike. Yet while the didactic, snobbish, and frankly nerdy aspects of this appeal suited visitors like Frank A. Polkinghorn and many Japanese, it held less appeal for other, often younger, visitors of all nationalities.

Postwar beach culture

The beach remained the most powerful leisure imaginary in the 1950s and 1960s. While splashing in the waves was already popular before the war, in the first three postwar decades, the scale of beach tourism increased by an order of magnitude. Photographs from that era show a crowd so dense that sunbathing must have been impossible because it required lying down. Once again beach tourism encompassed the entire Shōnan peninsula. Neighboring Enoshima energetically pursued this new way to interact with the seashore, negotiating a Sister City agreement with Miami Beach in 1959, and working together with the Odakyu company, owner of the Enoden train line, to build a water-skiing show like one in Florida.[96]

The sheer mass of people is mind-boggling. On Sunday August 2, 1959, to pick one representative summer weekend, 230 JNR trains carrying 263,000 riders stopped in Kamakura, nearly all heading for the shoreline. Others arrived by Enoden or by bus, a much more common transportation choice from the late 1950s. These numbers far outpaced the normal weekday commuting population:

Figure 1.5 View of Enoshima, a lively pilgrimage site with a character very different from that of Kamakura, and Mt. Fuji, from Shichirigahama. 2013. Photograph courtesy of Timothy S. George.

approximately 103,810 people regularly rode the JNR train to Kamakura, Kita Kamakura, and Ōfuna stations, according to station master Tanaka Hikōjūrō.[97] The beach remains a smaller but still major tourist attraction today, with annual visitor numbers peaking at over a million people in the 1990s, and then typically hovering just below that threshold annually in the twenty-first century.[98]

One reason for the huge surge in the popularity of Kamakura beaches was that, as Yoshimi Shunya has argued, American soldiers introduced new pastimes such as surfing and waterskiing, making Shōnan an American-inflected youth-culture space.[99] This tone was never entirely welcome to either Kamakura's cultural or political elite, continuing an ambivalence begun before the war. Men such as Osaragi Jirō and Yasuda Saburō still preferred the old-fashioned charm of Kamakura's woods and temples to the noisy crowded beach. Choosing another response to the same distaste, the mayor and governor hoped to turn the urban shoreline into an elegant European-style ocean resort rather than a mad crush of nearly naked bodies. In 1960 Governor Uchiyama and Mayor Yamamoto discussed their ideas for expanding beach-based tourism with local resident Sawada Setsuzō. Uchiyama wanted to make the coast "something like the French Riviera," studded with international hotels. Sawada, a retired diplomat, agreed, arguing that at many fashionable seaside tourist destinations around the world, natural conditions were not actually particularly hospitable. As he said,

> I lived overseas for 20 years and I've been all over the world—to the southern coast of England, France's north coast, near New York City in Oyster Bay, and other excellent places, and compared to them, where the water is cold, creating fog, the shore in Kamakura is wonderful. The city has mountains, ocean, an amazing history, and renowned gardens.[100]

They hoped to create a boardwalk promenade, modeled on Brighton and Deauville, where Uchiyama had visited in the 1920s when he was attached to the Paris Embassy. This was actually a prewar plan, one that had circulated in 1931 but was never implemented, in part because of pessimism that success required first instituting the social habit of a regular evening stroll to meet people. In fact, by 1960 in Europe this kind of resort was already in decline. In any case, neither group got what they wanted. Postwar Shōnan beach culture was no longer modeled on Brighton and Deauville, let alone classical China's reed-filled lakes.

The Kamakura Carnival returned in 1947 and at first seemed to recapture its cachet as an emblem of tasteful beach partying. Ever-attentive to transnational culture, it was one of the first events in Japan to feature beauty contests in bathing attire, starting in 1948. The Iwanami photobook took care to signal that its photograph of a postwar Miss Carnival surrounded by men on the beach depicted a high-culture ogling of young women, which the author seemed to think was somehow more appealing than other forms of leering. "The *bunkajin* who live in Kamakura participated and their influence is felt" (*haba o kikasu*).[101] One way their influence showed was the political tinge of postwar Carnivals; in 1952 the Japan Communist Party staged a Peace Festival in the water at Kamakura beach at the same time as the beauty contest portion of the Carnival; 20,000 men in bathing suits waving red flags and a leftist theater troupe livened the occasion with skits denouncing Japanese rearmament and engagement in the Korean War. It is unclear whether the organizers knew in advance about this embellishment but the 250,000 Carnival participants apparently took the whole thing in stride.[102]

In other years, the reigning deities were more serious figures too, such as the President of the Philippines, Elpidio Rivera Quirino in 1953, and Labor Minister Ishida Hirohide, who had just brokered an end to the Miike Coal Mine strike (and lived in Shōnan), in 1960. Kume died in March 1952 and was chosen as the Carnival god that year. He is buried at Zuisenji, famous for its plum blossoms and daffodils, a fittingly mixed classical East Asian and Western flower combination. But in the early 1960s, participation dwindled and Kamakura held its last Carnival in 1962.[103] For many younger Japanese, the tradition now felt too scripted and old-fashioned.

Despite considerable efforts by both the men of letters and city officials, an entirely different and much more unreservedly hedonistic sensibility increasingly animated postwar beach culture, imaginatively fueled by the cultural production of a youthful and fashionable in playboy set. In Kamakura and Zushi, the brothers Ishihara Shintarō and Yujirō were the key figures, especially after publication of Shintarō's Akutagawa prize-winning book *Season of the Sun* (*Taiyo no Kisetsu*) in 1955, and the movie version, which came out in 1956, closely followed by *Crazed Fruit*, set in the same milieu, also written by Shintarō and starring Yujirō. The protagonists of these two films—like their real-life creators—liked to fight, drink, drive fast cars and yachts, and chase after girls. They had no interest in working at a job or improving the lives of others and instead extorted money from men and wheedled it from women. Nor did they care much for family or for adult responsibilities. Their audience was young: the first generation raised in the new postwar environment. Based on the sales reports from a movie theater in Tokyo that sold tickets through a film club, about 80 percent of the people who saw *Season of the Sun* were between 17 and 23 years old.[104] None of these cultural products could have passed the censors before 1945 and so were quite different from the books and films encountered by previous cohorts of teens.

Not coincidentally, the early 1960s also marked the moment when postwar culture began to lose the implied political idea that freedom entails responsibility and self-restraint. In part, this was because many young people found the Ishiharas' unadorned image of self-confidence more appealing—and more accessible—than versions tied to any sense of being earned through acts of social responsibility. As Katō Atsuko explains, at precisely the moment when postwar Japanese were finally able to purchase and consume goods as they pleased, these films established new fashions in Japan, including Hawai'ian Aloha shirts and sunglasses for men and circle skirts and bikinis for women, as well as less glamorous items, such as wool-nylon blend socks. The jersey fabric required for tight sweaters and swimsuits was invented only in 1955 and Japanese people first saw these fashions at the movies. Indeed, the concept of "leisure wear" itself was newly imported from the United States and these outfits became hot fashion lines in both fancy Tokyo department stores and Kamakura boutiques.[105] One could vicariously participate in this version of the "Shōnan brand" simply by sporting trendy sunglasses or either brother's signature hair style.

Although Shintarō, who graduated from Hitotsubashi University, and Yujirō, who attended Keio University, had access to top-flight educations, they were uninterested in showing off a command of either classical Asian or European high culture, let alone endorsing the overt politics of European intellectuals such as Jean-Paul Sartre or Bertrand Russell, who inspired other elite Japanese. Such people did not know what to make of the Ishiharas' disinterest in—even disdain for—the Japanese literary tradition. Kamakura author Kawabata Yasunari, for example, both voted to give Shintarō a book prize and publicly criticized himself for doing so. In her study of the reception of *Season of the Sun* Ann Sherif reports that Kawabata, "one of the four decidedly ambivalent Akutagawa judges," was particularly troubled at having voted based on Ishihara's fame, spread as it was by mass media, and so had bestowed the Akutagawa prize on a novelist who "had barely read any of the canonical works of modern Japanese literature" and showed little interest in the men who had created them.[106] And yet Kawabata felt that Ishihara's open contempt for the past was itself reason to award him Japan's most prestigious literary prize, because that quality captured the historical moment.

The new Japanese style epitomized by the Ishihara brothers drew on American hedonism, disdain for tradition, and consumer products, rejecting the earnest postwar efforts—by both Americans and Japanese—to improve society or value self-restraint for the sake of others. The Ishiharas adopted the playboy style of Hugh Hefner and the Rat Pack (without the assimilationist backstory of the immigrant and African American strivers in Hollywood that democratized their image at home). They casually claimed the self-confidence that had eluded so many others without worrying about higher justifications. The members of this "sun tribe" were not unlike the people Osaragi had portrayed negatively a few years earlier in *Homecoming*, when young repatriates from the continent conducted mysterious deals with Occupation personnel while enjoying unusual access to American automobiles and expensive hotels.[107] But while Osaragi's wheeler-dealer characters were hungry entrepreneurs who were in it for the money, the carefree "swaggering" that had so repelled the Iwanami editor in 1950 was precisely what attracted the *Crazed Fruit* crowd. Ishihara Shintarō and his fictional creations retained the cosmopolitan stance, the sporty leisure activities, and the confidence of the older Kamakura "high-collar" style but firmly rejected the politics, the sense of responsibility, and the dorky earnestness of people such as Osaragi. Osaragi's idealization of Kamakura deliberately encoded a commitment to a democratic political community. He and his friends felt an obligation to preserve the natural environment, protect the right to self-expression, and establish a strong social safety net. They wanted to make leisure and cultural activities available to all Japanese, although, being human, they did not always live up to their own ideals.

By contrast Ishihara Shintarō courted celebrity through his performative stance of rejecting the cultural traditions of elite society while still actively participating in them as a novelist and later as a politician. Ishihara's taste for domination eventually brought him back to presurrender elite cultural styles and political tenets, although in the 1950s and 1960s, the "sun tribe" had as yet little interest in their national identity as Japanese. The tribe did quickly readopt the celebration of physical violence that had characterized military-dominated male culture before defeat. Like their uniformed elders, they asserted the right not only to dominate others by force but also to openly enjoy the ensuing submissiveness. Fueled by an anger at any obstacle to their immediate desires, they brawled for the pleasure derived from cowing others rather than for a larger cause.

As Ann Sherif has argued, this celebration of selfishness and violence as the epitome of virile masculinity, or the "aesthetics of speed," not only presaged Shintarō's later embrace of right-wing nationalism but also reframed the transnational cultural politics of its Cold War moment. In the 1950s, the Ishiharas already overlaid their attraction to contemporary American youth culture with scorn for Americans themselves, mirroring the Iwanami photobook's celebration of Kamakura tennis players while criticizing the people swaggering off to Camp McGill. In *Crazed Fruit,* the character played by Yujirō was openly contemptuous of the significantly older American husband of the woman he pursued and told one of his friends "Yankee go home!" when irritated by the other youth. In both cases, and when he raped the woman he desired, the intensity of his wish to dominate, married to his stronger physique, meant he got what he wanted.[108] When still a young man, Shintarō liked the sensation of dominance through personal violence but as he aged out of the years of peak physical strength, he turned to the power of the state to achieve the same effect. His later nationalism emerged, not out of ideological fervor but because he needed new enforcement mechanisms for the same gratifications. This naked celebration of power simply for the pleasure of exercising control over others was one of Shōnan's contribution to postwar political culture, undermining and sometimes overwhelming the post-fascist efforts of the Ishiharas' Kamakura neighbors.

The Kamakura Akademia and Humanities Education

The end of the Second World War changed life for nearly everyone. In Japan, as in other warzones, existence had shrunk down to a daily struggle for survival. When the war finally ended, optimistic people could at last turn their attention to the future, for themselves personally and for the people around them, a concern that quickly led to formal education. In Japan by mid-1945 schools had been integrated into the war effort at every level, making it necessary to rethink how they functioned. Since schools everywhere integrate children into society and instill in them appropriate notions of their responsibilities to each other and to the formal political system, defeat opened the questions: what kinds of education were appropriate for this new era? and how should young people prepare for postwar society?

While the story of postwar Japanese educational reform at lower levels is well known, less is written about postwar colleges, even though higher schools, technical institutes, and universities all had been sites of intense political polarization. Repression began early and never let up. A nation-wide wave of arrests in March 1928 revealed a larger group of left-wing students across higher education than authorities had anticipated, alarming both campus leaders and government officials. Over the next decade, what began as small groups of right-wing faculty and students gradually gained the tacit support of government officials. These activists agitated to expel teachers whose ideas they rejected as unpatriotic, with increasing success. They attended the targeted professors' classes, listening for anything that could be reported as seditious, protested the political tenor of their books, and complained when they did not behave in a sufficiently patriotic manner, for example, declining to lead a student group to Meiji Shrine to pray for victory over China in fall 1937. They also attacked other students. Their biggest victories against their teachers are well known: Kyoto University law professor Takigawa Yukitoki (1891–1962) lost his job in 1933, retired Tokyo Imperial University law professor Minobe Tatsukichi (1873–1948) saw his books banned in 1935, Minobe's son Ryōkichi, Arisawa Hiromi, Wakimura Yoshitarō, their teacher Ōuchi Hyōe, and several other economists were imprisoned in 1938, all for expressing ideas either in print or in the classroom that had been considered unremarkable a few years earlier. The campus right-wing activists, who had the sympathy of the Ministry of Education, functioned much as did fascist groups in Europe, where educational institutions were also important sites, not just for mobilizing and transforming public opinion, but also for silencing prominent dissidents.[1]

Education for a post-fascist future

Given this recent past, Japanese who feared the return of fascism after 1945 needed to not only articulate new strategies to create a sense of belonging along different lines—replacing fascism's key social appeal—but also establish new non-violent productive outlets for young people, particularly young men. The single most obvious way to do both was to reform secondary and tertiary education. Indeed, after the war many male higher school and university students were also military veterans, and so embodied both of the groups that Michael Mann identified as most likely to become fascist.[2] Like military and paramilitary organizations, educational institutions create feelings of belonging in two ways—through both the ideology of the educational content and the intensity of the interactions among participants. If postwar reformers hoped to redirect that sense of community, any successful post-fascist institution would have to provide satisfaction in both forms as well.

Two of the first postwar Ministers of Education explicitly worried that students from the military academies, whose education had been abruptly terminated when their schools closed on August 18, 1945 (army) and September 30, 1945 (navy), would cause trouble. As an Occupation official explained, Maeda Tamon (1884–1962), who served as Minister of Education from August 18, 1945, to January 13, 1946, moved quickly to enroll these students in other schools, "activated by a desire to remove this minority group from possible subversive influences and to disperse them widely in civilian institutions." Maeda feared that having "this large group of disillusioned young men around with not enough to do ... would 'constitute a grave problem for social equilibrium.'"[3] The navy's elite higher schools included the Military Aviation Academy, the Military Paymasters' School, the Naval Academy, and the Naval Engineering

School, and the army supervised an equivalent set. In addition to this top tier, the Ministry of Education and the Imperial Japanese Army jointly administered 15,000 technical middle schools, making this group a truly significant number of students.[4]

Morito Tatsuo (1888–1984), Minister of Education from May 1947 to March 1948, continued to track these students carefully for the same reason and also streamlined school admissions for newly demobilized soldiers. Maeda, who had represented Japan at the International Labour Organization in the 1920s, and Morito, who worked for many years at the Ōhara Institute for Social Research, had both thought carefully about social conflict and its causes. Neither man argued that veterans deserved priority because of their service to the nation. Rather, they feared their potential to disrupt society and sought to placate, rather than reward, them. Interestingly, the Occupation officials were not nearly as enthusiastic about enrolling the former military cadets in civilian schools, fearing they would ideologically indoctrinate others, and they insisted on limiting them to 10 percent of the student body of any school.[5] That small disagreement rested within a larger transnational consensus on the proper direction for educational change.

As Takemae Eiji reminds us, the early Occupation's philosophy of education dovetailed with that of postwar Japanese, to the point where "Occupation authorities found themselves working closely with their Japanese counterparts to implement what would turn out to be in some important respects a Japanese programme of reform."[6] The major educational reforms of the postwar years are so closely associated with the American occupation that it is easy to forget how many Japanese were passionately concerned with transforming what happened in schools. In 1955 Education Minister Morito noted that many people had worked to change educational institutions for decades and finally had the chance to enact their long-standing ideas after the war. As a typical example, although making secondary schools co-educational is often spoken of as an Occupation reform, Julia Bullock's recent work traces a history of Japanese efforts to merge Japanese all-male middle and higher schools with girls' schools long before 1945, and shows that, like Morito, these individuals worked closely with Occupationaires to finally make it happen.[7]

Because Kanagawa Prefecture housed the headquarters of the U.S. Eighth Army, educators there experienced an unusually large degree of American engagement, which did not necessarily mean conflict over educational content. For example, Occupation personnel, who thought Japanese officials did not move fast enough, found a space at Yokosuka for a group of Catholic nuns to reopen the Seisen girls' elementary school. On another occasion, the Occupation army decreed that a former Japanese navy storehouse be used to shelter one of the new middle schools, disrupting the prefectural government's plan to turn it into housing. Their opponents merely wanted the buildings for other purposes rather than disagreeing about the educational program itself.[8] Gordon Bowles, who was in charge of the education section of the Occupation bureaucracy and spoke Japanese, confirmed that local reformers shaped education policy more than did Americans when he estimated that Japanese individuals proposed 60 percent of the education-related reforms and shaped all the rest in discussions along the way, integrating American and Japanese ideas. That coordination explains why, in Takemae's words, "the Occupation's transformation of educational content was dramatic, thorough-going and enduring. Compared with the pre-1945 school programme, it was revolutionary."[9] Their actions marked a widespread Japanese repudiation of the education system in place during and before the war.

In pre-surrender Japan, teacher training was especially tightly controlled; government officials had an unusually broad range of ways to discipline future educators. The only institutions authorized to produce primary-school teachers were state normal schools, and young people who embarked on this career had to be recommended by their prefectural governor, county head, or city mayor. Once enrolled, they were required to live in dormitories, where their extra-curricular activities were monitored. Normal-school principals could and often did expel students for unacceptable political behavior, such as attending a lecture by an anarchist.[10] In return for paying for their training, the government assigned novice teachers to their first jobs, based on their professors' recommendations, so these judgments controlled where they lived as adults. Politically suspect individuals ended up in isolated villages far from their original homes. This history explains why the postwar reformers integrated the formerly separate normal schools into the new university system. The widespread popularity of this change also indicates that Paul Webb, an American Occupation official, was correct when in 1949 he stated that Japanese people "generally agreed that the normal schools were the breeding grounds of much of the prewar militaristic and ultra-nationalistic spirit in the Japanese people."[11] Dismantling this teacher-training system was an early post-fascist act.

Many adult Japanese in 1945 desperately wanted to convey to young people the message that education could encourage them to develop their own goals rather than just prepare them to die in war. This group included both professional educators and amateurs. Ienaga Saburō (1913–2002), who tirelessly argued that a different philosophy of education, one that emphasized peaceful communication, accuracy of information, the right to dissent, and respect for all the world's people, would have given Japanese citizens the tools to prevent war even though their leaders had desired it, was the most famous.[12] In addition, a surprisingly large number of postwar Japanese with no connection to professional education agreed with Ienaga so heartily that they started their own schools and universities.

One of the institutions created in this manner was the Kamakura Akademia. This short-lived humanities-centric college taught about 600 students for five years, before collapsing. Planning began on November 5, 1945, when a group of civic-minded Kamakura residents—none of them teachers—calling themselves the Kamakura Culture Committee (Kamakura Bunkakai) met to choose a collective postwar project and decided to establish a new college explicitly in order to redirect young adults away from fascist thought. Their founding statement explained that "the education of young people from here on requires avoiding the people whose hands were dyed with the formal education of the past," and they took responsibility for making that change. The group elected a committee consisting of three farmers, the abbot of a Zen Buddhist temple, one bureaucrat, a journalist, and the local librarian. Three of these men were also heads of neighborhood associations (*chōnaikai*). The librarian, Kimura Hikosaburō, explained that "avoiding Ministry of Education controls was essential although we also hoped to win certification as a university. So we decided to 'create something out of nothing.' "[13] They aimed to invent a new kind of educational institution to train post-fascist citizens.

The nicknames for the school, "college of the fields" (*nōzan no daigaku*) and "temple-school university" (*terakoya daigaku*), emphasized its location away from Tokyo and, more importantly, the desires of the founders to serve the needs of students whose lives had been blighted by the war. Their goal was to "create a new will among the Japanese people—new industry, new daily life, new culture"—by creating better formal educational structures that allowed students and teachers to jointly pursue knowledge. Like Maeda and Morito they actively recruited young men whose education had been cut short when the military academies abruptly closed, hoping to transform their thinking. In another consequential decision, they sought teachers "whose thinking was dialectical materialist," meaning politically left-wing, committed to a social-scientific system of knowledge, and informed by progressive education principles. This hiring priority explains why so many Akademia faculty members previously had been persecuted for their beliefs. More succinctly, as one of the seven men on the planning committee put it, "We wanted to create free-thinking people."[14]

The Akademia's founding organization, the Kamakura Culture Committee, represented the long-standing Kamakura elite, the *jimoto no hito*, whose families had lived there for centuries, often since Kamakura had been the Shogun's capital in the twelfth through fourteenth centuries. It had first formed in 1940 as the Kamakura Bunka Kyōkai but when they reconvened in 1945, the members changed their name to symbolize the changes in their views about life and society, as Kimura later explained.[15] The date of the first organization's founding—1940—signals that its original purpose almost certainly had been to mesh with national and imperial fascist mobilization campaigns. So does the presence of three heads of neighborhood associations. Moreover, this group had organized some of the displays of patriotism at sites like Tsurugaoka Hachiman Shrine described in Chapter 1. The Kamakura Culture Committee members were thus typical of the broad range of people who developed during the war what Rieko Kage and Sheldon Garon call "civic skills," such as planning events, public speaking, and managing finances.[16] This is a common outcome of major wars since civilians must take over the work that soldiers leave behind.

The Kamakura Culture Committee members were thus directly grappling with the problem of what to reject and what to retain from their personal recent pasts. Their sense of responsibility derived from a belief that they had been both victimized by the war fever and complicit in it. Establishing the Akademia was thus an act of collective self-criticism at the same time that it signaled their desire to continue as community leaders and to take responsibility for creating a society where everyone was free to explore their own desires. More than educational content itself, they identified the problem facing most Japanese individuals as a trauma that cut deepest because it was in part self-inflicted. Since they saw a school as the solution, we know they framed the problem fundamentally as one of ignorance. And, perhaps most impressively, they radiated confidence and optimism about changing the future by founding a new university amid the ruins of postwar Japan.[17]

The Kamakura Akademia was by no means alone in its philosophy of education; many schools and adult-education centers created after the war adopted the principles of progressive education and student-centered learning explicitly to help young people resist social conformity. One similar but larger school in Kyoto, the Jinbun Gakuen, opened its doors the month after the Akademia, in June 1946. The Jinbun Gakuen was actually more experimental in style than the Akademia—for example, students received no formal grades— but rested on a similar philosophy taught by a similarly politically progressive and highly educated faculty. The teachers included Mashita Shin'ichi (1906-

1985), Shinmura Takeshi (1905–1992), and Nakai Masakazu (1900–1952), all literature or linguistics scholars trained in Kyoto. Maeda Tamon, the first postwar Education Minister mentioned above, enrolled his daughter Mieko in that school, giving it national visibility.[18]

Similarly, the Shomin University in Mishima and the Ueda Free University in Nagano were also established by local people who responded to the war's end by creating post-fascist institutions of higher education. Both of those schools built on prewar local traditions of progressive academies that had been forcibly closed during the war. Other people, such as the staff of the Ōhara Institute, where both Morito Tatsuo and Ōuchi Hyōe spent the war years, helped reopen and expand urban night schools so that full-time workers could earn higher-school and college degrees. Meanwhile other individuals, often encouraged by SCAP, established adult-education centers that offered learning but not formal credentials. One of these, the Kamakura Citizens' Summer Institute, opened in the neighboring town of Fujisawa in 1946, and included on its faculty Hayashi Tatsuo (1896–1984), who also taught at the Akademia. In the 1970s, a former student, Kubota Jun, recreated the Kamakura Akademia on this "lifelong learning" model.[19]

Many other people across Japan who did not go as far as founding a new school still turned to the topic of the relationship between education and citizen activism because they were asking themselves how to prepare young people for democracy. One indication of such popular interest is their reading choices. Victor Kobayashi reports that between 1945 and 1952 at least 199 books and essays were published in Japan on the educational philosophy of John Dewey alone, not to mention eleven different translations of Dewey's own work. Kobayashi convincingly shows that these publications reflected widespread Japanese interest rather than enthusiasm by Occupationaires.[20] Dewey's central points were that good education creates empowered and creative individuals and that democracy requires these well-informed citizens. This post-fascist Japanese hunger for more knowledge extended beyond educational and political theory. Bookstores were thronged with readers who devoured works on many intellectually challenging topics, along with trashy novels and porn—also far more freely available than in the past.

Citizen-activists in Kamakura, as in other parts of Japan, institutionalized another Occupation-era educational reform, the Parent Teacher Association (PTA). As the official city history put it, "People really began to understand that the PTA could play an important role in helping schools in material ways... In addition, in an unanticipated development, a 'PTA activism' that could support the needs of the era began to take root in the region." The Kamakura parents who joined the PTA formed part of the huge surge of "civic engagement" documented by Rieko Kage in these years, just as the Americans had intended.[21] They first organized to advocate for funds to build six new middle schools in response to the March 1947 decree making that level of education mandatory. Next they focused on establishing a new co-educational high school to serve the newly expanded group of middle-school graduates. Several hundred parents visited the Mayor's office to ask for one in June 1947. Their pressure meant officials moved very quickly and by March 1948 the high school was up and running with 22 teachers, 113 freshmen, and 45 sophomores. Moreover, 180 graduates of the local middle schools were poised to move to the new high school on April 1st, bringing the total to 338 students. By 1950 the school boasted 407 students and 18 more teachers.[22]

In other words, Kamakura was one of many places where teachers, local citizens, national bureaucrats, American Occupationaires, and young people all recreated Japanese education as a post-fascist project. They cooperated to create new institutional structures that they hoped would protect them from the nationalist and imperialist juggernaut that had overwhelmed them and everyone they knew. Returning briefly to Michael Mann's explanation of fascism's rise in Europe, these individuals agreed that fascist movements would find it harder to seize control of an institution "whose everyday practices embodied liberalism."[23]

Choosing the humanities

This national surge of education-reform efforts was the context for the Kamakura Akademia's launch. The Akademia opened its doors in May 1946 with thirty-eight professors—impressively early, given the many challenges the organizers faced. Its local founders initially provided the school with a strong fiscal and administrative footing. Hisaeda Takenosuke gave 170,000 yen in cash while Enomoto Yoshinobu pledged 24.5 acres (30,000 *tsubo*) of land on Kamakura Mountain. Next they won accreditation from the Ministry of Education on March 21, 1946, partly by the savvy strategy of applying under the rules that governed girls' higher schools, technical institutes, and the old military schools, rather than as a more elite university. In addition to the blessing of the national government, the Kamakura Akademia also needed help from the prefecture and city to get off the ground. The founders went directly to Governor Uchiyama Iwatarō, who granted formal permission to create the university and also helped

Figure 2.1 Main gate of Kōmyōji Temple, the first home of the Kamakura Akademia. 2010. Photograph by Laura Hein

the school open within the grounds of Kōmyōji Temple, its first location. At that point, the Mayors of Kamakura and neighboring Fujisawa both joined the school's board of directors.[24]

The founders decided to establish a humanities college rather than a full-range institution because their highest priority was to create new kinds of cosmopolitan citizens. The school offered three degree tracks: literature, drama, and economics. The third track was intended to provide analytical framing for the expressive forms of culture stressed by the other two. They actually used the term *sangyō*, or industry, rather than "economics," which they treated as equivalent to "social science," encompassing economic and social thought in general, rather than the narrower term in general use today. The theater track, soon expanded to include cinema, attracted particularly creative and articulate students and was the most successful section. Numada Yōichi, in the literature classroom down the hall, wistfully reported that on the first day in 1946, "we could hear the people in the theater classes roaring with laughter as students introduced themselves."[25]

These individuals defined the humanities and social sciences jointly as the "cultural sciences," a widely used concept at the time. Indeed, Akademia President

Saigusa Hiroto, one of Japan's first historians of science, who also published extensively on literature and art, was part of the prewar group that had introduced the concept to the Japanese public sphere. He treated science as a historical human creation, born out of a desire for an internally coherent, secular way of understanding human society and its relationship to the natural world. Kevin Doak has traced the intellectual history of the term "cultural science," which came from German scholar Heinrich Rickert's (1863–1936) ideas about the nature of historical reasoning. Like his friends Miki Kiyoshi (1897–1945) and Hani Gorō (1901–1983), Saigusa had read Rickert's work in the 1920s and that of Rickert's colleague, Wilhelm Dilthey (1833–1911). Anticipating the central assumptions of twenty-first-century science studies, Rickert argued that the scientific method and empiricism were themselves historical creations, initiated by people who were expressing the values of their own era. Although as Doak notes, Rickert still thought he was making history more objective and thus more scientific, none of these twentieth-century Japanese men were positivists.[26] By 1945, moreover, they were painfully aware that the universalism and precision of scientific reasoning had been mobilized for war, empire, and fascism and that *no* form of modern knowledge had emerged unscathed. As Saigusa pointed out on the day the Akademia moved to its second location in Totsuka, even the chairs on which the students sat had a military pedigree, since the school had inherited the Naval Fuel Depot's furniture.[27] Nothing in their world was pure. In 1945 science seemed to them just a *better* tool to break the enchantment of fascism rather than a perfect one.

This concept of "cultural science" was widely accepted in postwar Japan as a tool to unmake fascism; for example, Nanbara Shigeru (1889–1974), president of Tokyo University, in his address of welcome on October 2, 1948 to an American delegation of experts, spoke for Japanese scholars in general when he said: "It is nevertheless a self-evident fact that the promotion of science, natural and cultural, is the *sine qua non* of Japan's rehabilitation as an enlightened and peace-loving nation."[28] Nanbara and the Akademia faculty were focusing not just on qualities intrinsic to the scientific method itself—rationality, universalism, replicability—but also ones that are more properly thought of as the culture surrounding science, such as curiosity about the natural world. The point of "cultural science" was as much to subsume science to humanism as the other way around.

The Americans Nanbara addressed fully understood and respected this interpretive strategy, incorporating the concept of cultural science into their own bureaucratic initiatives. In fact, the group he was speaking to signaled as much through its name, the United States Cultural Science Mission to Japan, which made recommendations for postgraduate education. Its head, Charles E. Martin, also understood "cultural science" as a response to the ideological mobilization of the fascist years. He deplored the capture of science and technology in Japan by "government and business ... which have made science and technology tools of bureaucracy, imperialism, authoritarianism, militarism, and war, [which] has impeded the development of Japan as a democratic country." Martin went on to explain that even more than redirecting the physical sciences, "It is only by the release of the humanities and the social sciences from such domination, whether political, military, or technological, that democracy may, as a long-range matter, displace totalitarianism, and peaceful intent displace aggression."[29] This set of beliefs explains why the Kamakura founders decided to establish the Akademia as a humanities institution, why Saigusa Hiroto was a good match for the fledgling school, and why the larger community, including many Americans, thought it an exciting new venture.

As scholars such as Ruth Rogaski, Todd Henry, and Aaron Stephen Moore have recently shown, science itself was the justification for much Japanese violence in the empire and occupied territories, primarily because it was yoked to disdain for local people. That disdain was the exact center of why imperialism for Japan, as for the other colonial powers, meant horrific violence in the name of scientific modernity. While the ideology of science itself, including the aesthetics of what James C. Scott has called "thin simplification," played a key role in normalizing and justifying that systemic violence, not all scientists shared the aesthetic of simplification. The Akademia faculty explicitly did not; when they championed rationality, they meant being realistic about events—such as a military defeat—rather than imposing uniformity on others.[30]

The social composition of the faculty also was distinctive. The planners began by asking Iitsuka Tomoichirō (1893–1983), an expert on Kabuki who was already active in the Kamakura Culture Committee, to serve as President of the Akademia, and to hire the rest of the faculty in consultation with other prominent intellectuals.[31] Many of the scholars he recruited, such as the man who was President for most of the institution's life and most influenced its character, Saigusa Hiroto, already had national reputations. Most had graduated from the elite higher schools and imperial universities. Saigusa was part of the wave of Japanese artists and scholars who moved to Kamakura in the 1920s, forming an urban nucleus of "the creative class," as discussed in Chapter 1. Other faculty members, such as theater scholar Endō Shingo (1906–1996), accepted the job in 1946 because the offer included housing, a welcome amenity given that the Endō family had been made homeless by Allied bombing raids.[32]

The Akademia was thus created by three distinct social groups, the local notables who founded the university, the educated elite who sank roots in Kamakura in the 1920s, and the new wave of urban refugees who had just arrived. These intellectual and social worlds overlapped through friendship networks and proximity. For example, the librarian Kimura Hikosaburō, born in Kamakura, and Akademia literature professor Takami Jun (1907–1965), a prewar transplant, met through a mutual close friend, Shimaki Kensaku (1903–1945), and shared a hospital vigil when he died just as the war ended.[33] All three groups also mingled at a Kamakura-yama bookstore, where the proprietor welcomed "higher-school students, workers, visual artists, performing artists, labor-union leaders, various hangers-on, and Kamakura [Akademia] students" according to one frequent visitor. Hattori Shisō (1901–1956), the Marxist historian and Dean of the Akademia who also had relocated to Kamakura in the 1920s, was particularly fond of the bookshop.[34] The small scale and density of Kamakura created an intimacy that crossed other lines—people met each other at the market, on the long train ride to Tokyo, strolling by the ocean, or in local restaurants and bars. Often their children attended school together; for example, the sons of Satomi Ton (1888–1983) and Ōmori Yoshitarō (1898–1940) became good friends.[35]

But the Akademia faculty members shared far more than a workplace, an exclusive education, and a mailing address in 1945. Many of them had seen their chances for a presurrender academic career ruined because they had been arrested and imprisoned for violating the 1925 Peace Preservation Laws, which typically also meant getting fired from academic posts and blacklisted from new ones. Hattori Shisō spent many years as the communications director for Kao Soap Company, which he must have hated because he quit the job on August 17, 1945, without lining up anything else first.[36] Murayama Tomoyoshi (1901–1977), a cultural theorist and multitalented visual and performance artist prior to his Akademia role as a theater professor, had spent some of the Pacific War years in prison. By the end of his sentence, Murayama recalled, "I was nothing but skin and bones and was too weak to do anything but sit in a chair. My hands and body looked like a skeleton's."[37] These men were chosen explicitly because of these experiences, since the Kamakura Culture Committee's desire "to avoid the people whose hands were dyed with the formal education of the past" shaped the nature of the faculty. The founders got precisely the kind of university they wanted.

The Akademia was also only one of a number of new Kamakura institutions with overlapping memberships, all designed to create "a self-aware citizenry

Figure 2.2 Kamakura Akademia faculty photograph. Saigusa Hiroto is in front. Behind him, from the left, are Yoshino Hideo, Yamaguchi Masao, and Hattori Shisō. In the third row, Yoshida Ken'ichi and Nagata Hideo are barely visible, next to Tanabe Sukatoshi and, mostly obscured, Sakabe Kiyo, then Murayama Tomoyoshi, and Sugai Jun'ichi. In the back row are Tashiro Michitoshi, Haruki Noboru, Kataoka Ryūichi, Torii Hirō, Kubō Shun'ichi, Hayashi Tatsuo (behind the others), Yamane Kiyomichi, Takami Jun in kimono, and Endō Tadashi. ca. 1947. Courtesy of the Kamakura City Central Public Library archive.

(*jikaku kokumin*) that understands the reason for defeat," as Saigusa put it.[38] Another, the Kamakura Bunko, was launched two weeks after the surrender on August 30, 1945, as a new post-fascist publishing house. Recognizing in July that the debacle in Okinawa presaged military defeat, a group of local writers, including Takami Jun and Osaragi Jirō, began quiet conversations about how to respond. By the end of September they had raised one million yen and hired Kimura Tokuzō, previously of *Kaizō* magazine, as editor to oversee both four monthly journals and a book series. As Takahashi Hideo explains, the Kamakura group wanted to create an institution that would serve as a bulwark against the return of fascism, or as they grandly put it, "we wanted to revolutionize publishing," particularly by challenging government censorship and by encouraging writers to publicly "explore self-reflection on human morals and self-criticism." By the third issue of *Man*, the translation they chose for *Ningen* magazine, the print run was 70,000 copies. In addition to Takami, Saigusa and other Akademia faculty published there.[39]

Like the Akademia, the Kamakura Bunko was part of a larger trend of new research and publishing institutions. In Tokyo at the same time Noma Hiroshi (1915–1991) invited Katō Shūichi (1919–2008) to establish a different publication, *Kibachi*, because "the most compelling thing for writers to do then was to start new literary journals based on pacifism and respect for human rights."[40] Similar discussions took place just before the war ended at economic policy think tanks such as the Ōhara Institute, another run by Takahashi Kamekichi (1894–1977), a third focused on finance, headed by Shibusawa Keizō (1896–1953), and a fourth at the Ministry of Foreign Affairs, all treating the disaster as a golden opportunity to reshape the economic relationship between the Japanese state and society along less fascist lines.[41]

In Kamakura, the publishing house, like the Akademia, was fundamentally designed to champion the humanities, that is, the "cultural sciences." The Kamakura Bunko started selling books in 1945, and still occasionally releases elegantly produced volumes in the twenty-first century. Early books included fiction by Japan's leading novelists, such as Akutagawa Ryūnosuke's *Rashomon* and Kawabata Yasunari's *Snow Country*, translations of Nikolai Vasilevich Gogol, Andre Gide, and Andre Malraux, and left-wing scholarship, such as the correspondence between Japan's first Marxist economists Kawakami Hajime (1879–1946) and Kushida Tamizō (1885–1934), edited by Ōuchi Hyōe. The name *Ningen* was repurposed from the small literary journal that Kume Masao, Takami Jun, Satomi Ton, and a few others had started in 1918, mentioned in Chapter 1, and the staff came mainly from the Kaizō publishing house.

The Kamakura Bunko was in the late 1940s a powerhouse, with a huge book list. By October 1948 the company had already published 120 books with a combined press run of 1.5 million copies.[42] Attesting to their good relationship with the Occupation, only one book had been censored, or, more precisely, the Bunko editors decided not to publish it because the fourteen major deletions ordered meant it was no longer coherent.[43] Another related venture was a children's literature series with a small press that defined itself as Kamakura-centered, although the editorial office was actually in Tokyo, the Shōnan Shobō. Osaragi published several beautifully illustrated volumes, while Kume Masao wrote one. The series also included a 1948 translation of a portion of Harriet Beecher

Stowe's *Uncle Tom's Cabin*, by Muraoka Hanako, *Dorei Tomu Monogatari*.[44] The Akademia faculty also resumed active publishing lives as individuals, both because they could now write in a much less constrained political environment and because they needed the money. Indeed, some of them enjoyed an enormous readership.

The "men of culture" created these institutions out of a complicated mix of responsibility, optimism, and shame. Osaragi and Takami invited Kume Masao, who had so enthusiastically supported the war, to become an officer of the Kamakura Bunko, joining Osaragi and Kawabata Yasunari. Their pledge to publish in a spirit of "self-criticism" both acknowledged their own cooperation with the censors and the military in the past and functioned to repudiate it. Similarly, the Akademia faculty acknowledged their sense of debt to younger people for depriving them of the chance to choose their own paths through life, and they hoped these new institutions would make amends for that. The historian Hattori Shisō later said he joined the Akademia because

> I wanted to provide an opportunity for young people after the war's end—especially the members of the unfortunate generation who had to abandon middle school or higher school during the conflict and those who graduated just before then. How often had they had the chance to talk about the freedoms they collectively possess as young workers?... The realities of defeated Japan and [the task of] accomplishing democratic revolution require a greater understanding than in the past of the meanings of modern Japanese history... The young generation has a much stronger passion for democratically rebuilding our country than do their elders. I want to encourage them because I think they can tackle—and steadily solve—our grave problems. And, as far as I am concerned, the classrooms of the Kamakura Akademia and the schools for workers being run by labor unions are places where this training is especially rigorous.[45]

This is why Hattori preferred a job at the Akademia rather than Kao Soap Company.

The Akademia's philosophy of education rested on the proposition that true learning took place when it was initiated by students, meaning that students had to first define their own goals, unconnected to national ones. One way the professors encouraged them to do so was to include students when writing and scoring the entrance exams and conducting interviews for the next year's class. The 1948 exam gives a good sense of the assumptions underlying the school's curriculum. The English portion required aspiring scholars to translate into

Japanese the following statements: "During those two centuries the Japanese were as completely cut off from the rest of the world as though they lived upon another planet," followed by, "In such cases we may admire the powers which are shown by the world's conqueror; but these must not blind us to the real nature of his deeds," and, finally, "Spring has restored to me something of the long-forgotten vigour of youth; I walk without weariness; I sing to myself like a boy, and the song is one I knew in boyhood."[46] In other words, they immediately telegraphed their desire to impart cosmopolitanism, rejection of violence, and an optimistic sense of renewal.

Their commitment to student-centered learning was also highlighted by President Saigusa's favorite metaphor: that students were like birds alighting on a tree branch: the student-bird "chooses where to land, not the branch."[47] Saigusa also described the school as a place to develop the skills to choose one's own life's direction, perennially one of the primary goals for humanities education. As he explained, the purpose of a university was to

> learn for ourselves—not for others. In feudal times we learned for our parents or our country. But now we learn for our own social education. If we want to change the direction of the country and family tradition, we must learn not to destroy ourselves. Develop ourselves as much as possible—that's the socially [important] thing. For that reason, you students must take responsibility for yourselves.[48]

Given that only a few months earlier, the government had defined acting on any desire other than for total self-destruction as selfishness, this was a profoundly liberating educational philosophy. In later decades, this stance would sometimes sound self-absorbed and privileged but in the late 1940s this was an important assertion, one that provided young people with the tools to demobilize themselves from the fascist enterprise.

Taking such responsibility required learning how to disagree constructively, another skill the faculty considered crucial. As one student, Takase Yoshio, recalled, "the Akademia teachers were not all of one philosophical school… The ethos was to encourage students to come to their own conclusions. For example, one professor might complain that '*tanka* poetry is the literature of slaves' while in the next room Professor Yoshino Hideo would erupt in anger if a student made the same assertion."[49] Any topic—poetic form, feudal land-holding patterns, mathematics—could lead directly to an exhilaratingly new experience. Because the stance of being passionate while also valuing dissent simply had not been an option in wartime fascist society, learning to disagree required a

Figure 2.3 Saigusa Hiroto, President of the Kamakura Akademia, who built on his study of the history of science to create a student-centered, open-education college. 1963.

complete reimagination of community and its rituals of belonging. People who only a year earlier had clustered around radios to participate in what Kenneth Ruoff has called "self-administered forms of citizenship training," such as all bowing to the emperor at the same time, could now simply refuse to participate in activities mandated from above.[50] Rather than "harmony" of opinion and behavior, they were free to choose their own attitudes, provided they respected each other's differences. For the first time in decades—meaning for the first time in the students' adult lives—the social space in which Japanese people could express their individual selves was expanding rather than contracting. Teaching students to constructively maneuver through that new space was another way in which the Akademia operated as a humanistic endeavor.

At the same time, all the teachers defined their task as community-building as well as imparting skills to individuals, so that their students would feel no desire for fascist belonging. Saigusa regularly invoked the model of Yoshida Shōin, one of the first individuals in the nineteenth century to become passionately interested in the world beyond Japanese shores. Saigusa admired Yoshida for his cosmopolitanism, his curiosity, and his willingness to defy authority, qualities that led directly to his execution in 1859 by the Shogun's government. Saigusa also praised his scientific turn of mind, which, in his opinion, made Yoshida an important exception to most Japanese of the era, who "lacked the quality of abstraction—preventing them from developing a modern concept of nature."[51] But when he invoked Yoshida Shoin as a model for the Akademia, Saigusa above all was celebrating his close relationship with his students at his rural academy of higher learning. As Iida Ken'ichi, an Akademia student, put it, "like Yoshida Shōin's Shōkason-juku, the teachers and the people being taught at the Kamakura Akademia forged strong bonds of human relations and trust between each other and were very close psychologically."[52] Saigusa wanted to create a community based on a sense of mutual responsibility and shared adventure that was "not clannish (*mibunteki*), conservative, or artificial."[53]

Cultural historian Hayashi Tatsuo (1896–1984) also offered Yoshida Shoin's school as a model, along with European Renaissance universities, as places where groups of people cooperated to "transplant" ideas developed elsewhere into their own societies.[54] In 1938, when celebrations of national cultural purity were on the rise, Hayashi had already argued in print that culture traveled well and that, like trees and shrubs, ideas that were transplanted from somewhere else were often more vigorous and desirable than native ones. Hayashi, the son of a diplomat, had lived in Seattle as a child, which must have contributed to this line of thought.[55] His postwar pupils soaked up his concept of "transplant culture" as though they themselves were thirsty plants. The imaginative community the professors created for the Akademia students was thus both global and trans-historical in ways designed to undercut the anti-Western grudges of wartime leaders, highlighting their conviction that the conflict had been unnecessary. It also deftly dismissed the problem of authenticity that had generated so much earlier anxiety.

Student–faculty engagements

The students brought their own agendas as well. Their desperate desire for education was common in 1945, as is typical for people whose schooling is disrupted by conflict. This hunger to return to the classroom is one of the many ironic, rather than direct, ways that the wartime experience contributed to what Hiraku Shimoda has called the "spirit of grit" that prevailed after defeat.[56] Rather than being built on the sacrifices made during the war, this energy came from anger at having been forced to make them. One young man recalled that wartime graffiti in the toilet at the Kanazawa Prefecture No. 4 middle school, by then an industrial workplace, read, "I want to study. I wish the teachers would let us do that, even just for an hour."[57] Clearly many young people agreed: by the end of September 1945, an astonishing 86 percent of Kamakura students were already back in the classroom. So many teens signed up for middle school in 1948 in Yokohama that double-shifts overtaxed the classroom space and they were split into triple shifts. By 1950 nationally 96 percent of elementary and middle-school-aged students were studying, while about a fifth of older teens—male and female—had enrolled in high school, far more than before the war. By 1956 the fraction was nearly a third and the Kamakura numbers were considerably higher.[58]

The single most important aspect of postwar educational reform was simply that a far greater percentage of young people could receive secondary-school and university education than in the past. In the old system, despite expansion in the 1920s, only around 10 percent of male and 8 percent of female elementary-school graduates had enrolled in academic middle schools, although when schools that trained boys for careers at such places as the Japan National Railroad and the military are included, about 40 percent of Japanese boys received some kind of formal training beyond primary school. But opportunities drastically narrowed again when young people graduated from middle school. About 60 percent of this group pursued higher education, mostly vocational training. The twenty-three public academic higher schools accommodated only 13.4 percent of them in 1925 and, even though the government added eleven more schools over the next fifteen years, in 1940 they still offered spaces to only 20.3 percent of male middle-school graduates.[59]

The daily experience of school changed too in ways that added to its transformational effect on participants. One reason the early postwar was such a culturally rich moment in Japanese history was that people of different ages and life experiences were thrown together in ways that had not happened before the war nor would last long after it. Higher education in particular attracted a broad range of people: demobilized soldiers, still dressed in khaki, civilians who had evacuated to villages that lacked secondary schools, so their education also had been interrupted, new graduates wearing their previous schools' uniforms, and older people who had started work already but decided to respond to the cosmic gift of survival by doing exactly what they wanted to do.[60] Many students kept their jobs while attending the Akademia, to pay tuition and put food on the table.

Another reason the Kamakura Akademia felt new was that, like other postwar schools, it was co-ed, something that few of the students had experienced since second grade.[61] It was exciting to share classes with potential romantic partners, especially knowing that war would no longer function to separate young men from women. For the students, gender-mixed classrooms symbolized "democratizing through and through," creating a new feeling of belonging that included at least the promise of more sex and much less violence. Moreover, the young military veterans saw the escape from the hierarchy of military life— and the notoriously high levels of "friendly" violence associated with that—as a central benefit of post-fascist society. A smaller but symbolically resonant decision was to dispense with a dress code.[62]

The experience of attending the Akademia was, of course, different for women. On one hand, they were included in the central activities of the institution on formally equal terms, which was still highly unusual. On the other hand, both faculty and students betrayed casually unself-conscious sexism in their actions and commentary, such as the student-run theater clubs that extended classical Japanese theater tradition by barring women. The Akademia hired only a few female faculty members, notably English professor Sakabe Kiyo, who had grown up in Seattle and later translated a book by Louisa May Alcott.[63] But the early postwar years comprised a heady moment for young women, who were suddenly much freer to express and act on their own desires than ever before, and the Akademia provided ways to do so that not only satisfyingly combined respectability and excitement but also were framed as democratization. The humanities curriculum itself offered many entry points for discussion of this fascinating topic, not to mention the fact that an educational philosophy that valorized self-expression for all human beings must have been especially exhilarating for women students.

The gender implications of connecting scholarship to socializing were obvious to all. According to Mark McClelland, "one's ability to engage in new, modern 'democratic' styles of courtship became an important way of acquiring social capital in postwar Japan." Magazines and newspapers published at least 700 articles on this issue in the first four postwar years.[64] Most Akademia students and faculty walked from the train station to campus, first at Kōmyōji and then in Totsuka, creating an ideal opportunity to discuss and implement the ideas they encountered. By all accounts, students took full advantage of this informal but still "educational" intellectual space of the commute to school. One student recalled that "the wide-ranging discussions on the road were one reason why it felt like open education—people engaged in them without thought to whether they were in a classroom or not." Indeed, it was hard to distinguish the open-air debates from formal learning, especially in the winter because it was often too cold to sit in the classrooms. Sometimes the students just roamed about in order to stay warm. "We were cold all the time. At Kōmyōji there were no stoves or heaters. We just wore lots of clothes. It is hard to remember today how hungry and cold we were all the time. We'd go anywhere where it was warm. If we saw a bonfire, we'd head for it," another student reminisced.[65]

Faculty also deliberately shaped the educational experience through their use of this penumbral time surrounding formal lessons. Co-education meant female inclusion in this ambiguous after-school socializing with the faculty, something that had long been a central component of elite university life for young men. Professor Yoshino Hideo (1902–1967) was particularly fond of this activity, and Yamaguchi Haruko remarked almost twenty years later that she was keenly aware that "unlike the male students, I would never have had the opportunity to go drinking with Professor Yoshino," the activity accompanying much of his teaching, if she had not joined the Akademia student body.[66] Yoshino, who was

Figure 2.4 Kamakura Akademia faculty and students commuting between the school and the railroad station, where many of the most interesting discussions took place. ca. 1947. Courtesy of the Kamakura City Central Public Library archive.

just establishing his reputation as a *tanka* poet, epitomized a romantic ideal of education that erased conventional boundaries in ways that would have explicitly excluded women in the past. He typically held his classes outdoors, taking the students on long walks into the hills or down to the ocean, where he read poems from the eighth-century *Manyōshū* aloud, keyed to the season and the locale. His unorthodox style modeled his visions of the creative genius and post-fascist intellectual community of empowered individuals. As one student recalled. "He'd stop in the middle of a lecture to give a student money to buy some sake," and then

> After the class, he'd bring all us students back to his home. While continuing to drink, he'd argue and engage with us all evening long. We'd sleep there that night. He simply didn't observe the distinction between the time formally set aside for class and free time. The official day for his class was Friday but he didn't pay much attention to that, and just invited us home whenever he wanted to. We'd spiritedly argue about literature all the time [as equals], not as a professor and his disciples. When we finally reached a conclusion, he'd send us on our way.

It seems likely that the women students enjoyed being part of this lively exchange but were also well aware that when Yoshino "invited us to stay the night, it created hardship for his poor wife."[67]

The students fully understood that they were being asked to create post-fascist selves. Years later Hirosawa Ei (b. 1924), a film scriptwriter, said that he was trying to sort out the issues of collaboration and war culpability for himself when he enrolled. Hirosawa's draft notice came on the same day that he was hired at the Tōhō movie studio and thus he had been able to combine soldiering and filmmaking. When the war ended, he started reading previously banned books and learned for the first time that some Japanese had opposed the war. Until then, "I thought of myself as a victim who had been deceived. But [I then realized] at the same time, I was also a perpetrator. I had worked on a film that supported the military police, for example, and I became a soldier. After 15 August 1945 I was sorting out the meaning of the war for myself." Hirosawa was attracted to the school for openly acknowledging the need to do so and also for presenting the teachers as "coaches" who were searching for answers to the same questions rather than as authority figures.[68]

Tsugami Tadashi (1924–2014), a theater student, was questioning his own wartime beliefs too. Tsugami had been rejected by the military and then lost his job because he had tuberculosis. While confined to a hospital, he began an intensive reading course, including Hattori's *History of Japanese Capitalism* (*Nihon Shihonshugi Hattatsu Shi,*) and concluded that "as I went deeper into these works, I realized how much the 'holy' war in Greater East Asia was an anti-Marxist strategy." Just after the war ended, Tsugami's elder brother died in Tokyo and he traveled there to collect his remains. It must have been sad to know that the 25-year-old had managed to stay alive through the long years of conflict but not lived to enjoy the peace. While in this reflective frame of mind, walking through Tokyo, Tsugami was asked directions by an American soldier in a jeep. They chatted amiably for a few minutes, and this chance encounter, layered on the sorrow of his brother's too-short life, affected Tsugami enough to send him to the theater whenever American or European plays were being staged, and to audition for *The Doll's House* in early 1946. As Tsugami put it, "I felt that I was like Nora, moving from doll to woman" as he rethought his life.[69] His encounter with the American in the jeep brought home to him how little he knew about the world beyond Japan and sparked a fierce desire to find out more.

Another student, Maeda Takehiko (1929–2011), came to the school after joining a youth-soldier corps, where he had served on the battlefield and "pledged to give away my life." As he put it, "the war left a big hole in my heart and I didn't know what I wanted." Maeda and the others who "returned from the realm of the dead" wanted to study with people who had not asked for that sacrifice.[70] Katō Shigeo's (b. 1925) personal wartime experience similarly had convinced him that something had gone terribly wrong. He had nearly finished a technical-school degree in airplane maintenance when he was drafted in mid-1945. Instead of using his skills, the army leaders expected him to fight the enemy furnished only with a bamboo pole, since there were no spare parts for the few aircraft still available. And, he added bitterly, "they didn't even have enough bamboo poles!" Katō also reflected on the irony that he was required to take an English-language class at the Akademia less than a year after it had been denigrated as the language of the enemy. "When I considered this, I began to think that how we live our lives is under our own power to change." He was drawn to the school's ability "to gather together various young people whose defeated hearts and bodies were in pain."[71]

These young men were searching for ways to heal the damage that fascism and war had done to them and also through them. Today we would use the therapeutic language of treatment for post-traumatic stress disorder but in the 1940s enrolling at the Kamakura Akademia performed that function for them, providing a structure in which they could make sense of their experiences in new ways, often for the first time. For at least one traumatized former military engineer and POW (prisoner of war) in China, the Akademia literally brought back his capacity to converse. Minamikawa Tadashi (1925–2001) was so moved by a stage performance that he broke the war-induced silence he had maintained at the school until then.[72]

When wars end, frequently such people are permanently lost to society; after years in uniform or in factories, some individuals find it difficult to return to an activity that now feels childish, others are traumatized to the point where they cannot muster up the necessary concentration, some see little point in deferring other life goals, while yet others have too many responsibilities to take any time for themselves. Veterans frequently develop a sense of injured hostility to civilians—especially women—because they feel their sacrifices are inadequately appreciated. Andrew Barshay has recently concluded that, in après-guerre Japan, the Japanese soldiers who returned after surviving years as POWs in Siberia had been rendered incapable of social engagement—that is, their ability to work with other people—but not of individualism by their experiences. One reason Japan successfully transitioned to a peaceful society surely is in part because, unlike the Siberian POWs, young men like Hirosawa, Tsugami, Maeda, Katō, and Minamikawa were able to advance their education in ways that reconnected them emotionally to a broad range of other human beings.[73]

Tsugami was also typical in that his longing to connect to others extended to a global imagined community, explicitly including members of the Occupation forces, not just other Japanese. Students also appreciated their professors' efforts to convey cultural developments from abroad; Takase Yoshio, who entered the Akademia in 1948, said that the most appealing aspect of the new university was that it invoked international culture in exciting ways, such as when historian Shimada Yūjirō explained that the faculty and students of medieval Italian universities, like the students huddled in front of him in their overcoats, had only improvised spaces in which to learn.[74] And the teachers who had been lucky enough to go overseas before the war talked about their travels often, precisely because that experience had so powerfully enlarged their own imaginative worlds. Saigusa was typical when he described his sojourn in Germany as "a transformative experience that gave me a worldwide perspective," even though he spent only six months there in 1930–1931. Saigusa, like most other Japanese who visited interwar Europe, forever after saw himself—and his nation—as full participants in global scientific, artistic, and political trends rather than mere followers.[75] This transnational community remained an important source of their identity as well as a wellspring of ideas for the rest of their lives.

Every aspect of society had been transformed in the war years to support state priorities, and both faculty and students put this profoundly disorienting fact at the center of their studies. Takami Jun was the faculty member who most openly grappled with the problem described by Jay Winter and Emmanuel Sivan: "Under Fascism ... the invasion of everyday private life by political agents contaminated memories of mundane events: how to write about family life under such circumstances was a profound challenge. Where 'normality' ended and the monstrous began is a question which may never be answered fully."[76] As Donald Keene has recently argued, Takami's prose provides a particularly clear window into postwar Japanese reassessments of their own recent behavior. Takami's popularity as a writer was based on his willingness to make explicit his ambivalence about his engagement with the war, and his shamed recognition that he had all too thoughtlessly enjoyed wartime activities that in retrospect seemed heartless, a predicament that serves as an elegantly succinct definition of post-fascism.

Takami's political thinking had developed over the decades. He had been a Marxist as a young man, but was frightened into renouncing leftist politics after arrest, torture, and brief imprisonment in 1933. Thereafter he avoided overt political engagement, and the troubled link between psychological and sociological experience became the central theme of his literary output for the rest of his life, often focusing on different forms of anxiety, particularly shame.[77] During the war, the government mobilized his skills as a writer, and he took two long overseas trips, traveling as part of an army "pen brigade" to Bali, Vietnam, and Burma in 1941 and to China in 1944. He returned to Japan just before the devastating air raid on Tokyo on March 10, 1945. While he was teaching at the Akademia, Takami was editing and revising his wartime diaries as well as re-examining his wartime beliefs. Although he did not publish them until later, he discussed this project with his students at the time.[78]

Takami's wartime diaries celebrated his feelings of comradeship within a national community, for example, when he saw Tokyoites patiently lining up for trains out of the city, the day after the firebombing.

> Before I knew it, tears had poured from my eyes. My heart was full of love and affection. I thought that I wanted to live with these people and die with them. No—though I was not the victim of a bombing, I was one with such people. These ordinary people have not been authorized to emit angry voices. They have no influence they can depend on, no money, but as they wait in patient silence they love and trust Japan from their hearts. I was one with them.[79]

The passage shows some distance from the state, although he takes for granted the fact that the national railroad was still functioning, but is characterized by generalizing about national character and a search for ways to merge emotionally with "these ordinary people." Over the next year, Takami's diary and his Akademia lectures show him struggling to disengage from what Tansman has called "the aesthetics of beauty defined as devotion to a horizontally imagined community," his definition of the aesthetics of fascism.[80]

Takami never fully broke these habits of generalizing about national character but he developed some tactics to interrupt them. In his postwar writing and teaching, he focused directly on the feelings of sincerity and authentic belonging that had so attracted him during the war, and explored both his rage at official hypocrisy and the reasons why he had so deeply desired that national community in the first place. The cynicism revealed by Japan's civilian and military enforcers when the war ended broke the enchantment of Tansman's cultural sublime for Takami as it did for many others. After Japan's military leaders not only failed to commit "glorious self-destruction" but also commandeered resources such as seats on the last departing trains in Manchuria, leaving civilians to walk to the coast across hostile territory, few people remained in awe of them. Back in Japan, some of the people who had most vociferously demanded sacrifice from others also revealed their opportunism. Japanese who were children and teenagers in

1945 often reported that they first understood the difference between principle and political jockeying when they watched a particularly jingoistic teacher become a champion of democracy overnight.[81] This was another ironic, rather than direct, contribution of the war to postwar society—and a lesson that could not be unlearned for those who absorbed it first-hand.

The selfishness of Japan's leaders in the face of defeat gave Takami solid ground to stand on that did not melt into a sense of inadequacy and isolation, the emotions that had fueled his support of the war and empire. Next, Takami came to think that Japan's national stance of aggrieved bravado itself had been the spur that drove the country into an idiotic conflict. In other words, the war's end gave Takami a new public voice, one that suggested a way to live without resentfully submitting to authority figures. While his previous strategies had been limited to empty assertions of strength and sullen acceptance of orders, for the first time Takami began to feel he could be part of an effort to change the structures—national, social, and familial—that had shaped his older responses of shame and thwarted rage. The central goal of his writing after 1945 was to explore this explicitly post-fascist agenda for his readers.

Takami brought this concern into the classroom, arguing that students could block the aesthetics of fascism by checking the relevance of abstract thought to their own lives. After explaining that study is the process of absorbing outside ideas, while writing involves externalizing personal creativity, Takami reduced the combination to a neat formula: A (book learning) leads to C (analytical knowledge), while B (experiential learning) leads to D (wisdom from emotions). But real understanding also requires using B to understand C and D to understand A, creating a self-sustaining cycle.[82] While this is amusingly presented as a scientific formula, it is actually a call to think as a humanist. Takami's equation also contributed to the school's emphasis on applying academic skills to the real world throughout the curriculum, a rare approach in presurrender elite education, but something intrinsic to the way that Saigusa and his prewar colleagues had understood "cultural science," as Kevin Doak has argued. This emphasis also meshed with their commitment to value the qualities that students brought to the educational enterprise as highly as the ones imparted by the teachers.[83] Their desire to directly link formal elite education to real-world applications, moreover, is another instance of the ways that progressive Japanese goals dovetailed with early Occupation education policy.[84]

In the late 1940s, the consequences of living under fascism that most disturbed Takami was the emotional exhaustion he both felt himself and observed in others, which, typically, he defined with pinpoint exactitude.

> We've undergone extreme indoctrination, and we feel it. At the same time, the expression on people's faces is one of profound resignation, seeming to say 'It doesn't matter what happens—no matter what happens, it can't be helped.' It is not, however, the blackness of despair...it is a colorless, tasteless, odorless expression of the belief 'things will work out somehow.' ... Not only our bodies but our spirits are at their twilight.

Takami was pointing out that, despite its promise, the war had—in the end—robbed people of the confidence that they could ever enjoy a community of belonging, just as did life in Siberian POW camps. Takami saw his postwar task as a way to reanimate the spirits of his students and readers without replicating the sugar-high effect of fascist mobilization. He was heartened when he observed Japanese being "mild-mannered, easy-going, basically not at all belligerent" to others, which he saw as evidence of the true self-confidence they needed for a post-fascist future.[85]

Takami's focus on encouraging self-confidence in his students was not just for the sake of improving domestic Japanese society. He also saw this quality as crucial to making Japan a better neighbor to Asia, because, in his view, suppressed rage—particularly the rage of thwarted masculinity—about slights Japanese men had endured when Westerners and Asians alike had failed to respect their authority—explained their cruelty on the mainland. In retrospect, Takami also thought the war—not just the ensuing Allied military occupation—had "emasculated" Japanese.

> In some ways, the reign of terror turned them into little lambs incapable of expressing openly their anger in either words or deeds—spiritless, strengthless human beings. But one can't say that...they are a gentle people who dislike cruelty...It might be more accurate to say that the Japanese were particularly cruel. The Japanese soldiers at the front in China indulged in acts of cruelty to their heart's content. The Japanese become cruel when they have power. When their power is taken away, they are docile as lambs, even servile...So when they were given power, they wanted to display it. They became inhuman. They became brutal. They overstepped the bounds. It was a kind of hysteria induced by the fact that power had never before been placed in their hands. The poor Japanese.[86]

Takami was making two points. First, a sense of emotional inadequacy had blinded people, including himself, to the impact of their own actions, and second, those feelings of inadequacy were generated by demands that they set their own desires aside to sacrifice for others. Abusing power abroad had felt like compensating for powerlessness under a fascist regime, and any effective way forward had to address that emotional reality. In short, Takami felt that most Japanese were perpetrators *because* they had been taken advantage of by the very people who had demanded they sacrifice for the community.[87] For him, exploring the ways that Japanese had been victimized at home was thus a stepping-stone to exploring their brutality abroad rather than an attempt to evade that task.

Takami found that even his personal memories shifted their valence as he re-thought wartime society in this light. Although he was a profoundly selfish man, in this regard he was an honest one. He admitted in print that by 1945 he understood that all hungry and homeless people behaved in ways he had breezily thought were unsavory characteristics of the Chinese national character. In an April 24, 1944, entry in his diary, Takami wrote that as his train south from Tokyo passed through Ōfuna, he saw women and children scrabbling among ash-heaps for coal that might still burn. He commented, "in China I saw such scenes everywhere. Although the Japanese looked down on the Chinese as backward, poverty and wartime shortages had driven even Japanese to desperate expedients." Similarly, Takami wrote in his August 16, 1945, diary entry that in November 1944 he had witnessed Japanese officers harassing Russian musicians and female taxi dancers in Harbin. At the time, he had felt briefly ashamed—and had fleetingly wondered whether a Japanese victory would encourage more such behavior—but had not given the incident enough importance to write down his reactions.[88] The day after the war ended, it seemed more significant. It is not clear whether Takami wrote these entries in 1945 or (more likely) added them later, but either way, they show the pathways of his reassessment and his perceptiveness.

As his frequent focus on emasculation suggests, Takami's perspective was deeply gendered. Takami had horrible relationships with women in general and his mother—with whom he lived his entire adult life—in particular. As Keene explains, Takami revealed in his published work that his personal sense of shame at his illegitimate birth and boiling-point rage at his mother underpinned his experience as a national subject and member of society as well. His mother, a domestic servant, had been impregnated by her employer, perhaps explaining why he was so focused on prostitution as a metaphor for occupied Japan, as explored by Michael Molasky, and why his imagined citizen was so obviously male.[89] When he nationalized issues of sexual shame and extra-marital sex, he really was working out his own story. Throughout his life he resented male authority figures whose self-confidence and power made him feel weak and ashamed, felt even more enraged at himself for having done their bidding, and was perennially contemptuous of women for their association with those men. Most of all Takami went white-hot ballistic to discover cynicism and hypocrisy in authority figures. The core of his incandescent rage was directed at Japan's wartime leaders but he expressed similar anger toward Occupation members when he saw them with Japanese women. His professional interactions with Occupation personnel through the Akademia and the Kamakura Bunko, however, were largely amicable, and his first impression of an American soldier in 1945 led to the comment that the Americans were respectful of Japanese as human beings.[90]

Despite being blessed with a sunnier personality than Takami, Mashita Shin'ichi, who taught at the Kyoto Jinbun Gakuen, described the effect of the surrender in similar ways. "I felt a strange kind of self-confidence... It was as though my head was filled with rainbow-colored images of life after having lived so long with a world of nothing but khaki." Later in the day Mashita passed the jail where he had been held for half a year and noticed white smoke rising from a bonfire. When he went closer, he realized that the Special Higher Police (*Tokkō*) were burning all the records of their investigations—confessions, mug shots, case notes, and trial transcripts. As Mashita put it,

> They were all being fed into the flames. I understood this in a flash. I was looking at the enforcers of fascism and militarism—who had steadily investigated lawbreakers such as myself—in the act of revealing themselves as people who had also engaged in criminal activities. Probably in anticipation of the 'occupying forces,' they collected all the evidence of their investigations and turned it into ashes when they had lost authority.[91]

For Mashita, this was a definitive "post-fascist" moment.

Mashita soon had one of the deeply weird experiences that revealed the degree to which wartime enforcers were motivated by self-interested cynicism. About three days later, two of the same Special Higher Police detectives who had once interrogated him came to Mashita's house requesting a favor. Using the respectful language they had pointedly avoided earlier, they asked "Sensei, you know how to fish, will you be kind enough to introduce us to the craft?" They then wrote a "free pass" for the train to Lake Biwa, and the three men traveled there late the same day. Mashita said that being treated like an important guest by men who had threatened and belittled him just a few days earlier was one of "the small ways that I could tell the entire society had shifted on its axis. I was so happy that I had lived to see this day. I felt completely rewarded."[92] Mashita did not publish this anecdote until 1975 but it is easy to imagine that his students would have been riveted by his words if Mashita had shared them earlier in the classroom.

Murayama Tomoyoshi is best known in English through Gennifer Weisenfeld's work on the MAVO art movement but in the postwar years he concentrated on other talents, particularly theater directing, script-writing, stage-set design, and drama criticism, all of which he taught at the Akademia. Murayama also illustrated children's literature, including translations of *Robinson Crusoe, Gulliver's Travels,* and stories by Anatole France and Hans Christian Anderson, extending his focus on education, as well as teaching at the Akademia. In fact, Murayama had a long-standing interest in progressive education dating back to his childhood. Both young Murayama and his mother had worked for Hani Motoko (1873–1957), who founded the progressive girls' school Jiyūgaoka Gakuen, and Murayama's wife, Kazuko (1903–1946), had been a student there.[93] The Jiyūgaoka Gakuen operated on John Dewey's principle that education should be the well-spring of democracy, and in the prewar years had responded to the national requirement to teach morality by holding "discussions in which the pupils criticized each other as well as themselves so as to instill-self-examination… They didn't have grades or final exams. Instead the teachers gave criticism and suggestions for improvement."[94] The school also arranged for students to integrate hands-on life experience with classroom study, such as working in a nursery to learn about human behavior through observations of young children, so Murayama was already familiar with both student-centered and experiential learning. The Murayamas remained close to the Hani family, in part because Murayama's good friend, Mori Gorō, married Hani Setsuko (1903–1987), Motoko's daughter, and took her family's name in 1926.

The prewar Jiyūgaoka Gakuen was only one of several ways Murayama encountered transnational movements in his youth. During his sojourn in Berlin in 1922, he socialized with the artists from across Europe who were creating Dadaism, Italian Futurism, Constructivism, and Expressionism. Murayama was lucky enough to be invited to exhibit in Dusseldorf and at the highly influential Berlin gallery *Der Sturm*, and to interact with modern-dance pioneers Mary Wigman and Niddy Impekoven. He clearly contributed ideas to the European artists as well as absorbing them. Omuka Toshiharu reports that "in [Russian artist El] Lissitzky's address book Murayama was entered, symbolically enough, just below Kasimer Malevich and Piet Mondrian, and above Filippo Marinetti. The Japanese artist had joined the international circle of the avant-garde."[95] Needless to say, many of the artistic and design movements flourishing in Berlin then carried explicit political meaning.[96]

Interestingly, Murayama also weighed in on the issue of Japanese self-confidence and its relationship to unhealthy nationalism in a short story he published in the 1920s, set in Weimar Berlin. In that era, due to an international treaty, Japanese traveling abroad exchanged their yen for British pounds, meaning that, because the British currency held its value during the hyper-inflation in Germany, the Japanese there were suddenly rich. Not everyone handled their good fortune well. In the story, Maruyama depicted Japanese visitors who lorded it over their hosts, insisting that a dance-hall orchestra play *Kimigayo*, and scattering devalued marks on the musicians' heads as an incentive. After quarreling with some equally boorish Americans, everyone involved was arrested.[97] Thus, despite his own well-deserved reputation as a flamboyant pain in the neck, Murayama was clearly able to distinguish between obnoxious jingoistic bravado and—sometimes also obnoxious—genuine personal self-confidence.[98]

Murayama and his friends in Berlin, including Mori Gorō, were also politically engaged observers of democratic Weimar society before the Nazis gained power. They were there earlier than Saigusa, but Mori kept in close touch with three Marxist economists in Heidelberg at the same time—Sakisaka Itsurō, Uno Kōzō, and Ōuchi Hyōe—as well as philosopher Miki Kiyoshi, who later worked closely with Saigusa. In those years, despite defeat in the First World War, Germany was at the pinnacle of global scientific, social-scientific, and technological achievement, explaining why so many Japanese—and Americans—studied there. All were keenly interested in the German post–First World War artistic scene and political culture. In particular, Murayama absorbed artistic commentary on the effects of military defeat on German society, for example, publishing an essay on visual artist George Grosz (1893–1959) in 1922 that stressed the ways that war dehumanized all its participants.[99] Grosz's signature themes also appeared in short stories Murayama published then, such as one that described a maimed veteran on the Berlin streets, who was nothing but a "machine made from a human" after losing both legs, an arm, and parts of his face.[100] Like Grosz, Murayama recognized that some of the horror of the "machine made from a human" derived from the modernity of the devastation. Two decades later, the resonances with post-surrender Japan in 1945 cannot have escaped him.

Murayama had plenty of opportunity to ponder the dehumanizing effects of modern conflict. He was arrested and imprisoned three times; for six months in 1930, then for twenty months in 1932–1933, and, finally, at Sugamo Prison, in solitary confinement for nearly two years, in 1940–1942. Senda Koreya (1904–1994), who briefly taught drama at the Akademia, was arrested in the same 1940 sweep. As Maruyama later recalled, prison conditions gradually worsened. The number of letters he was allowed to write each week steadily diminished, as did the permitted length. By the end, he could only send postcards. The hardest moment was when his mother died, in early December 1941, just before the attack on Pearl Harbor. Although he was not granted compassionate leave to see her while she was dying, he was allowed to attend her funeral with a police escort, knowing that she had surely worried about him in her last hours.[101]

Like Takami, Murayama both renounced his leftist beliefs in order to win release from prison and then published a slightly fictionalized examination of how miserable that act made him feel. Even though Murayama possessed one of the most robust egos on the planet, he emerged from the war feeling conflicted about his own actions, suggesting that no one was immune. Nor did he argue that his persecution exempted him from self-criticism even though he had spent the war years in terror of being murdered by the police. As he later explained, Murayama knew that his prosecutors and jailers harbored no compassion for him. "They felt that we prisoners had stepped beyond ethical behavior (*rongai*) and so it was fine to kill us all… That's why Miki Kiyoshi and Tosaka Jun both died although I didn't know this at the time."[102] After his release, Ōya Sōichi (1900–1970), the well-known journalist, visited Maruyama late in the war to urge him to flee to mutual friends in Korea, because "the military is planning to create concentration camps like those in Germany for people like you when Japan is defeated." Heeding Ōya's counsel, Murayama left for Seoul [Keijō], Pyongyang, and Dalian [Dairen] in March 1945, returning to Japan in December 1945.[103]

Murayama's experience in the wartime empire, like Takami's, troubled him later although he was not quite as honest about it as was Takami. Despite the steadily encroaching war, Murayama enjoyed both artistic recognition and a creative burst of energy with Korean partners. In 1944 he began painting portraits to earn a living and, despite a ban on publishing anything in writing, was successful enough as a painter to mount an exhibit in a Ginza gallery in October 1944 and in the Seoul Mitsukoshi Department Store gallery at the very end of the war, from August 1 to 6, 1945.[104] In Korea Murayama lived first with Jo Taekwon (Gen Michisawa) with whom he choreographed a dance, and then with a theater-director friend, Chun Hyang-Jeon (Chang Hokchu), while writing a play together.[105] Murayama claimed that he wasn't worried about his own safety after August 15, because, unlike other Japanese in Seoul, "I was completely different and was a friend of Koreans." Nonetheless, when his first host's mother started to complain that Murayama had outstayed his welcome, he found it prudent to move on.[106]

Murayama and Takami's discomfort about Japanese behavior in the Empire—and in Europe—was palpable and sincere, but they spent less time thinking about the war's harm to Asians than about the debts due to other Japanese. Their rhetorical stance repudiating Japanese imperialism was consistent but only occasionally tied to concrete actions, let alone institution-building. By contrast, Maruyama's postwar actions chosen to "make amends" domestically for his role in the war included taking Akademia students on tour around Japan to stage puppet shows. They charged only 99 sen and often drew 1,000 kids for each show. Murayama argued that "theater, of all the arts, is closest to daily life and to the actual conditions—the reality—of our existence, allowing us to reflect on and reenact those conditions ... so theater productions really pop with intensity." The experience of watching plays, he averred, helped people understand what was wrong in their lives and societies and imagine ways "to step-by-step get closer to an ideal society."[107]

In 1949 Murayama published a primer with a labor-union press on how amateurs could produce theater as a strategy for decoupling individuals from the fascist past. As he explained, "theater conveys the hardships and sorrows and joys and anger of many different kinds of people. Actors play all of these roles and try to think and act and feel like their characters... It's not enough to pretend to be sad when the script calls for shedding tears—you have to actually feel sad!" As he put it,

> for instance, during the recent Pacific War, didn't it seem that in general people in Japan conducted their lives as though they all thought the same way and felt the same way? That was mostly true but, starting with the Communists, some people never changed their perspective and could perceive the true nature of the war. They opposed it throughout the era even though they knew how workers were supposed to think and feel. Why were these people not pulled along in the riptide of the times? How did they hold fast to their principles?

Their individual resilience had great social relevance, he concluded, and theater was an excellent way to explore that fact.

But more important than insight into other people, working on a play led to self-examination.

> When people play the parts of individuals who are nothing like themselves and...really have to explore the feelings of those people, and really become the character, even more than finding the core of that character, they have to understand their own individual nature. Understanding their own thoughts, feelings, actions, and how they transition, and then recognizing the ways they themselves are similar to or different from the character they are studying—that is the only possible way to deduce how to play another individual.

Moreover, such self-knowledge is hard to achieve in any other way.

> "Reflecting on our own nature is something that, to be honest, we are all terrible at… No one wants to acknowledge one's own errors. This instinctive feeling is universal and is very strong in all of us. This is why it so hard to see ourselves clearly. Nearly everyone goes to their death without understanding his own true essence. But all humans are riddled with flaws."

Theater, because it teaches people about themselves by requiring that they understand the core motivations of another individual, "is really helpful for this process."[108]

In other words, for Murayama, this exercise in empathy and self-discovery was the central post-fascist task.

The end of the Akademia

Despite the earnest efforts of its faculty, the Akademia folded after five years. It failed because of a confluence of misfortunes, only some of which were intended. As mentioned earlier, the men who established the Akademia in 1946 set aside both land and a substantial cash grant as an endowment for the new school. Unfortunately neither form of wealth held its value for long. The cash donation came just before bank accounts were frozen and the rapidly inflating yen was revalued in February 1946, shrinking the endowment to a paltry size. The Occupation land reform dealt another unintended blow to the university's financial health when Enomoto's acreage was redistributed to tenant farmers.[109] The Akademia never fully recovered from these losses. The school initially had strong support from wealthy Japanese, led by Yamaguchi Masao, a prosperous businessman whose children went there. Other backers included Ichimada Hisato (1893–1984), who was President of the Bank of Japan at the time, Horikoshi Teizō (1898–1987), who soon became the Secretary-General of the Japan Business Federation (Keizai Dantai Rengokai), and future Prime Minister Ishibashi Tanzan (1884–1973), as well as Daiei Film Company President Nagata Masaichi (1906–1985), bankers Nishino Masahiko and Higuchi Kōyō, Shimizu Yasuo of Shimizu Corporation, and others. This list of heavy hitters from the ranks of national—not local—business leaders is remarkable, and shows how much was possible in those early postwar years. Yet partly because of changes in property and income-tax law, and because the national government denied the school's request for classification as a foundation (*zaidan hōjin*), by 1950 the school was unable to raise adequate money from its patrons, and it shut down after graduating its last class in March 1951.[110] A window of opportunity had closed for the Akademia to serve as a post-fascist model of higher education.

The Akademia's financial problems were compounded—and partly caused—by growing political hostility, mainly from the Ministry of Education, by then recaptured by conservatives, but also including the Occupation. Japanese analyses of the Occupation have long stressed a "reverse course," arguing that the Occupation's main thrust shifted from democratization in the first two years to distrust of progressive and anti-fascist initiatives due to an unreasonable fear of communism. This analysis holds particularly well for education. SCAP documents, such as the Civil Information & Education Section's *Monthly Reports*, show that through mid-1948 the Americans actively prevented right-wing teachers from presiding over Japanese classrooms. But they also reveal a gradually growing concern that communists would take advantage of idealistic young Japanese and usurp power under cover of democracy, a concern evident in the Americans' assessment of the Akademia by mid-1947.[111]

At first, SCAP and the Eighth Army encouraged the school but on July 1, 1947, the Kanagawa-based U.S. Military Government recorded in its *Monthly Report* that "leftist activities at Kamakura University increase." The report began with the puzzling assertion that "The Kamakura University was founded for profiteering purposes by some capitalists but due to the inexperienced managership, commercial motives, and lack of teachers, it has been easy for the formation of a leftist faculty. The school was originally called the 'Socialist University' but was changed to the 'Kamakura University.'" The author estimated that about 15 of the 450 students were communists, which, although probably correct, seems a small number to have generated the hysterical tone of the report, particularly since every institution of higher learning enrolled a few communists in 1947.[112] Many people joined the Japan Communist Party after the war to support political freedom and express a desire for social change rather than out of a deep commitment to the party itself. In Kanagawa Prefecture in 1948 one political officer, Major George M. Gaither, noted with alarm that local communists were attempting "to organize certain cultural and democratic organization[s] which will cooperate with labor[er]s and farmers," showing their ongoing anxiety that humanities and culture would be the vehicle by which these unwelcome opinions would spread in Japan.[113]

As Saigusa Hiroto patiently explained, "To the extent that the Kamakura Akademia was part of the international world and part of Japan, people were passionate about their ideas and politics. I never saw a problem at the time. If some students got too pushy, the other students would challenge them."[114] A few of the faculty, notably Hattori Shiso, also joined the Japan Communist Party after the war, alarming the Americans, although Saigusa did not. The bemused SCAP author also seems to have confused the transliterated Greek of "Akademia" with the homonym "aka" for the color red and assumed that "red" was a euphemism for socialism. This confusion was known at the time, and the students bitterly joked that the school should have been named "Kamakura White-iversity," or Shirodemia.[115]

Yet the Akademia had supporters within the Occupation structure who prevailed for a few years. Haruki Takeshi, one of the thousands of Japanese nationals who worked directly for the Eighth Army (and who deserve more scholarly attention than they have yet received), ran interference for the school, protecting it from American anti-communism. Haruki spoke excellent English, thanks to his education at the University of Southern California, and chose English-language texts for Akademia courses. He served as a direct conduit to Occupation decision-makers, helping the school to move to a second campus in April 1948 after the new Constitution required delineating spaces as unambiguously either religious or secular, which meant ejecting the school from Kōmyōji temple. At that time, the Americans, nudged by Haruki, decreed that the Akademia be allowed to lease land at the former Naval Fuel Depot in Totsuka, even though the Yokohama Technical Institute, which already used some of the navy's space, wanted all of it. This was a victory, since the Occupation forces had previously denied the Akademia's request.[116] Eventually, however, Haruki's influence waned.

And in Tokyo, as Yoshiko Nozaki has shown, the Ministry of Education officials under Prime Minister Yoshida Shigeru began reasserting their right to control textbook content at around the same time, soon becoming one of the bastions of postwar conservatism.[117] The real fight for them was over the classroom as a workplace, however. Ministry of Education hostility developed teeth in 1950 when it seized on the anti-labor-union "red purge" blacklist created that year and applied it to the entire Akademia senior class. In spring 1950, one new Akademia graduate reported that when he applied for teaching jobs at middle schools, he was told that no one trained at such "a red school" would be hired.[118] Private firms also refused to employ Akademia students for the same reason. The Akademia's close connection to the Tōhō film studio, with its militant trade union, cannot have helped. Another Akademia graduate, Hatakenaka Masahiko, was fired from his Asahi News job at the same time, making it clear that all their students—past, present, and future—had uncertain employment prospects. This was the final blow. In his obituary of Hayashi Tatsuo, Kimura Hikosaburō said that their conversation about Hatakenaka's disturbing news—so similar to the 1930s—was one of his strongest memories of Hayashi, because they both had been so appalled by it.[119]

The faculty members were eminent enough to continue their careers at more robust institutions—and at much higher salaries too—after the school closed. Hattori Shisō, the faculty member whose presence most disturbed the anti-communists in SCAP, moved to Hōsei University, invited by its new president, Ōuchi Hyōe. Several others, including President Saigusa Hiroto, moved to Yokohama City University, where he became its President in 1961. One of the technical institutes run by local governments that were upgraded to full university status as part of the postwar educational reforms discussed above, Yokohama City University was—and is—committed to training young people from families that did not enjoy access to higher education in the past. The school also stressed the ways that the urban setting creates opportunities for community-building, an argument championed by Saigusa. After Saigusa died in a train crash in 1963, Akademia student Yamaguchi Hitomi tied the tragedy to this belief, commenting that "President Saigusa wasn't riding in the [first-class] Green Car. I think that was because he had an 'opposition mentality' and was not interested in self-aggrandizement… He was not an ordinary person."[120] Saigusa's policies at the Yokohama school also included expanding the humanities curriculum, linking academic study to real-world applications, and articulating and disseminating a vision of egalitarian urban cosmopolitanism, making Yokohama City University the most direct heir to the Kamakura Akademia.

Reforming educational institutions seemed a crucial post-fascist task for the individuals involved in the Akademia. Democratic education would not just reintegrate veterans and young civilians into society but would also teach them to recognize their own individual desires and feel greater empathy for people different from themselves. The Akademia founders and faculty hoped to repay their debt to young people for permitting a culture that had implicated every aspect of their lives in violent repression. They turned to the humanities to accomplish that task, using abstract ideas such as "transplant culture" and "cultural science" to combat anxieties over authenticity without discrediting diversity or dissent. They participated in remaking the entire system of secondary schools and universities across Japan into purveyors of high-quality mass education, and setting formal learning as the main route to improving the quality of life for the entire population, not just the main route to social mobility for its most academically talented members.

3

Telling Stories in the Museum:
The Kamakura Museum of Modern Art[1]

The Akademia shuttered its doors in spring 1951, but a few months later, a new cultural institution, the Kamakura Museum of Modern Art (*Kanagawa kenritsu kindai bijutsukan*), established by Kanagawa Prefecture, opened to the public.[2] The museum founders and curators self-consciously set out to create a new institution that would reshape society by creating a democratic aesthetic. They also developed an argument for why Kamakura and Kanagawa Prefecture more generally were auspicious environments in which to do so. Much like the Akademia founders, many of the people involved saw art appreciation—and more literally museum buildings—as spaces where Japanese of different ages, classes, and life experiences could learn to productively engage each other, and so work out their differences in a socially constructive manner. Indeed, observers considered building a regional modern art museum "an act of bravery" for this reason.[3] Most fundamentally, the museum has never pretended that art is a refuge from politics. Rather it reveals the curators' agendas in a variety of ways; through the physical space, in the manner that people interact there, via national arts organizations invented in Kamakura, and within the exhibition narratives themselves.

The museum's greatest contribution has been a sophisticated historical narrative that reframed Japanese modernity as part of a universal but highly diverse experience. As Alicia Volk has recently argued,

> the value of Japanese modern art may be located not in relation to any particular artistic canon but in the very stuff of its historical and cultural situatedness. This is not mere historical contextualization …. art, along with visual and material culture more broadly, were grounded in, reactive to, and most interestingly productive of a distinctive modernity, one that evolved according to its own logic and that involved both proximity and distance from "western" and "Asian" others.[4]

This process by which distinctive modernities develop is, as argued here, universal rather than specific to Japan, but the *narrative* Volk summarizes so elegantly is in itself spatially and historically situated, and in significant part this idea that modernity is produced by intercultural dialogue was developed at the Kamakura Museum of Modern Art. Moreover, this narrative was designed explicitly to counter the fascist ones of wartime Japan.

What were the key elements of this "distinctive modernity?" First, as explored in more detail below, the curators argued for diverse and dynamic modernities, a concept that parried both the idea that Japan was artistically a pale copy of modern Europe and the notion of a single national culture in Japan or elsewhere. They also treated the *idea* of national culture as a historical product, created by deliberate human actions. Anticipating Hobsbawm and Ranger's explication of the ways that tradition is reinvented all the time for modern—and nationalist— purposes, the curators also strove to show other Japanese the extent to which such manipulation was ubiquitous throughout the world, not just in Japan.[5] They thus reframed the relationship between tradition and modernity as interactive rather than a simple one-way and one-time transition, anticipating one of the central insights of post-colonial studies.

Perhaps most crucially, the people at the Kamakura Museum of Art simply rejected the concepts of an injured or thwarted nationalism and the alignment of individual identity to national identity, assumptions that had formed the heart of fascist political culture. Only seven years earlier it had been both illegal and dangerous to suggest that Japan's nineteenth-century leaders had invented the modern emperor system, and so this stance was widely recognized as a powerful political statement. And these ideas were exciting to everyone involved; both the museum's internal commentary and outsiders' reactions to it exude a sense of intellectual engagement and relevance. The core driver of modernity portrayed by the museum became not the result of some stable and innate "Japaneseness," either ethnic or emperor-centered, but the striving of its modern inhabitants. It must have felt incredibly liberating to be able to think along such lines, even for, or perhaps especially for, people who had tried hardest to believe in the superiority of an undefinable "Japanese spirit."

Founding the museum

The museum, Japan's first dedicated to modern art, developed out of local efforts to create new kinds of institutions, like the Akademia. It is impressive that anyone had the energy to make fine arts a priority in the Occupation years, when money was scarce and daily life required great effort. As museum curator Yagyū Fujio recalled, when the museum opened, Yokohama was still full of shops selling whale-meat stew and *kasutori shōchū*, the cheap liquor distilled from fermented dregs left behind after sake is made. Even established museums struggled, such as the Okura Shukokan Museum of Art, which only managed to keep its doors open in the postwar years by renting out part of its building as office space.[6] Taking the time to visit an art museum, let alone pay for the experience, required real commitment.

The Kamakura museum got its start through the efforts of both Kanagawa's prefectural governor, Uchiyama Iwatarō, and the American Occupation forces. In his earlier career as a diplomat in Paris and Madrid, Uchiyama had decided that art appreciation was a public experience best shared by all community members and that government should support the arts. In August 1949, he convened local artists and asked them to name their biggest problem. Not surprisingly, given how intensively both Yokohama and Kawasaki had been bombed, the response was "exhibition space."[7] Uchiyama then allocated 28.5 million yen (almost $80,000) in 1950 to establish a new museum, a highly unusual move at a moment when most local governments were focused on building housing, schools, and commercial infrastructure. The museum was only one of a string of new spaces Uchiyama erected to enhance public life in the prefecture. Nicknamed the "assembly hall governor" (*kaikan chiji*), Uchiyama built a center for educators in 1948, a Workers' Building in 1949 at the joint request of the Sōdōmei and Sanbetsu labor unions, and then a Farmers' Hall in 1952. As his biographer explained, he built them because "his philosophy was that in a democracy people needed places where they could meet and talk with each other."[8] The nearby Occupation forces agreed, and hailed the opening of each of these new spaces as signs of political progress.

Uchiyama acted at an opportune moment, just when Occupation officials dismantled the powerful Home Ministry, giving prefectures considerable independence from the national government, although Tokyo later reconsolidated some of that power.[9] Uchiyama also had excellent connections with both SCAP in Tokyo and U.S. Eighth Army headquarters in Yokohama, where he regularly met General Robert L. Eichelberger and once took General Walton H. Walker boar hunting. The museum would soon benefit from these connections, from Uchiyama's "lack of an inferiority complex" toward all these authorities, and from his "amateur's bravery and passion," as Osaragi Jirō put it.[10]

SCAP's philosophy of decentralization and democratization explicitly included encouraging local museums at the expense of national ones. As Satō Kaori notes, the Americans issued a directive on August 10, 1946, to democratize art in Japan in this manner.[11] The Fine Arts Advisors to SCAP, first Sherman E. Lee and then James M. Plumer, wanted to block the efforts of the National Museum to establish ten regional branches. Plumer argued that establishing independent prefectural and municipal museums was preferable, explaining that "proposed branches of National Museum, (e.g. as at Fukuoka and Nagasaki) should be frowned upon as coming into conflict with basic SCAP policy of decentralization." In a later memo, Plumer argued even more forcefully that "no other branches should be permitted" of the National Museum. He went on to complain that the policy of sending to the Tokyo museum "broken-off heads and other fragments from the gradually crumbling Buddhist stone caves in Oita-ken" was problematic because it promoted the "unfortunate possibility of draining Kyushu of cultural objects that should remain in Kyushu."[12] Clearly, the idea that the artistic heritage of local regions could strengthen resistance to the national government and therefore aid democracy had adherents within SCAP as well as among Japanese.

Plumer had very little success in his drive to promote local art centers. Despite stated policy, in practice, most of SCAP's museum-related efforts aided the National Museum in Tokyo. In mid-1949, for example, Plumer traveled to Kyushu to inspect art-related activities in the region. He "noted with regret" that projects to establish prefectural museums in Kagoshima and Miyazaki were on hold, because the relevant buildings were temporarily occupied by a police training academy and a girls' school, respectively. Few of Plumer's superiors shared his view that SCAP resources—such as the cost of sending him to Kyushu—were usefully spent on local arts development, and his other travel requests were brusquely refused.[13]

Yet, in the case of the Kamakura museum alone, the Occupation seems to have played a significant role in establishing a local museum by securing an affordable location. Governor Uchiyama at first planned to use a building erected for the 1948 Yokohama Trade Fair, but it proved inappropriate. Another Yokohama building was too expensive. Uchiyama then somehow persuaded the Tsurugaoka Hachiman Shrine to rent 71,080 square feet (2,000 *tsubo*) of its land near Kamakura station at essentially no cost to the prefecture. While many people would have preferred to build the museum closer to the main population centers, the ideal price, together with proximity to a station on the national train line, eventually carried the day.[14]

The agreement with the shrine was highly unusual, and almost certainly involved Occupation officials. SCAP's structure shows the likely internal channel of communication. The Arts and Monuments Branch was housed within the Religions and Cultural Resources Division of the Civil Information and Education Section (CI&E) of SCAP, meaning that the officials monitoring art-related activity interacted with those who oversaw religious reform every day. Shintō shrines were just then under orders to privatize, and donating this land would have tempered SCAP criticism of a shrine dedicated specifically to the god of war. Although no records seem to exist today, this effort surely stands as one of many examples of the ways in which mid-level Japanese and Americans at times worked together to create an outcome that was a low priority for top officials in both Tokyo governments.

Uchiyama, Plumer, and others were all interpreting the Occupation goals of demilitarization and democratization to mean decentralization of cultural institutions away from Tokyo, establishing public support for artists at the local level, and creating new structures that would help Kanagawa citizens create a fresh collaborative public culture. And this arrangement endured despite the fact that shrine officials have openly regretted the lost opportunity to build a money-making enterprise on the museum site.[15] (In March 2016 the building was closed because it was no longer safe for crowds, but Hachiman Shrine, still the owner of the land, has pledged not to tear down what is today seen as an architecturally significant Modernist edifice.) Given the many obstacles, the museum planners showed impressive initiative and perseverance, not to mention speed, in choosing the site, hiring an architect, building the structure, and getting art up on the walls.

In 1950, Sakakura Junzō (1901–1969) won a design contract for his stark white, Modernist, two-story rectangle. Sakakura kept his budget at half the amount estimated by the other architects by using asbestos (an environmental hazard that contributed to the 2016 closure). He found other creative economizing strategies, such as painting the walls of the interior courtyard white, allowing the museum to screen movies without a dedicated cinema space. But by contemporary standards the building is completely inadequate as a museum. For one thing, it has no elevator, so curators must carry art works up and down a steep flight of stairs. This deficiency, however, is dwarfed by the omission of climate control, a problem built into the original structure. Since even Sakakura's design had required expenditures higher than the budgeted amount, the committee decided to go without air conditioning or heat to make it affordable. While this meant that the museum was sometimes too hot or too cold for visitors, a far bigger problem was the lack of any mechanism to control humidity—the great enemy of fragile art. The curators combated the damp with charcoal braziers, a strategy that would be inconceivable in a professional museum anywhere in the world today.[16]

Nonetheless, early commentators invariably stressed the beauty of the structure in its natural surroundings. Often to their surprise, they found they liked the contrast between the stark white rectangle of the building and the lush greenery around the pond on which it seemed to float. Poet Ikeda Katsumi noted that, although people had feared that the museum would detract from the atmosphere of antiquity in Kamakura, he felt that it showed faith in contemporary culture and the strength of the human spirit.[17] Osaragi Jirō put it more succinctly when he commented that "the building is small but is inspired by a large muse."[18]

One important influence for the Kamakura museum was the Stedelijk Contemporary Art Museum founded by the city of Amsterdam. Sakakura used estimates by postwar director Willem Sandberg (1897–1984) on how much space would be needed for various functions when he was designing the museum building, as well as endorsing Sandberg's pledge to "overcome the past" by offering visitors a fresh approach to art.[19] Sandberg, who had been active in the Dutch resistance to the Nazis, specifically meant fascism when he used this phrase. The assistant director of the museum, Hijikata Teiichi, praised the Amsterdam museum for "doing something really important, which is to question the very concepts of tradition and modernity," an insight that transformed Hijikata's own thinking when he first encountered it there in 1930.[20] Satō Kei, another museum founder, also cited the Amsterdam museum as a model for "its commitment to work with citizens rather than dictating to them."[21]

Sakakura hoped the intimacy of the building itself would socially mobilize people in a variety of ways: "Unlike… monumental museums, this new museum can have an intimate relationship with people." Sakakura was particularly interested in its ability to foster local identity and create a dialogue between the past and the present. "The museum now built in Kamakura not only functions as a center for the interaction between the region and beyond, it also introduces local classical art and displays contemporary art for study and discovery. By shaping both artistic production and taste, the museum 'functions almost as cultural policy,' at the local rather than national level." Most of all, Sakakura concluded, "the museum can operate as a cultural center not just for Kanagawa prefecture but can be seen as a stroke of good fortune for all of Japan's regions. If this Kanagawa Prefectural Modern Art Museum becomes a pioneer,

Figure 3.1 Kamakura Museum of Modern Art building exterior, designed by Sakakura Junzō to be an intimate space in which to rethink the nature of modernity and modern communities. 2012. Photograph Courtesy of Timothy S. George.

then it will have fulfilled its purpose." Hopefully, visitors would feel both that their independent judgment mattered and that local solidarity could counter nationalist pressure from Tokyo. Sakakura wanted to capture all of this in the building's form.[22]

Hijikata's intellectual journey

Once the museum was built, the single most important individual who shaped its message was assistant director, and later director, Hijikata Teiichi (1904–1980). Although he was the "last man added" to the founding group, he soon dominated the intellectual profile of the new institution.[23] Hijikata, then in his late 40s, was a published poet and had earned a living as a journalist, editor, and arts bureaucrat. He also had written or translated eighteen books, but had never worked as a curator before the Kamakura museum opened. He had first attracted notice as a brilliant literature student at the Mito Higher School, then at Tokyo Imperial University, graduating in 1930 with a degree in aesthetics. In late 1930 Hijikata traveled to Berlin to study Hegelian aesthetics, the subject of his first book. Like both Murayama Tomoyoshi and Saigusa Hiroto, discussed in Chapter 2, he spent only a few months in Berlin, but somehow found time to learn about such European artistic and literary trends as Brechtian theater, German Expressionism, and the Bauhaus movement, as well as to visit museums—all activities that would shape his postwar projects.

Just before his European trip, Hijikata collaborated with Murayama on Edwin Hornle's German-language book, *The Fundamental Issues in Proletarian Education*. Hijikata translated the text and Murayama designed, illustrated, and bound the volume.[24] Although Hijikata was in Germany at the same time as Saigusa, they may not have met there but they certainly had begun their long friendship by the following year when Hijikata briefly joined the Marxist Society for the Study of Materialism (*Yuibutsuron kenkyūkai*), when Saigusa edited its journal. Hijikata was at first attracted by the group's interest in theorizing the relationship between culture and everyday life, but rather than identifying with their Marxism, Hijikata soon began to refer to himself as an anarchist. For the next few years he edited art books at a publishing house and wrote essays that explored the social relevance of European and Japanese cultural trends.

Hijikata shifted his primary focus from literature to visual art in the late 1930s, probably because he was attracted to the wider intellectual spaces surrounding that topic than for literary studies.[25] At the same time, he became increasingly interested in Chinese art, and used his Tokyo Imperial University connections to get paid to learn more. In April 1938, Hijikata began writing research reports about Chinese artistic and intellectual heritage for the Foreign Ministry. Hijikata was then based in Tokyo, although he traveled to China several times, and was in Shanghai on December 8, 1941 when the Pacific War began. He thus simultaneously began focusing directly on art history, the Chinese cultural tradition, and Japan's ambitions in Asia, opening up whole new vistas of scholarship and their relevance to Japanese imperial policy.

Like his trip to Europe in 1930, this constellation of new influences was intellectually productive for Hijikata, as we know because he picked up the pace of his publications. In 1941 Hijikata brought out three books in his new field: one on oil painter Kishida Ryūsei, another analyzing Western-style Japanese modern art, and a third that surveyed Chinese, Korean, and Japanese art history. These volumes collectively treated modern artistic traditions as a global phenomenon, while also tracing the ways that various individual modern artists engaged with the European, Asian, and Japanese past. Hijikata's months in Germany had already convinced him that it made no sense to think of modernity as something that occurred separately in different countries, and attention to China only confirmed that insight for him.[26] The first two of these books stressed the ways that ideas, techniques, and images moved from their original to new contexts, or what today we call "transnational flow." Hijikata was excited to be part of this process and understanding his wartime actions requires, as Alicia Volk put it, "a sense of the exhilarating revolutionary potential that the war represented" for individuals like him.[27] At that point, Hijikata focused on identifying nationally distinctive sources of global modernity, a topic he first explored in his translations of German works by Pierre Ramus, Franz Mehring, and Karl Wittfogel.[28] His interest in those authors make it clear that he was still banging his head against the conceptual box of belated modernity. On the other hand, he was already aware that Japanese discourse about its national culture closely resembled the German one, an observation that eventually became his first step toward a different framework.

Yet, when he turned to an in-depth study of one artist, Hijikata chose Kishida Ryūsei for his individual singularity. He was curious why a twentieth-century Japanese painter would find more inspiration in the Northern Renaissance painters Albrecht Dürer and Jan van Eyck than in contemporary European art, and then used that observation to stress Kishida's modernity and independence of thought. Hijikata's reasons for singling out Kishida remain influential; the artist's most recent biographer, Michael Lucken, agrees with Hijikata's analysis, treating Kishida's portraits of his daughter as "the sign of modern thought taking root in Japan." As both Hijikata in 1941 and Lucken in 2016 argue, "Kishida adopted the method of openly distancing himself from both local traditions and European fashions. In this way, he inscribed Japanese art … in a logic of rupture necessary for the assertion of a local and autonomous genius. Kishida allowed Japan to adopt a modernity that was all the more genuine for being indigenous."[29] (Lucken adds a striking argument about Kishida's use of the uncanny to destabilize realism and locates his creativity there.) Hijikata later wrote that Kishida's aesthetic choices reminded him of a story his mother used to tell, of someone who traversed the 88-stop Shikoku pilgrimage route backward so that he would see the comings and goings of all the other pilgrims. As Hijikata put it, "that was the kind of self-confidence and courage Kishida showed."[30] In other words, the arguments of this 1941 book about the independence of the modern individual failed to fully mesh with those of the other two, which generalized about broader nation-based trends. Later he would address this dissonance more successfully.

In 1941, the same year that he published three books on three different topics, Hijikata moved to the Yenching University campus outside Beijing, which housed several Japanese government research institutes.[31] Like the broader policy within which he operated, Hijikata's work was steadily militarized. That institute merged with several others into the North China Research Institute (*Kahoku sōgō chōsa kenkyūjo*) in 1942 and Hijikata became Assistant Director of its Cultural Section (*Bunka kyoku*). Later the whole operation was absorbed into the Ministry of Greater East Asia (*Daitōashō*).[32] Japanese imperialists justified their project on the basis that Japan was the conservator of and rightful heir to Asian civilization; and Hijikata's wartime assignments helped substantiate that claim. For example, he led a team that traveled to remote temples to photograph Buddhist art in situ, and the government used these images to argue that Japan was protecting and modernizing study of the paintings and statues. When hostilities increased, such visits became more hazardous, and Hijikata traveled with intensified army protection.[33] As part of his official duties, Hijikata also met contemporary Chinese artists in Beijing and Shanghai. In early 1945, as a counter-insurgency assignment for the Japanese government in China, Hijikata collected anti-Japanese woodcuts, presumably for military analysis, although the whole collection burned when the Chinese bombed the train transporting it.[34] By then, since the work itself as well as the conditions under which Hijikata operated shone an insistent spotlight on the intensity of Chinese resistance, it must have taken considerable psychic energy to ignore the contradiction between Japanese rhetoric and actions.

Japan's military defeat raised sharp questions about all these activities and pushed Hijikata in yet again a new direction. Hijikata wrote little about those years, although he never lied about his involvement with the wartime imperial state in China. Nonetheless, I would concur with Aoki Shigeru's opinion that "Hijikata-san was someone who was always keeping one eye on that past," and that this concern explains not just his postwar energy and creativity but also the new directions—institutional and intellectual—for his work.[35] After the war, Hijikata became a veritable fountain of original ideas, even by his previous impressive standards. In one of his first postwar publications in 1946, Hijikata had lambasted Japanese art critics, himself included, for having been too timid before the war. "In the past, bold critical judgment was possible; today it is necessary," he wrote, continuing, "up to now art critics have been, to put it negatively, like comic entertainers (*hōkanteki*), or to be more positive, concerned with abstract interpretation (*kaishakugaku*)." After the disastrous war, "we must re-secure and enlarge the space for the field of criticism, *including fundamentally re-securing and enlarging freedom for the critics*."[36] Hijikata thought ordinary citizens needed to exercise more bold judgment too, as he made clear in a December 1945 diary entry, when he first glimpsed the ruined city of Hakata from the deck of the ship that returned him to Japan. Hijikata thought that "the Japanese state domestically and the Japanese people as individuals both have to develop a little more independence (*jishusei*)" and decided then to work toward that goal.[37] Hijikata may have been rebuking himself for the intellectual crimes of accepting sloppy reasoning and dubious evidence more than for ignoring Chinese suffering, but his work over the next thirty-five years can be—indeed, should be—summarized as challenging and revising his own former positions as an act of redress. The passion with which he did so, and the imaginative ways in which he undermined the fundamental assumptions about national cultures and civilizations that had underwritten his earlier work, explain why his books and exhibits excited other people. In the context of postwar Japan, offering a new way to think about Japan's place in the modern world functioned as post-fascist redress, although Hijikata did not go far enough to explore Chinese modernity, let alone explicitly apologize for the war and colonialism, to satisfy most East Asians today.

Hijikata's intellectual contributions included a sophisticated understanding of the mutually constituted relationship between institutions and abstract knowledge and of the ways that museum-going was a democratic social practice. Hijikata described his task as bringing contemporary art into being not only by recognizing, organizing, and displaying it, but also by working with visitors to create demand for it. This was the first museum in Japan to explicitly include two-way interaction with the general public as a goal. Hijikata explained that everyone benefited from this interaction: contemporary art museums needed the input of "a society of modern citizens" in order to avoid "becoming mausoleums."[38] His framing of the relationship between the museum and its audience as one of shared meaning-making sounds very fresh in the twenty-first century, especially given that museum educators, such as Lisa Roberts, have generally presented this insight as a major new development of the 1990s.[39] To be clear, when Hijikata argued that the curators should work with the general public to design exhibits, he meant experts, collectors, and educated elites outside of the museum more often than ordinary citizens; he did not, in other words, push this argument as far as museum studies scholars such as Tony Bennett have in recent years.[40] But, as with the concept of multiple modernities, such expansion is consistent with the logic of his worldview.

In practice, Hijikata pursued this goal by highlighting the ways in which aesthetic categories and artistic conventions were ever-changing historical human creations, meaning that culture originated in the activities of citizens, rather than the gods, the emperor, or the state. His sophisticated exhibition strategy was unusual for Japan, although it echoed what leading modern-art curators were saying elsewhere in the world at the time.[41] Hijikata's interest in using museums for social education also dovetailed with SCAP policy to introduce the idea that museums should meet "the convenience and needs of the public." While Hijikata may have picked up some of his ideas from American officials in Japan, this seems more an alignment than active cooperation. The Occupation was winding down as the museum got started and, at that point, the first director, Murata Ryōsaku, would have handled negotiations with the Americans rather than his second-in-command.[42]

Satō Kei, an artist and critic who served on the Kamakura museum's founding Board of Directors, concurred with Hijikata in 1951 when he explained that "the concept behind the role of museums in Japan in the past has been to collect and display a historic art object in order [to show] its eternal value… This is similar to the mission of the Louvre and the British Museum and other national art museums. We will leave that role to them." Instead of defining a national canon, he explained, the Kamakura museum had chosen the task of developing an empowered public: "This social role stretches from training children to develop their aesthetic awareness [*bi-ishiki*] to enlarging the general public's sense of what is socially possible."[43] Satō's explanation of how the intended social functions of this adventurous modern art museum differed from those of the national museums was very exciting to future curator Sasaki Seiichi, who, when he read these words, thought, "It really is the start of a new era and I want to work at this museum!" Later, he did.[44]

Figure 3.2 Hijikata Teiichi, the intellectual heart of the museum for thirty years. Photograph by Sakai Yoshiyuki. 1958. Used by permission of Bijutsu Shuppansha.

Exhibition themes

The first twenty-five years of exhibits expressed a consistent narrative that rejected the assumptions that had driven both the war and the empire before 1945. This narrative displayed the highlights—and limits—of the museum's intellectual leadership. At the Kamakura museum, "modern culture" and "Japanese culture" meant an amorphous, ever-changing collection of overlapping regional and class entities that incorporated elements from elsewhere in a variety of ways at different times. The only boundaries to this view of culture arose from the limits to human abilities to trace and describe the full range of possibilities, not the objects of interest themselves. The core of this idea's appeal was its rejection of fascist aesthetics, and, as Nagasu Kazuji, Uchiyama's successor as Governor of Kanagawa Prefecture, said in his eulogy for Hijikata: "You encouraged us to see local and regional culture as brimming over with individuality and originality."[45]

Every category was fair game. Two very popular exhibits in the 1950s, for example, questioned the definition of art itself. A 1956 show focused on the difference between "real and fake" art (*honmono to nisemono*), while another in 1958 was on "authentic and legendary art" (*honmono to den-ten*). For the "real and fake" exhibit, the curators borrowed objects from collectors who specialized in forgeries, upsetting contemporary artists who were made uneasy by the idea of displaying these counterfeits in a museum. Artists such as Hayashi Takashi, however, took the attitude that "since forgeries of my works have appeared I have come to appreciate them for what they are."[46] The curators published no catalog for either exhibit, fearing that a document pointing out the blurriness of the boundaries of "art" would be used in ways they did not condone, such as in lawsuits.[47] Nonetheless, the implications of their claim that objects did not have stable forms of "authenticity" was precisely what they found intriguing, because it supported their central assumption that culture is an ever-changing invention of disparate individuals who get their ideas from the natural world, books, travel, friends and families, dreams, the dissonance between what they learned in and out of school, and sometimes even from thin air. Rather than signifying a fascist sense of belonging to a fixed community, both artistic invention and appreciation were constantly on the move.

This was without question a minority view at the time. Just after the Kamakura museum opened, art critic Imaizumi Atsuo, who had already been appointed as assistant director for the planned national modern art museum, roiled the art world by proclaiming the Japanese paintings displayed at international art shows in Paris and Venice to be "drab" (*donyori*) and unappealing. His judgment, and the sense of crisis his words represented, sparked a major debate in 1952 on whether Japan and its art had achieved true modernity yet, with most artists and critics agreeing with Imaizumi that it had not. Many of them also thought this inadequate modernity had explained fascism's rise.[48] In the early postwar years, Imaizumi was only one of many art critics to express the anxiety that Japan was not yet modern or, for Marxists, still feudal. For example, in 1953, the distinguished architect Tange Kenzō (1913–2005) called the first exhibit at the new national modern art museum "a chance to someday achieve modernity," although he dismissed Maekawa Kunio's renovations to the building as having rendered the paintings "nothing more than brightly colored artificial flowers. Beautiful living blossoms may have existed there once but mysteriously they all seem to have died." An important issue lurked beneath the obvious professional jealousy. After a lengthy celebration of French culture, Tange commented that "the meaning and the role of the Japanese modern art museum cannot be the same as of the Parisian one. Why? In a place where there is no domestic lineage [for modernity] one cannot start with historicism, nor be able to proceed in a straight line from the past… Japan is still in the stage of pre-Impressionism."[49]

Hijikata not only disagreed that Japan was at an earlier historical stage than was Europe, but also by 1952, he saw Imaizumi and Tange's anxieties themselves as having been produced by modernity rather than by realistic observation. Fundamentally, Hijikata not only rejected a Japanese national canon, he rejected the idea of a canon itself. If all kinds of art are in the process of being revalued retrospectively all the time by many different people, a stable core tradition cannot exist. As he put it, "in Kamakura rather than placing importance on the existence of objective worth from the past, we focus on what contemporary people see and value, and what people in future might get out of it."[50] His shows often emphasized the ways that new art-historical categories gave older images modern meanings (*keimō no imi*), a line of thought that the national museum, by the way it framed its mission, necessarily neglected.[51] For Hijikata, as for the Akademia faculty, individuals expressed their modernity when they used cultural resources in an "autonomous" or "independent" manner (*jishusei*), incorporating them into their mental frameworks or daily lives. By contrast, Imaizumi Atsuo at the national museum, as art historian Mitsuda Yuri explains, treated "the nation" as a unified entity that yearned for cohesion and produced art that furthered this goal, a concept that Hijikata had found attractive before 1945 but later rejected. Imaizumi championed a single abstract notion of "the modern"—which Japanese painting had not yet achieved—while Hijikata sought out many different moderns and found them everywhere.[52]

Over the next decades, Hijikata's exhibits at the Kamakura museum parried Imaizumi's and Tange's doubts about the completeness of Japanese modernity, by arguing that Japan and Europe participated equally in the modern experience through individuals who drew on cultural resources from beyond national borders. Hijikata shared the view that the Japanese displayed their modernity whenever they participated in the global exchange of ideas and techniques with his long-time friends, Akademia professors Hayashi Tatsuo and Saigusa Hiroto. He adopted Hayashi's terminology of "transplant culture" (*ishoku bunka*) when he argued that, when individuals combined ideas, techniques, and environments in new ways, they often energized their surroundings enormously. As he explained, "The process of tensions between old and new is natural when successive waves are transplanted and, with each successive wave, what was once new in Japan, such as impressionist-style painting … became accepted." Hijikata was especially critical of the Japanese art establishment for not recognizing that culture is dynamic and instead—tragically—trying to root out "anti-Japanese" painting styles. "The quest for recovering a holistic national identity for Western-style oil painting (*yōga*) was merged with political compulsion in a terrifying way" during the war, he opined.[53] Rather, he advocated for treating national culture as something that was repeatedly cobbled together out of a variety of disparate activities by people acting both locally and transnationally.

From the beginning, Hijikata and the other curators showcased the ways in which traffic between Europe and Japan continually changed the meanings of the art in each place. They hosted two exhibits in 1952 that examined this interaction in different ways. One was an exhibit of modern Japanese ceramics that had just returned from France, which focused on why the French were interested, drawing viewers' attention directly to transnational meaning-making.[54] The museum's earliest show dedicated to a single artist was on Isamu Noguchi, and was also Noguchi's first significant exhibition in Japan. Bert Winther-Tamaki has argued that Noguchi sought to treat Japanese and American artistic nationalisms as mutually constituted and impossible to disentangle, a stance very compatible with Hijikata's concept of universal, malleable, and reciprocal modernity. Hijikata also liked the way that Noguchi invoked and reinterpreted ancient art.[55] Yet, as Winther-Tamaki explains, many visitors were uncomfortable with what would today be termed Noguchi's multi-racial identity and cultural hybridity. They rejected his art as a pathetic attempt to be more Japanese than "real" Japanese; some expressed the view that Noguchi's racially diluted blood hampered his artistic expression. In this case, according to Winther-Tamaki,

Figure 3.3 The Kamakura Museum's internal courtyard and two Noguchi Isamu sculptures. The walls were painted white so they could be used as a cinema screen. 2012. Photograph courtesy of Timothy S. George.

the architect Sakakura "policed the native-alien border" when he warned that Noguchi's work was "moving in a dangerous direction."[56]

Although most of Hijikata's work was on European and Asian art, his reach was global. He produced a show of African prints in 1959 and one on modern Mexican prints in 1960. Both exhibits depicted the artists as participants in a worldwide modern conversation on art. In early 1952, Hijikata traveled to Europe where he saw a show on Mexican art in Paris and met sculptor Henry Moore, who, like Noguchi, had "transplanted" Mexican art. The fact that both artists found inspiration there intrigued Hijikata, and he published a short book on that subject in 1955, just before the first big Mexican art show in Japan opened at the Tokyo National Museum. Once again, Hijikata's view of this art as an example of universal, globally simultaneous modernity starkly contrasted with the opinions of other experts. In Winther-Tamaki's analysis of the 1955 Tokyo exhibit, most Japanese critics lingered on the power of the images in ways that telegraphed nationalist anxiety: "Indeed, perhaps the repetition and intensity of the rhetoric of expressive strength was driven by a desire to suppress an alternate reading of Mexican culture as impure hybridity, an impression that was demoralizing because it resonated with insecurities about the hybridity of Japan's own modernity."[57] Hijikata simply did not think that hybridity was either deviant from a stable norm or a problem.[58] On the contrary, it was the solution to the cultural anxieties that had undergirded fascism's appeal.

In exhibits that focused entirely on Europe, too, Hijikata emphasized the heterogeneity of artistic trends, such as one show on contemporary Dutch woodcuts in 1953 and a large exhibit on Yugoslavian medieval wall paintings held in 1957. By the end of its first decade, the museum was widely recognized for introducing an exceptionally broad range of European art to Japan, and for presenting Europe as the site of many modernities.[59] Many of the exhibits focused on Eastern Europe. Hijikata also made the case for urbane modernity in sixteenth-century Netherlands in his prize-winning book on Pieter Bruegel. Hijikata fleshed out this approach by consistently presenting artistic developments as having been motivated by the same broad historical contexts in Japan and Europe. For example, in both a 1952 exhibit of Sharaku and Utamaro prints, and a large show of European prints in 1953, Hijikata argued that prints, as a reproducible art, had permeated early modern society in ways that contributed to modernity and Enlightenment thinking in both places. Hijikata soon began exhibiting Asian and European artifacts together to emphasize this argument, such as a 1958 show on "extraordinary pottery" (*mezurashii yakimono*), which included pieces from Great Britain, France, Iraq, Iran, Cambodia, Vietnam, China, Korea, and Japan, again suggesting that modern reinvention was a global phenomenon.[60] Hijikata said that a major inspiration for his exhibition philosophy was his work in the late 1920s and early 1930s as an editor on the thirty-nine-volume Heibonsha *Comprehensive World Art* series (*Sekai bijutsu zenshū*).[61] Rather than emphasizing area-specific art through time, it was divided chronologically, and presented art produced simultaneously all over the world as a globally interconnected creative panorama. The series, for example, paid close attention to the artistic impact of travel along the Silk Road of central Asia on European and Asian societies.

Yet it was in his Japanese shows that Hijikata's historical ideas about the arrival of modernity emerged most clearly. In these exhibits he contended that both modern concepts and art objects predated the establishment of the Meiji state in 1868 and came from people only loosely affiliated with the new central government. His exhibits traced many diverse traditions within Japan, making the same argument as with the global scale: all regions were sources of modernity rather than examples of a unified national canon. One long-running theme celebrated the centrality of Kanagawa prefecture to Japanese modernity.[62]

Emphasizing Yokohama's role as one of the first official treaty ports, or "Japan's front door" (*nihon no genkan*), Hijikata framed Kanagawa prefecture as more international than Tokyo. He suggested that Kanagawa had enjoyed more cultural resources to overcome feudalism, because its practical and realistic values were rooted in mercantile rather than samurai society, giving Kanagawa culture greater flexibility on issues of honor and identity than that of Tokyo. Sawatari Kiyoko has made this argument recently in essays and exhibits at the Yokohama Museum of Art and was praised by Ellen Conant in 2006 because "Her research ... challenges previous scholarship stressing the role of Edo/Tokyo and government institutions there," but Hijikata consistently preceded her for thirty years from 1951 to 1980.[63]

Many of Hijikata's exhibits and publications, such as *A Short History of Late Tokugawa and Meiji Art* (*Bakumatsu Meiji Shoki*) of 1970, ranged across artistic genres to present a synthetic analysis of nineteenth-century Kanagawa's contribution to modern Japanese art history, in order to "prevent [this modern art] from being forgotten."[64] He mounted a large November 1957–January 1958 show that focused on 100 years of Japanese crafts, such as metal vases, glass from early-Meiji glassworks, sketches by Japanese of exhibits at nineteenth-century European trade fairs, woodcarving, and Western-style dining sets, already an unusual set of choices. Many of the objects originated in Kanagawa, and most included attribution to individual artists, erasing the class distinction between the artist and the artisan often used to assign low status to these genres, and to denigrate the modernity of their creators. Hijikata was also integrating Kanagawa prefecture spatially with this argument, by linking its twentieth-century urban centers of manufacturing, such as working-class Kawasaki, to the artisanal and artistic communities in elite Kamakura, and treating both as cosmopolitan.[65]

These exhibits, like Hijikata's other shows, built on a significant research base, and were accompanied by books that extended Hijikata's claim that contemporary Japanese benefited from a long history of democratic and diverse narratives of modernity. A 1972 volume on Takahashi Yūichi (1828–1894), timed to appear concurrently with a big show of his work at the museum, focused on his life rather than the exhibit itself, and represented major scholarship, as evidenced by the list of twenty-one archives that Hijikata consulted while researching the book.[66] Another example was the fourteen-volume *Record of Local Art and Culture* (*Bijutsu fūdoki*) series on local artists. The individual titles focused on such topics as early photography's relationship to painting, architecture, and industry in Yokohama, and on artists themselves. The 1970 *Short History*, for example, emphasized the interaction between local and foreign artists in the late Tokugawa period, the importance of Kanagawa to national artistic and intellectual life then, and the meager role played by either the old or the new national government in those developments. To put the same point another way, Hijikata broadened Saigusa's claim—that a few individuals in Tokugawa Japan comprehended the scientific spirit—by arguing that these ideas were widespread enough in Yokohama to affect artisans as well as artists, making the city a center for modern aesthetics and proto-capitalist manufacturing a century before it became a treaty port in 1858.[67]

In fact, Hijikata pushed this argument several centuries deeper into the past, dating the origins of bourgeois culture in Japan to roughly the same era as in Europe. He organized an enormous two-part exhibit in 1956 on the cultural history of the prefecture in the twelfth through seventeenth centuries, and another in 1959 on *The Japanese City*, of maps and genre paintings of urban scenes from the fourteenth through late nineteenth centuries, particularly of Yokohama. In these exhibits, Hijikata argued that ancient and medieval Japan was less a centralized national culture than a highly diffuse and varied society. He located the origins of Japanese modernity in the century of early contact with Europe, noting that in 1550–1650, Europeans too were just beginning to think in terms of a world history that involved Asia and the Americas. He also pointed out that European expansion was built on the plunder of older American civilizations, another argument that is far more common today than in the 1950s. Hijikata presented Kanagawa as an important meeting place for cosmopolitan people interested in foreign cultures in that "era of the eastward advance of Christianity" (*Kurisutokyō tōzen jidai*). This historical analysis highlighted Hijikata's (and the Akademia's) fundamental argument that the path to modern political subjectivity lay through the capacity to make sound aesthetic judgments.

These arguments excited younger critics and artists, such as *nihonga* painter Hirayama Ikuo, who reviewed a 1967 Hijikata exhibit for *Mizue*. He began by praising the museum for using the history of *nihonga* to challenge the standard story that Japanese history was stagnant until the Meiji Restoration ushered in modern political and social change. Hirayama reported how stimulating he had found it just to encounter this *question*, let alone the conclusion that the fifty years before 1868 were already crucial to *nihonga*'s modern development. As he explained, the narrative proposed by the exhibit began with the stresses and strains faced by the Tokugawa authorities as their "closed country" policies began to break down. Individual Japanese became more aware of international currents of thought and eagerly seized on anything new that managed to slip through the

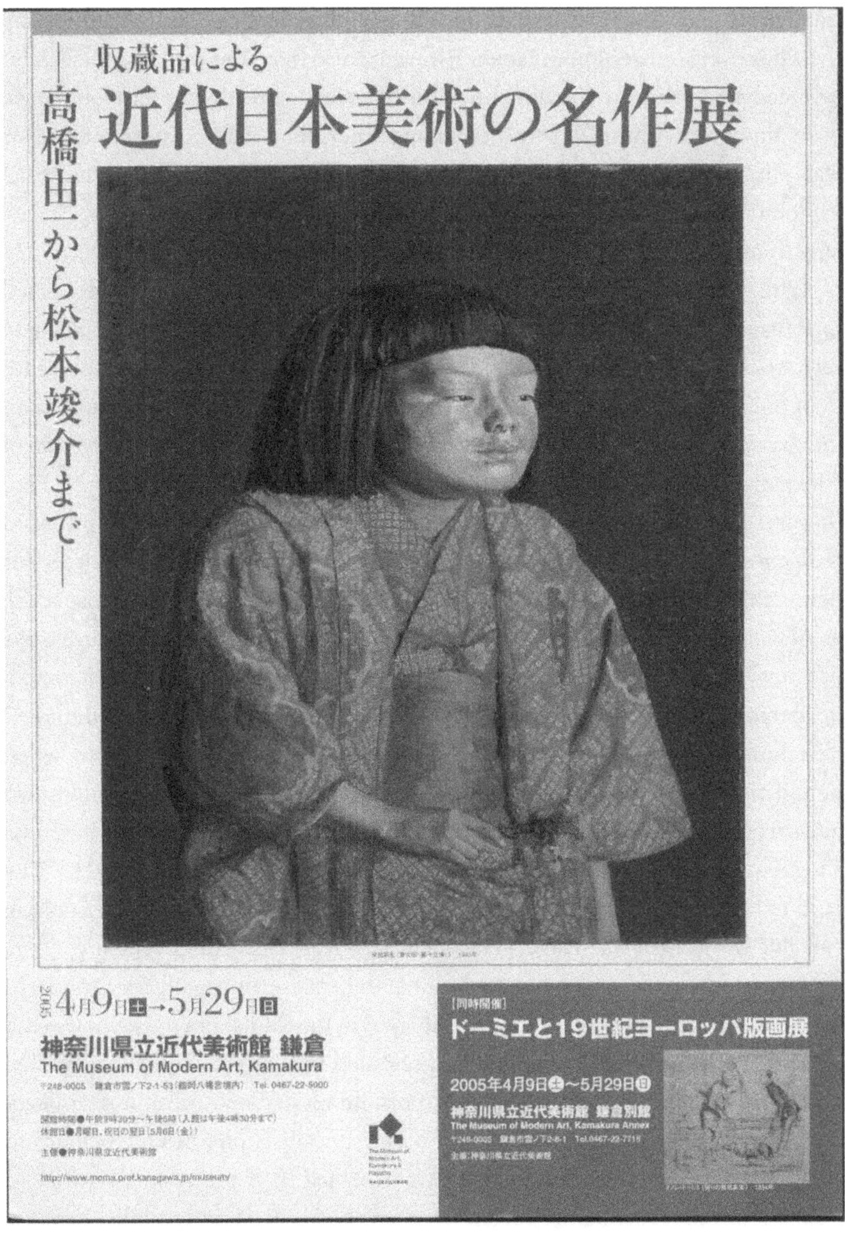

Figure 3.4 Poster with painting by Kishida Ryūsei from "Masterpieces of Modern Japanese Art: From Takahashi Yūichi to Matsumoto Sannosuke" exhibit. The museum was instrumental in elevating the status of all three artists and treating them as creators of distinctive and cosmopolitan forms of local identity. The inset is for a concurrent smaller exhibit on Honore Daumier and nineteenth-century European prints. 2005. Courtesy of the Modern Museum of Art, Kamakura & Hayama.

tiny aperture of Deshima island, translating, transplanting, and disseminating their discoveries throughout Japan. Hirayama also liked the way that the exhibit revalued Buddhism by showing how it influenced—already modern—*nihonga*, even though it was officially denigrated after the Meiji Restoration.[68] Nor was Hirayama alone. As Hijikata's disciple Sakai Tadayasu wrote, curatorial explorations such as this one inspired many others in postwar Japan. "That's why so many kinds of people visited us at the Kamakura museum."[69]

While the museum founders had a formal responsibility to present art related to Kanagawa prefecture, they extended the same philosophy to other Japanese regions as well, showing that their approach was based on a social vision rather than mere local boosterism. A 1973 show featured Wakayama prefecture as an incubator for creative modern innovation, in part because of its long tradition of elite patronage of the arts. It foreshadowed the argument recently made by Eiko Ikegami that Tokugawa artistic communities (many in Wakayama) provided indigenous models of egalitarian community that later became resources for democratic modern society.[70] The museum also began a series of retrospective exhibits in the mid-1960s—notably one on "150 years of modern western-style painting" in 1966 and another on "150 years of *nihonga*" in 1967—that were a deliberate resistance and counterpoint to the national celebration of the Meiji centennial.[71] As Hijikata explained in a June 1966 essay in *Asahi Jyanaaru*, when he and his colleagues visited outlying prefectures, they found over thirty unknown but surprisingly well-documented treasures, such as a 1912 painting by Fujita Tsuguharu and a 1919 work by Sekine Shoji, who died that year at age 21.[72] The rush to centralize cultural and political power in Tokyo had meant overlooking valuable works held elsewhere, even when they were easily discoverable.

This research had a very wide range, in part because, unusually for a modern-art museum, at least a third of the art displayed in the Kamakura museum was not created in the modern period but was presented in order to show the ways that much older art objects, such as ceramic pots, developed new meanings. Hijikata typically brought in archeologists and other specialists on ancient societies to create these exhibits and, by doing so, transformed their professional worlds as well. As Yasuko Tsuchikane's recent research shows, ceramic specialist Koyama Fujio completely changed the way he thought about Japanese pottery between 1952 and 1964. Koyama, who curated the exhibit mentioned earlier that began in France and moved to the Kamakura museum in 1952, was involved in all the ceramics shows held there. (The Kamakura museum—with no dehumidifiers— devoted an unusually large percentage of its shows to exhibits of pottery, stone, and metal because those sturdy media could withstand Kamakura's humid summers better than could paper or canvas.) As Tsuchikane explains, in the early 1950s, Koyama's opinions and exhibits were "marked by his defense of Japan's cultural insularity in ceramics, as he exalted antique Asian works as the world's supreme achievement in ceramics. Toward the early 1960s, however, Koyama's thinking underwent a radical shift, as he engaged with the contemporary international ceramic art scene and the Euro-American modernists most influential within it."[73] Tsuchikane sees that change as beginning when Koyama's show returned from France. As a gesture of thanks, the French exhibitors had added three pottery works by Pablo Picasso, which appeared in the Kamakura show. She explains that two other Picasso exhibits in late 1951 also included ceramics pieces, so museum-goers in Kamakura, Tokyo, Osaka, and Kurashiki were all able to see this avant-garde art, helping to explain why it sparked a huge debate among Japanese ceramics aficionados. Picasso had only begun exploring this medium four years earlier, so they confronted his innovations essentially at the same time as critics elsewhere in the world.

Many of the steps of Koyama's intellectual journey took place within the cramped space of the curators' office after the museum closed for the night. Hijikata used the Kamakura museum as a salon, where local "men of culture" spent long evenings arguing about art, culture, and politics, marinated in a river of alcohol and billowing clouds of tobacco smoke. As one participant recalled, "we would drink whisky and nibble cheese and argue with gusto."[74] Koyama, a spirited participant in the "Picasso debate," was a frequent visitor, as were literary lions Kobayashi Hideo and Kawabata Yasunari, who also collected ceramics.[75] All three men prized pottery for its elegance and high level of craftsmanship, a view expressed in Koyama's 1951 exhibit in Kamakura, on Chinese Black Porcelain, which emphasized its delicacy of form. At that time they still treated innovation "not as a manifestation of each maker's artistic originality, but as having initiated and developed a distinct historical lineage that archeologists identified through their material and technical analyses of ceramic fragments." Koyama and Kobayashi, according to Tsuchikane, defined such lineages as manifestations of pure culture, either "Japanese" or "East Asian" in 1951. This is why they were so unprepared for criticism from avant-garde artists and the Parisian visitors to the Japanese ceramics show, who defended Picasso's pottery for its unique individual expression and simply did not mind that he was no master of the craft. Nor did they care which pots best showcased an "authentic" civilizational lineage. In short, this was essentially the same debate about "drabness" versus authentic modernity raging elsewhere in the Japanese art sphere at the same time.[76]

Hijikata was not just throwing boozy parties with talkative friends. He thought the research, the analytical processes, and the debates they sparked all *created* local community that gave meaning to both the museum and modern art. In addition to scholars like Koyama and novelists such as Kawabata, the group regularly included editors from Heibonsha, Shinchōsha, Iwanami, and other publishing houses as well as musicians, screenwriters, and artists. As Sakai Tadayasu explained,

> We wanted to enrich the regional art museum by engaging with problems that come from our times so we consulted with lots of people and used many archives for our exhibitions. Ever since it opened, this museum has had the foresight to engage in this deep planning... We seized on this new function for museums and have been putting such planning at the center of the art museum ever since.[77]

The coherent set of ideas that radiated out from the Modernist box of the museum functioned for the participants—and for everyone who encountered their cultural productions—as a blueprint for a post-fascist community.

These interventions were genuinely exciting in postwar Japan because they made trivial the problem of belated modernity, and they made intellectual and emotional sense in other important ways too. Positing many modernities and decoupling individuals from national culture acknowledged the copious evidence that modernity was highly uneven in the West as well as in Japan. This stance also eliminated the barrier between "high art" and "folk art," resituating them both as different kinds of locally inflected modern art. Finally, Hijikata acknowledged the social context in which individuals operated while still celebrating personal creativity, bridging the tension between Marxist and liberal views of social change. In Sakai's words, "The theme that Hijikata chose to explore in his critical writing over many years was 'art and society.' Hijikata was a person who enthusiastically embraced the dream of a new 'form' for society and engaged in the work of consulting others to discern that."[78] Because these postwar breakthroughs made coherent intellectual sense, they were far more emotionally satisfying than was the unsustainable narrative that Japan was the pinnacle of Asian civilization, or even itself a unified cultural entity.

Museums as urban policy

Hijikata's visionary leadership extended to the institutional framework for the arts throughout Japan. One reason for the strong esprit de corps at the Kamakura museum was that the assistant curators knew they were getting professional training unavailable anywhere else in Japan at the time. Yagyū Fujio described his introduction to museum work as "blindly reading documents from foreign modern art museums, studying advice from our elders [*senpai*], and then trying to figure out what to do."[79] Hijikata not only provided intellectual leadership but also taught his subordinates the craft of museum management, which he had taught himself. Other museum professionals described the Kamakura museum as completely free of "the stink of bureaucracy" (*kanryōshū*), and many prefectures and municipalities modeled their institutions on it in later decades.[80] The young assistant curators at Kamakura, such as Yagyū Fujio, Asahi Akira, and Sakai Tadayasu, who reveled in the opportunity to "slip away from the reach of meddlesome conservative bureaucrats," later went on to head up other museums. Yagyū's commitment must have been high because he accepted a substantial salary cut of 2,000 yen from the 7,000 yen he made as an editor at Heibonsha.[81]

In fact, as architect Sakakura had hoped, Hijikata advised other localities on starting museums, established a professional association for curators, and created a museum consortium that provided institutional support and shared costs.[82] Here too, Hijikata was extraordinarily clever at coming up with solutions that helped everyone, including his own museum. For example, as other prefectures established museums, when he came up with a new exhibition idea, Hijikata would invite curators at two or three of them to collaborate by working with him to identify interesting objects, write the catalog, and design the show. Then he would ask the other museums to shoulder the financial costs among themselves, defining the Kamakura museum's contribution as providing both art-history expertise and hands-on training. And while the benefits to Kamakura's bottom line were obvious, at a time when there were essentially no other places to learn these skills, most people seem to have considered this a reasonably fair trade. These ingenious systems meant that Hijikata mounted exhibits at very low expense to the prefecture—at a time when there were no well-established conventions for what an exhibit should cost. In terms of museum management as well as exhibit philosophy, Hijikata was far ahead of his time.[83]

In the first thirty years, the museum hosted 300 exhibits—an exhausting round of ten per year. The assistant curators did everything themselves.[84] They collected artworks from lenders, cut the mats and framed the art, hung it on the walls, designed the posters, took them to the printers, wrote captions, washed the floors, and boxed everything back up again at the end. Clean tissue paper and tape were luxuries used only for particularly valuable items. Since they had no automobile, borrowed objects had to be wrapped in a big cloth and carried by hand. Simply sourcing art was a huge task, and if an item was in Kyoto or Osaka, a curator would go down in the morning and take the last train back, napping with the art at his feet. It is remarkable how loyal Hijikata's subordinates are to his memory given that he was a horrible boss in any conventional sense. He not only selfishly shirked these tasks, he habitually insisted that someone run out to buy him cigarettes, made people wait hours for him at inconvenient locations, and threw legendary tantrums.[85]

In contrast to his unwavering support for prefectural and municipal museums, Hijikata made deft use of legal structures to disadvantage the national ones. Although he never mounted a major show on Kishida Ryūsei, he secured the rights to exhibit his work from Kishida's heirs early on. In 1979, the National Modern Art Museum curated a huge exhibit on Kishida in both Tokyo and Kyoto. Despite the rivalry between the Tokyo and Kamakura museums, Hijikata is listed as one of the authors of the exhibit volume because he had veto power over which images they could display. Hijikata also retained exclusive control over Kishida's ten-volume *Complete Works*, which appeared at the same time as the exhibit. The staff at the national museum could neither take credit for nor influence that parallel project.[86]

Other people took the lead in using the museum to affect social interactions in other ways. Wakimura Yoshitarō, who joined the museum's founding board of directors in 1951 and chaired its management committee from 1969 until his death in 1997, thought the museum should encourage cross-class interactions in order to defuse the antagonisms that had dominated public life in the 1930s. Wakimura anticipated and shared Pierre Bourdieu's insight that cultural capital operates as an invisible form of power, but he thought those processes were susceptible to alteration.[87] Wakimura believed that by democratizing access to aesthetic experience, wise social planners could diminish the distance between classes, particularly when they combined such efforts with national policies— such as a minimum wage and unemployment insurance—that eliminated economic insecurity, policies that Wakimura also worked on establishing, as I have discussed elsewhere. In museum studies, Tony Bennett has pushed Bourdieu's insight further by observing that public museums ostensibly welcome all comers but still enforce class distinctions in subtle ways. His point is that this contradiction is built into the museum because it models a "correct" way to interact with art. Wakimura, however, was not just trying to expose "the working classes to the improving mental influence of middle-class culture," as Bennett has disapprovingly observed, although that was one of his goals.[88] He also wanted to push middle-class culture into developing a sense of engagement with and obligation to all Japanese through the shared activity of museum-going. Although his personal tastes were "high-collar," the point was to encourage all parties to adjust to each other. As Wakimura made clear in his business histories, he thought that capitalists had too often viewed workers with mistrust and did little to make them feel as if they were valued members of the national community. On the other side of the class divide, many poorer Japanese thought of their rich compatriots as rapacious and evil men. While supporting workers' rights to better wages and working conditions was the most important step toward a good society, Japanese also needed to engage in egalitarian human contact to transform their class prejudices, Wakimura believed, and he hoped that mutual enjoyment of art could be an important vehicle for that process.[89]

Governor Uchiyama shared this goal with Wakimura for the museum and for the other public spaces he created. In his introduction to Uchiyama's authorized biography, Osaragi Jirō praised Uchiyama for "without prejudice, immersing himself in the customs and society of each place he was assigned, for sharing the feelings of the people of that country, doing as they do, and fully experiencing their lives … something that is impossible for [those who] stay within the walls of the embassy." He was particularly impressed that, as a diplomat and governor, Uchiyama did not limit himself to the elegant parts of town, but also "lightheartedly walked the back streets among the local crowds, entering into their moods."[90] In other words, Osaragi valued Uchiyama for his ability to connect with both elites and working-class individuals in a transnational context. All these men hoped that art appreciation could help prevent the class-based fears that had driven people apart in the 1930s. Nor were they unique. Another cultural product of the same moment, the 1962 full-color remake of *The 47 Ronin*, directed by Inagaki Hiroshi at nearby Tōhō studio, presents the protest against Lord Kira as succeeding because it rested on a cross-class coalition of individuals who sought justice rather than the traditional presentation of the story as a tale of samurai honor.

To return to Hijikata, post-fascist arts management also meant pioneering ways to incorporate art into modern urban life, particularly sculpture parks. He started thinking about this issue on a 1952 trip to Europe when he visited an outdoor sculpture garden at the Middelheim Museum in Antwerp, and learned that creating one involved negotiating with city officials.[91] After teaching himself enough about public art to claim expertise, Hijikata began providing advice to local governments and museums beyond Kamakura on how to introduce more public art into their communities. In 1958 Hijikata argued that outdoor sculpture gardens mattered because "sculpture, which has been neglected in this century, must escape artists' workrooms and move out into the open air for it to play a social role. Then architects and sculptors and painters can work together to make the spaces of daily life more beautiful in a rational way." And, as he added in 1960, "sculpture by its power and architectural volume necessarily contributes to larger plans to brighten and enliven open spaces." When art professionals collaborated with urban planners and park managers, they could improve the built environment by creating beauty. Moreover, because the setting affected the experience of interacting with the art, these outdoor exhibitions, Hijikata argued, had the capacity to change the way people see sculpture too, and so spark exciting new directions in that medium. When that happens, the show's contribution is not just "harmony" but also "development" for the art itself as well as for urban daily life, he continued.[92] It seems overwhelmingly likely that Hijikata—and anyone else interested in the social functions of art—was aware of the contrast to the war years when bronze statues were "drafted" into the war effort by being melted down and then celebrated for their "self-sacrifice" in accepting immolation for the nation.[93] His post-fascist vision of art retained the social relevance but granted human creations—and their creators—permission not just to live but also to thrive.

Japan's first major outdoor sculpture installation was in Ube City in Yamaguchi Prefecture, which began holding biennial exhibits in Tokiwa Park in 1961 and continues to do so today. Ube was in terrible shape in the late 1950s. Bombed during the war, it tried to rebuild as a coal-mining center but that strategy failed when the last coal mine closed after the Korean War cease-fire in 1953. Moreover, Ube City suffered from exceptional environmental degradation, another legacy of the mining and cement industries. In 1958, a group of city residents decided to begin a massive flower-planting campaign, interestingly as a response to a spike in youth crime. They added sculpture two years later, an expansion that began with a controversy over replacing a damaged statue. At first someone suggested buying a cheap replica of the original, but Ueda Yoshie, the city's librarian and head of the flower-planting group, reframed the issue as one of democratic rights: if the citizens were paying for art, they should have a high-quality statue that conveyed recognition by city officials that local citizens were worthy of aesthetically significant objects. Ube City residents were clearly in the midst of their own post-fascist re-evaluation of political and social relations. These civic reformers saw their role not as social uplift but as championing the democratic right to enjoy beauty in places like Ube as much as in Kamakura.

At that point city officials brought in Hijikata, who transformed this modest plan into an innovative urban planning strategy of national cultural significance. He organized a sculpture competition and recommended that the city award a prize of several thousand dollars to encourage high-quality submissions. In another first for Japan, the sculptors had free rein over what their images would look like. The willingness of Ube provincials to put their trust in the hands of artists particularly impressed sculptor Mukai Ryōkichi, and his was among a large number of experimental and daring submissions. The openness of that aesthetic stance was, by all accounts, due to Hijikata's ability to convey a compelling vision of Ube's contribution as patron of an endangered art. It surely helped that the specific medium of sculpture fit well with the gritty self-image of a mining town whose traditional main industry had involved hacking through rock. Hijikata's message fed the souls of his listeners: despite its impoverishment, Ube could contribute something significant—and distinctive—to postwar political culture.

According to local official Kitakawa Rinmei, by evoking this goal, Hijikata "created harmony" among the diverse figures involved, and "the passion with which he conveyed his ideas" inspired the mayor, librarian Ueda Yoshie, the key city assemblyman, and many capable city bureaucrats "to cooperatively embrace the idea of supporting sculpture through these coordinated activities from the time the program was founded through today [1993]."[94] Hijikata also suggested themes for later competitions, sometimes focusing on new media, such as 1969's "Stainless Steel, Aluminum, Plastic" exhibit, and sometimes on other qualities, such as the 1973 entries chosen on the basis of "Form and Color." Ube's strategy of distinguishing itself from other rough mining centers through flowers and sculpture is not unlike Fort Worth, Texas, which differs from other American cattle towns by hosting the Van Cliburn classical piano competition and three major modern art museums. Both regional centers sponsored cultural activities often derided as intrinsically elitist as a source of civic pride for all their inhabitants, creating a strong local community with a distinctive public culture.

The Ube competition significantly affected the wider Japanese art world too, especially for sculptors. The winner of the first competition, Shimizu Seiji (1928–2005), had previously worked only in wood and his submission for Ube was his first in stone. Ever since, he gratefully described this as the event that truly launched his career. The resulting publicity led to new commissions for many of the other sculptors too, and raised the status of the medium in the art world. Hijikata characteristically piggy-backed on the Ube shows to mount follow-up exhibits in Kamakura, another example of his ability to get as much impact as possible from every unit of effort and expense. When he did so, he was always careful to showcase "the winners of the Ube City open-air sculpture competition," deliberately lending Kamakura's cosmopolitan cachet to both the art works themselves and Ube City.

In part because of his decades' long friendship with Wakimura, Hijikata knew how to think about art and museums as generators of economic value as well as shapers of modern culture. The Kamakura museum has since 1951 been an important economic draw for the city, and was highly valued for that contribution by the urban planners and city administrators of Kamakura, the subject of the next chapter. Hijikata's local economic influence extended beyond the museum walls too. Chita Kenzō, who worked for neighboring Fujisawa City, described how Hijikata lobbied for a sculpture in front of the train station there, saying that

> I'd like to display an amazing sculpture in that spot so please let me introduce you to a wonderful artist. I know Fujisawa is not a rich city and I won't pick an expensive big shot. I'll choose someone who is just making his mark now and has a long career ahead of him, someone who one day will be one of Japan's leading sculptors. So by spending just a little bit now you will have an artwork that will be really valuable in the future.[95]

Hijikata was confident that he could make good on this promise not just because he trusted his own judgment but also because he recognized that by securing the commission, purchasing work by the same artist for his own museum, and encouraging other museums to display him, the Fujisawa City choice would indeed become more valuable over time. And his confidence was not misplaced: the artist in question, Yamamoto Masamichi, did become very famous.

Coming to terms with modern China

The range and sophistication of both Hijikata's shows and his outreach to places like Ube City make all the more striking the museum's largest blind spot: the complete absence of attention to Asian modernity other than in Japan until the 1970s. If one accepts the argument Hijikata made about Japanese history, then the same must hold true for the rest of Asia. Yet Hijikata did not create or commission exhibits on modern Asia for over twenty years, even though he and his friends were deeply informed about Chinese art in particular. While many of the early exhibits focused on Asian art, nearly all of it was ancient. On their own terms, these were innovative shows. The first three on China were Koyama's 1951 exhibit on Black Porcelain, another in 1953 on metal and rock rubbings, and a third on Buddhist sculpture the following year. The curators also developed one exhibit about Central Asia in 1952, another on the "Orient"—by which they meant Cyprus, Egypt, Syria, Iraq, Iran, and Afghanistan—in 1955, and a show on art from Karakoram, a mountainous region straddling parts of Pakistan, China, and India, in 1957, all of which helped establish the idea of the "Silk Road."[96] But despite Hijikata's oft-stated conviction that all twentieth-century societies participated in the same modern moment, he was exceptionally

Figure 3.5 Poster for Art of Central Asia exhibit. 1952. This was one of the many exhibits focusing on modern meanings of objects created long ago that helped create the story of the transnational "Silk Road." Courtesy of the Modern Museum of Art, Kamakura & Hayama.

slow to explore this through exhibits of modern Asian art. The lack of attention to modern Korean art is particularly surprising since Japan and South Korea had full diplomatic relations from 1965.

The Kamakura museum mounted its first exhibit of Chinese modern art—on woodcuts from the collection of Uchiyama Kakitsu (1900–1984)—only in 1975, after Hijikata had been diagnosed with the cancer that later killed him. In that exhibit and catalog essay, he made the same case for Chinese artistic modernity as he had for Japan over the past twenty-four years: autonomous individuals used transnational contacts to envision something new, they productively yoked art and modern technology to develop novel artistic techniques, and their art was received as socially relevant visual culture. As is well known now, but was not when Hijikata published this essay, Uchiyama had taught woodblock printmaking in Shanghai in 1931 at the invitation of the writer Lu Xun (1881–1936). Many of his students, who included Lu Xun's younger brother Zhou Zuoren (1895–1967), went on to make powerful anti-Japanese woodcuts during the war. Hijikata recounted this story in the 1975 exhibit catalog and explained that Lu Xun had also published about thirty volumes of European and Soviet prints with his own translations by such artists as Käthe Kollwitz and Frans Masereel.[97] Further emphasizing the way that information and objects were global, Hijikata quoted Lu Xun, who wrote in 1934 that some of these art books had been printed in Japan while others, such as works that Lu asked the American journalist Agnes Smedley to request from Kollwitz herself, came from Europe. Drawing on Lu Xun's own writings, Hijikata explained that, after being told that Soviet artists favored Chinese paper for their prints, Lu checked the illustrations in Aleksandr Serafimovich's *Iron Flood*, and found that they were indeed printed on Chinese-made paper.[98] Hijikata concluded that twentieth-century Chinese printmakers had quickly absorbed a variety of techniques developed elsewhere (but resting on local paper-making technology) and had successfully integrated them into their own styles and agendas. He used this anecdote to show that "transplant culture" was multidirectional and multifaceted. In the catalog for this exhibit, Hijikata also emphasized Chinese wartime resistance to Japan. He was frankly admiring of the anti-Japanese movement in China, treating the 1940s as "an age of heroes," and praising the artists for their ability to connect visually and emotionally with the Chinese people. Hijikata foreshadowed a 2008 analysis: that by the mid-1930s the Chinese woodcut movement "began to emerge as a self-consciously avant-garde movement with a political impact," and, precisely because of this quality, he defined the artists' impact as more modern than that of mid-century Japanese artists.[99] Hijikata's 1975 catalogue text, which was reprinted in his *Collected Works* two years later, was actually first published in a 1948 book on modern art and realism. In the afterword to the 1948 book, Hijikata made his position on modern Chinese art even clearer. He argued there that the wartime prints derived their enormous emotional power from the artists' clarity and compassion for the suffering caused by Japanese aggression. The impact of the prints was further enhanced by the liveliness of the dialogue between Chinese and European printmakers, in his view. These three factors—autonomous expression by the artists, participation in transnational culture, and emotional engagement with their viewers—explained the greater degree of modernity of Chinese over Japanese art, in his opinion. In another essay in the 1948 book, Hijikata made a similar case for the painter Jiang Zhaohe. Yet, although he had said this in print early on, Hijikata did not call attention to his own beliefs until 1975, when he reiterated them unchanged.[100]

Nonetheless, Hijikata's exhibits in the intervening years show that he was critically reflecting on his wartime activities in China throughout the 1950s and 1960s. He exhibited Georges Rouault's (1871–1958) anti-war print series, *Misèrere*, in 1951, which, as Hijikata well knew, Lu Xun had published in China but was not yet well-known in Japan.[101] The ironic implications of showing in defeated Japan the images that had motivated Chinese resistance could not possibly have been lost on Hijikata, although he did not share them with the public. It seems likely that much of Hijikata's thinking about the development of Japanese art was shaped by his experience in China. Indeed, in one of his first postwar publications, he said that he first worked out his argument that "the history of Japanese oil painting is by nature a transplant culture" while living in Beijing and pondering artistic development in Asia as a region.[102]

Why then did Hijikata avoid shows on Chinese modern art for the first quarter-century of the museum's existence? Almost certainly shame about his wartime activities played a part, hindering his ability to find appropriate language for the topic. As Sakai Tadayasu put it, "that was really hard to talk about" (*hanasu koto wa muzukashii*).[103] Hijikata had found China fascinating but in retrospect could feel not confident that his own role there had been constructive. Uchiyama Kakitsu, who only met Hijikata in the 1970s, was in a similar position. Both men had known Zhou Zuoren, who had worked with Hijikata at the North China Research Institute. In November 1945, before he left China, when Japan had already lost the war, Hijikata visited Zhou to say goodbye. Even though Zhou correctly feared that he would soon be arrested for cooperating with the Japanese, Hijikata reported, he was sad but calm and composed. In 1975 Uchiyama Kakitsu and Hijikata expressed their joint ambivalence by dedicating the last room of the exhibit to photographs of Zhou, Lu Xun, and their extended family, including images that showed the postwar punishments Zhou had endured. By 1975 they also knew that Zhou had died after being beaten and confined to a shed for seven months by Red Guards during the Cultural Revolution.[104] As Ōkochi Kikuo put it, this exhibit was Hijikata's acknowledgment of his last meeting with Zhou, the very complicated emotions that memory evoked, and the larger context that it symbolized.[105]

But another probable reason why Hijikata took so long to criticize Japan's wartime policies in China and only did so in an oblique way was that his exhibit really was more daring in 1975 than it would be today. At that time, museum-goers still remembered an era when being more forthright would have landed Hijikata in prison. Hijikata's muted language and visual reminders of Zhou's sad life, combined with his claims for Chinese modernity, powerfully evoked post-fascist regret to members of his generation but conveyed less meaning to younger people. As such, the Kamakura museum reflected the self-protective ambivalence of his generation without making out the case in rich detail that mainland Asia was equally modern, even though doing so would have been consistent with Hijikata's postwar philosophy of history. Hijikata thus laid the educational groundwork for repudiating Japanese wartime attitudes toward China but went no farther. His postwar work strongly implied a rebuttal of wartime and colonial justifications for attacking Asia—one that resonated with attentive museum visitors—but it did not establish an explicit reckoning with Japanese actions in China, let alone articulate a convincing apology and redress for them.

In retrospect, the 1970s, just when Hijikata's generation was ceding the public sphere to younger people, was a missed opportunity for Japan to repair relations with China. Not only were individuals like Hijikata and Arisawa Hiromi, as discussed in the Introduction, making the case to do so, but President Richard Nixon reversed U.S. foreign policy toward China in 1972, creating the first real opportunity for the Japanese government to directly engage with its Chinese counterpart. There were many reasons why this did not happen. Some of Japan's most powerful leaders had pressing personal reasons to avoid drawing attention to the wartime past. When the Lockheed Aircraft Company bribery scandal erupted in February 1976, which revealed that the American manufacturer had hired gangster Kodama Yoshio, who made his first fortune plundering China, to bribe Prime Minister Tanaka Kakuei, Hijikata told his wife, "I saw the beginning of this scandal in China! I should write about it!"[106] Moreover, at the time few Japanese leaders could imagine China becoming an economic powerhouse of the twenty-first century and so felt little urgency on those grounds. But another cause is that the language and symbols chosen by the wartime generation to talk to each other about the recent past failed to engage younger people, who set off in different directions. If intellectual clarity on the part of individuals such as Hijikata had been enough to revise Japanese political culture, contemporary East Asia might look very different. That, however, would have required a level of explicit self-criticism that Hijikata expressed as an individual but not through the institution on which he so deeply left his stamp. The gap between those two things is especially striking because Hijikata was so successful at institutionalizing his post-fascist worldview in every other way.[107]

4

Urban Administration:
Social Science and Democracy

The social scientists and policy activists who focused on public administration shared the stance of welcoming dissent with the Akademia faculty and the narrative of transnational modernity with the museum curators but their main efforts went to expanding access to and respect for specialist knowledge. They were wrestling with one of the great conundrums of democracy—how to build effective public policy while honoring democratic input. While genuine democracies allow their citizens to shape the social conditions of their lives and negotiate choices through non-violent dialogue, well-designed policies lead to much better outcomes than do others. And democratic debate is a difficult way to achieve that result. The fundamental problem is that most policy problems are complex: remedies can fail for many reasons and must be both carefully structured and competently implemented to succeed. The social science disciplines are largely dedicated to coming up with strategies for anticipating and addressing this problem. Experts understand technical challenges, are aware of previous attempts to do something similar, have tools to estimate costs, and can anticipate likely future complications. They possess both formal and informal knowledge about their chosen subject. Because they are essential, experts are also ubiquitous in the modern world. All but the smallest societies delegate authority to specialists to accomplish such public needs as creating a functioning sewage system, setting well-timed traffic lights, and adjudicating property disputes.

Yet either relying exclusively on specialists or bypassing them altogether leads to predictable problems. Experts are notoriously poor at listening to people outside their little circle, for example, generating jargon that excludes others. Typically, while experts often have excellent knowledge about some parts of a social institution, they lack it for others—how it is used, why different groups respond differently, or who is made more vulnerable by its adoption. Yet highly democratic systems also produce their own predictable challenges. No plan will satisfy everyone. Even when people agree on which problems to tackle first, they frequently are unable to choose a coherent strategy. Sometimes individuals focus on symbolic issues that are only tangentially relevant to the problem actually requiring a solution. Others base their decisions on unrelated goals, such as building a political alliance in anticipation of the next election. Still others reject all courses of action without proffering alternatives. An even larger group finds topics such as property tax assessment adjustments so boring that they refuse to pay even minimal attention.

In recent years, much scholarship on Japan as elsewhere has focused on the problems created by the "rule of experts," and treats expertise as incompatible with democracy because experts are so often attracted to what James C. Scott has called "high-modernist ideology." Scott names high modernism as one of the four key elements that together caused disastrous "great utopian social engineering schemes of the twentieth century." As he explains, this ideology "is best conceived of as a strong, one might even say muscle-bound, version of the self–confidence about scientific and technical progress, the expansion of production, the growing satisfaction of human needs, the mastery of nature (including human nature), and, above all, the rational design of social order commensurate with the scientific understanding of natural laws."[1] In the 1930s and 1940s, as recently shown by Aaron S. Moore, Janis Mimura, and others, Japan's educated elite, particularly those working directly for the increasingly authoritarian imperial state, enthusiastically adopted high modernism, with tragic results for colonial subjects, occupied peoples, and, ultimately, all Japanese.[2]

Yet expertise is essential in complex societies, a point that is often missed by the critics of "rule by experts." Indeed, although Scott is frequently misrepresented as critical of both the practices required to make national subjects visible to the state, such as passports and statistics, and what he calls the "thin simplification" of high modernism, he is actually quite comfortable with modern experts, their tools, and their ideology. He points out that the various activities that make up the "administrative ordering of nature and society" "are the unremarkable tools of modern statecraft … They undergird the concept of citizenship and the provision of social welfare just as they might undergird a policy of rounding up undesirable minorities." Moreover, as Scott explicitly states, "nor was this utopian vision dangerous in and of itself. Where it animated plans in liberal parliamentary societies and where the planners therefore had to negotiate with organized citizens, it could spur reform."

Rather, Scott's recipe for disaster required four ingredients: "In sum, the legibility of a society provides the capacity for large-scale social engineering, high-modernist ideology provides the desire, the authoritarian state provides the determination to act on that desire, and an incapacitated civil society provides the leveled social terrain on which to build."[3] As Scott's formulation suggests, the particularly dictatorial conditions of direct military rule in Japan's colonies and occupied territories had encouraged more intensive—and more destructive— high-modernist experiments than in the archipelago. High modernist plans were not brought home until late in the war, by which time their sheer wishful thinking was painfully obvious to informed observers, that is, experts. Ensconced in the Imperial Navy's economic planning body, Wakimura Yoshitarō, for example, could easily see that desperate attempts in 1944 and 1945 to produce airplane fuel domestically could not possibly compensate for the petroleum imports that never materialized from Southeast Asia.[4] While some in Kamakura were inspired by the symbolic sacrifice of the sentinels of Wakamiyaōji Avenue for their pine-root oil and only later understood that cutting them down had been pointless, experts like Wakimura immediately knew that the trees' collective contribution could never do more than keep one plane briefly in the air. This is why after August 1945 so many postwar Japanese experts fully comprehended and agreed with Scott's point that bold projects "only became lethal" when administered to "an incapacitated civil society" by a powerful state. Many of them felt a responsibility to reinvigorate civil society as atonement for having personally participated in those bold projects. Yet rationality itself was not the fundamental problem in their view for two reasons. First, the irrationality of relying on pine-root oil to keep planes aloft had obviously contributed to "becoming lethal." Second, they saw no way to solve Japan's pressing postwar problems without relying on social-science expertise.

The Kamakura social scientists were typical in that—like Scott—their chosen strategy was to democratize expertise rather than eliminate it. They sought to increase the legibility of state and society to each other. Theirs was a fivefold approach: in both Kamakura and Tokyo these experts first set the goals of raising standards of living, eliminating poverty, and rejecting war as national priorities. These goals included protecting the needs of future generations, especially via environmental preservation. Next, they developed policies to meet these social goals. Third, they created mechanisms to educate the general public on how to evaluate policy proposals and responded to the ensuing comments. Fourth, they established a symbolically dense narrative that reinforced those solutions, and, finally, they institutionalized the processes through which they pursued them. In sum, this web of mutually reinforcing actions was the policymakers' contribution to post-fascist political culture. And, when they ran into problems, over-reliance on high-modernist ideology was rarely the cause.

Making democracy by empowering local government

Progressive experts in Kamakura worked hard to shift power from the national to local governments. The prewar state had been highly centralized and wartime consolidation had further accentuated Tokyo's power. They had good reasons to treat devolving power downward as democratization. Because prefectural, municipal, and village governing units were relatively small, it was easier for citizens to communicate with officials at the local, rather than the national, level, and for people in and out of office to understand and respect each other's goals and spheres of knowledge. When local governments are responsive to citizens, they also can act as a democratizing force upon the central government, not least by pioneering new policies that later can be adopted nationally after proven viable on a smaller scale. Kamakura was only one of many places where citizens quickly seized the opportunity to change how such decisions were made, but its high numbers of educated experts made Kamakura a leader in the fight for more local autonomy. Local experts there organized into civic groups to pressure all levels of government on a variety of issues, including education, as discussed in Chapter 2. Other people focused on urban planning, land use, municipal services, historic preservation, and environmental protection, all of which remain central to Kamakura politics to this day.

The Japanese who wished to empower local governments in 1945 had a powerful ally in SCAP. The Occupation forces made it clear that they expected the active cooperation of local governments—not just the national one— immediately. On August 28, 1945, just one day after the battleship *Missouri* arrived in Tokyo Bay, a jeep carrying three American military policemen visited each Shōnan town to deliver new "rules for compliance" to the mayors. The soldiers were under the command of the Eighth Army based in Yokohama, and began by requisitioning places for the Americans to live and work. The first spaces to be repurposed in Kamakura were naval installations, including the Navy Cadet barracks in Fujisawa, which became home to about 600 American sailors.[5] It must have seemed odd to the local population to have the Americans replace the Japanese military, and then use the spaces in just the same ways. Military bases remained military bases, as did military hospitals, ship docks, supply depots, airfields, and recreation centers.

But once they were confident that their power was secure, Occupation government officials also began looking for ways to strengthen, not just command, local government. As Cecil G. Tilton, Division Chief of the Local Government Division of Government Section, SCAP, put it "As for local government, we knew one thing and we stuck to it. We were going to take as much power out of the central government as possible."[6] Enhancing the clout of localities vis-à-vis national officialdom was one of the central strategies of Occupation policy because the Americans thought that a significant institutional barrier to democratization in Japan had been their inability to protect themselves from Tokyo's dictates. Juha Saunavaara has recently shown that SCAP was very active in Japanese local politics, trying hard to establish "moderate conservative leaders" at every level of government, often behind the scenes. Although Saunavaara does not stress this point, that strategy required working with individual Japanese closely enough to learn their preferences and to pressure other individual Japanese to support them.[7] Within SCAP just as among Japanese, the political reasoning for this emphasis on local government varied widely from individual to individual. Tilton himself advocated strong local autonomy from a radical right-wing perspective. "Here. I grew up before that damnable Roosevelt started socialists running across the country, bothering everybody… I've always thought you want a local answer for local problems. That's the main tenet."[8] By contrast, Carl Shoup, who overhauled Japan's tax system and created independent revenue sources for towns and villages to help them resist Tokyo, was a classic "New Dealer" who, in sharp contrast to Tilton, believed that national government policy should structure a wide range of civic relationships.[9] Like the Japanese economists profiled here, Shoup also advocated for progressive taxation structures, which at the time meant they favored property taxes, on the grounds that poor people generally did not own property.

As with educational and cultural policy, many Japanese experts in local administration worked amicably with the Americans on these issues because their goals aligned even though their politics also varied tremendously among themselves. One milestone was the September 27, 1946, arrival of new rules for governance in prefectures, cities, towns, and villages that allowed, among other things, public recall of officials and the direct election of mayors. As Takemae Eiji explains, SCAP officials drafted these administrative codes but many of the provisions had had Japanese advocates since the 1920s. Suzuki Shin'ichi (1910–2010), a bureaucrat in the Local Affairs Section of the Home Ministry and later Governor of Tokyo, also stressed the Japanese origins of these rules in a 1982 essay.[10] The new Constitution and the concurrent Local Autonomy Law consolidated this trend, including dissolving the Home Ministry on December 31, 1947, and dividing its expansive portfolio into four new ministries. Prefectural governors such as Uchiyama Iwatarō went from being Home Ministry appointees to locally elected public servants, answerable to residents. These were consequential changes. Together with agricultural land reform, as Andre Sorensen put it, these "reforms to local government structure had the most important long-term impact on urban planning and urban growth" of any Occupation-era legal changes.[11]

The interactions with Occupationaires were particularly intense in Kamakura because it was one of three Kantō-area cities chosen by the Americans as "test cases" for participatory democracy, along with Utsunomiya and Chiba City. This "test case" designation meant that SCAP officials not only stopped by to chat with town officials quite often, but they also encouraged other residents to organize into pressure groups and regularly lobby municipal and prefectural officials. One new civic organization that formed with the blessing of the Occupation forces was the Mikkakai, established as an "advisory board to the mayor" in 1951 with Katō Yasuhira as its first chair. Kume Masao and the first director of the modern art museum, Murata Ryōsaku, were also founding members. The Mikkakai members wanted to "examine city government," "discuss and publicize what is happening in local governments," "create a space for citizens to talk among themselves," and act as "a small group of citizens who formed into an association to improve city administration."[12]

As Katsura Takashi, the second Mikkakai head (from 1955 to 1957) explained later: "GHQ officials looked for people in the city assemblies and for appropriate individuals elsewhere in these localities and gave them advice about starting groups to establish democracy. They also set up meetings between us and the prefectural Governor, Uchiyama Iwatarō, who lived in Kamakura." Katsura went on to say that he had not needed SCAP's introduction to either the mayor, Asama Tokimitsu, or the head of the city council, because he already knew them both well. "So it all went very smoothly." Another activist explained, "basically the Mikkakai was full of opinion leaders" and "this was the era when people really wanted to limit the power of government and SCAP assistance meant we could do so."[13] Moreover, rather than being created by the Occupation from nothing, the Mikkakai formed by merging several existing groups, including the venerable Kamakura Dōjinkai, which first met in 1915. Some of these individuals had begun working with SCAP in September 1946 to consolidate transport and educational services for Kamakura, Fujisawa, and Ōfuna.[14] Nor did the end of the Occupation markedly change the Mikkakai's relationship with the municipal and prefectural government or with other new civic associations such as the PTA, showing that the Americans were relevant but never indispensible to any of these efforts.

The Mikkakai's main efforts focused on land-use policy, urban planning, and the city budget, an expansive agenda that remains its main preoccupation today. The organization's monthly journal—started in 1960 with a circulation of 3,000 copies—explained that, in addition, the organization also

> monitors the various offices of municipal administration, relevant activities in the prefectural government, important developments in Kamakura and in adjoining cities, evaluates surveys and other data relevant to Kamakura city produced by the central government, scans mass media regarding these issues, reports on civic activities at both the Mikkakai and local book stores ... and supports the benefit association for the JNR stations in Kamakura, North Kamakura, and Ōfuna, including the little stores inside Ōfuna station and on the platform at Kamakura.[15]

The Mikkakai's roughly 280 active members included many individuals, often retired, who had significant experience as policy analysts. They saw their role as managing the interface between official experts and the general public, including conducting their own public opinion surveys and other kinds of social-science research, analyzing the results, and then lobbying for specific policies.

In 1951, the economy was beginning to recover but, as the Mikkakai's historian, Hashizume Yukiome, put it, "our lunch boxes still consisted mainly of sweet potatoes with just a garnish of rice."[16] By then, urban problems were increasingly caused by economic recovery, primarily because investment in infrastructure of many kinds failed to keep up with economic growth. Traffic jams defined life in Kamakura. Although one of the first issues Mikkakai tackled was improvements to road and rail infrastructure, rush hour gridlock at both the western and eastern approaches to the Kamakura train station has been an ongoing headache since the 1950s. Not only are most of Kamakura's streets narrow and winding, but the city itself is nestled within a ring of hills, creating chokepoints for cars, busses, trains, and trucks. The Yokosuka JNR line was also exceptionally hazardous until three trains collided at Tsurumi Station on November 9, 1963, killing 162 people, including Saigusa Hiroto.[17] After that disaster, Japan National Railroad upgraded the tracks.

The group's first major victory was improving long-distance telephone service. Placing a call to Tokyo or Yokohama routinely took over an hour, because there were only ten cables to Tokyo and five to Yokohama, which could not support much traffic. Mikkakai delegates went directly to the Minister of Posts and Telecommunications, Satō Eisaku, in 1954 to make their case for

Figure 4.1 The eastern entrance to the JR Kamakura railroad station, the center of town. 2012. Photograph courtesy of Timothy S. George.

expansion. Hashizume noted with satisfaction that this victory marked the moment when the organization moved from "participation in government" to having a "guiding role in government." In the 1950s, people joked that one could tell when the organization was particularly active by the frequency with which "you heard the subject of the Mikkakai being discussed in the train cars of the Yokosuka line."[18] As the Mikkakai's ability to get on the Minister of Posts and Telecommunications' calendar suggests, the organization made good use of Kamakura's unusually large number of well-connected experts, in this case a retired bureaucrat from the same ministry. The Mikkakai members not only seized the opportunity to make their voices heard, as people did all over Japan, but—less commonly—were able to directly engage Tokyo-based *national* experts in public administration as equals as well as local officials.

The early postwar was an auspicious time for these efforts in other ways too. Not only were Kamakurans supported by Occupation forces when they demanded greater say in their community, they also had the ear of reformers within the national government. Two key sites for officials interested in such matters were the Bureau of Statistics, then in the Prime Minister's Office, and the Economic Stabilization Board, which later became the Economic Planning Agency. Under the 1947 Constitution, the Home Affairs Bureau, created to deal with local government issues after the Home Ministry was broken up, was housed in the Prime Minister's Office.[19] As I have argued elsewhere, the economists at the Bureau of Statistics saw the establishment of an integrated statistics system based on modern social-science assumptions and techniques as the most important act of political democratization they could accomplish in the "storm-tossed chaos" of the postwar period. Creating reliable data was for them not just a knowledge-making activity but also a strategy to give citizens more power relative to experts within government.[20]

The men at the Statistics Bureau wanted to open up access to the process of economic policymaking so that people would trust the government to act in their interests, trust that had been destroyed during the war. As statistician Yamanaka Shirō explained in March 1946,

> In order to get the cooperation of a broad spectrum of the population, first each government unit must have a clear and united plan. Those plans and ideas for implementing them must have democratic force to get support and participation. We need to make a recognizable system that is comprehensive and that in its daily operations strengthens democracy through its functioning and its flexibility. That means that even when we have to provide an incomplete "rough estimate" we do so in a fair way.[21]

So, for example, the Statistics Commission pursued transparency by releasing weekly information on its activities to journalists, a very unusual practice in 1946.[22]

This agenda required citizens to actually understand the implications of policy choices. Ōuchi Hyōe, the key figure who was particularly determined to "democratize Japan through statistics," also pioneered the visual language of statistics: as he explained in the introduction to a textbook on regional economics, photographs and statistical graphs were powerful teaching tools. Deploying them "means ideas that are hard to say in sentences can be summarized visually in easy-to-understand ways. Also graphs make the subject less abstract, which is good" because democracies work only when people understand what is at stake.[23] As professors, policymakers, and public intellectuals, Ōuchi and the men around him patiently explained economic concepts and the implications of economic policies to the general public at every possible opportunity. They tried to make sure that everyone had access to reliable information and knew how to interpret it. Ōuchi's goal was the opposite of a "nanny state," since, even though he believed in using government to distribute economic benefits, his larger goal was to assist informed citizens in imposing their priorities on bureaucrats rather than the other way around.

Ōuchi also argued early on that reliable statistics systems rested on data-gathering at the local level. His 1930s pedagogy had vividly demonstrated this point to his students, many of whom later worked in the postwar bureaucracies. As one alumnus reminisced decades later, Ōuchi had assigned each pupil the task of researching his own hometown. Then he visited them all during the winter break, accompanied by an assistant and an enormous box of books, helping them finish their homework and undoubtedly also admiring the local scenery, charming their families, and leaving gifts of calligraphy behind. The final class product demonstrated how much one place differed from others and how many of those differences would have been missed if the students had used only documents available in Tokyo.[24]

By 1945, however, none of these men thought producing and disseminating good data alone was enough, because the wartime political leaders had stopped relying on that resource, preferring to base policy on sheer wishful thinking. One of the most disturbing aspects of fascism, as they saw it, was this refusal to face reality. After the war they also worked hard to institutionalize information systems at every level of government and require their use. When Ōuchi wrote the October 21, 1946, document outlining how to reconstruct the statistics system, he included mandates that obligated the national government to pay the salaries of statisticians hired by localities throughout the country, as well as all other statistics-related costs, such as funds for the Statistics Bureau to train employees at other ministries of the national government and in prefectural and municipal administrations. These expenses were significant. In 1948 the prefectures employed 5,030 statisticians and the largest cities hired 1,200 more. The national government funded all 6,230 individuals and coordinated their activities so that their results would be compatible as well as accurate.[25] The deputy head of the Statistics Bureau, Masaki Chifuyu, in his diary on May 24, 1949, celebrated completing one such stint at the Ministry of Commerce and Industry (just before its name changed to the Ministry of International Trade and Industry). He commented, "It feels like graduation day from school. I've left things in the hands of a progressive Bureau Chief so I'm not worried at all. And, in a special arrangement, Mr. Shiino is about to transfer to Kanagawa Prefecture's Economics Division." Masaki also visited Sapporo in June 1949 where "it looked as though there were plenty of people out of work," and in July he traveled to assist the prefectural governments of Hokkaido and Hyōgo. In the same month, Masaki also met with statisticians from Aiichi and Kagoshima prefectures, issued guidelines on how to improve training for staff in all the regional bureaus, and went to at least one meeting to write the forthcoming Regional Administration Law.[26] All these efforts were designed to make society more legible to citizens and to establish new norms of political culture that favored decision-making based on accurate data.

These postwar statisticians turned to municipal, rather than national, administration in the 1950s because they lost some of their power at the national level. The Cold War had already made the Americans more sympathetic to Japanese conservatives, allowing them to recapture control of the national government in October 1948. Then, when the Occupation ended, Prime Minister Yoshida's administration seized the opportunity to reverse several American priorities, including clawing back some of the power that had devolved to localities. It did so mainly by recentralizing control of tax revenue but, in addition, as Ōhashi Ryūken put it, conservative bureaucrats "rooted out" the Ōuchi group from its entrenchment within the Prime Minister's Office.[27] These men remained phenomenally influential in such areas as employment and labor policy, energy and industrial structure, fiscal and statistical systems, and peace and civil liberties activism but no longer from positions within the national bureaucracy.

Indeed, a surprisingly long list of local government leaders got their start at the Statistics Bureau or the Economic Stabilization Board. Two future mayors worked at the Statistics Bureau: Masaki became mayor of Kamakura from 1970 to 1978 while the Bureau's head, Minobe Ryōkichi (1904–1984), served as Governor of Tokyo from 1967 to 1979. Ninagawa Torazō (1897–1981), who became Governor of Kyoto for twenty-eight years, from 1950 to 1978, was at the Occupation-era Economic Stabilization Board, as was Masaki for a year. So was Tsuru Shigeto (1912–2006), who later advised both Masaki and Minobe. Other Occupation-era statisticians went on to work for local governments in other capacities, such as Ōhashi Ryūken (1912–1983), who conducted policy analysis for Ninagawa for decades in Kyoto, and Takahashi Masao (1901–1995), who worked in the Price and Statistics Division of SCAP's Economic and Scientific Section, which closely coordinated with these Japanese government bodies.

Mayor Masaki's intellectual journey

Typically these men learned technical skills in the prewar years in order to reduce poverty and inequality but became interested in local administration only after the war, when they also first grappled with the task of actually integrating their expertise with the day-to-day challenges of democratic practices. Masaki fit this profile: by the 1960s he had excellent preparation for public service as Kamakura's mayor. Masaki's student activism and first jobs provided him with practical knowledge of the real problems facing real people. Meanwhile, his early postwar work gave him policymaking experience—and the combination taught him how both political power and social knowledge were shaped by ostensibly technical decisions. The years in between, spent in prison, provided a very personal sense of where wartime society had gone wrong.

Masaki Chifuyu was born into privilege in 1903 as the oldest son of Masaki Naohiko (1862–1940), president of Tokyo Art College (*Tokyo Bijutsu Gakkō*, now *Nihon Geijutsu Gakkō*) and a third-generation Ministry of Education bureaucrat. The family was run along traditional lines: Naohiko's idea of interacting with his teenage children was to summon them at 10 PM every evening, when he would formally serve tea and lecture them about topics such as the brushwork of one artist or the properties of a certain kind of pottery.[28] In due course young Chifuyu attended a Tokyo City middle school, the First Higher School, and, eventually, the Economics Department of Tokyo Imperial University, graduating with a degree in statistics and public finance in 1926. Like nearly all progressive social scientists of his generation, Masaki first discovered economics through the work of Kawakami Hajime but his lifelong intellectual mentor soon became Ōuchi Hyōe. Masaki was one of many young men who drew inspiration from Ōuchi for decades. He also joined the left-wing student group Shinjinkai, and then in his third year, the communist-friendly Student Federation of Social Sciences (*Gakusei Shakai Kagaku Rengōkai*), the first organization to be investigated under the new peace preservation law of 1925.[29]

The event that really politicized Masaki and focused his thinking on the challenges of daily life was the Great Kantō Earthquake of 1923. The 2011 Tohoku earthquake reminds us that such disasters inspire people to take stock of their lives and can permanently change their outlook, so it is not surprising that it had this effect on Masaki. Charles Schenking has argued that the 1923 earthquake "cosmologically legitimated an interpretive construction of reality, which suggested that urban, consumer-oriented culture in Japan had become increasingly immoral and degenerate and threatened both individuals and the nation." As he explains, many economists and urban planners thought along these lines, and even Fukuda Tokuzō, a highly rational thinker most of the time, called the earthquake "a form of purification."[30] Masaki shared the sense of urgency of these moral reformers but interpreted the quake as a call to

Marxist rather than national spiritual renovation, demonstrating the ideological polarization that characterized the Japanese public sphere in the 1920s and the way the earthquake heightened that divide. What seemed immoral to him was the suffering of poor people when society offered so much to others, not the hedonism of his peers.

Masaki threw himself into helping the hundreds of destitute refugees who lived on campus lawns until they could find housing. "The light poles and walls were covered with notes written by people trying to find their families," he recalled.[31] At first the students disseminated information about first-aid stations and compiled lists of dead and injured, but they soon moved on to a more ambitious long-term project. Law professors Suehiro Izutarō and Hozumi Shigeto suggested that the students follow the model of Christian activist Kagawa Toyohiko and build a settlement house for earthquake survivors. The settlement, in Yanagishima Motomachi, Tokyo, offered food, shelter, an orphanage, education, legal representation, and a medical clinic.[32] Masaki said, "I lived that movement for three years," and it was clearly more exciting to him than were his classes. He put most of his efforts into the settlement's labor school, headed up by Hattori Shisō, who later became the Kamakura Akademia Dean. Masaki liked being involved in something socially useful and also enjoyed sharing the experience with teachers and students from other departments in the university. The settlement house lasted for twenty years but police forced an end to student involvement there through a wave of arrests in February 1939.[33]

When Masaki graduated, his father's connections delivered a job as an economics editor and reporter at the Osaka *Mainichi* newspaper, a relocation that focused Masaki's attention on regional as well as national problems. He also worked at *Economisuto*, which published his first book on bank consolidation after the financial panic of 1927. Then in 1929 he lost his job after he was detained by the police and spent a few days in the Osaka jail, where the bedbugs feasted on him. The police investigated him because he had given his friend Murayama Fujishirō an internal telephone list and an employee badge for the newspaper, which they found when they arrested the prominent Communist, Fukumoto Kazuo, on April 16, 1929.[34]

In fact, Masaki was a bit reckless, getting pulled in by the police more than once for such things as enthusiastically participating in a May Day parade. He also boasted to his future wife that he was "notorious" (*fudatsuki*). Interestingly, she found this romantic although she did comment that he hid his political activities in Osaka from his parents.[35] Masaki later wrote in his memoir that he did not have the courage to become a labor organizer before the war, which—as his audience understood—was code for not joining the Communist Party. But this was a lie. By 1929 he had already joined the party, sponsored by Noro Eitarō, whom he knew through the Industrial Labor Research Institute (*Sangyō Rōdō Chōsajo*), another communist-backed organization. (In 1967 Masaki wrote of his sorrow that neither Noro nor Inomata Tsuneo, whom he also met there, had lived to see postwar Japan.[36]) Masaki managed to stay out of real trouble in the 1930s only because he was protected by his uncle, Shiono Suehiko, the Minister of Justice, who minimized the damage.[37]

Masaki's luck ran out in 1941, although before then he worked at the heart of the wartime bureaucracy, making him yet another figure who later would—correctly—consider himself both complicit and resistant to the wartime state. He was offered a new job in November 1935 at the Cabinet Research Office (*Naikaku Chōsakyoku*), which later was combined with another unit, the Resources Bureau (*Shigen Kyoku*, created in 1927) into the Cabinet Planning Board (*Naikaku Kikakuin*), designed to impose central planning on the economy. Masaki served under Wada Hirō (1903–1967), conducting research on how best to allocate economic resources, together with other young men much like himself: Katsumata Seiichi (1908–1989) and Inaba Hidezō (1907–1996), who had both been active in left-wing politics at Kyoto University, and Sata Tadataka (1904–1980), one year behind Masaki at Tokyo University and a fellow Shinjinkai activist. As the war intensified, their assignments shifted more and more to meeting military priorities. Masaki, Inaba, and Katsumata all worked on expanding industrial production and such consequential acts as writing the 1938 National General Mobilization Law (*Kokka Sōdōin Hō*). They also planned a national healthcare system, something that Masaki would revisit as mayor.[38] Then the whole group, including Masaki, was arrested in January 1941. After languishing for nearly a year in jail, Masaki was charged and moved to Sugamo Prison on December 8, 1941, the day Japan attacked Pearl Harbor, where he remained until offered bail in October 1944. He was found innocent a few days after the war ended, in a makeshift courtroom because the Tokyo District Court had burned in a May air raid.

Next Masaki was hired by Ōuchi to gather and analyze statistics and, from 1947, by Wada Hirō, who became head of the Economic Stabilization Board and rehired many of his former employees. Then, in the early 1950s, Wada, Katsumata, and Sata entered the Diet as legislators, while a few other comrades, like Masaki himself, moved there as expert staffers. Masaki worked at the Budget Committee of the House of Councillors from 1953 through 1966.[39] Masaki's direct engagement with Kamakura local politics was minimal until 1963 when he and Arisawa Hiromi both moved there to join Ōuchi Hyōe but he was already on a track parallel to the Mikkakai a decade earlier.

The key institutional link between the overlapping groups around Ōuchi and Wada, on one hand, and local organizations such as the Mikkakai, on the other, was the Research Center on Tokyo Administration (*Tokyo Tosei Chōsakai*), established by Komori Takashi in 1955. Like the Mikkakai, this organization was designed to bridge the gap in expertise between citizens and state by producing policies that were both democratic and professionally informed and then winning public approval through an extensive education program. Simon Avenell, in *Making Japanese Citizens*, describes the Research Center on Tokyo Administration as the most important intellectual and institutional foundation for local citizens' movements in postwar Japan because of both its attention to practical problems and the dense web of personal connections enjoyed by the researchers there.[40] Despite the Tokyo-centric name, the Research Center, like the Kamakura Modern Art Museum, also trained people in other parts of Japan to replicate their activities.

A similar body, the Institute for Public Policy in Kanagawa Prefecture (*Kanagawa Ken Chihō Jiji Kenkyū Sentaa*) was an early partner of both the Tokyo organization and the Mikkakai. The Tokyo and Kanagawa organizations brought together architects, urban planners, economists, and political theorists, who worked with citizen's groups such as the Mikkakai to create step-by-step, concrete proposals for new policies. One of the most famous participants was Matsushita Keiichi, who articulated the concept of a "civil minimum" guaranteeing health, safety, and financial security to all inhabitants as the baseline principle on which policies should rest. Another active attendee was architect Tamura Akira, who designed several of Yokohama's subway stations. The Kanagawa institute had several hundred staffers in the 1970s and 1980s and generated a steady stream of reports and policy proposals based on their own research within the prefecture and on best practices elsewhere in Japan and abroad.[41]

These groups all set out to create a culture around policymaking that combined democratic access and high standards of professional expertise. They wanted to instill respect for careful informed assessment based on good data because without protecting standards, people were far too easily led in unproductive or even destructive directions. So, for example, they pushed citizens to assess how taxes were being spent rather than simply complaining about them. As Ōuchi explained in 1965, anticipating James C. Scott by thirty years, learning about local government was key to understanding the fundamental social contract between democratic states and their citizens: "We Japanese, who are capitalists and workers on the one hand, are on the other hand national citizens (*kokumin*) and citizens (*shimin*) of local units, that is, cities, towns, and villages." As such, "we have the responsibility to pay taxes and the modern state—both socialist and capitalist—has a responsibility to improve standards of living for us."[42]

The Mikkakai was typical of this approach in that the organization regularly expressed a pragmatic recognition that providing services required revenue. Indeed, its members put considerable effort into educating the voting population on this point, focusing on both specific policy recommendations and basic principles. In a 1960 essay that began by documenting the fact that Kamakura residents paid unusually high property taxes, the unnamed Mikkakai author concluded by telling his neighbors to be more realistic and stop grousing. "The taxes in Kamakura are high because many properties are on the beach, citizens have substantial incomes, and their land and homes are expensive. The high taxes show that many people want to move here and we should be using this fact for its public-relations value as evidence of how desirable Kamakura is." Kamakura's dearth of manufacturing and its many non-profit institutions also meant that the city had no choice but to rely on high property taxes, he concluded.[43] Such pragmatism is typical of discussions *among* experts, in great contrast to most discussions with the general public.

The Mikkakai focused attention on how the Kamakura city administration spent revenue as well, and similarly insisted that its readers be well informed. Another 1960 study analyzed total personnel costs, noting that, while they were higher than the national average of 24.7 percent of municipal budgets, residents should not assume that all city employees had high salaries. "Kamakura doesn't pay the education people particularly well—they get a bit less than the prefectural average. Where we really spend more than other places is for fire safety personnel."[44] Once again, the author wanted citizens to know precisely how their money was being spent, not in order to cut back, but so that they would understand why the expense was necessary in a city with an unusually large number of centuries-old wooden buildings.

The unstated author of the first 1960 essay also made Ōuchi Hyōe's signature argument that warfare drove up taxes, reminding his readers that, before 1945, national taxes had been 65 percent and local taxes 35 percent of the total burden—exactly the reverse of the postwar ratio—and that "if the national government has to build a strong military, then the averages will go back to the prewar ones," with predictable tax hikes and loss of regional autonomy. He was reframing healthy municipal budgets as a bulwark of democracy in two different ways: not only did they pay for the amenities that citizens cared most about but also money collected at that level was hard to divert to wasteful military spending.[45] This was a major theme of Ōuchi's public speeches and general-interest publishing in the 1950s and 1960s, all easily accessible to Kamakura residents. Masaki too had made this point in print as early as 1932 and repeated it often as mayor.[46]

Land use and the environment

The most significant postwar urban planning development for Kamakura was the intertwined evolution of the environmental and historic preservation movements, and Mayor Masaki's main achievement was to integrate what started as two independent citizens' movements with municipal administration and formal land-use planning. Fights over land use had become intense around 1960 when the city began to grow at an accelerated pace. Kamakura's population grew only modestly from 93,000 in 1950 to 98,617 in 1960, but then swelled to 139,249 in 1970, and picked up the pace to reach 165,552 in 1975 and 173,331 in 1979. Since then, the population has stayed roughly the same, however, clocking in at 172,491 in 2016.[47] The stable number of people did not mean that activism ebbed away; in 1999, the Mikkakai was one of twenty-three separate Kamakura-based organizations (with much overlapping membership) that made land use and environmental protection their central mission, and one of 188 local bodies that listed the natural environment as one of their concerns.[48]

Although in the 1950s and 1960s Japanese localities as yet had few tools to control land use, Kamakura residents aggressively used what they had. The city administration, spurred on by the Mikkakai, deployed the Land Readjustment Act of 1954 (*Tochi Kukaku Seiri Hō*), which gave municipalities power to rezone and exercise eminent domain and provided mechanisms for them to decide how to use central government subsidies and new revenue from the gasoline tax. As Andre Sorensen explains, "The law has been widely used and in an extraordinary variety of circumstances, primarily for urban expansion into agricultural areas, but also for downtown redevelopment, new town building, public housing projects, railway and mass transit development, and others."[49] Kamakura used it to develop public transportation systems and reinforce buildings. Because of its proximity to Tokyo, Kamakura was also included in the National Capital Construction Law (*Shuto Kensetsu Hō*) of 1950 and the National Capital Region Development Law (*Shutoken Seibi Hō*) of 1956. These Kantō-area laws created a regional planning process that was designed to encourage greenbelts around

Tokyo and control sprawl. Although their overall impact was disappointing, Kamakura residents made particularly effective use of their provisions, and later Mayor Masaki steadily increased their capacity by expanding their geographic reach and by slowing down construction permits. By then Masaki could also take advantage of the new City Planning Law of 1969, the most important of these mandates.[50] Under Masaki's watch, the city created additional zoning regulations in 1973 that limited all commercial development to the areas around the two big train stations, with only minimal expansion at Kamakura station, making Ōfuna the commercial hub. Masaki unveiled the first comprehensive plan for the city, which supported preservation of both historical and natural sites, and also affirmed the importance of citizen participation in government in 1976.[51]

Kamakura's most important contribution to national land-use policy was to introduce new strategies to protect green spaces within urban environments. Mikkakai members, Osaragi Jirō, and others created the *Kamakura Fūkei Hozonkai* in 1964 modeled on the British "national trust" system, which was then adopted elsewhere in Japan, and now is integrated into national government policy. The system uses tax breaks to encourage landowners to sell properties with significant historical or environmental value to the non-profit National Trust for Places of Historic Interest or Natural Beauty. Japanese citizens support these transactions by buying memberships in the National Trust, paying to purchase and maintain the protected lands. This was a clever expert-led solution, one that adjusted incentives to a variety of actors based on the proven results of land-use planning in another country. The first purchase was 1.5 hectares of land on the hill behind Tsurugaoka Hachiman Shrine in 1966, supported by contributions from 1,330,000 individuals from around the country.[52] Other Mikkakai members carved out smaller projects for themselves within this framework. For example, Takahata Shōzō, vice president of the Mikkakai in the late 1960s, focused on mapping all the city's woods, including each tree's species, health, and estimated age, with special protections for groves of 150-year-old trees. He also successfully lobbied the city to plant more roadside trees, bringing Kamakura's tree count to over 2.5 million.[53]

The Mikkakai also deserves credit for contributing to both the national 1966 Historic Land Preservation Act and the Green-space Conservation Act of 1970, and for using those legal protections to keep new development within Kamakura's already densely populated core rather than continuing its outward sprawl. The same groups took advantage of Kamakura's status as a former Shogun's capital to help enact another law that protected the archeological and historic sites of Nara, Kyoto, and Kamakura. As a 2017 official Japanese government publication

Figure 4.2 Tsurugaoka Hachiman Shrine was the ritual center of Kamakura when it was the Shogun's capital, and during the Asia-Pacific War, and is a major tourist site today. The hillside behind it was the first area in Japan to be protected from development through a National Trust procedure. 2012. Photograph courtesy of Timothy S. George.

aimed at English speakers acknowledged, when private developers tried to build on the hill behind the Hachiman shrine, "local people fought back, leading to the green space's permanent protection. This movement ultimately led to the Ancient Capital Preservation law … and to the protection of all Kamakura's landscapes, officially establishing a balance between natural and historical heritage."[54] Kamakura residents were exercising the same civic activism as when building new schools soon after the war.

In the fast-growing 1960s and 1970s, the biggest problem was not inadequate regulation but illegal construction of shoddy buildings with insufficient infrastructural support—including parks, utilities, roads, schools, and such basic precautions as terracing hillsides to prevent mudslides. Rather than legislation, Kamakura needed someone to make sure that the new rules were obeyed. When Masaki became mayor, the city administrators began enforcing existing rules much more enthusiastically.[55] He also explored tactics such as paying landowners to maintain forests on steep slopes, rather than selling to developers. But at other times, groups such as the Mikkakai have had to pressure the city administrators when land developers tried to evade compliance. The central importance of enforcement is why authors of a 2006 study warn that Kamakura's relatively successful urban planning still requires continued vigilance even as they offer it as a superlative model of land-use planning for other places.[56]

The Mikkakai's complaints were not about minor infractions. One serious issue was water pollution, which was a major priority for Masaki in the 1970s. The problem itself was not unusual: Andre Sorensen reports that in 1970 only 16 percent of the national population was connected to sewage systems.[57] Much of the untreated waste ended up in the waterways. The Mikkakai had agitated for better sewage management since the 1950s, choosing the rhetorical strategy of lamenting the way that current conditions made the city look unsophisticated. The first issue of *The Kamakura Citizen* in 1960 included a letter from an unnamed Zaimokuza resident who related the tale of "Patricia," who rented a nearby home for the summer but abandoned her plans after a week. She discovered that, because the city had provided only one public toilet near the ocean, weekend crowds used the shoreline instead, destroying her interest in swimming there. As the letter writer asked, "Why does a city that is full of educated people and famous for its beauty tolerate this situation?"[58] Kamakura's responsibility for environmental protection, the letter argued, was greater than just providing services to its own residents and catering to tourists. It also had an obligation to future generations. The beach pollution was a major reason why the last Kamakura Carnival was held in 1962 and its organizers turned to environmental activism instead.

In response to these circumstances, one of Masaki's first mayoral actions was to commission a three-stage plan to bring sewers to different parts of the city, first in the historic district and then in outlying areas. He relied on both the Research Center on Tokyo Administration and the Institute for Public Policy in Kanagawa Prefecture to create this plan. Like the Mikkakai, Masaki included the task of educating the public about their findings as part of effective policymaking. Comprehensive planning, such as to bring sewers to Kamakura, was precisely the kind of work Masaki had done at the Cabinet Planning Board before his arrest in 1941 but this time he harnessed it to the goal of raising the quality of life for residents rather than waging total war. He evoked this contrast when he carefully explained to residents the need for a new city levy to pay for the installation of sewers, because the national government would not provide the funds. On the contrary, as he complained on several occasions, local governments had to challenge Tokyo, which typically supported land developers over towns and "colluded in industry efforts to evade responsibility," to borrow Andre Sorensen's acid prose.[59] Rather than an excess of high modernist ideology, the Tokyo government simply didn't care enough that new construction overloaded Kamakura's sewage system to make land developers shoulder more of the cost of solving that problem.

Similarly, in a long essay on the 1976 development plan, Masaki spent ten pages educating local citizens about the many factors that affected the aesthetic quality of urban streets, such as height of buildings, their overall design and facades, placement of trees, and neon signage. He also explained that banning cars from the perennially congested central part of the city would be a mistake because, although one might think that pedestrians would welcome no-car zones, in fact, where this solution had been tried, few people liked it. This is a perfect example of using expert knowledge to discern true public preferences, since some policy measures—such as banning cars—often seemed more attractive in the abstract than when actually experienced. But what comes through most powerfully in Masaki's communications with citizens is the high level of sophistication and tolerance for technical detail he expected from his audience.[60] His goal was to democratize expertise, not by simplifying the message, but by increasing the sophistication with which his readers received it.

In a recent study, geographers Oh Iwata and Takashi Oguchi called Kamakura "a typical example of an Asian historic city which has been subjected to recent urbanization, and which therefore deserves detailed analyses of its land use patterns," but they misidentify the ways that Kamakura is typical. Iwata and Oguchi theorize that Kamakura's unusually strict limits to private property rights are the legacy of traditional farming-village customs of sharing property rights in timber, charcoal-making, and thatch, but their guess is not just wrong; it obscures the political culture of postwar Kamakura.[61] Kamakura's zoning regulations, particularly its rules on building height, preservation of historical monuments, and control over its residential zones, were all the result of decades of twentieth-century activist organizing. Moreover, such activism succeeded by appealing to the most modern and cosmopolitan aspects of Japanese society, not to ancient village customs. Or, as Ueno and Sonobe put it more accurately, Kamakura developed "a social mechanism to promote environmental conservation, as well as technologies to solve the problems."[62] This modern history explains why the politics of zoning, economic development, and preservation became very explicit and contested in Kamakura. Soon other places began using the "Kamakura model" to block haphazard development and protect green spaces. At the prefectural level too, under two successive socialist governors, Kanagawa started

Figure 4.3 Enoden train passing Shichirigahama. 2017. Kamakura residents have worked hard to control sprawl and preserve urban greenery and the city is home to over 2.5 million trees. Photograph by Kajiwara Yuji, used by permission of Getty Images.

integrating industrial development with environmental planning and basic scientific research well before the national government did so. Later Kanagawa became a leader in planning for the shift to knowledge-intensive industries, as firms in Kawasaki and Yokohama moved factory production to Asia.[63]

Masaki also worked very hard to encourage two-way transmission to allow citizens to educate experts. As he said in December 1970, when institutionalizing systems for getting feedback from the community, his aim was to "widen the pipeline" into city hall, so as to help transform his constituents "into citizens who demand things." One of the provisions of the 1968 New City Planning Law was that both municipal administrations and land developers were required to solicit citizen opinions, and Masaki enthusiastically adopted this directive.[64] Nor did he listen only to the most powerful constituents. In addition to problems like sewage that affected daily life for everyone, Masaki emphasized social-welfare services that lightened the burden on women because, as he pointed out, citizens themselves—clearly meaning women—most often asked for assistance to care for the very young and the very old. In his first speech as mayor, he promised to improve these services, adding that "men don't take this responsibility seriously enough." Among other steps, Masaki expanded educational and vocational programs for children with special needs and established daycare services for the elderly, particularly places for them to socialize.[65] While this was a common theme for progressive mayors of the era, Masaki acted much more aggressively than did the Minobe administration in Tokyo, perhaps because of his prewar settlement-house experience.

Peace activism, democratic spaces, and urban diplomacy

The policymakers in Kamakura also shaped the culture around policymaking by replacing fascist rituals with ones that affirmed the value of individual life and the freedom to enjoy it as one pleased. They developed new civic rituals around peace activism, individual rights, and international amity, integrating these efforts into the "Kamakura brand." Kamakurans were—and remain—very engaged in the peace and Constitution-protection movements. Local activists organized to declare Kamakura a peace-promoting city, officially doing so on August 10, 1958, when "the city council unanimously voted to support the spirit of the Japanese national constitution, ban nuclear weapons, and work with the globe's population to make eternal world peace a reality. We declare that Kamakura and its many historical heritage sites and cultural legacies is an eternal city of peace." To mark its status as one of the first Japanese "Peace Cities," Kamakura also paid to carve this message on a rock, in the elegant calligraphy of painter Hirayama Ikuo, which sits in front of City Hall.[66] Another peace statement, produced by local woodcarvers, bears the calligraphy of Ōuchi Hyōe and was mounted in the public library for many years. This was a repudiation of the municipality's stance during the war, when Tsurugaoka Hachiman shrine, not the secular spaces of city hall and the library, had been the center of civic mobilization.

The Kamakura City Central Public Library is another key post-fascist institution, serving as a democratic and cosmopolitan space for community "capacity-building" of all kinds. Its precursor had actually opened in 1911, when it was Kanagawa prefecture's first public book-lender. But, although open to all, only about four people a day visited the prewar institution because they had to pay to use it. The library closed when the military requisitioned its building in 1944 and reopened only on June 1, 1946. Soon thereafter Kimura Hikosaburō, one of the Akademia founders, took a job there, and Sawa Jurō, a Mikkakai activist, later also served as librarian, showing the interconnections of these post-fascist networks.[67] Around the same time, the American military set up two "kamaboku libraries" named for their Quonset-hut housing, shaped like a fish-cake loaf, in Hase and Ōfuna. The Hase space was later donated to the city, becoming a branch of the municipal library.[68] The library became truly popular when borrowing became free in 1951, and has ever since provided a variety of other cultural activities for citizens, such as staging "record concerts" from 1954 and screening films from 1962. The library also hosts a staggering number of citizen's group meetings, now announced on its website, which reveals considerable social-science and media expertise. In recent decades, the librarians have developed a strong online presence, host a volunteer network on their server, and provide free Wi-Fi and resident computers to patrons. The physical library building is packed every day with people of all ages, reading and working on personal projects.

Unusually for a small city, the Kamakura Library is also an active research center and archive, with some significant collections. The 1976 *Kamakura Dictionary*, edited by Shirai Eiji, was created at the library, for example.[69] Kimura Hikosaburō and Sawa Jurō wrote and edited the official city history there in 1959, an achievement *The Kamakura Citizen* marked by boasting that the result was "scholarly to a degree one cannot find elsewhere."[70] The following month's issue announced Sawa Jurō's donation of a trove of historical maps to the public library, followed by the editor's comment that, while history buffs would want to explore the primary sources themselves, for people "who just want to know the essentials, there is no one better than Sawa Jurō to introduce them" to Kamakura's past through his own publications.[71] Sawa also coordinated with Mayor Masaki to create the Kamakura Museum of Literature (*Kamakura Bungakukan*), and transferred the library's literary-related holdings there when it was established in 1986.[72] That institution also now frames elite Kamakura history as both locally and nationally significant. The current archivist at the library, Hirata Emi, is a modern Japan specialist and has published two books on the Kamakura Akademia, with the cooperation of a research group she runs, and has curated several photography exhibits highlighting different elements of Kamakura's modern past.

Action to develop public libraries as a central institutional home for democracy is something these individuals shared with Ōuchi Hyōe and Morito Tatsuo, the postwar Minister of Education discussed in earlier chapters. Together with two other men, Muira Yoshiaki (who lived just outside of Kamakura) and Takano Iwasaburō, they submitted a formal request to the Prime Minister on July 31, 1946, to establish a library with a permanent budget line for the use of Diet members and the general public, based on the model of the U.S. Library of Congress. Later Suehiro Izutarō, who founded the prewar settlement house where Masaki and Hattori Shisō volunteered, and a former Minister of Finance,

Shibusawa Keizō, also signed the petition, which resulted in establishing the National Diet Library. The petition specified that the library absorb the archives of the South Manchuria Railways Research Department, the Imperial Army, and the Navy, as well as the research holdings of the Home Ministry, the Ministry of Education, the presurrender Statistics Office, and the official censorship bodies, explicitly in order to make visible the irrationality of past policy and prevent its repetition. Later, when the new Constitution was in place, Representative Hani Gorō arranged for Library of Congress employees to visit Tokyo to advise the staff of the new library, which opened its doors in February 1948 as a public research institution, open to all.[73] The National Diet Library was designed to function in many of the same ways as its municipal counterpart in Kamakura. All the individuals involved saw libraries as capacity-building institutions that taught citizens to understand modern problems and so provided them the skills as well as the facts to challenge their leaders by proposing well-informed, creative post-fascist solutions.

Masaki carried these priorities into City Hall, making it too a capacity-building space that reinforced awareness of civil rights, such as by instituting the first formal celebration of Constitution Day by city officials. On May 3, 1971, he gave a short speech at City Hall on the postwar constitution, emphasizing popular enthusiasm for the document when it was passed in 1947. As he put it, "The events held today commemorate the blossoming of our consciousness that this Constitution would be the means by which we ordinary people (*ippan no hitobito*) built a new Japan." He focused on Article 12, which states "the freedoms and rights guaranteed by the people by this Constitution shall be maintained by the constant endeavor of the people, who shall refrain from any abuse of these freedoms and rights and shall always be responsible for utilizing them for the public welfare." Constitution Day was an opportunity to remind his listeners that "constant endeavor of the people" was crucial to safeguarding the freedoms they enjoyed, and that all citizens bore responsibility for "the public welfare."[74]

Like Hijikata at the museum, Masaki turned to the issue of redress to Asia in the 1970s in his official capacity as mayor. In a speech on August 15, 1971, Masaki recalled the hardships of the war years and noted that nearly everyone in the audience had lost someone dear to them. But then he reminded his listeners that

> we must not forget that the white flowers represent other faces as well...It was not just people on our side who were sacrificed to the war. During the fifteen years Japan waged aggressive war on the continent, the blood of hundreds of thousands of Asians was spilled—something for which we have not yet

made reparations. The postwar era has exposed numerous acts of brutality and misconduct by Japan's old military, and we should not avert our eyes from them. At the same time, given the extreme conditions on the battlefield, major responsibility belongs less to individual perpetrators of these crimes against human rights (*jinken hanzai*) than to the government leaders and the warmongers who spurred on Japanese citizens, took them away from their peaceful lives, and tossed them into the scary battlefield.[75]

Masaki then argued that Japanese commitment to global peace and an anti-nuclear future, while important, was not enough. Japan should work with China toward peace in the region and also help accomplish the reunification of Korea.

Masaki had struck a similar note in another speech six months earlier denouncing a proposed law to bring Yasukuni shrine back under national government administration. He focused on the disproportionate attention to military deaths by the state as opposed to Japanese civilian deaths both from aerial bombardment in Japan and on the Asian mainland. The same misallocation occurred for the living, he thought, since soldiers but not civilian repatriates had preferential access to state pensions.[76] Masaki also had harsh words for the security alliance with the United States, which he saw as detrimental to Japan.[77] The alliance was particularly unfair to Okinawa, he argued in another speech, since, even though the Japanese government had just regained sovereignty over Okinawa Prefecture, it still gave the United States "a free hand" to do what it pleased there, meaning that Okinawa was now tied to American aggression in Indochina far more than to economic reconstruction in Japan. While the Okinawans bore the brunt of this policy, their difficult lives destabilized peace in the rest of Japan as well. Masaki almost certainly knew Okinawan rights activist Senaga Kamejirō, who was mayor of Naha in the 1950s personally, since they worked for the *Osaka Mainichi* at the same time before the war and both were then secretly Communists, meaning that he had been following this issue for decades by the time he became mayor.[78] Masaki also regularly spoke out on other peace-centered topics, such as opposition to government support for the U.S. war in Vietnam, not to mention U.S. military bases in Shōnan, and to the repressiveness of the South Korean government. While mayor he visited both Vietnam and North Korea, and met with the mayors of Hanoi and Pyongyang.[79]

On these issues Masaki pursued a policy of symbolic statements and international "citizen's diplomacy," which he clearly saw as compatible with the expertise-led strategy he preferred for urban planning. He also used the physical space of City Hall for both kinds of activities, in a nod to his somewhat unusual political coalition. While Masaki "drew on the accumulated wisdom" of

Ninagawa Torazō, Minobe Ryōkichi, the Yokohama mayor Asukata Ichio, and the Tokyo Research Center, and had the endorsement of both the Socialist and Communist Parties, he did not win on the basis of industrial-labor-union votes. Instead, Masaki had relied on cultural leaders such as Osaragi Jirō, Komaki Ōmi, Hatta Motō, and Maeda Seison, local citizens' groups such as the Mikkakai, and public-sector unions, in a campaign strategy that became known as "the Kamakura method" when it was copied elsewhere.[80] The policy difference can be summed up as focusing on "quality of life" beyond the workplace concerns of the labor unions.

The Mikkakai also prioritized quality of life in ways that included attention to cultural style. *The Kamakura Citizen* interspersed its dense technical articles about the city budget and the nuances of cost-sharing for regional transportation plans with artwork by local citizens, providing small opportunities for its readers to enjoy culturally rich lives and reinforce "the Kamakura brand." The front page of the first few issues featured a beautiful woodcut design of stylized ivy leaves, reminiscent of William Morris and Leonard Woolf's Hogarth Press publications, while a line drawing of a boat by Katō K. graces page 3 of the inaugural issue. Many of the advertisements also are lovely little images, such as the one for the Yua Inn, whose punning English name also acknowledges Kamakura's self-presentation as an elegant cosmopolitan center. Finally, the editors found amusing little news items to fill awkward spaces, such as a report on the main cause of house fires in the United States, which turned out to be "smoking in bed."[81]

One of the long-time Mikkakai members, political cartoonist Nasu Ryōsuke (1913–1989), whose line drawings often appeared in *The Kamakura Citizen*, made the post-fascist quality of their thinking particularly clear when he explicitly connected environmental protection to peace activism. He argued in *The Kamakura Citizen* that environmental and historical protection should be treated as the national defense of Japan—saving it internally from rapacious development. In a 1965 essay he argued that 90 percent of the national defense budget should be reallocated to cultural and environmental protection rather than the Ministry of Defense. As he explained,

> It is said in the last war that the Japanese military didn't shoot down even one bomber over Tokyo—that's why Tokyo turned into a vast burned-out plain. When we hear that Japan lost because of its material disadvantages, this is the first thing we should think about… I spent eight years as a soldier, being made to support the slogans about prosperity and peace in Asia and the Kingly Way and now I can't believe in these beautiful words being uttered by the government.

Nasu went on to argue that the greatest security threats to Japan were the possibility of "war in the name of peace," unregulated economic growth, and government policies that supported corporate profits rather than the lives of citizens, which he saw as three aspects of the same problem.[82] Based on his own bitter experience—that the military had not tried to protect Japanese civilians—Nasu reframed environmental preservation as a post-fascist task.

Locating the sources of political rancor

As Masaki and the Mikkakai soon discovered, however, bringing democracy into administrative decision-making sometimes solved problems but at other times simply generated political rancor. Importantly, although tension erupted between experts and the general public and ugly personal rifts also drove wedges between the experts themselves, few of these fights were because experts were imposing one-size-fits-all, high-modernist policies on citizens. In 1968 Masaki narrowly lost his third election after his coalition broke apart over anger that he had failed to control his subordinates within the government. A scandal had erupted because city employees had accepted money from a developer to allow a substandard project, precisely the kind of corruption Masaki had unsuccessfully but sincerely tried to stamp out. Although no one thought Masaki was personally involved, he had just raised the wages of municipal workers substantially, intensifying the frustration of Kamakura residents.[83] Another source of tension was the splintering of both the Socialist–Communist alliance and the Socialist Party itself nationally in the 1970s, which contributed to local conflicts everywhere. Writing about the effect of these clashes on Tokyo's municipal government at the same time, Takahashi Masao described the battle years later as "like a fever. Now looking back, I can't understand it." Shibata Tokue, in a similar reaction, described the battle as "like the Cultural Revolution, no reason. But that lasted ten years and ours lasted only one."[84] The partisan battles took their toll in Kamakura too. Everyone walked away angry and bruised.

These conflicts also reached within the community of experts, even those who had worked amicably together at the Statistics Bureau. Ōhashi Ryūken, who had two decades earlier published lively, sympathetic, and highly personal profiles of his colleagues, later lambasted them in print for "having lost the fighting spirit to criticize and resist American type modern economic theory and modern statistical theory." While his concern was fundamentally political, his chosen battlefield was highly technical. Ōhashi was angry that Ōuchi Hyōe and his circle had adopted statistics techniques such as sampling and quality-control analysis, as well as concepts like "normal distribution," all of which he associated with monopoly capitalism.[85] While Masaki agreed with his fellow Communist that monopoly capitalism was dangerous—because it established conditions conducive to fascism—he embraced these techniques and resented Ōhashi's personal attack on his mentor. In this case, everyone involved understood the technical issues and agreed on the policy implications of the various available choices. They also agreed on desired outcomes. They disagreed only on the impact of accepting compromises in an imperfect world, but treated those differences as if they signaled deep conflicts in value systems. That was enough to destroy decades-long personal relationships.

The attacks from the Left were matched by equally ferocious sorties from the Right, ones that also felt like personal betrayals to Masaki and Ōuchi. When Minobe decided to step down in 1978, Suzuki Shun'ichi, who was one of Minobe's deputies in the Tokyo Municipal Government, ran for Governor on the Liberal Democratic Party platform against the Socialist Party candidate, labor leader Ōta Kaoru. Ōuchi had not only taught Suzuki but also presided at his wedding, and he convinced Minobe to withhold an endorsement of Ōta because of his respect for and trust in Suzuki's professionalism. That act almost certainly clinched Suzuki's electoral victory, recapturing Tokyo for the Liberal Democratic Party. Suzuki immediately repudiated many of Minobe's policies and the priorities that Minobe and Masaki shared. He also allowed publication of a nasty interview which described 91-year-old Ōuchi as so frail that he pulled himself around his house in Kamakura by a rope, unable to walk without it, and characterized Minobe as nothing but the "puppet" of Komori Takashi, the head of the Research Center on Tokyo Administration. Suzuki claimed he had never met Komori but that was such a blatant falsehood that the interviewer responded, "Oh, come on, be honest. It isn't like you to flat-out lie for your own advantage, nor is that acceptable behavior either." Suzuki next described himself as far more experienced than Minobe, and therefore less reliant on public input into administrative matters, implying that democratizing expertise was useful only to the unprepared.[86] After twelve years of close collaboration, the venom in Suzuki's remarks placed him in the ranks of unattractive "sore winners." This incident also marks a moment when relying on shared professionalism went very wrong for Ōuchi and his former students.

In Kamakura, however, what is most striking is the vagueness of the complaints about Masaki, from both the general public and experts, suggesting that the tension was about political stance and tone rather than policy content. Koizumi

Chikataka, who worked at the Kanagawa public policy institute, was typical when he groused that "Masaki was such a stubborn old man," but produced no concrete examples even when prodded. The editor of *The Kamakura Citizen* similarly complained that Masaki did not listen to anyone, without ever being specific.[87] My guess is that style more than substance separated Masaki from his harshest critics because he was obviously sincere about "widening the pipeline" and providing much-needed services to the city. His mix of symbolic and practical causes also fit very comfortably with larger patterns of Kamakura activism.[88] Yet his constituents were increasingly irritated by him. Probably Masaki thought he was being inclusive when he piled on details about how to structure the sewer tax or regulate building heights, but the more he emphasized the technical challenges, the more his constituents felt he was either ignoring their actual concerns or condescending to them. And he was incapable of understanding why they reacted in that manner. Despite his Communist Party membership, Masaki was "born in the Meiji era" as the eldest son of an elite bureaucrat; learning to listen and expressing gratitude to subordinates were not stressed when he was growing up. Four years in prison probably also contributed to his impatience with demands that he constantly reaffirm his democratic credentials. By 1978, Masaki was also seventy-four years old and visibly growing tired of daily life as a public servant.[89]

Nor did Masaki indulge in the rhetorical praise of Kamakura as a uniquely charming and significant place, even though he often expressed pleasure in its ancient buildings, abundant greenery, and interesting modern culture. That omission may have been his biggest tactical error. By contrast, nearly everyone else who wrote about Kamakura seemed to boast about it constantly. National Trust members' willingness to pay in order to retain Kamakura's charm, as well as the campaign for the Ancient Capital Law, intensified Kamakura residents' sense of themselves as stewards of sites important to all Japanese, a belief they regularly stated in print. The Mikkakai, like so many other Kamakura institutions, often exuded a self-congratulatory civic pride. For example the first issue of *The Kamakura Citizen* featured a message from Mikkakai Chair Sawada Setsuzō, declaring that "we want to emphasize the many special features of Kamakura and ... the ways that our daily life is blessed by being here." A few pages later another officer, Katō Yasuhira, began his remarks by noting that "Kamakura has qualities that are praised throughout the world." In the next issue, Governor Uchiyama lectured Mayor Yamamoto along the same lines:

> In any case people want Kamakura to retain its refined character and stay the way it is. They can see rowdy people and factories everywhere else. But it would

be a problem if we could no longer say 'the Japanese character is most at home in places like Kamakura.' I beg of you from the bottom of my heart not to sully dignified places like Kamakura with factories.[90]

The self-satisfaction dished up with the savvy policy recommendations must have grated on outsiders' ears. I think it grated on Masaki too and every time he displayed that response, his Kamakura listeners saw him as an outsider once again. In the end, it was not the high-modernist ideology or the policies that damaged Masaki and deprived Kamakura of an environmentally protective, social-welfare-oriented urban administration for the next fifteen years; it was the cultural politics.

By 1978, Japan had changed too, in many positive ways because of the hard work detailed in these pages. But another—ironically related—reason was also the direct outcome of post-fascist political culture; most Japanese had tired of the soul-sapping political fighting of the past thirty years. The sheer intensity of the political engagement meant that no one had escaped without battle scars. It surely did not help that so many of the clashes were between people who shared most of their political commitments and knew each other personally. And yet this political engagement and activist interaction with governments were precisely the developments that Scott identifies as the difference between benign and lethal planning. They were integral to maintaining an informed and activist democratic citizenry. For better and for worse, that shift was generated in places like Kamakura.

Conclusion

The leftists in Kamakura, as in Japan more broadly, can claim an impressive legacy—for a generation. Japan became a far more hopeful and egalitarian place after 1945, a transformation heightened and intensified at the local level where most political transactions among individuals actually took place. For the first time ever, most young people had access to good-quality secondary education and therefore to the main route to social mobility. Fueled by the ever-rising skill level of the workforce, the economy expanded, and, due to the new institutions that disseminated the economic rewards across the population, standards of living steadily rose too. The same high skill levels also served Japanese in their private lives: by international standards, they managed their health, their finances, and such tasks as following intricate instructions for assembling objects, very effectively. The violence that had characterized presurrrender Japan, including both "government by assassination," and the daily experiences of soldiers and poor civilians, was vastly diminished. One of the most appealing qualities of postwar Japanese society was—and remains—the physical safety its inhabitants enjoyed. People felt secure on the streets and they no longer feared arrest, torture, and imprisonment for their ideas. Not only did they keep their nation out of wars, their consistent political opposition to atomic weapons, although denigrated as "Japan's nuclear allergy" by the U.S. government, meant that Japan is the rare major power today without such a weapons program. Japan after 1945 was also characterized by a rich cultural and intellectual life. New institutions such as the Kamakura Akademia, the modern art museum, and Japan's vibrant reading culture all contributed their share to improving quality of life. By the 1970s, this also included strong environmental protections and expanding social-welfare measures, most of which were adopted first by local urban governments and then, in a defensive response, by the national one. Building those new institutions required determined political organizing and reestablishment of social trust among Japanese along new lines. None of this was easy.

However, enormous challenges remained, including the fact that the leftists really did have enemies. The capacity-building institutions of democratic society they erected were more resilient than were prewar structures but time was shorter than they realized. Some of their opponents were ideological, such as the cluster of people who wanted to keep reverence for the Emperor at the center of national life. Others, such as Kamakura-based economist Koizumi Shinzō (1888–1966), president of Keio University from 1933 to 1947, thought that stopping global communism was so essential that he was willing to trade away nearly everything else.[1] Some, like novelist-turned-politician Ishihara Shintarō, enjoyed the sense of domination over others so much that he later joined forces with the overtly "reactionary modernists." Still others wanted to get rich fast, which in Kamakura usually meant questionable land development projects.

Nor did Japanese political battles occur in global isolation. Some of the leftists' opponents derived their success from the influence they wielded beyond Japan's shores. As elsewhere around the globe, the scales were tipped by American willingness to meddle in Japanese domestic affairs out of a fear of communism, expressed through the Cold War. It proved impossible to exclude from national policymaking even deeply disliked former wartime leaders such as Kishi Nobusuke because he had American overt and covert backing.[2] Postwar Japanese have never had the luxury of deciding their political fate without such interference from abroad. From the late Occupation years, American government actions consistently were designed to weaken the Socialist and Communist parties, undercut labor unions, and involve Japan in U.S. wars in Asia.[3] These policies, unlike American actions in the early postwar period, made the always difficult task of conducting democratic governance far harder by installing and protecting unpopular, irresponsible, and self-interested leaders.

Japanese conservatives used American anti-communism and domestic discomfort with social change to suppress critics, roll back the new labor laws, and conduct mass dismissals of labor union activists in the early 1950s, a crucial moment for Japan's postwar political culture. Since the urban labor unions were the main supports of the Japan Socialist Party, doing so was about political control as much as economic power. Some conservatives simply were uncomfortable with the pace of social change rather than its direction. As Masuda Hajimu explains, older and rural Japanese in particular were discomfited by the tone of labor protesters even when they thought the content of their demands was reasonable. "In other words, the actual dynamics of the mass firings around 1950 were not necessarily about ideology but about a desirable style of order and harmony at workplaces and in society."[4] It is hardly surprising that young adults were less respectful of their elders than in the past, given the history they had all just shared, but this shift was nonetheless much resented.

The Kamakura Akademia was a victim of this 1950 "Red Purge" because it collapsed when all its students were blacklisted from employment in both the private and public sectors. Since speech and publication were by then formally protected in Japan, and other postwar reforms made it very difficult to fire workers for political reasons, hostile employers focused on ways to avoid offering jobs to politically engaged applicants in the first place. In the postwar system, very few employers ever took on mid-career hires. Instead, they tied the selection process very tightly to school graduation, making it easy to blacklist certain categories of job candidates. The Akademia thus functioned as a canary in the coal mine of Japanese labor relations by revealing the moment when presurrender political tests for access to jobs were indirectly but effectively reestablished. While the intensity of opposition to the Akademia seems wildly out of proportion to its impact today, the entire postwar system by which schools fed young people into their careers was at stake. Nationally, the "Red Purge," of which this was one small part, would have failed if more public and private employers in communities across the country had ignored the blacklist. There was little that the Akademia faculty themselves could do to overcome this hurdle.

Yet, in a countervailing effort, the "Red Purge" attack on labor unions and the concurrent American-led push for Japanese rearmament re-energized the Japanese labor, human rights, and peace movements, because so many people saw these developments as "nothing but the revival of fascism."[5] Despite the advantages of American backing and control of the central government, the conservatives could maintain their power over the next few decades only by regularly acceding to pressure from the leftists. Although the Akademia was soon gone, Yokohama City University picked up the torch and produced a steady stream of well-educated young people from modest backgrounds who continued to expand opportunities for the next generation, as did similar public, low-tuition schools elsewhere, such as Osaka City University. Like the curators at the Kamakura Museum of Modern Art, the faculty in those places presented local culture as "brimming over with creativity" and trained young people to democratize both policy and politics. They also encoded a strong consciousness of the dangers of fascism in a huge variety of institutional practices, which young graduates carried with them into their adult lives.

In fact Japan retained most of the early postwar reforms and their attendant political culture because of the strength of this opposition. In its first three decades, when the Liberal Democratic Party adopted social welfare measures, it did so explicitly—and grudgingly—in order to deprive opponents of a powerful political weapon. Japan's pacifist policies, such as the pledge to limit defense spending to 1 percent of GNP, were universally acknowledged to be the result of leftist pressure. So were the environmental and heritage protection bills of the 1960s and 1970s. Even the Income Doubling Plan of 1960 was, in Masumi Junnosuke's perceptive analysis, "first and foremost a regional development program," designed to bind local governments to the ruling party.[6] All of these actions show the power of the opposition.

But the leftists still faced an uphill battle for a variety of reasons. One problem was that, as they became more experienced and effective in the 1950s, so did their opponents, who found creative new ways to disenfranchise urban leftist voters and disproportionately reward their smaller core constituencies, particularly farmers. After the various factions of the Japan Socialist Party unified in 1955, conservatives responded by merging into the Liberal Democratic Party later the same year. The Liberal Democrats then maintained control of government by self-interested redistricting that gave rural voters—few of whom were labor union members—far more power than urban ones. Because the postwar era was characterized by a steady exodus from villages to Japan's urban centers, the pernicious effect of this manipulation was to steadily widen the disparity between the impact of a rural versus an urban vote. Once the leftists lost control of the Diet and Prime Minister's post, it was hard to reclaim it.

Other enduring problems for the leftists emerged because their commitment to democracy made it hard to control internal bickering. Political battles were exhausting and the constant, often personal, criticism of each other's actions cut its own distinctive swath of damage. As Masumi Junnosuke ruefully explained, the Japan Socialist Party "squandered its energy on self-destructive factional infighting and lost the strength it needed to nurture and expand its support base," explaining why it peaked at one-third of the voting population in Japan. The Communist Party leadership was equally willing to waste the energy of its own members. This globally common failing of left-wing movements regularly hobbled activists and complicated their relationships to sympathetic policymakers in Kamakura and throughout Japan.

Another challenge derived from the leftists' strategy of relying on direct democracy rather than the traditional channels of power controlled by their opponents. In Masumi's concise summary, this approach was inherently "precarious" because "the progressive leaders attempted to introduce institutions for citizen participation, thereby creating further friction with existing institutions. Channeling a form of energy that rejects formalization into institutions and then stabilizing and sustaining it was a formidable task."[7] Enabling greater democratic participation, ironically, often made it far harder to effect change. Moreover, since, as this book argues, making institutions fairer and building trust in them were both essential post-fascist tasks, the leftists had the challenging assignment of critiquing LDP-dominated structures without undermining trust in all civic institutions.

Another set of challenges unfolded as a direct result of the leftists' earlier successes. Greater democratization, broader upward social mobility, and higher standards of living all made Japan into a more successful society but also rendered their most potent strategies less effective in crucial ways. The expanded public sphere weakened the cohesiveness and intimacy of elite culture simply by vastly enlarging it. The quiet offers of cooperation to individuals across political lines in the name of post-fascism had worked best when they occurred off-stage and with listeners who fully appreciated the generosity of the gesture. Indeed, leftists in Kamakura, like Kyoto, were able to maintain that intimacy more than could their counterparts in places like Tokyo and Yokohama because their communities were smaller and had not been disrupted in 1945 by bombing raids. One reason both cities became left-wing bastions was that their inhabitants continued to interact with the same neighbors as before surrender, forming a basis of personal trust that sustained cohesive long-term political communities. Iguchi Kazuki stressed the importance of this place-based personal trust in explaining Kyoto politics, where leftist Mayor Ninagawa Torazō governed from 1950 to 1978.[8] His unusually long tenure in office rested on just such intimate engagements among his constituents.

A different way to characterize the impact of these vast changes is that they caused a particularly strong generation gap in Japan between those who remembered "fascist society" and those who did not. Surviving a regime of lies, censorship, and, ultimately, great violence meant sharing a powerful visceral experience that was difficult to convey to others. In particular, the strategy of establishing a post-fascist atmosphere of oblique reminders was not durable, because the passage of time changed the extent to which communication in this register could take place. For older generations, allusiveness had real disciplinary power, which is why they could not comprehend how much their habitual circumlocutions sounded evasive—and eventually obscure—to younger people. Instead, younger Japanese often experienced such indirectness as smug exclusivity, precisely what older folk were trying to avoid in their dealings with each other. (They may also have perceived that cohesive but allusive atmosphere—"political correctness"—as disturbingly parallel to the reigning fascist aesthetic of the 1930s.) The generational divide—as it so often is—was also in part about style: young people read the earnestness that undergirded both conciliation and militancy by their leftist elders as uncool. They were not wrong: the historical record shows enormous amounts of sincere dorkiness and far less cynical self-interest than in conservative ranks. Minobe Ryōkichi, the most media-savvy of the economists, acknowledged this when he described his circle in 1970 as resembling Don Quixote, deeply committed to their cause even when they seemed to others like badly dressed men tilting at windmills.[9] They had no response to people who thought the playboy persona epitomized by the Ishihara brothers looked like a lot less work and a lot more fun.

The rapid pace of change after 1945 continued to intensify this generation gap, explaining why the "1968 generation" rejected existing leftist organizations—both working-class and elite. According to Oguma Eiji, the most visible groups of young activists in 1968 significantly expanded the range of ways to express a stance of resistance but generated neither a new narrative of urban modernity nor concrete policy goals. Rather, they pushed the rejection of formal organizations much more than had their predecessors. Oguma's subjects neither learned to master existing political institutions, nor adopted the cultural protocols that older leftists had used to renegotiate political life after 1945.[10] To be clear, while such impatience and formlessness were much celebrated in avant-garde culture, this was never the whole story; for example, activists for environmental-protection policy followed a more traditional path. As Simon Avenell argues, the "long 1960s" (through 1973) was the "formative moment in the development of environmental consciousness in postwar Japan," and since then has been sustained by people of every generation who doggedly worked through political institutions to achieve their goals.[11] But the largest left-wing movement dominated by young people in 1968, the struggle against the Vietnam War, epitomized this anti-institutional style: as a contemporary observer, Tsurumi Yoshiyuki, explained, "Beheiren has deliberately acted in ways that challenge the long-accepted patterns of left-wing action." Capable of calling huge demonstrations, Beheiren rejected all established political organizations, and was "a movement uniquely and strongly infused with concepts of cultural revolution."[12] Yet because members shied away from institution-building, Beheiren's long-term impact was to extend for another quarter-century the world the post-fascist leftists made without leaving its own distinctive political stamp.

And, just as fascism had been powered by an emotional desire for systemic "feelings of belonging," the dissatisfaction that powered the 1968 protesters, according to Oguma, was a sense of alienation in high school and especially university because these institutions had become large and impersonal. Ironically, the protesters longed for the intense purpose that the tiny groups of presurrender university students had experienced and responded to that desire by focusing on protest for its own sake and on partisan issues that seemed like splitting hairs to more distant observers. Yet presurrender universities had conveyed such a powerful aura of belonging precisely because studying there had been a privilege restricted to a lucky few. The people who had gone through that experience correctly identified it as the wellspring of their own energy, courage, and optimism. Ironically, recreating that formative community was incompatible with the very changes that brought the 1968-ers into higher education, even though the older leftists wished above all to do so. Perhaps it was inevitable that the 1968-ers interpreted their own frustration at that impossibility as anger at their elders' elitism.

Post-fascism, because it rested on the shared experience of living through a traumatic era, could never fully make sense to the generations born after 1945. But the war still cast an enormous shadow on the lives of younger twentieth-century Japanese. Marianne Hirsch explores related terrain in her study of the "postmemory" of the children of survivors of the European Holocaust. As she explains, these children, her "postrememberers," also must manage their own distinctive and intense relationship to the wartime past because those difficult experiences marked survivors in ways that profoundly affect their child-rearing practices. Properly speaking, "postmemory" refers only to a single generation: the people who pursue remembrance in order to make the baffling conditions of their own upbringing more comprehensible. In Hirsch's formulation, their response to that dilemma is "postmemory," which is "a powerful and very particular form of memory precisely because its connection to its object or source is mediated not through recollection but through an imaginative investment and creation."[13] Most valuably, she calls attention to the profound emotional investment in the past by people too young to remember it and explains why this occurs. Postrememberers feel an intense desire to make their own sense out of that past to address the profound cognitive dissonance created by growing up in the homes of people still responding to already-vanished events.

Fundamentally what was needed in Japan in the late 1960s and 1970s was greater intergenerational dialogue—which functions as a kind of talk therapy. Hirsch identifies family photographs and family stories as key to postremembrance but this misdirects attention to the talismanic object when the emotional power comes from the *process* of conveying historical knowledge. And that did happen in some areas, such as peace education, which is particularly well developed for learners of all ages in Japan. But often it did not.

The mutual incomprehension across Japan's postwar generations had many implications, but the most significant may have been the effect on efforts to reconcile with Asia. Since the 1980s, a long-running critique of the post-fascist leftists is that they failed to acknowledge responsibility for colonialism and war in Asia. Yet this is not quite fair. In particular, Japanese public debate included a spike of honest and contrite engagement with China in the 1970s, just after U.S. President Richard M. Nixon's 1972 trip to Beijing made it far easier for individual Japanese to travel there or to advocate for more contrite and constructive policies. Most who did so were younger people, such as journalist Honda Katsuichi, who reported on the Nanjing Massacre, but it also included late-in-life efforts by individuals who had been adults during the war years.[14] In Kamakura, Ōuchi Hyōe, Masaki Chifuyu, Arisawa Hiromi, and Hijikata Teiichi were among the many people who reopened the subject of war responsibility in the 1970s in ways that were intended as redress to China.

In fact, this topic was not new for Ōuchi and Arisawa. They had first tackled it in 1945 when both men joined a high-level commission intended to explore not just the reasons for Japan's defeat but also to establish responsibility for war crimes. The commission planned to spend five years on this task but was soon forced to disband after the Soviet delegate to the Far Eastern Commission, Lieutenant-General Kuzma Nikolayevich Derevyanko, complained that the Japanese were "making preparations for the next war and acting as though they were not completely defeated."[15] In this case, a Japanese attempt to reflect self-critically on the war was blocked not by Japanese intransigence or by U.S. Cold War concerns, but by Soviet desire to punish perceived Japanese arrogance. This anecdote is a reminder that the obstacles to accomplishing political change internationally were at least as formidable as were domestic ones, since Derevyanko's negative reaction derailed precisely the process that his government desired.

But both Ōuchi and Arisawa persisted. Like many other peace activists, over the next thirty-five years, Ōuchi regularly mobilized Japanese citizens not just for pacifism but also to express penitence for Japan's wartime crimes in Asia. In 1960, the year he moved to Kamakura, Ōuchi criticized the 1952 peace settlement and security treaty for having upended the international hierarchy of responsibility: those agreements had resolved war issues with the United States and Great Britain but not with China or Southeast Asia, where Japan's wartime depredations were far greater. Why, he asked, did the Japanese government agree to repay money borrowed before the war from the United States and Britain before offering reparations to China to fulfill a debt that was a higher moral responsibility? This should make Japanese feel ashamed. And, Ōuchi continued, Americans should accept some of the blame for Japan's slowness in resolving wartime restitution, since the U.S. government had cooperated with Japan to jointly wrong the world (*ayamari o okashita*) by pushing through the partial San Francisco Peace Treaty rather than resolving Chinese, Soviet, and other Asian claims at that time.[16] Similarly, when Masaki visited Pyongyang and Hanoi in a mayors' delegation to encourage "urban diplomacy," he also proffered an apology for Japan's wartime acts.[17]

Arisawa published less consistently on this topic but he too turned his energy to war responsibility to Asia in the last decade of his life. He chaired the Sino-Japanese Joint Committee on Culture, Science, and Society from 1979 until he passed away in 1988. In 1987, he gave 20,000 volumes from his personal library to the Chinese Academy of Social Science (including a first edition of *Das Kapital*), expressing his reasons at a ceremony on May 25, 1987. Arisawa took pains to explain that he did not make this gesture to help a less developed country. Rather, he acted out of a sense of obligation to China, based on debts of both guilt and gratitude. First, he wanted to urge all Japanese to take responsibility for the "crimes, destruction, and damage" they had inflicted on China during the war.

But, in addition, Arisawa carefully explained, Japanese also owed a separate debt of gratitude to *postwar* China, because the Chinese had relinquished claims to reparations. Arisawa knew just how valuable that act was to Japan because his own research showed that German resentment at reparations after the First World War had significantly contributed to Hitler's rise to power. He told his audience not to take credit for Japan's extraordinary postwar economic growth: "We did not build that. America and China did it for us. We must not, must not forget this." Arisawa ended by pledging his remaining time on earth to repaying those debts.[18] Hiraiwa Gaishi, chairman of the business federation Keidanren, later said that Arisawa's depiction of China's decision not to pursue reparations as "one of the great overlooked sources of Japanese growth" profoundly changed his thinking.[19] Hiraiwa did not miss the point that acknowledgment of this debt could serve as a sturdy foundation on which to build a strong East Asian community, based on Chinese magnanimity and Japanese respect. Undoubtedly he also recognized that Arisawa's emphasis on Chinese generosity aligned with Arisawa's own post-fascist overtures as an individual to his wartime persecutors.

In retrospect, the 1970s were a crucial lost opportunity because these scattered post-fascist efforts did not coalesce. By then, Arisawa's generation was too elderly to sustain the attempt. In hindsight, of course, Arisawa's warning that postwar Japanese should not take China's relatively forgiving stance for granted was prescient. Japan did act as though China would forever retain the policy of renouncing claims to war reparations, which had begun with the Nationalist government in 1945 and then was maintained by the Peoples Republic of China for thirty years. At that time, as Takashi Yoshida explains,

> the PRC leaders regarded ordinary Japanese citizens, including rank-and-file soldiers, as the victims of Japan's militarism and differentiated the general population from the relative handful of militarists whom they held responsible for the aggression. In addition, until the early 1980s, the government generally suppressed the memory of Japanese aggression and atrocities, believing that overlooking past offenses was the best way to maintain peaceful Sino-Japanese relations.[20]

Since 1982, by contrast, Chinese remembrance of the Asia-Pacific War has come to mean something more closely resembling the aggrieved and militant remembrance practiced by the Spanish Civil War exiles, who, it should be recalled, "appear to be obsessed by the fear of being forgotten … and are very reluctant to forgive and forget." This great shift in Chinese (and Korean) remembrance in the 1980s regarding the war responsibility of ordinary Japanese was in part a horrified reaction to Japanese government actions in 1982, when Ministry of Education officials sought to erase from Japanese textbooks criticism of the Asia-Pacific War. At first it seemed as though—for the sake of a common Asian future—the Japanese population and even other portions of the government would respond positively to Chinese demands for redress, and reject the Ministry of Education's dishonesty about the recent past. The 1989 end of the Cold War, the death of the Shōwa emperor, and the model provided by European unification all nudged Japan in that direction. But then so many Japanese became frightened by China's growing global power that a backlash against expressing contrition developed political muscle. Next in an increasingly vicious spiral of blame, Chinese commemoration of the Nanjing Massacre and other sites grew in scale and intensity in the early twenty-first century, and became far more critical of Japanese society in general, not just the military-dominated government of the 1930s and 1940s. The shift in Chinese public opinion had other causes too, such as the death of Chiang Kai-shek in 1975, which made it easier to ignore the conflict between the Communists and the

Nationalists in the 1940s. Not coincidentally, the textbook battle took place at exactly the same time that Japanese policymakers began warning that a looming labor shortage was resolvable only by relaxing immigration barriers. On that topic too, a government-orchestrated panic about foreigners committing crimes led to a cruel policy in which outsiders were admitted but disempowered through legal restrictions that made it impossible for most of them to settle down, learn Japanese, and integrate into the community. Now many Japanese communities have too few young people to sustain their existence. Clearly, for a variety of reasons, it would have been far easier to resolve the lingering tensions of the Asia-Pacific War if Japan had followed the leftists' lead in the 1970s than at any time in the subsequent thirty-five years.[21]

The cost of not reconciling with Asia became clear when Japan faced both a severe economic downturn in the 1990s and an increasingly hostile international environment, much like the conditions that had encouraged the rise of fascism in the 1930s. Since then, Japan's foreign policy has become more belligerent without any coherent diplomatic strategies or even consistent goals. At home the extraordinary postwar improvements in standards of living for all Japanese reversed in the new millennium, and today income inequality and poverty rates are both on the rise. Perhaps most insidiously, Japanese educational standards have plummeted in the last twenty years too.[22] Intellectually and psychologically the worldview established by the post-fascist generation retreated, and was replaced by the discredited fascist fantasy, that if Japan only regained ethnic purity, all would be well.

Shockingly, the earthquake-tsunami-nuclear disaster on March 11, 2011 revealed both the emptiness of that utopia and the cynicism of Japan's leaders, just as did the end of the war. In recent years, the Liberal Democrats have presided over a return of what Takahashi Tetsuya has dubbed "a sacrificial system" that not only forces some people to choose between "life and livelihood" but also presents that choice to everyone else as necessary to Japan's national survival. Over 130,000 people still lived as displaced refugees six years after the quake; workers at the damaged nuclear plants toiled in shockingly poor conditions, and the measures in place to prevent large-scale release of irradiated water are almost certainly doomed to fail. While the government sank vast financial and human resources into decontamination around Fukushima Daiichi nuclear plant, little of that effort realistically addressed the health and environmental threats still posed by the complex. The Abe Shinzō administration next doubled down on its plans to destroy a pristine Okinawan coral bay at Henoko for an American military base that Okinawans unanimously had rejected. As Takahashi argues, the government's stance that the people harmed in these ways were "necessary sacrifices" for the nation was chillingly close to the fascist logic of the 1940s.[23]

Prime Minister Abe not only expressed precisely the same anxieties and illogically belligerent priorities that characterized Japan's leaders in the 1930s, but also began recreating 1930s-style legal institutions of oppression, such as awarding the government the right to prosecute any journalist it deemed annoying.[24] The government also used its prosecutorial power to intimidate political protest. It arrested and held incommunicado without charges for six months an elderly non-violent protester against the Henoko base, Yamashiro Hiroji, in 2016–2017, depriving him of liberty while ostensibly investigating whether he had committed a minor property crime.[25] Equally alarmingly, the Abe administration openly encouraged right-wing violence against both critics and minorities, reestablishing the influence of Mann's core enforcers of fascist politics. The return of a "sacrificial system" is particularly horrifying because 1945 really was a watershed moment, when, thanks to the constructive energy of its postwar citizens, Japan rejected such tactics. And, far more than in the 1930s, as one of the richest nations on earth, Japan has more than sufficient resources to provide for all its inhabitants' needs but has not deployed them in ways that do so.

But even as the national government abandoned its responsibilities to its citizens, local political institutions continued to sustain the bodies and spirits of individuals in Kamakura and elsewhere by enacting a caring social community. The Kamakura City Central Library, for example, functions as archivists Kimura Hikosaburō and Sawa Jurō would have hoped. Today the library staff uses Twitter to encourage desperate high school students to "take the day off from school and visit the library" when they feel overwhelmed. As their August 2015 tweet continued, "Even if you spend the whole day here, no one will try to chase you off. If the prospect of heading back to school in September has you ready to die, remember you've got a place of refuge at the library." Rather than scolding them for skipping school, the Twitter message explained, "To those of you who are carrying painful emotions, we would like the library to be a place where you feel like you belong… You just might find a book that comforts your exhausted heart." And, after promising human community, the staff directed readers to "a special selection of life-affirming books. One of them could be extremely significant for you." Frankly acknowledging grim reality, the message embedded a hot link to a support site for suicidal teens. As the news report on this announcement stressed, the response to the library's overtures was overwhelmingly positive. Teens retweeted comments such as: "I'm deeply moved by these words … Please keep up the good work." "I've heard that child suicides peak around the end of summer vacation" and "this kind of simple kindness could really help some kids." "I wish there were more places like this, close by, that people could turn to in times of distress," and, simplest of all, "Thank you. Thank you. Thank you."[26] Keeping teenagers alive is only a first step but a sadly needed one in Japan today. On a small scale, Kamakura remains a post-fascist place.

Notes

Introduction

1 Gavan McCormick, "'All Japan' versus 'All Okinawa'—Abe Shinzo's Military-Firstism," *The Asia-Pacific Journal* 13, issue 10, no. 4, March 16, 2015. Tessa Morris-Suzuki, "Freedom of Hate Speech; Abe Shinzo and Japan's Public Sphere," *The Asia-Pacific Journal* 11, issue 8, no. 1, February 25, 2015.

2 Edward W. Soja, "Writing the City Spatially," *City* 7, no. 3 (November 2003): 269–280. Soja is making a case for a larger and more heterogeneous urban agglomeration but Kamakura operates in his model "as a new centre in the urban periphery." Like other such centers, it "contributed significantly to a dramatic spatial re-organization of the modern metropolis" creating "expanding constellations of local synekisms," by which he means political civic organizations that maintain a sense of responsibility to inhabitants. Quote page 279.

3 Prasenjit Duara has made this argument for Manchuria, but it holds for localities within the home islands as well. Prasenjit Duara, "Local Worlds: The Poetics and Politics of the Native Place in Modern China," *South Atlantic Quarterly* 99.1 (Winter 2000): 13–45.

4 Saigusa Hiroto, "Fūhyō Daigaku o Tsubusu," *Chūō Kōron*, February 1951, 141–150, 149.

5 For two American examples, see Michael J. Allen, *Until the Last Man Comes Home* (North Carolina University Press, 2009) and David W. Blight, *Beyond the Battlefield: Race, Memory & the American Civil War* (University of Massachusetts Press, 2002).

6 Akiko Hashimoto, *The Long Defeat: Cultural Trauma, Memory, and Identity in Japan* (Oxford: Oxford University Press, 2015), 14 and 47.

7 Gaspar Miklos Tamas, "What Is Post-Fascism?" Open Democracy website, https://www.opendemocracy.net/people-newright/article_306.jsp (accessed July 8, 2017).

8 Mashita Shin'ichi, "Ichi Tetsugakusha no Kaisō," in Murayama Tomoyoshi, *Hachi-ichigo haisen zengo* no. 5 in series: *Gendaishi no Shōgen* (Tokyo: Sekibunsha, 1975), 20.

9 Reto Hofmann, *The Fascist Effect: Japan and Italy, 1915–1952* (Ithaca and London: Cornell University Press, 2015).

10 Maggie Clinton, *Revolutionary Nativism: Fascism and Culture in China, 1925–1937* (Durham and London: Duke University Press, 2017).

11 Laura Hein, *Reasonable Men, Powerful Words: Political Culture and Expertise in Twentieth-Century Japan* (Berkeley: University of California Press, and Woodrow Wilson International Center for Scholars, 2004).

12 Ōmori Yoshitarō, "Antantaru Nihon Keizai no Tenbō," *Kaizō* 19, no. 9 (September 1937): 2–19.

13 Kamakura-shi Shishi Hensan Iinkai, *Kamakura shishi–kindai tsūshi*, 7 vols, vol. 7 (Tokyo: Yoshikawa Kōbunkan, 1994), 395.

14 Harry Harootunian, "Time, Everydayness and the Specter of Fascism," in *Re-Politicizing the Kyoto School as Philosophy*, ed. Christopher Goto-Jones (London: Routledge, 2008), 96–112. Naoki Sakai, "Imperial Nationalism and the Comparative Perspective," *positions: east asia cultures critique* 17, no. 1 (Spring 2009): 159–205, which also takes up the issue of fascism. Ken C. Kawashima, Fabian Schafer, and Robert Stolz, eds., *Tosaka Jun: A Critical Reader* (Honolulu: University of Hawai'i Press, 2013). See also Iwakura Hiroshi, *Aru Senjika no Teikō—Tetsugakusha Tosaka Jun to "Yuiken" no Nakamatachi* (Tokyo: Kadensha, 2015).

15 Jeffrey Herf, *Reactionary Modernism: Technology, Culture, and Politics in Weimar and the Third Reich* (Cambridge: Cambridge University Press, 1984). And, as Janet Hunter has argued in a recent essay summarizing scholarship on earthquakes in Japan, the 1923 quake had already created a sense that the core problem was that Japanese had little social trust in each other. Janet Hunter, "Earthquakes in Japan," *Modern Asian Studies* 50, no. 1 (January 2016): 415–435.

16 Hofmann, *The Fascist Effect*, 87. Federico Finchelstein makes a similar argument in *Transatlantic Fascism: Ideology, Violence, and the Sacred in Argentina and Italy, 1919–1945* (Durham: Duke University Press, 2010).

17 Murayama Tomoyoshi, "Georuge-gurotsusu," *Atorie* 3, no. 1 (January 1926): 87–133, reprinted in *Murayama Tomoyoshi: Bijutsu Hihyō to Handō*, ed. Takizawa Kiyouji (Tokyo: Yumani Shobō, 2013), 411–422. See also Katō Tetsurō, *Waimaaruki Berurin no Nihonjin: Yōkō Chishikijin no hantei nettowaaku* (Tokyo: Iwanami, 2008), 84.

18 Michael Mann, *Fascists* (Cambridge: Cambridge University Press, 2004), 24–25.

19 Herf was arguing against the idea that the key trigger was a failure to develop economically and instead argued that a better predictor of fascism was "late political development." He was refuting another widely held theory, that fascism is best understood as a failure to develop into a properly modern—that is, rational—society. Thirty years ago he coined the phrase "reactionary modernism" specifically in order to drive a silver stake through the heart of this view, which is sometimes labeled "modernization theory." See also Peter Hayes, *Why? Explaining the Holocaust* (New York: W.W. Norton, 2016), 147–154. Yoshimi Yoshiaki, *Grass Roots Fascism* (New York: Columbia University Press, 2015). (Originally published 1987 in Japanese.)

20 Mann, *Fascists*, 24–25. See also Mark Mazower, *Dark Continent: Europe's Twentieth Century* (New York: Vintage Books, 1998), 401–402. This is also the demographic that commits most crimes, especially violent ones—and the steep drop in Japanese crime rates that began in the early 1950s is another indication that life really changed for young men at that time.

21 Mann thinks Japan was "'corporatist' heading toward 'fascist,'" 46.

22 Ethan Mark, "The People in the War; Translator's Introduction" to Yoshimi, *Grass Roots Fascism*, 1–39, esp. 18–20. As Mann notes, European fascists exploited the common sense among Protestant church leaders and congregants that they had lost a "sense of the sacred" "by managing to transfer some of the sense of the sacred from God to the nation-state," 86–87. This quasi-religious element certainly operated around the Emperor in Japan. Kenneth J. Ruoff, *Imperial Japan at its Zenith: The Wartime Celebration of the Empire's 2,600th Anniversary* (Ithaca: Cornell University Press, 2010).

23 Two of them returned to this issue decades later showing that they had been thinking about the modern transnational causes of fascism all along. Arisawa Hiromi—between ages 82 and 88—published over 900 pages of densely researched text on why the Weimar Republic weakened and fell in 1933. Arisawa Hiromi, *Waimaaru kyōwakoku monogatari* two vols, (Tokyo: Tokyo Daigaku Shuppankai, 1978), *Waimaaru kyōwakoku monogatari yowa*, (Tokyo: Tokyo Daigaku Shuppankai, 1984). Takahashi Masao also analyzed the reasons for the fall of the Weimar Republic in various publications, including *Happō Yabure—Watakushi no Shakaishugi* (Tokyo: TBS-Buritanika, 1980), 172–176.

24 Ōuchi Hyōe, Arisawa Hiromi, Wakimura Yoshitarō, Takahashi Masao, and Minobe Ryōkichi, *Nihon Keizai wa Dō Naru ka: Zoku Nihon Infureshyon no Kenkyū* (Tokyo Ōdōsha, 1946), 7.

25 Mark Mazower, *Dark Continent: Europe's Twentieth Century* (New York: Vintage Books, 1998), 401–402.

26 Alan Tansman, "Introduction: The Culture of Japanese Fascism," in *The Culture of Japanese Fascism*, ed. Alan Tansman (Durham and London: Duke University Press, 2009), 1–29, quote 7.

27 Tansman, "Introduction," 18. The essay is Aaron Skabelund, "Fascism's Furry Friends: Dogs, National Identity, and Purity of Blood in 1930s Japan," 155–182.

28 Susan Sontag, "Fascinating Fascism," in *Under the Sign of Saturn* (New York: Vintage Books, 1972), 91. Tansman, "Introduction," 4.

29 Osaragi quoted in Fukuda Kazusuke, "Kurama Tengu to Hitoraa Yūgendo no Tō Jihyō," *Shūkan Shinchō*, August 24, 2006, 140–141. George Mosse, *The Image of Man: The Creation of Modern Masculinity*, 1996, also George Mosse, *Fallen Soldiers: Reshaping the Memories of the World Wars* (New York: Oxford University Press, 1990).

30 Osaragi Jirō, *Osaragi Jirō Zenshū*, vol. 3 (Tokyo: Asahi Shinbunsha, 1974), 194.

31 James Orr, *The Victim as Hero: Ideologies of Peace and National Identity in Postwar Japan* (Honolulu: University of Hawai'i Press, 2001).

32 Like their counterparts globally, by the mid-twentieth century, this was not new. See Sabine Frühstück, *Colonizing Sex: Sexology and Social Control in Modern Japan* (Berkeley: University of California Press, 2003); Jordan Sand, *House and Home in Modern Japan: Architecture, Domestic Space, and Bourgeois Culture, 1880–1930* (Harvard University Asia Center, Distributed by Harvard University Press, 2003); Louise Young, *Beyond the Metropolis: Second Cities and Modern Life in Interwar Japan* (Berkeley: University of California Press, 2013); Sheldon Garon, *Molding Japanese Minds: The State in Everyday Life* (Princeton, NJ: Princeton University Press, 1997).

33 Most higher schools were much smaller, about 60–100 students. Takeuchi Yō and Inose Naoki, "Kyōyōshugi to iu 'kabe,'" *Geppō* 4 (April 1999): 1–12. Insert to Takeuchi Yō and Ito Takashi, *Nihon no Kindai*, vol. 12 (Tokyo: Chūō Kōronsha, 1999). See also Donald Roden, *Schooldays in Imperial Japan: A Study in the Culture of a Student Elite* (Berkeley: University of California Press, 1980).

34 Masaki Harue, "Sazanbara No Saku Koro: Masaki Haruesan Ni Kiku Chifuyu to Seishun," 1998. Deposited at National Diet Library, 151–152.

35 Andrew Gordon, *Labor and Imperial Democracy in Prewar Japan* (Berkeley: University of California Press, 1991), 177–181.

36 Mashita, "Ichi Tetsugakusha no Kaisō," 18, 20.

37 As they stress, the process of establishing collective memory is a complex one, "greatly enhanced by the retelling of these narratives, either by individuals alone or in public. Conversation is a fundamental social act." Jay Winter and Emmanuel Sivan, "Introduction," in Winter and Sivan, *War and Remembrance in the Twentieth Century* (Cambridge: Cambridge University Press, 1999), especially 6, 10, 14, 28, 32–33.

38 Murayama Tomoyoshi, "Kaisetsu: 8.15 no Ishiki," in Murayama Tomoyoshi, *Hachi-ichigo haisen zengo*, 291.

39 Mashita, "Ichi Tetsugakusha no Kaisō," 13.

40 Maruyama Masao, "Author's Introduction to the English Edition," in *Thought and Behavior in Modern Japanese Politics*, ed. Ivan Morris (Oxford: Oxford University Press, 1963), xii; J. Victor Koschmann, *Revolution and Subjectivity in Postwar Japan* (Chicago: University of Chicago Press, 1996); Andrew Barshay, *The Social Sciences in Modern Japan: The Marxist and Modernist Traditions* (Berkeley: University of California Press, 2004).

41 Tony Judt, *Postwar: A History of Europe since 1945* (New York: Penguin, 2005), 61.

42 Vaclav Havel, "New Year's Address to the Nation," speech, Czechoslovakia, January 1, 1990, Czech Republic Presidential Website, Speeches, http://old.hrad.cz/president/Havel/speeches/index_uk.html (accessed April 13, 2017).

43	Ōuchi Hyōe, Arisawa Hiromi, Wakimura Yoshitarō, Takahashi Masao, and Minobe Ryōkichi, "20 Nen Mae," *Sekai* 1958, 127–128. Philosopher Kosai Yoshishige said nearly the same thing in "Haisen no Hi," in Murayama Tomoyoshi, *Hachi-ichigo haisen zengo,* 279–289, esp. 286–287.

44	Ienaga Saburō, "Preface," in *The Pacific War: 1931–1945* (New York: Pantheon, 1978), xiv–xxv.

45	Masaki Chifuyu, *Zuihitsu Kamakura Shichō* (Tokyo: Chūō Kōronsha, 1983), 17–18. See also Tanabe Kotarō, "Kakushin Kanryō no Senzen to Sengo—Masaki Chifuyu Nikki ni Miru Sengo Kaikaku," *Kinki Daigaku Tandai Ronshū*, March 2003, 43–45.

46	Timothy Brook, "Collaboration in the Postwar," in Timothy Brook, ed., "Collaboration in War and Memory in East Asia: A Symposium," special issue *Asia-Pacific Journal-Japan Focus* vol. 6, issue 7, July 2, 2008. http://apjjf.org/-Timothy-Brook/2802/article.html (accessed December 29, 2016).

47	Ōuchi Hyōe, "Watakushi no Shinjō," *Sekai*, no. 64 (April 1951), reprinted in *Ōuchi Hyōe Chosakushū*, vol. 12 (Tokyo: Iwanami Shoten, 1975), 3–8.

48	Paloma Aguilar, "Agents of Memory: Spanish Civil War Veterans and Disabled Soldiers," in Winter and Sivan, *War and Remembrance in the Twentieth Century,* 84–103, quotes from 102–103.

49	For example, see Philip Seaton, "The Nationalist Assault on Japan's Local Peace Museums: The Conversion of Peace Osaka," *The Asia-Pacific Journal* 13, Issue 30, no. 2, July 27, 2015. http://apjjf.org/2015/13/30/Philip-Seaton/4348.html (accessed December 29, 2016).

50	Louise Young, *Japan's Total Empire, Manchuria and the Culture of Wartime Imperialism* (Berkeley: University of California Press, 1998). Janis Mimura, *Planning for Empire: Reform Bureaucrats and the Japanese Wartime State* (Ithaca, NY: Cornell University Press, 2011), Annika Culver, *Glorify the Empire: Japanese Avant-Garde Propaganda in Manchukuo* (Vancouver: University of British Columbia Press, 2013). See also Yoshimi, *Grass Roots Fascism.*

51	One example is Arisawa's *Sangyō Dōin Keikaku* (Tokyo: Kaizōsha, 1934). While the book starts out sounding like an endorsement of Nazi policy, Arisawa provides a vigorous rebuttal in the later 2/3 of the book. See also Arisawa Hiromi and Takahashi Masao, "21 seiki o mae ni shite," in *21 Seiki no Gunzō: Takahashi Masao Sensei no Shōgen*, ed. Takahashi Masao Sensei Seibi Kinen Kankōkai (Tokyo: Daiichi Shorin, 1989), 195–237. Hatenaka Shigeo, "Bringing the Liberals to Heel," in Haruko Taya Cook and Theodore Cook, *Japan at War* (New York: The New Press, 1992), 68.

52	Rachel Hutchinson, "Introduction: Negotiating Censorship in Modern Japan," in Rachel Hutchinson, ed. *Negotiating Censorship in Modern Japan* (London: Routledge, 2013), 1–12. See Michael Emmerich, *The Tale of Genji: Translation, Canonization, and World Literature* (New York: Columbia University Press, 2013) for literary imaginativeness under censorship in Tokugawa Japan. For Meiji, see Jason G. Karlin, *Gender and Nation in Meiji Japan: Modernity, Loss, and the Doing of History* (Honolulu: University of Hawai'i Press, 2014).

53 Wakimura Yoshitarō, "*Sekai* no 50-nen to watakushi—'Sekai no Ushio' Shuppatsu no Koro," *Sekai*, no. 617 (January 1997): 121–123.

54 Yonekura Mamoru, "Tokujiku Nohahikae—Wakimura Yoshitarō" part 19 "Hasegawa Jin: Garō, Gaka, Shūshūka," *E*, no. 345 (November 1992): 16–19, esp. 18–19. For another example, in the official Tokyo Daigaku Keizaigakubu, ed., *Tokyo Daigaku Keizaigakubu 50-nen shi* (Tokyo: Tokyo Daigaku Shuppankai, 1976), the participants were circumspect as to the identities of particularly troublesome colleagues even though the same individuals had disclosed this information in other group interviews published years earlier. By contrast, see Wakimura Yoshitarō and Minobe Ryōkichi, "Danatsu no Arashi," in Andō Yoshio, ed., *Shōwa keizai shi e no shōgen*, vol. 1 (Tokyo: Mainichi Shinbunsha, 1966), 146–176.

55 Leith Morton, "Self-Censorship: The Case of Wartime Japanese Poetry," in Hutchinson, ed., *Negotiating Censorship in Modern Japan*, 112–132, quote 129.

56 Ann Sherif, "The Politics of Loss: On Etō Jun," *positions: east asia cultures critique* 10, no. 1 (Spring 2002): 111–139, and Jay Rubin, "From Wholesomeness to Decadence: The Censorship of Literature under the Allied Occupation," *Journal of Japanese Studies* 11, no. 1 (1985): 71–103.

57 Ōuchi, Wakimura, and Arisawa helped establish Tokyo University Press, Takami Jun and others set up the Kamakura Bunkō, as discussed in Chapter 2, and Ōuchi edited one of the first volumes they published. Takahashi Masao founded the Ōdo publishing house where the other economists all published. Other new journals they started included *Sekai, Fabian Kenkyū, Heiwa Keizai*, and *Shakaishugi*. The Kamakura PEN chapter was established in 1936, the first in Japan. Documents on exhibit at the Kamakura Museum of Literature and interview with its director, Yamanouchi Shizuo, November 11, 2011. Osaragi was the first president of the chapter and Ōmori Yoshitarō and Kume Masao were also founding members.

58 Mann, *Fascists*, 72.

59 Frederick R. Dickinson, *World War I and the Triumph of a New Japan, 1919–1930* (Cambridge: Cambridge University Press, 2013), 8–9.

60 Hiromi Mizuno, *Science for the Empire: Scientific Nationalism in Modern Japan* (Stanford, CA: Stanford University Press, 2008), Aaron Stephen Moore, *Constructing East Asia: Technology, Ideology, and Empire in Japan's Wartime Era 1931–1945* (Stanford, CA: Stanford University Press, 2013). Hein, *Reasonable Men*. John W. Dower registers the same process when he notes that, while wartime "ideologues and propagandists ransacked the past for usable images and ideas— and came up with the cherry blossom, for example, and the mystique of a unique Yamato spirit (*Yamato damashii*) and a great deal of flowery language about purity," they also presented Japan's war as highly modern "and this positive, forward-

looking vision was the real key to mobilizing popular sentiment." John W. Dower, "Japan's Beautiful Modern War," in *Ways of Forgetting, Ways of Remembering: Japan in the Modern World* (New York: The New Press, 2012), 80–81.

61   She argues that in Japan neighborhoods were seen as self-managing units. Carola Hein, "Machi: Neighborhood and Small Town. The Foundation for Urban Transformation in Japan," *Journal of Urban History* 35 (2008): 75–107.

62   Discussed in "Ochiai Dōjin" neighborhood blog. http://chinchiko.blog.so-net.ne.jp/2011-02-19 (accessed April 19, 2017).

63   Masaki's wife Harue was an unacknowledged co-translator. Masaki Harue, "Sazanbara no saku koro," 157. Masaki Chifuyu, "Honsho no yakushutsu ni tsuite," 1–5. Amerika Gasshūkoku Senryaku Bakugeki Chōsadan, *Nihon Sensō Keizai no Hōkai—Senryaku Bakugeki no Nihon Sensō Keizai ni Oyobaseru Sho Kōka* (Tokyo: Nihon Hyōronsha, 1950). The original is The United States Strategic Bombing Survey, *The Effects of Strategic Bombing on Japan's War Economy: Over-all Economic Effects Division*, December 1946.

64   Arisawa Hiromi, "Nihon Sensō Keizai no Hōkai ni Tsuite," in Amerika Gasshūkoku Senryaku Bakugeki Chōsadan, *Nihon Sensō Keizai no Hōkai—Senryaku Bakugeki no Nihon Sensō Keizai ni Oyobaseru Sho Kōka*, 1–3.

65   Arisawa, "Nihon Sensō Keizai no Hōkai ni tsuite," 3.

66   Takahashi Masao, *Tenkeiki no Seiji to Keizai* (Tokyo: Ōdōsha, 1947), 101.

67   Also, a higher percentage of Japanese went to college than anywhere except Canada and Israel. Lucien Ellington, "Japanese Education," Japan Digest, National Clearinghouse for United States-Japan Studies, Indiana University, available at Stanford University SPICE website: http://spice.fsi.stanford.edu/docs/japanese_education (accessed April 17, 2017). Thomas P. Rohlen, "Education in Japanese Society," in Daniel I. Okimoto and Thomas P. Rohlen, eds., *Inside the Japanese System: Readings on Contemporary Society and Political Economy* (Stanford, CA: Stanford University Press, 1988), 26.

68   Quote from "Kamakura Akademia Nyūgaku annai," 1950, reprinted in Hirata Emi and Kamakura-shi Kyōiku Iinkai, *Kamakura Kindaishi Shiryō Daijūnishū: Seishun Kamakura Akademia* (Kamakura: Kamakurashi Chūō Toshokan, 1997), 20.

69   Prasenjit Duara, *Rescuing History from the Nation: Questioning Narratives of Modern China* (Chicago: University of Chicago Press, 1997).

70   Oguma Eiji, *A Genealogy of Japanese Self-Images* (Melbourne: Trans Pacific Press, 2002).

Chapter 1

1   Kiyohito Kokita, "Majority of Tokyo Urbanites Crave Escape to Coastal Kanagawa Area," *Asahi Shinbun,* January 9, 2016.

2   Young, *Beyond the Metropolis*; Christoph Brumann and Rupert Cox, *Making Japanese Heritage* (London: Routledge, 2010), 2–3.

3   Yukiko Koshiro, *Imperial Eclipse: Japan's Strategic Thinking about Continental Asia before August 1945* (Ithaca: Cornell University Press, 2013), 73. See also Tamotsu Sugao, "Conservation of Russian-Born Ballerina's Memorabilia at Issue in Kamakura," *Asahi Shinbun*, May 15, 2014. http://ajw.asahi.com/article/ behind_news/social_affairs/AJ201405150001 (accessed January 27, 2016). Normal School and orphanage are from Iso Mutsu, *Kamakura Fact & Legend* (Tokyo: Maruzen, 1918), 26. See also Kamakura-shi Shishi Hensan Iinkai, *Kamakura shishi–kindai tsūshi*, 7 vols, vol. 7, 396–397. For relevant statistics, see Kamakura City, http://www.city.kamakura.kanagawa.jp/soumu/toukei/kamakuratoukei/ top2/26toukeishotop.html (accessed January 27, 2016).

4   There are currently forty-six Catholic churches in Kanagawa prefecture. http:// www.jcarm.com/jpn/directory/prefecture2.htm (accessed January 27, 2016).

5   Ayumi Oya, "Enoden no Kaihatsu," in *Shōnan no Tanjō*, ed. Shōnan no Tanjō Kenkyūkai (Fujisawa: Fujisawa Kyōiku Kenkyūkai, 2005), 84–85.

6   Interview Aoki Shigeru, Tokyo Bunka Zaidan Kenyūjo, Tokyo, April 27, 2016.

7   Ernest Mason Satow, *A Diplomat in Japan: The Inner History of the Critical Years in the Evolution of Japan When the Ports Were Opened and the Monarchy Restored*. http://www.archive.org/details/diplomatinjapani00sato pp. 135–136. Also see Kokaze Hidemasa, "Yokohama Kyoryū to Enoshima," in *Shōnan no Tanjō*, pp. 6–26.

8   Kokaze Hidemasa, "Shōnan no Tanjō," in *Shōnan no Tanjō*, 91–93.

9   Erwin Baelz, *Awakening Japan: The Diary of a German Doctor: Erwin Baelz*, ed. Toku Baelz (New York: The Viking Press, 1931), 44.

10 Baelz opened a medical school in Tokyo in 1896 and summered in Hayama. Kokaze, "Shōnan no Tanjō," 91–93.

11 Shimamoto Chiyo, "Shōnan no Bessō Chika–Kugenuma Chiku o Chūshin ni shite," in *Shōnan no Tanjō*, 63.

12 Kokaze, "Shōnan no Tanjō," 102–103. Before then it took about 2½ hours from Shinbashi to Kamakura. Kusumoto Katsuji, *Naruhodo Kamakura Jiten* (Tokyo: Jitsugyō no Nihonsha, 2002), 152. Hyung-il Pai, *Heritage Management in Korea and Japan: The Politics of Antiquity and Identity* (Seattle: University of Washington Press, 2013).

13 Motomiya Ichirō, "Gōrakuchi Shōnan no Kakuritsu–taishūka no hinten to 'Kankō' chi," in *Shōnan no Tanjō*, 112.

14 The Yokosuka line had been extended to Kamakura and Zushi in 1889. Kokaze, "Shōnan no Tanjo," 96–97. See also Sugiura Yasuhei, *Shōnan no Gojūnen: Shōnan o Tsukiageta Senkushatachi* (Tokyo: Bara Shuppan, 1977), 11.

15 Kusumoto, *Kamakura Naruhodo Jiten*, 208–209.

16 Kusumoto, *Kamakura Naruhodo Jiten*, Manju, 216–217, Ham and box lunch, 218–219.

17 Angela Yiu, "'Beautiful Town': The Discovery of the Suburbs and the Vision of the Garden City in Late Meiji and Taishō Literature," *Japan Forum* 18, no. 3 (2006): 315–338. Stephen Dodd, *Writing Home: Representations of the Native Place in Modern Japanese Literature* (Cambridge, MA: Harvard University Asia Center, 2004), 76. Tokutomi Rōka first published *Shōnan Zuihitsu* in serialized form in 1895. Antonia Brooks Saxon translated it as "Random Notes from Shōnan," MA thesis, Cornell University, 1998.

18 Natsume Soseki, *Kokoro*, trans. Edwin McClellan (South Bend, IN: Gateway, 1957). Shimamoto Chiyo, "Bessochi no bunka," in *Shōnan No Tanjō*, 141–143. See also Kota Inoue, "Uneven Space of Everyday Modernity: The Colonial Logic of the Suburb in Tanizaki Jun'ichiro's *A Fool's Love*," *Japan Forum* February 2015, 189–212.

19 Shimamoto, "Shōnan no Bessō chika," 144–146. Yiu, "'Beautiful Town.'"

20 The waves created by the tsunami rolled all the way to the torii near the main post office on Wakamiyaōji Avenue, according to Ōuchi Tsutomu, who watched the debacle from his grandparents' home in the Kamakura hills. Personal interview. March 17, 2006, Tokyo. Of the 4,138 buildings in the city in 1923, about 3,400 collapsed, while 412 residents were killed and 341 seriously injured. Kadota Isao, "Kamakura Zakkan," in *Kamakura Shito Sanpo*, ed. Asahi Shinbunsha (Tokyo: Asahi Shinbunsha, 1966). "Ginza by the Sea" from Tsurisuto Gaidobukksu Meibundō Henshūbu, *Kamakura* (Tokyo: Meibunshō, 1955), 33. See also Kamakura City Central Library website https://lib.city.kamakura.kanagawa.jp/ (accessed March 11, 2016).

21 Richard Florida, *The Rise of the Creative Class and How It's Transforming Work, Leisure, and Everyday Life* (New York: Basic Books, 2002).

22 Exhibit at Kamakura Museum of Literature, viewed November 11, 2011. Nikkatsu also had a film studio in Ōfuna. The Tōwa Shōji film distribution company, which imported European films to Japan, had an office nearby, where Kawakita Nagamasa arranged private screenings for Wakimura and Ōmori. Arisawa Hiromi, Miyazaki Toshiyoshi, and Wakimura Yoshitarō, "Eiga wa Tanoshi," *Fujin Kōron*, 1953, 166–171. For Kawakita see Poshek Fu, *Between Shanghai and Hong Kong* (Stanford, CA: Stanford University Press, 2003). The Kawakita Film Museum, which opened in 2010, also emphasizes the portrayal of Kamakura in film.

23 Ozu Yasujirō, *Tokyo Chorus* (Shōchiku Kinema, 1931), Criterion Collection, 2008.Ozu set the last scene of his 1941 *Brothers and Sisters of the Toda Family* at a Shōnan villa. In that picture, the beach house symbolized the fact that the rest of the family did not want the widow and youngest daughter around. Ozu's first postwar film after being repatriated from Southeast Asia in March 1946 was *The Record of a Tenement Gentleman* (Nagaya Shinshiroku) 1947, which sets a key scene in Chigasaki. Later films include *Late Spring*, which opens at the Kita Kamakura railway station and exactly matches the journey to Ginza, and *Early Summer*, which begins on a distinctive Shōnan beach. Donald Richie, *Ozu* (Berkeley: University of California Press, 1974), 165–166, 217, 222–224.

24 For salaries, see Glenda Roberts, "Shifting Contours of Class and Status," in *A Companion to the Anthropology of Japan*, ed. Jennifer Robertson, 2nd edn (London: Blackwell, 2008), 104–124.

25 This material is drawn from Edward Mack, *Manufacturing Modern Japanese Literature: Publishing, Prizes, and the Ascription of Literary Value* (Durham: Duke University Press, 2010).

26 Osaragi Jirō was the pen name of Nojiri Haruhiko while Satomi Ton was in daily life known as Yamanouchi Hideo. Takami Jun was the alias of Takama Yoshio. Kume Masao, "Tiger," translation in Donald Keene, ed., *Modern Japanese Literature* (New York: Grove Press, 1956), 288–299.

27 Sugiura, *Shōnan no Gojūnen,* 55–58.

28 Murakami Mitsuhiko, "Fukkatsu: Kamakura Kaanibaru," *Misuzu*, no. 486 (September 2001): 91.

29 Philip Seaton and Takayoshi Yamamura, "Japanese Popular Culture and Contents Tourism-Introduction," *Japan Forum*, December 13, 2014, 1–11.

30 *Kamakura Shishi–Kindai Tsūshi*, 432. To this day, many Kamakura denizens view these day-trippers with frustrated disdain, an emotion clearly written on their expressions as they watch self-sufficient visitors stream out of the train station, with their tea thermoses, backpacks, and sturdy walking shoes, setting out on their frugal day of pleasure. The largest category of one-day visitors is schoolchildren on class trips, who are particularly unlikely to make major purchases.

31 Youth groups, *Kamakura Shishi–Kindai Tsūshi*, 432.

32 Most of Kamakura's religious institutions were founded in the thirteenth century when it was the shogun's seat of power, including the "big five Zen temples": Kenchōji, Enkakuji, Jufukuji, Jōchiji and Jyōmyōji. For flower-blossom sightseeing, see http://www.kamakuratoday.com/e/sightseeing.html (accessed February 10, 2012).

33 These figures come from a 1934 report of the Kanagawa prefecture's Tourism Commission, as quoted in Motomiya, "Gōrakuchi Shōnan no Kakuritsu," 120. But according to Kadota, "Kamakura Zakkan," only about five million people visited Shōnan in 1935.

34 Motomiya, "Gōrakuchi Shōnan no Kakuritsu," 118, 120–124.

35 Shimamoto, "Shōnan no Bessō chika," 134, 141. In 1955, local historian Suzuki Takashi boasted that "no fewer than seven million visitors come to Kamakura every year." Suzuki Takashi, *Gakuen to Kankō no Kamakura* (Kamakura: Shimamura Shoten, 1955), 21. By 1990, this had tripled to twenty-two million people, although in the mid-1990s the numbers dipped, only reaching twenty-two million again in 2013. Figures on contemporary Kamakura tourism from http://www.city.kamakura. kanagawa.jp/kamakurakankou/0803kankoukyakusuu.html (accessed March 11, 2016).

36   Natsume, *Kokoro*, 2–3.

37   *Kamakura*, photos by Nagano Shigeichi (Tokyo: Iwanami Shashin Bunkō, 1950), 23
     includes a photo of a postwar Miss Carnival. In 1935 some dance squads performed
     Japanese dances but according to Osaragi Jirō the most popular squad was
     Yukinoshita's Blackamoor group (Kurombo). Takayanagi Hidemaru, "Kamakura
     Kaanibaru," *Shōnan Bungaku*, no. 14 (Spring 2001): 143.

38   Sugiura, *Shōnan no Gojūnen*, 57–58.

39   David W. Hughes, "The Evolution of Traditional Japanese Folk Song in Modern
     Japan," Lecture, SOAS, University of London, March 9, 2016. See his *Traditional
     Folk Song in Modern Japan: Sources, Sentiment and Society* (Folkestone: Global
     Oriental, 2008).

40   Carnival also featured two Japanese heroes who appeared courtesy of the Kōdansha
     publication *Shōnen Kurabu*, Norakuro and Bōken Dankichi. Norakuro was a
     hapless perennial underdog, like Charlie Brown, while Boken Dankichi was a small
     boy who ruled over an African kingdom peopled by black-skinned natives and
     elephants. About 10,000 people came to the first Carnival and JNR added 6 special
     trains. http://www1.ocn.ne.jp/~kamakura/meisan.html (accessed August 11, 2015).

41   The *Kamakura Shishi–Kindai Tsūshi*, 476 defined the pillbox as "a structure built by
     Chinese to resist the Japanese invasion."

42   Ruoff, *Imperial Japan at its Zenith*, 4, 84.

43   Hyung-il Pai, "Romancing the 'Conquered Other' in the Korean Peninsula:
     Photography, Travel, and the Imperial Tourist Gaze." Presentation, Association for
     Asian Studies, Honolulu, April 2, 2011.

44   E. Taylor Atkins, *Primitive Selves: Koreana in the Japanese Colonial Gaze, 1910–
     1945* (Berkeley: University of California Press, 2010), 44.

45   See images at http://en.wikipedia.org/wiki/Wakamiya_%C5%8Cji#cite_note-
     kamiya15-0. See also Kamiya Michinori, *Fukaku Aruku—Kamakura Shiseki
     Sansaku*, vols 1 & 2 (Kamakura: Kamakura Shunshūsha, 2008); John Breen and
     Mark Teeuwen, *A New History of Shintō* (Chichester: Wiley-Blackwell, 2010), 42.

46   Japan Travel Bureau, *Pocket Guide to Japan* (Tokyo: Japan Travel Bureau, 1953), 46.
     Kamakura Shishi–Kindai Tsūshi, 440.

47   Ruoff, *Imperial Japan at Its Zenith*, 5; *Kamakura Shishi–Kindai Tsūshi*, 448–449.
     Maki Kaneko, "New Art Collectives in the Service of the War: The Formation of
     Art Organizations during the Asia-Pacific War," *positions: east asia cultures critique*
     21, no. 2 (Spring 2013): 309–350. Ruoff, *Imperial Japan at Its Zenith*; Tansman,
     "Introduction," 1–29.

48   *Kamakura Shishi–Kindai Tsūshi*, 462–463 includes a reprint of one of the many
     congratulatory telegrams that were delivered to Yamashita from Kamakura citizens,
     while page 476 discusses wartime tourism.

49   *Kamakura Shishi–Kindai Tsūshi*, 459.

50   Garon, *Molding Japanese Minds*, 141, 145.

51 Allen Hockney, *Felix Beato's Japan: An Album by the Pioneer Photographer in Yokohama*, "Places" reproduces it on the *Visualizing Cultures* website at MIT. http://ocw.mit.edu/ans7870/21f/21f.027/beato_places/fb1_visnav01.html (accessed January 29, 2016).

52 Japan Travel Bureau, *Pocket Guide to Japan*, 108.

53 For context, see John S. Brownlee, *Japanese Historians and the National Myths, 1600–1945: The Age of the Gods and Emperor Jimmu* (Vancouver: UBC Press and University of Tokyo Press, 1997), 118–130.

54 *Kamakura Shishi–Kindai Tsūshi*, 432–439.

55 *Kamakura Shishi–Kindai Tsūshi*, 444–445. Osaragi himself met them in Kyoto, not Kamakura.

56 Andrea Germer, "Visual Propaganda in Wartime East Asia—The Case of Natori Yōnosuke," *The Asia-Pacific Journal* 9, 20, no. 3 (2011). Paul Barclay found similar efforts to attract Western visitors to Taiwan and then invite them to join in deploring the picturesque backwardness of the local people. Paul Barclay, "Peddling Postcards and Selling Empire: Image-Making in Taiwan under Japanese Colonial Rule," *Japanese Studies* 30, no. 1 (May 2010): 81–110.

57 *Kamakura Shishi–Kindai Tsūshi*, 449. In mid-1939 only nine local soldiers had been killed, so people were still enthusiastic about the war.

58 *Kamakura Shishi–Kindai Tsūshi*, 453.

59 Faye Yuan Kleeman, *Under an Imperial Sun: Japanese Colonial Literature of Taiwan and the South* (Honolulu: University of Hawai'i Press, 2003), 42–43. One such friend was Takami Jun. Donald Keene, *So Lovely a Country Will Never Perish* (New York: Columbia University Press, 2010), 4, 58.

60 Mack, *Manufacturing Modern Japanese Literature*, 218–219.

61 *The Most Beautiful*, Akira Kurosawa, Toho Studios, 1944; *Kamakura Shishi–Kindai Tsūshi*, 470–471.

62 *Kamakura Shishi–Kindai Tsūshi*, 484–486 and 458.

63 *Kamakura Shishi–Kindai Tsūshi*, 484–485 and 494. For photograph of students getting military training, see Kimura Hikosaburō, *Me de miru Kamakura-Zushi no 100 Nen* (Shizuoka: Furusato Shuppansha, 1992).

64 City government officials were privy to information not always available to others, such as a briefing on September 17, 1940, when the mayor and other notables from Kamakura were told "last year in Manchukuo the Nomonhan incident occurred and there are false rumors about it circulating" that it had been a great defeat, but since the lecture included the sobering information that 18,000 Japanese had died, they remained skeptical. *Kamakura Shishi–Kindai Tsūshi*, 459–460, 469.

65 Takashi Nishiyama, "Transformative Power of Peace," presentation AAS, Toronto, March 17, 2012 described Yokosuka as the most militarized city in Japan during the war, e.g. it was illegal to carry a camera there.

66 Uchiyama Iwatarō, *Hankotsu 77 Nen* (Yokohama: Kanagawa Shinbunsha, 1968), 7.

67 *Kamakura Shishi–Kindai Tsūshi*, 459–460.

68 Food scarcity in Kanagawa remained a problem into 1949. *Kamakura Shishi–Kindai Tsūshi*, 471–472. Uchiyama *Hankotsu 77 Nen*, 146–150.

69 Hirata et al. and Kamakura-shi Kyōiku Iinkai, *Kamakura Kindaishi Shiryō Daijūnishū*, 307.

70 Mire Koikari, *Pedagogy of Democracy: Feminism and the Cold War in the US. Occupation of Japan* (Philadelphia, PA: Temple University Press, 2015), 16.

71 For one extended example of amicable interaction—among tax economists—see the essays in W. Elliot Brownlee, Eisaku Ide, and Yasunori Fukagai, eds., *The Political Economy of Transnational Tax Reform: The Shoup Mission to Japan in Historical Context* (Cambridge: Cambridge University Press, 2013). Osaragi Jirō, *Kikyō* (Tokyo: Shinchōsha, 1948), translated by Brewster Horwitz as *Homecoming* (Rutland, VT: Tuttle, 1956) and *Tabiji* (Tokyo: Kadokawa Shoten, 1954), translated by Ivan Morris as *The Journey* (New York: Knopf, 1960).

72 Yoshimi Shunya makes the point that the Occupation forces can be invisible today but were not at the time, for example the MPs who stood behind the Emperor as he traversed his realm. *Posuto Sengo Shakai* (Tokyo: Iwanami, 2009).

73 Frank A. Polkinghorn, "Diary and Memoirs of Two Years with the Occupation in Japan," Verona, NJ: unpublished transcript, 1969, 8–12, 13–3, and 24–27. Director of the Research and Development Division of the Civil Communication Section, SCAP. Manuscript at Claremont College Digital Library. http://ccdl.libraries.claremont.edu/cdm/search/collection/khp/searchterm/Polkinghorn/order/nosort (accessed July 2, 2016).

74 Takase Yoshio, *Kamakura Akademia Danshō: Nōzan no Daigaku* (Tokyo: Mainichi Shinbunsha, 1980), 22.

75 *Life Magazine*, 19, no. 15 (October 8, 1945): 22. One of the first English-language guidebooks, published by the semi-official Tokyo Welcome Society, *A Short Guidebook for Tourists in Japan* (Tokyo: The Welcome Society, 1905) identifies Kamakura as "Famed for Its Great Buddha," xxviii.

76 *Kamakura*, Iwanami Shashin Bunkō, 1950 for "fascinating," 12, Tsurisuto Gaidobukksu Meibundō Henshūbu, *Kamakura*, frontispiece, for "everyone's list."

77 Kusumoto, *Kamakura Naruhodo Jiten*, 178–179.

78 For Morito, Peter Siegenthaler, "Looking to the Past, Looking to the Future: The Localization of Japanese Historic Preservation, 1950–1975," Ph.D. dissertation, University of Texas, Austin, 2004; Uchiyama Iwatarō, Yamamoto Shōichi, and Sawada Setsuzō, "Zadankai," *Kamakura Shimin* 1, no. 1 (January 1960): 6.

79 Siegfried R.C.T. Enders and Niels Gutschow, *Hozon: Architectural and Urban Conservation in Japan* (Stuttgart: Axel Menges Press, 1998).

80 Peter Siegenthaler, "Architecture, Folklore Studies, and Cultural Democracy: Nagakura Saburō and Hida Minzoku-mura," in *Making Japanese Heritage*, ed. Brumann and Cox, 60–61, 65.

81 Ichinohe Yoshiyuki, "Masu Rao-tachi no michinori," in *Kamakura Mikkakai 60 Shūnen Kinenshi*, ed. Kaneko Tsutomu (Kamakura: Kamakura Mikkakai, 2010): 12–23.

82 Hiroshi Sawa, *Kanagawa Picturesque* (Yokohama: Tourist Section, Kanagawa Prefecture, 1953).

83 It is clear from the text that the photographer did not write the captions. *Kamakura*, Iwanami Shashin Bunkō, 6–7.

84 *Kamakura*, Iwanami Shashin Bunkō, 26–27 and 30. The author specifies the cherry trees but it was actually the pines that were sacrificed to the war effort. The cherry trees that run up the median of the avenue were planted in 1918. *Kamakura Shishi-Kindai Tsūshi* noted that Kamakura residents tried to forget this past after the war in "an effort that embodied its own tragedies and comedies," 449.

85 Yasuda Saburō, Nagai Michiko, and Yamada Kimio, *Kamakura Rekishi Sansaku* (Osaka: Hoikusha Kara Bukkusu, 1976), 33.

86 Asahi Shinbunsha, "Kamera no Tabi: Kamakura to Kaigansen," *Asahi Gurafu*, July 26, 1950, 17. In 1961–1967 beach visitors remained steady at about five million but numbers at other sites grew. Visitors to the Great Buddha, for example, doubled in these years.

87 *Kamakura*, Iwanami Shashin Bunkō, 11. Kimura Hikosaburō, the author of the official city history, also wrote books that framed the area as a place for literary tourism, such as *Hase Kannon Yukari no Bungakusha* (Kamakura: Hasedera, 1956). The first postwar guide to Kamakura, by Saida Moriuji, *Shito Kamakura* (Kamakura: Tsurugaoka Hachimangu Shamusho, 1946) focused exclusively on the historical ruins. After that, eight guidebooks were published in the 1950s and six in the 1960s, which are very like the earlier ones except that the photographs are in color and are printed on higher quality paper. In the 1970s the genre exploded with eighteen new books on a variety of topics geared to different kinds of visitors. Sawa Jurō published two book-length guidebooks, one to local historical and archeological sites that appeared in 1955, and a more literary disquisition on the city's past, organized around visits to its most famous shrines and temples in 1976. Sawa Jurō, *Tsurezure no Kamakura* (Kamakura: Kamakura Shunjūsha, 1976).

88 Sylvie Guichard-Anguis and Okpyo Moon, "Introduction," in *Japanese Tourism and Travel Culture*, eds. Sylvie Guichard-Anguis and Okpyo Moon (London; New York: Routledge, 2009), 7–8.

89 The English translation of Natsume Sōseki's 1909 travelogue, "Mangan tokoro dokoro," in Inger Sigrun Brodey and Sammy I. Tsunematsu, *Rediscovering Natsume Sōseki: celebrating the centenary of Sōseki's arrival in England 1900–1902* (Folkestone: Global Oriental, 2000).

90 Osaragi Jirō ed., *Kamakura Rekishi Sanpō* (Tokyo: Kawade Shobō Shinsha, 1961), 8–9.

91   *Kamakura*, Iwanami Shashin Bunkō, 3–4. This booklet was in its eleventh printing by 1959. Although clearly meant for visitors, it was more a venue for contemporary photography than a formal guidebook, since it did not include recommendations for restaurants and hotels.

92   *Kamakura*, Iwanami Shashin Bunkō, 11, 14–15.

93   *Kamakura*, Iwanami Shashin Bunkō, 11, 13.

94   *Kamakura*, Iwanami Shashin Bunkō, 33.

95   The book, with its detailed maps, was, in his words, "a way to remind us of the middle ages, and the samurai homes and ruined temples that are forgotten by most people today." Yasuda Saburō et al., *Kamakura Rekishi Sansaku*, 23. Yasuda also contributed to Nagai Tatsuo, *Shirarezaru Kamakura* (Tokyo: Yomiuri Shinbunsha, 1978) and to Katō Osamu, *Koto Kamakura annai* (Tokyo: Yōsensha, 2002). In 2002 there were 4.8 temple or shrine visits in Kamakura, 5.1 million in 2010, and 5.8 million in 2014. Tourists generally go to more than one location unlike religious visitors. http://www.city.kamakura.kanagawa.jp/kamakura-kankou/0803kankoukyakusuu.html (accessed March 11, 2016).

96   Sugiura, *Shōnan no Gojūnen*, 10. See also Motomiya, "Gōrakuchi Shōnan no Kakuritsu," 178–179.

97   Tanaka Hikōjūrō, "Kamakura Arinomama," *Kamakura Shimin* 1, no. 2 (1960): 14–15. Shiota Masashi and Hasegawa Masahiro, eds., *Kankōgaku* (Tokyo: Dōbunkan, 1994).

98   For relevant statistics, see Kamakura City Home page, http://www.city.kamakura.kanagawa.jp/soumu/toukei/kamakuratoukei/top2/26toukeishotop.html

99   Yoshimi, *Posuto sengo shakai*.

100 They were particularly interested in attracting international luxury travelers and encouraging them "not to leave without scattering their foreign currency here." Uchiyama Iwatarō, Yamamoto Shōichi, and Sawada Setsuzō, "Zadankai zoku," *Kamakura Shimin* 1, no. 2 (1960): 5–6.

101 *Kamakura*, Iwanami Shashin Bunkō, 23. Masako Nakamura, "'Miss Atom Bomb' Contests in Nagasaki and Nevada: The Politics of Beauty, Memory, and the Cold War," *Japan-U.S. Women's Journal*, no. 37 (2009): 3–29.

102 Their presence was cause for sending 1,500 policemen to the shoreline as well. *Asahi Gurafu ni Miru Shōwa no Sesō* (9) (Tokyo: Asahi Shinbunsha, 1976), 119.

103 Sugiura, *Shōnan no Gojūnen*, 57–58. Changes in leisure culture also contributed to declining interest in the Carnival. Takayanagi, "Kamakura Kaanibaru," 143. Murakami, "Fukkatsu: Kamakura Kaanibaru," 89–93.

104 Shintarō Ishihara, *Season of Violence: The Punishment Room, The Yacht and the Boy*, transl. by John G. Mills, Toshie Takahama, and Ken Tremayne (Rutland, VT: Charles E. Tuttle Co, 1966); *Crazed Fruit*, directed by Ko Nakahira, Criterion Collection: Home Vision Entertainment, 2005, DVD (*Kurutta Kajitsu*, Nikkatsu,

1956); *Season of the Sun (Taiyō no Kisetsu)*, directed by Takumi Furukawa, Nikkatsu, 1956. Also Katō Atsuko, "Shuppan bunka to wakamono," in *Shōnan no Tanjō*, 206.

105 Katō, "Shuppan bunka to wakamono," 207–209.

106 Ann Sherif, "The Aesthetics of Speed and the Illogicality of Politics: Ishihara Shintarō's Literary Debut," *Japan Forum* 11, no. 2 (2005): 198.

107 Osaragi, *Kikyō*.

108 One of Ishihara's closest friends was Etō Jun, the critic of American censorship in the Introduction.

Chapter 2

1 Byron K. Marshall, *Academic Freedom and the Japanese Imperial University, 1868-1939* (Berkeley: University of California Press, 1992). Hans Martin Kramer has recently pointed out that in the 1930s a number of people called for school access based on egalitarianism without democracy for all Japan's young people in order to strengthen the state rather than to develop diverse and well-rounded individuals. Hans Martin Kramer, "The Prewar Roots of 'Equality of Opportunity': Japanese Educational Ideals in the Twentieth Century," *Monumenta Nipponica* 61, no. 4 (Winter 2006): 521–549.

2 Mann, *Fascists*.

3 Robert King Hall, *Education for a New Japan* (New Haven: Yale University Press, 1949), 424–428.

4 These mostly rural schools were established in 1937 and boys devoted a third of class time to military drill. The restriction to 10 percent lasted until July 1946. Ronald S. Anderson, *Education in Japan: A Century of Modern Government* (Washington, DC: U.S. Government Printing Office, 1975), 42–45. See also Hall, *Education for a New Japan*, 44–45.

5 Hall, *Education for a New Japan*, 424–428.

6 Takemae Eiji, *Inside GHQ: The Allied Occupation of Japan and Its Legacy* (London: Continuum, 2002), 347.

7 Morito Tatsuo, "Education Reform and Its Problems in Postwar Japan," *International Review of Education* 1 (1955): 342. Julia Bullock, "Coeducation in the Age of 'Good Wife, Wise Mother': Koizumi Ikuko's Quest for 'Equality of Opportunity,'" Association for Asian Studies, Philadelphia, March 28, 2014.

8 The girls' school moved to Kamakura in 1953. Yoshino Miyako, Interview, October 2011. For middle school, see Kamakura-shi, *Kamakura Shishi-Kindai Tsūshi*, vol. 7, 501.

9   Bowles in Supreme Commander for the Allied Powers, Civil Information and Education Section, Education Division, "Post-War Developments in Japanese Education, Education in Japan 1945–1952," *Education in the New Japan* 1 (Tokyo, April 1952), 136. The Japanese Education Reform Council, created on August 9, 1946, worked with both the Japanese government and SCAP, and was headed by Abe Yoshishige and Nanbara Shigeru. SCAP declared itself "substantially in agreement with" their first report. Hall, *Education in the New Japan*, 145.

10   Donald R. Thurston, *Teachers and Politics in Japan* (Princeton, NJ: Princeton University Press, 1973), 18–22. Academic middle schools did the same. Laura Hein, "Takahashi Masao: Flexible Marxist," in *The Human Tradition in Japan*, ed. Anne Walthall (Wilmington, DE: Scholarly Resources Press, 2001), 175–194.

11   Paul E. Webb, Director of Institute for Educational Leadership (IFEL), 27 quoted in Charles E. Martin, "Report of the United States Cultural Science Mission to Japan," to Supreme Commander for the Allied Powers: Civil Information and Education Section, published by University of Washington, Institute of International Affairs, January 1949.

12   Ienaga Saburō, *Japan's Past, Japan's Future: One Historian's Odyssey*, translated by Richard H. Minear (Lanham, MD: Rowman & Littlefield, 2001). The educational bureaucracy had been directly integrated with the military, especially after Army General Araki Sadao was named Minister of Education in May 1938.

13   Hirata Emi, interview Kamakura Library, April 1, 2009. Quotes from Kimura Hikosaburō interview in Maekawa Kiyoharu, *Kamakura Akademia: Saigusa Hiroto to Wakakikamometachi* (Tokyo: Simul Shuppankai, 1994), 13–15.

14   Kimura in Maekawa, *Kamakura Akademia: Saigusa Hiroto to Wakakikamometachi*, 12–13.

15   *Kamakura Shishi–Kindai Tsūshi*, 510.

16   Rieko Kage, *Civic Engagement in Postwar Japan: The Revival of a Defeated Society* (Cambridge: Cambridge University Press, 2011), 6–7. Garon, *Molding Japanese Minds*, 141, 145.

17   *Kamakura Shishi–Kindai Tsūshi*, 509–514.

18   Masako Yamazaki, *Kyoto Jinbun Gakuen: Seiritsu o Meguru Senchū Sengo no Bunka Undō* (Tokyo: Kazama Shobō, 2002). Mieko went to both the Jinbun Gakuen and another progressive school, Seijo, in Setagaya, Tokyo. Hall, *Education for a New Japan*, 424–428.

19   Takahashi Hiroto, *Sengo Kyōiku Kaikaku to Shidō Shuji Seido* (Tokyo: Kazama Shobō, 1995). For Fujisawa, see Hirata et al., *Kamakura Kindaishi Shiryō Daijūnishū*, 309. Kubota Jun, *Kamakura Shimin Akademia: Mō Hitotsu no Seishun Gakushū* (Tokyo: Gendai Keikakushitsu, 1991), 20. Nakai Masakazu also started a non-degree adult school. Leslie Pincus, "A Salon for the Soul: Nakai Masakazu and the Hiroshima Culture Movement," *positions: east asia cultures critique* 10, no. 1 (Spring 2002): 173–194.

20 Victor N. Kobayashi, *John Dewey in Japanese Educational Thought* (Ann Arbor, MI: The University of Michigan School of Education, 1964), 113.

21 *Kamakura Shishi–Kindai Tsūshi*, 501–502. Kage, *Civic Engagement in Postwar Japan*. Both authors see the PTA as a major democratizing force, unlike the gloomy assessment of Jacob van Staaveren in 1949. Jacob van Staaveren, "The Growth of Parent-Teacher Associations in Japan (A Prefectural View)," *Peabody Journal of Education* 27, no. 3 (November 1949): 162–166.

22 *Kamakura Shishi–Kindai Tsūshi*, 501–502.

23 Mann, *Fascists*, 72.

24 Their accreditation status meant they could not use the name Kamakura University. Kimura Hikosaburō, *Kamakura Kiokuchō*, ed. Kamakura Kyōdōshi Kenkyū Shiryōkan no Kamakurashi Kyōiku Iinkai (Kamakurashi Chūō Toshokan, 1986), 79.

25 Interview with Hattori Hiroaki, Katō Shigeo, and Watanabe Aira, Kamakura Public Library May 23, 2009. Maekawa, *Kamakura Akademia: Saigusa Hiroto to Wakakikamometachi*, 47 for Numada.

26 Kevin Doak, "Under the Banner of the New Science: History, Science, and the Problem of Particularity in Early Twentieth-Century Japan," *Philosophy East and West* 48, no. 2 (April 1998): 232–256.

27 Saigusa, "Fūhyō Daigaku o Tsubusu," 142.

28 Charles E. Martin, "Report of the United States Cultural Science Mission to Japan," to Supreme Commander for the Allied Powers: Civil Information and Education Section, Seattle: University of Washington, Institute of International Affairs, January 1949, 3.

29 The mission was in Japan for four months, from September 1948 to January 1949 and worked with seventy-eight Japanese scholars and translators. Charles E. Martin, "Report of the United States Cultural Science Mission to Japan."

30 Ruth Rogaski, *Hygienic Modernity: Meanings of Health and Disease in Treaty-Port China* (Berkeley: University of California Press, 2004); Todd Henry, *Assimilating Seoul: Japanese Rule and the Politics of Public Space in Colonial Korea, 1910–1945* (Berkeley: University of California Press, 2014); Moore, *Constructing East Asia*. James C. Scott, *Seeing Like a State: How Certain Schemes to Improve the Human Condition Have Failed* (New Haven: Yale University Press, 1998).

31 Iitsuka also translated Karl Mantzius' six-volume *History of Theatrical Art in Ancient and Modern Times* (London: Duckworth, 1903). He proved to be a poor leader and the students successfully agitated to replace him a few months after the school opened. Hirata et al., *Kamakura Kindaishi Shiryō Daijūnishū*, 307.

32 Maekawa, *Kamakura Akademia: Saigusa Hiroto to Wakakikamometachi*, 28–33. Many of these people already knew each other. For example, Murayama Tomoyoshi, Toyoda Shirō, Satomi Ton, and Endō Shingo all had worked on the 1941 film *Record of Our Love*. Takase, *Kamakura Akademia Danshō*, 37. Yanaihara

Isaku, a sculptor who is best known for his personal and artistic interactions with Alberto Giacometti, taught German and philosophy. Minoue Jirō taught Asian History. Shigemune Kazunobu, Hattori's higher-school classmate, taught film, as did Iijima Tadashi who later founded *Kinema Junpo*. Toyoda Shirō, a director at Tōhō Film Studio, lectured, as did Kataoka Ryūichi, a costume expert. Satō Takeo taught Mori Ōgai, while Yoshida Ken'ichi, the son of Prime Minister Yoshida Shigeru, taught English Literature, and Shigemune Kazunobu taught film. For full list of faculty, see Hirata et al., *Kamakura Kindaishi Shiryō Daijūnishū*, 77–83.

33 Kimura, *Kamakura Kiokuchō*, 70 reprints Kimura's obituary of Takami from the *Kamakura Times*, August 15, 1964. Takami and Shimaki had been arrested and recanted together. Donald Keene, *So Lovely a Country Will Never Perish* (New York: Columbia University Press, 2010), 130–131.

34 Takase, *Kamakura Akademia Danshō*, 39.

35 Interview Yamanouchi Shizuo, November 11, 2011.

36 Takase, *Kamakura Akademia Danshō*, 40.

37 Murayama Tomoyoshi, "Chōsen de no Haisen," in *Hachi-ichigo Haisen zengo*, ed. Murayama Tomoyoshi (Tokyo: Sekibunsha 1975), 100.

38 Saigusa, "Fūhyō Daigaku o Tsubusu," 149.

39 Takahashi Hideo, *Kamakura Bunko to bungei zasshi "Ningen"* (Tokyo: Ōzorasha, 1993), 14–15. See also the permanent exhibit at Kamakura Museum of Literature, viewed November 11, 2011.

40 Katō Shūichi, *A Sheep's Song: A Writer's Reminiscences of Japan and the World* (Berkeley: University of California Press, 1999), 235.

41 Laura Hein, *Reasonable Men, Powerful Words: Political Culture and Expertise in Twentieth-Century Japan* (Berkeley: University of California Press, 2004), 76–100.

42 Takahashi, *Kamakura Bunko* contains the complete list. Other books include a translation of Pinocchio, translations of the works of Edmond Goncourt, Clyde Eagleton, and a text on educating women, the exploits of the manga character, *Fukuchan no ochi* by Yokoyama Ryūichi, Irimajiri Yoshinaga's *Nihon Nōmin Keizai Kenkyū*, and Nakayama Ichirō's *Keizai Shaken no Kadai* 1948. The other journals were *Fujin Bunko*, from May 1946, *Shakai*, from October 1946, and *Yoroppa*, from March 1947.

43 The censored book, "Light of the Sea," was written during the war. Takahashi, *Kamakura Bunko*, 15. SCAP, "Kamakura Bunko" Civil Censorship Detachment Press, Pictorial Broadcast District One, Memorandum for Record, October 7, 1948, CIS-04450, and CIS-04450, SCAP records, National Diet Library.

44 Osaragi Jirō, *Suishōyama no Shōnen* (Tokyo: Shōnan Shobō, 1948); Osaragi Jirō, *Ōkami Shōnen: Shin Kanazukaiban* (Tokyo: Shōnan Shobō, 1947); Kume Masao, *Aozora Shōnen* (Tokyo: Shōnan Shobō, 1948?). Muraoka Hanako, *Dorei Tomu Monogatari* (Tokyo: Shōnan Shobō, 1948).

45 Hattori Shisō, "Kindai Nihon no naritachi," in *Meiji Isshin No Hanashi; Kindai Nihon no Naritachi* (Tokyo: Aoki Shoten, 1990 [1948]), 3. Hori Takahiko, interview June 22, 2009, Kamakura Central Public Library.

46 Hirata et al., *Kamakura Kindaishi Shiryō Daijūnishū*, 29.

47 Maekawa Kiyoharu, *Saigusa Hiroto to Kamakura Akademia: Gakumon to Kyōiku no Risō o motomete* (Tokyo: Chūō Kōronsha, 1996), 37.

48 Maekawa, *Saigusa Hiroto to Kamakura Akademia*, 50–51.

49 Takase, *Kamakura Akademia Danshō*, 53.

50 This point was emphasized by Hattori Hiroaki, Katō Shigeo, and Watanabe Akira, Interview. Ruoff, *Imperial Japan at its Zenith*.

51 Mizuno, *Science for the Empire*, 126–128.

52 Iida is quoted in Maekawa, *Kamakura Akademia: Saigusa Hiroto to Wakakikamometachi*, 8. The Shinzō Abe government included this school in a cluster of places collectively nominated as a UNESCO World Heritage site in 2014.

53 Saigusa, "Fūhyō Daigaku o Tsubusu," 149.

54 Takase, *Kamakura Akademia Danshō*, 24.

55 Michael Bourdaghs, *The Dawn That Never Comes* (New York: Columbia University Press, 2010), 194.

56 Hiraku Shimoda, "Memorializing the Spirit of Wit and Grit in Postindustrial Japan," in *Japan since 1945: From Postwar to Post-Bubble*, ed. Christopher Gerteis and Timothy George (London: Bloomsbury Press, 2013), 242–256.

57 Takase, *Kamakura Akademia Danshō*, 16.

58 Kamakura officials initially closed all the girls' schools on September 1, 1945 so that the teenagers could flee in advance of the occupation forces. Kamakura-shi. *Kamakura Shishi–Kindai Tsūshi*, 493–494. Yokohama figures from Civil Information and Education Activities MG-12, February 1948, "Monthly Military Government Activities Report," February 1, 1948 to February 20, 1948, 1 in "Senryōki Todō Fuken Gunsei Shiryō," vol. 41, Tokyo-Kanagawa-ken (3), National Diet Library. National statistics from Harold E. Snyder and Margretta S. Austin, eds., *Educational Progress in Japan and the Ryukyus; a Report of a Conference of Major American Non-Governmental Agencies* (Washington, DC: American Council on Education, 1950), 12. The number of children actually getting an education dwindled in the 1940s since by 1945 three million were laboring in factories and fields doing war work. Anderson, *Education in Japan*, 49. Also http://www.stat. go.jp/english/data/chouki/25.htm. Japan Statistics Bureau, *Japanese Government Historical Statistics*, accessed December 11, 2014. By 1950, 42.5 percent of students advanced to high school (48 percent of boys and 36.7 percent of girls). In 1954, 50.9 percent did so (55.1 percent of boys and 46.5 percent of girls) and about 10.1 percent of students entered college (15.3 percent boys and 4.6 percent girls).

59 In 1930 about half of the 159,648 middle school graduates who continued their education enrolled in private technical higher schools. The rest attended 208 public

and private higher schools and universities. Takeuchi Yō, *Gakureki Kizoku no Eiko to Zasetsu* (Tokyo: Chūō Kōron Shinsha, 1999), 26–30.

60 Hirosawa Ei decided to go to college in part because his brother, who died during the war, had not had that opportunity. See Hirosawa Ei, *Waga Seishun no Kamakura Akademia* (Tokyo: Iwanami Shoten, 1996), 20.

61 Anderson, *Education in Japan*, 42–45. Hall, *Education for a New Japan*, 43.

62 Takase, *Kamakura Akademia Danshō*, 14.

63 Probably she contributed to Louisa May Alcott, *An Old Fashioned Girl*, published as *Bara Monogatari*, Matsumoto Keiko translator (Tokyo: Shōnan Shobō, 1950).

64 Mark McClelland, *Love, Sex, and Democracy in Japan during the American Occupation* (New York and Basingstoke: Palgrave Macmillan, 2012), 2.

65 Takase, *Kamakura Akademia Danshō*, 30–31, 50. Photos show the faculty teaching in their overcoats. Hirata et al., *Kamakura Kindaishi Shiryō Daijūnishū*, 90.

66 Yamaguchi Haruko, "Manyō," *Shōwa Manyōshū. Kan-9 Geppo*. December 1965, quoted in Hirata et al., *Kamakura Kindaishi Shiryō Daijūnishū*, 91. Meanwhile lacking a blackboard, Hattori Shisō used the sand on the beach as his writing surface. Takase, *Kamakura Akademia Danshō*, 32.

67 Takase, *Kamakura Akademia Danshō*, 33–34.

68 Hirosawa, *Waga Seishun no Kamakura Akademia*, 211.

69 Maekawa, *Kamakura Akademia: Saigusa Hiroto to Wakakikamometachi*, 42–43.

70 Takase, *Kamakura Akademia Danshō*, 19.

71 Maekawa, *Kamakura Akademia: Saigusa Hiroto to Wakakikamometachi*, 47–50. Katō in Watanabe Nobuyuki, "Kamakura Akademia Sokuritsu 70 Shūnen," *Asahi Shinbun* Digital edition, http://www.asahi.com/area/kanagawa/articles/ MTW20160530150280001.html May 16, 2016 (accessed July 10, 2016).

72 Minamikawa broke his silence at the wake for Murayama Kazuko, who passed away in 1946. Maekawa, *Saigusa Hiroto to Kamakura Akademia*, 150–151.

73 Andrew Barshay, *The Gods Left First: The Captivity and Repatriation of Japanese POWs in Northeast Asia, 1945–1956* (Berkeley, CA: University of California Press, 2013).

74 Takase, *Kamakura Akademia Danshō*, 14, 48.

75 Saigusa in Katō, *Waimaaruki Berurin no Nihonjin*, 84.

76 Jay Winter and Emmanuel Sivan, "Setting the Framework," in Winter and Sivan, eds., *War and Remembrance in the Twentieth Century*, 7.

77 Donald Keene believes that he was tortured by Amakasu Masahiko, the man who had murdered Ōsugi Sakae and Itō Noe a decade earlier. Keene, *So Lovely a Country Will Never Perish*, 59.

78 Sakashita Keihachi comments at May 16, 2009 Akademia reunion, Kōmōyji Temple, Kamakura.

79 Quoted in Keene, *So Lovely a Country Will Never Perish*, 80.

80 Tansman, *The Culture of Japanese Fascism*, 19.

81 Sodei Rinjirō, *Were We the Enemy? American Survivors of Hiroshima* (Boulder, CO: Westview Press, 1998) provides examples.

82 Takase, *Kamakura Akademia Danshō*, 23.

83 Doak, "Under the Banner of the New Science," 239 stresses Miki Kiyoshi's commitment to being useful. Takase, *Kamakura Akademia Danshō*, 55–56.

84 The Occupation emphasis on practical education is a major theme of Takahashi, *Sengo Kyōiku Kaikaku to Shidō Shuji Seido*.

85 Keene, *So Lovely a Country Will Never Perish*, 142–143.

86 Keene, *So Lovely a Country Will Never Perish*, 143–144.

87 John Dower makes this point in "Japan's Beautiful Modern Wars," 101.

88 Takami Jun, *Haisen Nikki* (Tokyo Chūō Kōronsha, 2005 [1959]), Entries from April 24, 1945, and August 16, 1945, are translated in Donald Keene, *So Lovely a Country Will Never Perish*, 60, 109–110.

89 Michael Molasky, *The American Occupation of Japan and Okinawa: Literature and Memory* (London: Routledge, 1999). Osaragi and Takami—both womanizers—each commented acidly in their diaries in late August that Japanese officials were preparing brothels for the incoming forces. Takami not only blamed the women when he saw them with GIs but also thought this showed their unworthiness of the vote. Keene, *So Lovely a Country Will Never Perish*, 125, 149.

90 Takahashi, *Kamakura Bunko*, 11–28. Keene, *So Lovely a Country Will Never Perish*, 126–127.

91 Mashita, "Ichi Tetsugakusha no Kaisō," 18.

92 Mashita, "Ichi Tetsugakusha no Kaisō," 19.

93 Murayama and his friend Hijikata Yoshi restarted the journal *Teatoro* in December 1946, originally launched in 1934, where he drew some of the art and wrote theater reviews. *Murayama Tomoyoshi: Gurafikku no shigoto* (Tokyo: Hon no Izumisha, 2001), timeline at back of book. *Gulliver's Travels* was brought out by Iwanami in 1951. See also Gennifer Weisenfeld, *MAVO: Japanese Artists and the Avant-Garde, 1905–1931* (Berkeley: University of California Press, 2002), 31.

94 Kobayashi, *John Dewey in Japanese Educational Thought*, 78–83.

95 Murayama also encountered the Bauhaus, stage designs by Georg Kaiser, and the multimedia work of Alexander Archipenko. Toshiyaru Omuka "Tada=Dada (Devotedly Dada) for the Stage: The Japanese Dada Movement 1920–1925," in *The Eastern Dada Orbit: Russia, Georgia, Ukraine, Central Europe and Japan, Crisis and the Arts: The History of Dada*, ed. Gerald Janecek (New York and London: G.K. Hall & Co. and Prentice Hall International, 1998), 234.

96 Matthew S. Witkovsky, Carol S. Eliel, and Karole P. B. Vail, eds., *Moholy-Nagy: Future Present* (New Haven: Yale University Press, 2016)

97 Junko Ikezu Williams, "Visions and Narratives: Modernism in the Prose Works of Yoshiyuki Eisuke, Murayama Tomoyoshi, Yumeno Kyuusaku, and Okamoto Kaneko" (Ph.D. diss. Ohio State University, Columbus, 1998), 129, 131–132.

98   Weisenfeld, *MAVO*, e.g. page 1.

99   Murayama, "Georuge-gurotsusu," 87–133, reprinted in *Murayama Tomoyoshi: Bijutsu Hihyō to Handō*, 411–422.

100   Junko Ikezu Williams, "Visions and Narratives," 129.

101   Mrs. Murayama was widowed young and had raised Tomoyoshi as a single mother. Murayama, "Chōsen de no Haisen," 98.

102   Murayama, "Chōsen de no Haisen," 100.

103   Murayama, "Chōsen de no Haisen," 104.

104   After he was released in December 1942, Murayama was banned from publishing. He concentrated on visual art, designing at least one theater set (under an alias), and also drew book illustrations. Murayama Tomoyoshi, *Seitan 100 Nen Murayama Tomoyoshi 'Shōzōga' Ten* (Tokyo: Tokyo Daichi Seimei Hoken Kabushiki Kaisha, 2001).

105   E. Taylor Atkins argues that their play merely nodded to pan-Asianism by studding an essentially Japanese production with a few stereotypical markers of Koreanness while fundamentally remaining aligned with the war's ethos. Atkins, *Primitive Selves*, 135–136.

106   Murayama, "Chōsen de no Haisen," 104, 108. He also visited the Manchurian capital in August, probably after his show closed on August 6th, where he saw Amakasu Masahiko, who killed Ōsugi Sakae, reviewing the troops, and Harbin where he had a run-in with a Kempetai officer that scared him enough to rush back to Seoul, fortunately for him, because a few days later most of the Japanese men still in Harbin were sent to Siberia.

107   Murayama Tomoyoshi, *Engeki Nyūmon Tadashii Shibai no Yarikata-Mikata*, Kumiai Raiburari (Tokyo: Rōdō Kyōiku Kyōkai, 1949), 8. Matsuba Shigeyasu, from the Kanagawa prefecture's education department also conducted a workshop in Kamakura teaching teens how to stage puppet shows in September 1947. As an approving SCAP officer explained, "the purpose of the training courses and demonstrations is to encourage amateurs to use the puppet shows as one means of raising the cultural standards of young people and at the same time offering them entertainment that is worthwhile at a very nominal expense." Annex E. Monthly Military Government Activities Report, September 1947, 8, Monthly Military Government Activities Report, February 1, 1948 to February 20, 1948, 1 in "Senryōki Todō Fuken Gunsei Shiryō" vol. 41, Tokyo- Kanagawa-ken (3), in National Diet Library.

108   Murayama, *Engeki Nyūmon*, 15–18.

109   Kimura Hikosaburō, "Kamakura Daigaku no koto," in Kimura, *Kamakura Kiokuchō*, 79. See also *Kamakura Shishi-Kindai Tsūshi*, 513–514.

110   Saigusa, "Fūhyō Daigaku o Tsubusu," 149–150.

111   See, for example, Supreme Commander for the Allied Powers, Civil Information and Education Section, Education Division, *Education in the New Japan*, vol. 1,

Tokyo: Tokyo, General Headquarters, Supreme Commander for the Allied
Powers, Civil Information and Education Section, Education Division, May 1948.

112 "Leftist activities at Kamakura University Increase." Kanagawa Military
Government CIC, 1947.7.1, reprinted in Hirata et al., *Kamakura Kindaishi
Shiryō Daijūnishū*, 282. Oddly, and almost certainly inaccurately, the same
report estimated that there were only 277 Japan Communist Party members in
Kanagawa Prefecture in 1948.

113 Headquarters Tokyo-Kanagawa Military Government Team APO 503, Political
and Government Activities Annex A Monthly Military Government Activities
Report, "February 1, 1948 to February 20, 1948, 6–7 "Senryōki Todō Fuken
Gunsei Shiryō," vol. 41. Tokyo-Kanagawa-ken (3) in National Diet Library.

114 Saigusa, "Fūhyō Daigaku o Tsubusu," 145.

115 Hattori Hiroaki, Katō Shigeo, and Watanabe Akira, Interview, said that SCAP was
most concerned about Hattori Shiso.

116 Hattori Hiroaki, Kato Shigeo, and Watanabe Akira, Interview. Kimura, "Kamakura
Daigaku no koto," 511.

117 Yoshiko Nozaki, *War Memory, Nationalism, and Education in Post-war Japan,
1945-2007: The Japanese History Textbook Controversy and Ienaga Saburo's Court
Challenges* (London: Routledge, 2008).

118 Saigusa, "Fūhyō Daigaku o Tsubusu," 149.

119 Kimura Hikosaburō, "Hayashi Tatsuo Sensei," in Kimura, *Kamakura Kiokuchō*, 96.

120 Takase, *Kamakura Akademia Danshō*, 59, 29.

Chapter 3

1 Portions of this chapter first appeared in "Reckoning with War in the Museum:
Hijikata Teiichi at the Kamakura Museum of Modern Art," *Critical Asian Studies*
43, no. 1 (March 2011): 93–110. Reprinted by permission.

2 Although the formal Japanese name of the museum is the Kanagawa Prefectural
Modern Art Museum, since the 1950s exhibition posters and other materials
have called it the Kamakura Modern Art Museum because the official name
suggested to many people that the museum was in Yokohama. Sakai Tadayasu,
"Kaisō no Bijutsukan Funtōki," in *Chiisa na Hako: Kamakura Kindai Bijutsukan
no 50 nen, 1951-2000*, Kamakura Kenritsu Kindai Bijutsukan (Tokyo: Kyūryūdō,
2001), 15–16. The official English translation of the museum's name became The
Museum of Modern Art, Kamakura & Hayama when a new building was added in
2003. In 2016, although the first building closed, a third smaller exhibition space
remained in Kamakura and so the name is unchanged.

3 Ikeda Katsumi, "Kindai Bijutsukan ni tsuite," in Kamakura Kenritsu Kindai
Bijutsukan, *Chiisa na Hako*, 81–84.

4   Alicia Volk, review *Art Bulletin* 45, no. 4 (December 2015): 457–461.

5   Eric Hobsbawm and Terence Ranger, eds., *The Invention of Tradition* (Cambridge: Cambridge University Press, 1983).

6   Yagyū Fujio, "Wasurenagusa," in Kamakura Kenritsu Kindai Bijutsukan, *Chiisa na Hako*, 68–70. Okura from Charles F. Gallagher, Report of Conference, September 25, 1947, "Okura Museum," CIE (C) 06251, NARA RG 331, SCAP, CI&E, Religion and Cultural Resources Division. Arts & Monuments Branch.

7   Sasaki Seiichi, "Kamakura Kinbi Bijutsukan no Shuppatsu," in *Kanagawa Kenritsu Kindai Bijutsukan 30-nen no Ayumi: Shiryō-Tenrankai Sōmokuroku, 1951–1981* (Kamakura: Kanagawa Kenritsu Kindai Bijutsukan, 1982), 12–16.

8   Uchiyama, *Hankotsu 77 nen*, 222.

9   Takemae, *Inside GHQ*.

10 Uchiyama, *Hankotsu 77 nen*, 165–167. Osaragi Jirō, "Jo" in Uchiyama, *Hankotsu 77 nen*, 3–5.

11 Satō Kaori, "GHQ no Bijutsu Gyōsei: CIE Bijutsu Kinen Bukka ni yoru 'Bijutsu no Minshūka' to Yashiro Yukio," *Kindai Gasetsu* 12 (2003): 80–95. Yashiro focused on improving Japan's international image by sending art abroad, while Uchiyama was more concerned about giving Japanese people opportunities to view art.

12 "Report on Field Trip to Fukuoka, Saga, etc." in folder "Reports of Staff Visits" by James M. Plumer May 6, 1949, 6, RG 331 UD 1647 5074 and "Report on Arts and Monuments: Recommendations of Outgoing Adviser in Fine Art," in folder "Correspondence and Memoranda" by J. M. Plumer, June 20, 1949 UD 1698–5848, both NARA RG 331, SCAP, CI&E, Religion and Cultural Resources Division. Arts & Monuments Branch.

13 Plumer, "Reports on Staff Visits," 6. Later when SCAP CI&E officials planned but then canceled a two-month trip for museum professionals to the United States, they only considered staff members at the National Museums despite being dissatisfied with their English-language abilities. SCAP CIE (C) 06714–5 documents related to National Leaders Project no. 150—Museum Education. "Objectives of Visit to the United States," May 1950.

14 Sasaki, "Kamakura Kinbi Bijutsukan no Shuppatsu," 13. Interview with Hijikata Yukue, Kamakura, February 27, 2009. Kamakura and Yokohama City fought over where the museum should be located. SCAP, Civil Information & Education. Religion and Cultural Resources Division. Arts and Monuments Branch. "Museum Project Okayed—*Nippon Times* article," in *Museums, Art Galleries, Research Material* (Tokyo, 1950).

15 Interview Associate Director, Mizusawa Tsutomu. Kamakura April 16, 2005.

16 Yagyū, "Wasurenagusa," 68.

17 Ikeda, "Kindai Bijutsukan ni tsuite," 81–84.

18 Osaragi Jirō, "Saisho no chihō bijutsukan," *Mainichi News*, November 21, 1951, reprinted in Kamakura Kenritsu Kindai Bijutsukan, *Chiisa na Hako*, 75.

19 Sakakura Junzō, "Kamakura no Gendai Bijutsukan," *Geijutsu Shinchō*, (March 1951): 90–93. For Sandberg, see Ad Petersen, *Sandberg: Designer and Director of the Stedelijk* (Rotterdam: 010 Publishers, 2004). Sakakura's career took off after he designed the prize-winning Japanese pavilion at the 1937 Paris world exposition. He later worked with Charlotte Perriand.

20 Hijikata Teiichi, "Amusuterudamu no Kindai Bijutsukan to Gendai Oranda Bijutsu," *Mizue* (November 1952); reprinted in vol. 9 of *Hijikata Teiichi Chosakushū* (Tokyo: Heibonsha, 1976): 217–226.

21 Satō Kei, "Gendai Bijutsukan e no kibō," *Asahi*, March 6, 1951, quoted in Sasaki, "Kamakura Kinbi Bijutsukan no Shuppatsu," 14.

22 Sakakura, "Kamakura no Gendai Bijutsukan," 92–93. As David Tucker has argued, Sakakura Junzō's postwar international architectural vision was rooted in his wartime service in the empire. David Tucker, "Learning from Dairen, Learning from Shinkyō: Japanese Colonial City Planning and Postwar Reconstruction," in *Rebuilding Urban Japan after 1945*, ed. Carola Hein (London: Palgrave, 2003), 156–187. Sakakura also designed prefabricated housing for the navy during the war. The preparatory drawings were in the exhibit *Junzo SAKAKURA, Architect*. May 30–September 6, 2009 at the Kamakura museum.

23 Sasaki, "Kamakura Kinbi Bijutsukan no shuppatsu," 12.

24 Hijikata used the pen name Yai San'ichi, a plausible man's name in both Japanese and Chinese, when it was pronounced Oi San-pin. It also functioned as an elaborate joke, with each character suggesting several meanings, all of which fit under the general rubric of "from best to worst" or "full range" (*pin kara ichi made.*) The book is Edwin Hornle, *Puroretaria Kyōiku no Konpon Mondai*, trans. Yai San'ichi (Tokyo: Sekaisha, 1930). Aoki Shigeru, interview April 27, 2016 and Aoki Shigeru, "Yanase Masamu Nenpu III Hijikata Teiichi no Yakusho," *Isshun* 61 (March 2015): 5.

25 This is also the opinion of Aoki Shigeru, who first was an assistant curator at the Kamakura museum and then became a curator at The National Museum of Modern Art, Tokyo. Interview April 27, 2016.

26 Kon Hidemi, "Hihyōka Hijikata Teiichi no Tōjo," in *Hijikata Teiichi: Bijutsu Hihyō, 1946–1980*, eds. Kon Hidemi, Kagesato Tetsurō, and Sakai Tadayasu (Tokyo: Keibunsha, 1992), 2–9.

27 Volk, review *Art Bulletin*, 460.

28 Hijikata co-translated, with Asō Shuei, Franz Mehring's biography of Gotthold Lessing, *Die Lessing-Legende*, as *Resshingu Densetsu* (Tokyo Mokuseisha Shoin, [1929] 1932). The English version is Franz Mehring, *The Lessing Legend* (New York: Critics Group Press, 1938). He also translated Karl Wittfogel's study of Mehring as a literary critic which appeared in *Hihyō* in 1932. Hijikata wrote another biography, of scholar Tsubochi Shōyō, in 1934, which was published under the name of another individual, Chiba Kameo. For more on this topic, see Laura Hein, "The Art

of Bourgeois Culture in Kamakura," in *Japan from 1945: From Postwar to Post-Bubble*, eds. Christopher Gerteis and Timothy George (London: Continuum Books, 2013).

29 Michael Lucken, *Imitation and Creativity in Japanese Arts: From Kishida Ryūsei to Miyazaki Hayao*, trans. Francesca Simkin (New York: Columbia University Press, 2016), 106.

30 Hijikata Teiichi, "Atogaki," in *Hijikata Teiichi Chosakushū*, vol. 7 (Tokyo: Heibonsha, 1976), 429–436.

31 Sugiura Minpei, "Kuraiya no Jidai no Fureai," in *Hijikata Teiichi Tsuisō*, ed. Hijikata Teiichi Tsuitō Kankōkai (Tokyo: Heibonsha Kyōiku Sangyō Sentaa, 1981), 54–55.

32 Takeda Taijun identified him as having military rank, quoted in Ōkochi Kikuo, "Chūgoku Kanren no Tenkan," in Kamakura Kenritsu Kindai Bijutsukan, *Chiisa na Hako*, 71. However, Aoki Shigeru said that this was not the case; rather, Hijikata dressed in puttees and other random bits of military gear. Interview, April 27, 2016.

33 The 1954 show on Buddhist art built on this experience without ever mentioning it. Fujita Sada, "Hijikata Teiichi-kun to Senji," in Hijikata Teiichi Tsuitō Kankōkai, ed., *Hijikata Teiichi Tsuisō*, 84–86.

34 Hijikata Teiichi, *Gendai Bijutsu: Kindai Bijutsu to Rearizumu* (Tokyo: Azuma Shobō, 1948).

35 Aoki Shigeru, "Wasurenu uchi ni—Hijikata Teiichi nenpu," *Isshun*, issue 56 (November 2013): 4. In 1943 Hijikata also published a major study of Albrecht Dürer.

36 Emphasis in original. Hijikata Teiichi, "Nittenhyō—kore wa hitotsu no jōzetsu saidan," *Bijutsu*, April 1946, quoted in Kon, "Hihyōka Hijikata Teiichi no Tōjo," 2–9.

37 Hijikata, 1945 diary, quoted in Kon, "Hihyōka Hijikata Teiichi no Tōjo," 5–6.

38 Hijikata Teiichi, "Kindai Bijutsukan Sōseiki," *Geijutsu Shinchō* (July 1951): 56–69.

39 Lisa C. Roberts, *From Knowledge to Narrative: Educators and the Changing Museum* (Washington, DC: Smithsonian Institution Press, 1997).

40 Tony Bennett, *The Birth of the Museum: History, Theory, Politics* (London: Routledge, 1995).

41 Sakai, "Kaisō no Bijutsukan Funtōki," 13; Tsuruta Heihachirō, "Kanagawa Kenritsu Kindai Bijutsukan," in *Nihon Yōga to Kanagawa Kenritsu Kindai Bijutsukan*, ed. Asahi Shinbunsha (Tokyo: Asahi Shinbunsha, 1983), 125–135.

42 For SCAP critique of Japanese museums for ignoring the needs of the public, see SCAP CIE (C) 06714–5 documents related to National Leaders Project no. 150-Museum Education. "Objectives of Visit to the United States," May 1950.

43 The museum pursued this goal in its art classes for young people and annual exhibits of their work from 1953 to 1974. Satō, "Gendai Bijutsukan e no kibō," quoted in Sasaki, "Kamakura Kinbi Bijutsukan no Shuppatsu," 16.

44 Sasaki, "Kamakura Kinbi Bijutsukan no Shuppatsu," 17.

45 Nagasu Kazuji, "Chōji," in Hijikata Teiichi Tsuitō Kankōkai, *Hijikata Teiichi Tsuisō*, 4.

46 Yagyū Fujio, "1950 nendai no Omoide," in *Kanagawa Kenritsu Kindai Bijutsukan 30-nen no Ayumi*, 17–20.

47 Interview, Sakai Tadayasu, Setagaya Museum of Art, February 24, 2009. Unfortunately, the museum retained almost no documentation of its early exhibits, and the museum has no correspondence files from the 1950s.

48 For the debate, see Mitsuda Yuri, "'*Bijutsu Hihyō*' (1952–1957) shi to sono jidai—'*Gendai Bijutsu*' to '*Gendai Bijutsu Hihyō*' no seiritsu," *Fuji Xerox Art Bulletin* 2 (2006): 1–52, and, briefly, Bert Winther-Tamaki, *Art in the Encounter of Nations: Japanese and American Artists in the Early Postwar Years* (Honolulu: University of Hawai'i Press, 2001): 16–17.

49 Tange Kenzō, "Kokuritsu Kindai Bijutsu ni tō," *Geijutsu Shinchō* 4, no. 1 (January 1953): 32 and 34–35. Sasaki Seiichi summarized Tange's stance as taking "the opportunity created by the national art museum to address what had been unstated and so breathe out the great pain of self-condemnation regarding Japanese modernity that had been lodged in his heart up until then." Sasaki, "Kamakura Kinbi Bijutsukan no Shuppatsu," 15.

50 Hijikata, "Kindai Bijutsukan Sōseiki," 57–58.

51 Hijikata Teiichi, "Kanagawa Kenritsu Bijutsukan," *Atorie* 303 (February 1952) Reprinted in Kamakura Kenritsu Kindai Bijutsukan, *Chiisa na hako*, 38–39.

52 Mitsuda, "'*Bijutsu Hihyō*' (1952–1957) shi to sono jidai," 27. As recently as 2008, the national museum described its central task as showing the "maturity of Japanese-style and Western-style paintings" by Japanese artists, a characterization that presupposes exactly the kind of unified path to national modernity that the Kamakura museum questioned. Website of the National Museum of Modern Art, Tokyo. http://www.momat.go.jp/english/artmuseum/index.html (accessed September 17, 2008).

53 Sakai Tadayasu, Interview February 24, 2009. The transplant metaphor referred to botanical species, including the argument that plants sometimes were more vigorous in their new location than were long-standing local species. As such, it still retained in the 1930s some of the biological determinism of racial thinking of its day, although this element withered away in subsequent decades. Hijikata Teiichi, "Ishoku bunka to shite no yōga: 'Pari no shutten' ron no konkyo," reprinted in Hijikata Teiichi, *Hijikata Teiichi: Bijutsu Hihyō, 1946–1980* (Tokyo: Keibunsha, 1992 [1947]), 26–31.

54 Murata Ryōsaku, "Kamakura Kindai Bijutsukan—1-nen no seiseki," *Geijutsu Shinchō* (January 1953): 165–167. "Paris Exhibiting Nippon Ceramics," *Nippon Times*, December 18, 1950. Beginning in 1954, the national museum in Ueno also mounted "homecoming shows" (*satogaeri ten*) of Japanese art that had

toured overseas, but Hijikata's essays do not reveal the same desire to rehabilitate Japan's image in the world that Shimizu finds in those actions. Shimizu Yoshiaki, "Japan in American Museums—but Which Japan?" *Art Bulletin* (March 2001): 129. Shimizu's argument is somewhat undercut by the fact that, as he reports, the government officials in charge of choosing the works to send overseas initially wanted to send a motley collection of artifacts that they themselves did not think of as "masterpieces." See also Warren I. Cohen, *East Asian Art and American Culture* (New York: Columbia University Press, 1992).

55 Hijikata, "Kanagawa Kenritsu Bijutsukan."

56 Winther-Tamaki, *Art in the Encounter of Nations,* Chapter 4, especially 140.

57 Bert Winther-Tamaki, "'The Mexico Boom' in the Japanese art world, 1955." Paper given at Japanese Art Since 1945: The First PONJA GenKon Symposium, Yale April 2005. Summary at http://www.yale.edu/macmillan/ceas/japanartabstracts. pdf (accessed October 13, 2010). Hijikata Teiichi, *Mekishiko kaiga* (Tokyo: Misuzu, 1955).

58 Hijikata Teiichi, *Kuree* (Tokyo: Misuzu Shobō, 1955).

59 Sakai, "Kaisō no Bijutsukan Funtōki," 28.

60 Yagyū, "1950 nendai no Omoide," 17–20.

61 Hijikata, "Atogaki," 429–436.

62 Sakai, "Kaisō no Bijutsukan Funtōki," 29.

63 Ellen P. Conant, "Introduction: A Historiographical Overview," in *Challenging Past and Present: The Metamorphosis of Nineteenth-Century Japanese Art*, ed. Ellen P. Conant (Honolulu: University of Hawai'i Press, 2006), 3. See also Sawatari Kiyoko, "Innovational Adaptations: Contacts between Japanese and Western Artists in Yokohama, 1859–1899" in the same volume, 83–113.

64 Kanagawaken Bijutsu—Bakumatsu Meiji Shoki hen, *Kanagawaken Bijutsu— Bakumatsu Meiji Shoki* (Kamakura: Kanagawa Kenritsu Kindai Bijutsukan, 1970), 1.

65 For more, see Laura Hein: "The Art of Bourgeois Culture in Kamakura;" "Reckoning with War in the Museum: Hijikata Teiichi at the Kamakura Museum of Modern Art;" and "Modern Art Patronage and Democratic Citizenship in Japan," *Journal of Asian Studies* 69, no. 3 (August 2010): 821–841.

66 Hijikata Teiichi, *Takahashi Yūichi Gashū* (Tokyo: Kōdansha, 1972).

67 Hijikata Teiichi, "Maegaki," in *Kanagawa ken Bijutsu Fūdōki*, ed. Kanagawaken Bijutsu—Bakumatsu Meiji Shoki (Kamakura: Kanagawa Kenritsu Kindai Bijutsukan, 1970), ix–xiv.

68 Hirayama Ikuo, "Kindai Nihonga no 150 nenten—Minzokuteki kosei to dentō," *Mizue* (October 1967): 35–37. The show also made the case that art sparked scientific innovation, which Hirayama found very appealing.

69 Sakai Tadayasu, *Sono toshi mo mata—Kamakura Kindai Bijutsukan o meguru hitobito* (Kamakura: Kamakura Shunjūsha, 2004), 19–20.

70 Eiko Ikegami, *Bonds of Civility: Aesthetic Networks and Political Origins of Japanese Culture* (Cambridge: Cambridge University Press, 2005).

71 Sakai notes that this showed not only Hijikata's "resistance" to national narratives of art history, but also his excellent "journalistic sense." Sakai, "Kaisō no Bijutsukan Funtōki," 29.

72 Hijikata Teiichi, "Kakurete iru Meisaku," *Asahi Jyaanaru* (June 1966): 26–27.

73 Yasuko Tsuchikane, "Picasso as Other—Koyama Fujio and the Polemics of Postwar Japanese Ceramics," *Review of Japanese Culture and Society*, 26 (December 2014): 34.

74 Isaki Masakaki, "Hitokoto-Omoidasu koto nado," in Kamakura Kenritsu Kindai Bijutsukan, *Chiisa na Hako*, 100. Sakai, *Sono toshi mo mata*, 33 called the intellectual impact of the drinking sessions "the Hijikata typhoon."

75 Interview with Tanaka Atsushi, April 27, 2016.

76 Koyama was one of the individuals who established the 1952 Living National Treasure system for potters, identifying people who most fully realized the perfection of the Chinese or Japanese past. Tsuchikane, "Picasso as Other."

77 Sakai Tadayasu speech, quoted in Nishimura Takaaki, *Bijutsukan Sanpō in Kanagawa* (Yokohama: Kanagawa Shinbunsha, 1993), 13–15.

78 Sakai, *Sono toshi mo mata,* 19–20.

79 Yagyū, "1950 nendai no Omoide," 17–20.

80 Sasaki Kōzō, "Hijikata Ikka," 48–49 and Awaki Kōjirō, "Teatoru-kukura sono hoka," 44–46 in Hijikata Teiichi Tsuitō Kankōkai, *Hijikata Teiichi Tsuisō*.

81 Yagyū, "Wasurenagusa," 68. Yagyū, "1950 nendai no Omoide," 17.

82 Sakai, "Kaisō no Bijutsukan Funtōki," 30. This organization is the Bijutsukan Keikaku Kyōgikai.

83 Aoki Shigeru, Interview, April 28, 2016.

84 Most exhibits were up for five to six weeks. Yagyū, "Wasurenagusa," 69.

85 Hein, "The Art of Bourgeois Culture in Kamakura."

86 Aoki Shigeru, Interview, April 28, 2016. Hijikata probably did this in the 1950s because Kishida's widow refused to let Hijikata quote from the diaries when he was writing his 1941 book. Hijikata, "Atogaki," 429–436. For National Museum exhibit, see Asano Toru et al., *Kishida Ryūsei ten: botsugo 50-nen* (Tokyo: Asahi Shinbun, 1979). The national museum also held an exhibition on Kishida in 1966. See Oka Isaburō, ed., *Kishida Ryūsei Zenshū*, 10 vols. (Tokyo: Iwanami, 1979–1980).

87 Pierre Bourdieu, *Distinction: A Social Critique of the Judgment of Taste*, trans. Richard Nice (Cambridge, MA: Harvard University Press, 1984). For more on Wakimura's museum-related activities, see Laura Hein, "Modern Art Patronage."

88 Bennett, *The Birth of the Museum*, 90, 100.

89 Wakimura Yoshitarō, ed., *Wakimura Yoshitarō Taidanshū: Sangyō to Bijutsu to* (Tokyo: Nihon Keieishi Kenkyūjo, 1990).

90 Osaragi Jirō, "Jo," 4.

91 Sakai Tadayasu, Interview February 24, 2009.

92 Takeda Naoki, "Ubeshi ni okeru Chōkoku Setsubi Jigyō no Kaisho," *The Japanese Institute of Landscape Architecture* 65, no. 3 (2002): 259–267.

93 Hirase Reita, "War and Bronze Sculpture," in *Art and War in Japan and Its Empire, 1931–1960*, ed. Asato Ikeda, Aya Louisa McDonald, and Ming Tiampo (Leiden: Brill, 2013), 229–240.

94 Takeda, "Ubeshi ni okeru Chōkoku Setsubi Jigyō no Kaisho," 262.

95 Chita Kenzō, "Hijikata Sensei o Shinobu," in Hijikata Teiichi Tsuitō Kankōkai, *Hijikata Teiichi Tsuisō*, 68–69.

96 The exhibits are listed in Museum of Modern Art, Kamakura *Kanagawa Kenritsu Kindai Bijutsukan 30-nen no Ayumi*. The key advisor for the Karakoram exhibit was Mikami Tsugio.

97 Tang Xiaobing, *Origins of the Chinese Avant-Garde: The Modern Woodcut Movement* (Berkeley: The University of California Press, 2008); Michael Sullivan, *Art and Artists of Twentieth-Century China* (Berkeley: University of California Press, 1996), 80–82.

98 Hijikata, "Chūgoku no Kikoku," in *Hijikata Teiichi Chosakushū*, vol. 11 (Tokyo: Heibonsha, 1977 [1948, 1975]), 373–392.

99 Tang, *Origins of the Chinese Avant-Garde*, 116.

100 Hijikata, *Gendai Bijutsu*. Although Hijikata states in several places, such as on pages 376–377 of this source, that the essay on woodcuts appeared even earlier in *Chūgoku Bunka*, no. 2 (1948), it is not there.

101 The curators were pleased that the Rouault exhibit attracted 6,267 visitors, given his low profile. Yagyū, "1950 nendai no Omoide," 20.

102 Kon, "Hihyōka Hijikata Teiichi no Tōjo," 6.

103 Given that he published several essays on China between 1946 and 1948 and then abruptly stopped until 1975, the victory of the communists in China and the ensuing Cold War probably also contributed to his silence. Late in life Hijikata often declared his intention to write more about China. Interview with Hijikata Yukue, Kamakura, February 27, 2009 and interview with Sakai Tadayasu, February 24, 2009. Maki Kaneko treats Hijikata's postwar attention to painter Matsumoto Sannosuke as an attempt to atone for his own wartime actions. Maki Kaneko, *Mirroring the Japanese Empire: The Male Figure in Yōga Painting, 1930–1950* (Leiden-Boston: Brill, 2015), 146–148.

104 Uchiyama Kakichi donated 348 prints to the museum, its first major gift.

105 Ōkochi Kikuo, "Chūgoku Kanren no Tenkan," 73.

106 Interview with Hijikata Yukue, Kamakura, February 27, 2009.

107 The museum first tackled this topic in a 2013 exhibit when Mizusawa Tsutomu became Director. Kanagawa Kenritsu Kindai Bijutsukan/The Museum of Modern Art, Kamakura & Hayama, *Sensō/Bijutsu: 1940–1950: Modanisumu to Rensa to Henyō* (Kamakura: Kanagawa Kenritsu Kindai Bijitsukan, 2013).

Chapter 4

1   James C. Scott, *Seeing Like a State: How Certain Schemes to Improve the Human Condition Have Failed* (Berkeley: University of California Press, 1998), Introduction. Timothy Mitchell, *Rule of Experts: Egypt, Techno-Politics, Modernity* (Berkeley: University of California Press, 2002) is a well-known critique of expertise.

2   Moore, *Constructing East Asia*; Mimura, *Planning for Empire*.

3   Scott, *Seeing Like a State*, 4–5.

4   Wakimura Yoshitarō, "Kaisō no senchū-sengo-Sensō to gakusha," Interview by Mitani Taichirō, *Chūō Kōron*, nos. 1332–1333 (November and December 1995): 157, 167–175.

5   Officers were billeted at the Seaside Hotel until one of them accidentally sparked a fire that destroyed most of the building. As in the rest of the country, Japanese officials in Yokohama, Yokosuka, Atsugi, and Kamakura immediately ordered that brothels be organized for the Allied soldiers, although in Kamakura this directive was never carried out. Kamakura-shi Shishi Hensan Iinkai, *Kamakura Shishi-Kindai Tsūshi*, vol. 7, 471.

6   Tilton's original goal was to give local governments full tax powers and the right to maintain their own police forces but other SCAP officials, notably Deputy Chief of Government Section, Charles Kades, thought that was too autonomous and "something like a Greek city state." Takemae Eiji interview of Tilton, "C.G. Tilton and the Occupation of Japan," *Tokyo Keidai Gakkai Shi* 146 (1986): 552. Also see Takemae, *Inside GHQ*, 301–302; Amakawa Akira, "The Making of the Postwar Local Government System," in *Democratizing Japan: The Allied Occupation*, eds. Robert E. Ward and Sakamoto Yoshikazu (Honolulu: University of Hawai'i Press, 1987), 253–283.

7   Juha Saunavaara, *In Search of Suitable Political Leadership: Japanese Conservatives in Occupation Plans and Policies, 1942–1947* (Ph.D. diss., Acta Universitatis Ouluensis. B, Humaniora 93, Oulu: University of Oulu, Finland, 2010).

8   Takemae interview of Tilton, "C.G. Tilton and the Occupation of Japan," 556.

9   Brownlee et al., eds., *The Political Economy of Transnational Tax Reform*.

10 Takemae, *Inside GHQ*, 301. Suzuki Shun'ichi, "Minshushugi to jihō jiji," discussion with Matsuyama Yukio, in *Suzuki Shun'ichi Chōsakushū*, vol. 6 (Tokyo: Ryōsho Fukyūkai, 2001 [1979]), 108–109. Suzuki worked extensively with SCAP's Tilton, who expressed his respect for Suzuki in Takemae, "C. G. Tilton and the Occupation of Japan," 557.

11 Andre Sorensen, *The Making of Urban Japan: Cities and Planning from Edo to the Twenty-First Century*, The Nissan Institute/Routledge Japanese Studies Series (London & New York: Routledge, 2002), 154–156.

12 "Mikkakai to wa," *Kamakura Shimin* 1, no. 1 (January 1960): 3 and Hashizume Yukiome, "Kamakura Mikkakai o Hajimatta Jidai to Hitobito," in *Kamakura*

Mikkakai Rokujū Shūnen Kinenki, ed. Hashizume Yukiome (Kamakura: Kamakura Mikkakai, 2010), 62. The Mikkakai's first large meeting was on September 3, 1951, and its name came from that date. Hashizume Yoshiome, "Kaihō Daiji no Nazo," *Mikkakai Kaihō*, December 1992, 23. See also interview with Hashizume at http://www.kcn-net.org/my_kamakura/my_kama40/mykama_40.html (accessed August 17, 2015).

13   Hara Minoru, "Kamakura Mikkakai no Ugoki," *Kamakura Shimin* 1, no. 2 (February, 1960): 17; Hashizume Yukiome, ed., "Kamakura Mikkakai no Gojūnen: Kamakura Mikkakai Kaihō to Sono Jidai: Sokugō 50 Shūnen kinen (1)," 2001, manuscript deposited at the Kamakura Central Public Library, 9.

14   Hara, "Kamakura Mikkakai no Ugoki," 17. Japanese at both the local and national levels—separately—had actually tried two versions of this method of reducing the tax burden in the late 1930s but the two initiatives had clashed with each other. Then, although Kamakura and Zushi officials discussed combining forces in 1943, Tokyo decided to merge each town with some outlying villages instead. Kamakura-shi Shishi Hensan Iinkai, *Kamakura shishi—Kindai Tsūshi*, 489, 491.

15   Kamakura Mikkakai, "Mikkakai to wa," *Kamakura Shimin*, 3.

16   Hashizume, ed., *Kamakura Mikkakai Rokujū Shūnen Kinenki*, 62.

17   https://en.wikipedia.org/wiki/Tsurumi_rail_accident (accessed August 17, 2015).

18   Other members had formidable social capital in different forms, such as the third Mikkakai chair, Sawada Setsuzō, 1884–1976, who had been an Ambassador to Brazil when Uchiyama Iwatarō served as Counselor in his embassy. Earlier Sawada had been Consul General in New York and he was a UN observer after the war. Hashizume, "Kamakura Mikkakai no Gojūnen," 2, 10. Joke from Hashizume, ed., *Kamakura Mikkakai Rokujū Shūnen Kinenki*, 39.

19   Takemae, *Inside GHQ*, 305.

20   Laura Hein, *Reasonable Men, Powerful Words: Political Culture and Expertise in 20th Century Japan* (Berkeley and Washington, DC: University of California Press and Woodrow Wilson International Center for Scholars Press, 2004). For one of many "storm-tossed" comments, see Yamanaka Shirō, "Tōkei Kondankai Izen no," in *Nihon Tōkei Seido Saiken Shi—Tōkei Iinkai Shi*, vol. 1, ed. Nihon Tōkei Kenkyūjo (Tokyo: Nihon Tōkei Kenkyūjo, 1963 [1946]), 1–4.

21   Yamanaka, "Tōkei Kondankai Izen no," 1–4.

22   For press releases, minutes from third meeting of the group June 6, 1946, in Nihon Tōkei Kenkyūjo, ed., *Nihon Tōkei Seido Saiken Shi—Tōkei Iinkai Shi*, vol. 1 (Tokyo: Nihon Tōkei Kenkyūjo, 1963), 14. See also Kitada Hirōyuki, "Postwar Reconstruction of Statistical System in Japan," *Forty-Year History of the Statistics Council* (1995): 67–119, 2002 rev. edn. posted at http://www.soumu.go.jp/main_content/000327474.pdf (accessed August 17, 2015).

23   Ōuchi Hyōe, Itō Takeo and Chiiki Keizai Kenkyūjo, eds., *Nihon Sangyō Zusetsu*, vol. 9 of *Zusetsu Zenshū* (Tokyo: Iwasaki Shoten, 1956), 1–2. Ōuchi and his students

also wrote a series of pamphlets on statistics in the early postwar years to make their arcane subjects accessible to general readers, models that were the inspiration for Iwanami's Booklet series, inaugurated in 1982. Itō Narihiko, "Bukkuretto Sokkan no koro," in *Kiokushū Yasue Ryōsuke: Sono Hito to Shisō*, ed. Yasue Ryōsuke Kiokushū Kankō Iinkai (Tokyo: *Sekai* Henshūbunai Jimukyoku, 1999), 163.

24 The assistant was Minami Kinji, another colleague who died as a result of his prison experience during the war. Hama Masanari, "Ōuchi Sensei to Shinshū," in *Sanrokushū*, eds. Ōuchi Hyōe Sensei Kiju Kinen Zuisō Shūshutsuban Sewaijini Daihyō and Arisawa Hiromi (Tokyo: privately published, 1965), 208–214.

25 Japan actually had had a very good statistical system earlier in the century, but most of the forty-seven prefectural offices had been shut down during the war, and by 1945 only fourteen remained. Kitada Hirōyuki, "Postwar Reconstruction of Statistical System in Japan," 85.

26 Masaki Chifuyu, *Masaki Chifuyu Nikki*, eds. Tanabe Kōtarō and Miyazaki Masayasu (Tokyo: Chiiki Kenkyūkai, 2003).

27 Ōhashi Ryūken, "The Study of Statistics in Japan: Its Development, Present State and Future Task," *Kyoto University Economic Review* 29, no. 2 (1959): 52.

28 See Masaki, *Zuihitsu Kamakura Shichō*. Tanabe Kōtarō, "Kamakura no Midori to Masaki Chifuyu," *Nihon Rekishi*, no. 687 (August 2008): 86–87.

29 Masaki, *Zuihitsu*, 10–13; Wakimura Yoshitarō and Masaki Chifuyu, "Nihon Keizai no 45 nen no Fūsetsu: 'Ekonomisuto' no ayunda jidai," *Ekonomisuto* 46, no. 13 (1968): 120. Elise Tipton, *The Japanese Police State: Tokko in Interwar Japan* (London: Bloomsbury, 2012), 51. Tanabe, "Kamakura no midori," 86.

30 J. Charles Schencking, "The Great Kanto Earthquake and the Culture of Catastrophe and Reconstruction in 1920s Japan," *Journal of Japanese Studies* 34, no. 2 (2008): 301, 316–317. Masaki was certainly aware of Charles Beard's lectures on urban administration at Tokyo Imperial University in 1922, when Beard argued that Tokyo was a harsh environment because three groups were excluded politically: labor unions, intellectuals, and women. Minobe attended and said that these comments later guided his policies as Governor of Tokyo. Minobe Ryokichi, "Watakushi no Kakushin Toseiron–Ninenme no Kadai ni Mukatte," *Sekai*, no. 272 (July 1968): 47–59.

31 Masaki, *Zuihitsu*, 10.

32 This area is now split between Tokyo's Kuroda and Edo wards. The labor school closed in 1932. Key texts are Fukushima Masao and Kawashima Takeyoshi, eds., *Hozumi Suehirō sensei to setsurumento* (Tokyo: Tokyo Daigaku Setsurumento hōritsu sōdanbu, 1963); Fukushima Masao, *Kaisō no Tokyo Teidai Setsurumento* (Tokyo: Nihon Hyōronsha, 1984); Kami Shōichirō and Ōmori Toshio, *Tokyo Teikoku daigaku setsurumento jūninenshi* (Tokyo: Kyūzansha, 1998). For brief remarks in English, see Elyssa Faison, *Managing Women, Disciplining Labor in Modern Japan* (Berkeley: University of California Press, 2007), 82–83 and Sally

Ann Hastings, *Neighborhood and Nation in Tokyo: 1905-1937* (Pittsburgh and London: University of Pittsburgh Press, 1995), 59–62. Hastings notes that even earlier Katayama Sen had worked at the South End Settlement in Boston and then founded the Kingsley Hall settlement in Kanda, Tokyo, p. 24. Manako Ogawa, "'Hull-House' in Downtown Tokyo: The Transplantation of a Settlement House from the United States into Japan and the North American Missionary Women, 1919-1945," *Journal of World History*, 15, no. 3 (2004) describes a third settlement house in Tokyo that was much more closely tied to American missionary efforts.

33 Masaki, *Zuihitsu*, 10–13.

34 See Wakimura and Masaki, "Nihon Keizai no 45 nen no Fūsetsu," 117–118. Employee list from Tanabe, "Kamakura no midori," 86. Bedbugs from Hatta Motō, "Masaki Chifuyu no Koto—kōyū 50 nen," in Masaki, *Zuihitsu*, 187–189.

35 Tanabe Kōtarō and Miyazaki Masayasu, "Ko Masaki Chifuyu-shi no Omoide o Kataru: Masaki Harue Intaabyū," in Masaki, *Masaki Chifuyu Nikki*.

36 Masaki, "Wasuregataki Hitobito," Masaki, *Zuihitsu*, 32.

37 Wakimura and Masaki, "Nihon Keizai no 45 nen no Fūsetsu," 124.

38 Johnson emphasizes the impact this group had on postwar economic planning. As he and others have pointed out, they were influenced less by Nazi than by Soviet economic philosophy and focused on managing the supply of commodities to industry and on rapid industrialization. Chalmers A. Johnson, *MITI and the Japanese Miracle: The Growth of Industrial Policy* (Stanford, CA: Stanford University Press, 1982). See also Yoneyuki Sugita, "Universal Health Insurance: The Unfinished Reform of Japan's Healthcare System," in *Democracy in Occupied Japan: The U.S. Occupation and Japanese Politics and Society*, eds. Mark E. Caprio and Yoneyuki Sugita (London and New York: Routledge, 2007), 148.

39 Masaki, *Zuihitsu*, 19–21, 32.

40 Simon Andrew Avenell, *Making Japanese Citizens: Civil Society and the Mythology of the Shimin in Postwar Japan* (Berkeley: University of California Press, 2010), Chapters 2 and 4. See also Hein, *Reasonable Men*, 182–187.

41 Narumi Masayasu, "Matsushita Keiichi no 'Jijitai Kaikaku Toshi Seisakuron' no Genryū," *Jiji Ken Kanagawa Geppō* (August 2016): 11–19. Koizumi Chikataka, Kamibayashi Tokurō, and Kubo Takao, Interview, Institute for Public Policy in Kanagawa Prefecture, Yokohama, June 4, 2009.

42 Ōuchi Hyōe and Naito Masaru, *Nihon Zaisei Zusetsu* (Tokyo: Iwanami 1965), iv. Carl Shoup expressed similar views in *Federal Finances in the Coming Decade: Some Cumulative Possibilities, 1941-1951* (New York: Columbia University Press, 1941).

43 Kamakura Mikkakai, "Shisei memo," *Kamakura Shimin* 1, no. 8 (August 1960): 14–15.

44 Kamakura Mikkakai kōhōbu, "Zeikin no hanbun ijō o kū—Kamakura shi jinkenki no Jittai," *Kamakura Shimin* 1, no. 9 (September 1960): 14.

45 Kamakura Mikkakai, "Shisei memo," 14–15.

46 Masaki, "Seijinshiki no hi ni attate," Masaki, *Zuihitsu,* 58–60.

47 The population in the late 1930s was about 30,000 but wartime mergers with surrounding villages mean that the population increase by 1950 appears larger than it actually was.

48 Junko Ueno and Masahisa Sonobe, "Urban Sustainability: A Case Study of Environmental Movements in Kamakura," in *Sustainable Cities: Japanese Perspectives on Physical and Social Structures,* ed. Tamagawa Hidenori (Tokyo: United Nations University Press 2006), 208, 211.

49 Sorensen, *The Making of Urban Japan,* 159.

50 Sorensen, *The Making of Urban Japan,* 183–184, 188–191. The National Capital Region Development Plan of 1958 was also significant. Thomas R. H. Havens stresses how aggressively Minobe moved to create parks in Tokyo through this mechanism in *Parkscapes: Green Spaces in Modern Japan* (Honolulu: University of Hawai'i Press, 2011), 141–143.

51 Ueno and Sonobe, "Urban Sustainability," 226.

52 Ueno and Sonobe, "Urban Sustainability," 226. Hashizume, ed., "Kamakura Mikkakai no Gojūnen," 6.

53 Hashizume, ed., *Kamakura Mikkakai Rokujū Shūnen Kinenki,* 81.

54 Osamu Sawaji, "Carving Out a Balance in Kamakura," *Highlighing Japan* 108 (April 2017): 30–31.

55 Tanabe Kotarō, "Kakushin Kanryō no Senzen to Sengo—Masaki Chifuyu Nikki ni Miru Sengo Kaikaku," *Kinki Daigaku Tanki Ronshū,* 35, no. 2 (March 2003): 43–54. Hara Minoru, *Rekishiteki Fūdo no Hozon: 'Kamakura shimin' no hibi* (Odawara: Akansasu Kenchiku Kobō, 1989).

56 Ueno and Sonobe, "Urban Sustainability," 188, 212. They argue that the 1990s' environmental movement was much more effective and well integrated with the municipal government than earlier efforts. After Masaki, the next pro-environmental mayor was Takeuchi Ken, elected in 1993.

57 Sorensen, *The Making of Urban Japan,* 302.

58 "Zaimokuza Kaidan," *Kamakura Shimin* 1, no. 1 (January 1960): 8–9.

59 This was in the context of a larger urban development plan, created by a committee headed by Yokoyama Mitsuo. Masaki, "Shimin ga Tsukurisodateru Bikan Chizu," Masaki, *Zuihitsu,* 75–80. Sorensen adds, "the experience of the 1960s had resulted in the development of a general consensus in support of the need for increased planning and stricter controls over development." Sorensen, *The Making of Urban Japan,* 202–203, 213–214, and 206. The key national figure to integrate environmental issues into economic and urban planning was Tsuru Shigeto, who advised Masaki personally. Miyamoto Kenichi, "Kōgai Kenkyū Iinkai to Tsuru Shigeto Kyōju," special issue on "Tsuru Shigeto o Yomu: Sono Hito to Shisō to Miryaku," of *Shisō no Kagaku,* no. 126 (March 1990): 38–39.

60 Masaki, "Yōkyū suru Shimin o Tsukuru," in Masaki, *Zuihitsu*, 49–52. See also Tanabe, "Kamakura no midori," 86–87; Tanabe, "Kakushin Kanryō no Senzen to Sengo;" Hara, *Rekishiteki Fūdo no Hozon*. In another example, Masaki laid out the perverse incentives in land reclamation laws—while fishing groups and the prefecture were compensated at 3 percent of the value of the new land, towns received nothing until 1973. "Kamakura no Umi wa Dare no mono ka," in Masaki, *Zuihitsu*, 81–85. Masaki's citizen-input group was the Kamakura Citizens Round Table Conference on Urban Planning, established with 200 members in 1972. Sonobe and Ueno, "Urban Sustainability," 212.

61 Oh Iwata and Takashi Oguchi, "Factors Affecting Late Twentieth Century Land Use Patterns in Kamakura City, Japan," *Geographical Research* 47, no. 2 (June 2009): 177, 225.

62 Ueno and Sonobe, "Urban Sustainability," 208–209.

63 Koizumi Chikataka, Kamibayashi Tokurō, and Kubo Takao, Interview, June 4, 2009.

64 Masaki, "Saisho no Chisei Hōshin Ensetsu," Masaki, *Zuihitsu*, and "Yōkyū suru Shimin o Tsukuru," 39–48 and 49–52; Ueno and Sonobe, "Urban Sustainability," 214–215; Iwata and Oguchi, "Factors Affecting Late Twentieth Century Land Use Patterns in Kamakura City, Japan."

65 He emphasized mainstreaming special needs children, which was very rare in 1970. Masaki, "Saisho no Chisei Hōshin Ensetsu."

66 See Kamakura's official website: http://www.city.kamakura.kanagawa.jp/danjo/ heiwatoshisenngen.html (accessed August 10, 2015). In 2015, Kamakura officials reaffirmed this message, adding an artistic installation to emphasize its timeliness. http://headlines.yahoo.co.jp/hl?a=20150807-00002973-kana-l14 (accessed August 10, 2015). Hiroshima and Nagasaki both became Peace Cities in 1949.

67 Hirata et al., *Kamakura Kindaishi Shiryō Daijūnishū*, 309.

68 In Kanagawa prefecture, the Occupation forces also established libraries at Atsugi, Fujisawa, Hiratsuka, Oiso, Chigasaki, and four sites in Yokohama. "Civil Information Activities, OCIE-02 Major Graydon J. Jones, Annex E-2 Monthly Military Government Activities Report," April 1948, p. 5 in Monthly Military Government Activities Report, February 1, 1948 to February 20, 1948, pp. 6–7 in *Senryōki Todō Fuken Gunsei Shiryō*, vol. 39. Tokyo-Kanagawa-ken (1), in National Diet Library.

69 Shirai Eiji, ed., *Kamakura Jiten* (Tokyo: Tokyodō Shuppan, 1976). See also http:// www.city.kamakura.kanagawa.jp/kamakura-kankou/0803kankoukyakusuu.html (accessed March 11, 2016).

70 Inoue Fusao, "Kamakura ni Kansuru Chihō Shiteki Kenkyū no Dōko," *Kamakura Shimin* 1, no. 2 (February 1960): 16.

71 Hara Minoru, "Kamakura Mikkakai to wa," *Kamakura Shimin* 1, no. 4 (April 1960): 17. Sawa advised Hijikata on museum exhibits that featured such maps. Nagai Ryūo, "Chō," in Sawa Jurō, *Tsurezure no Kamakura, Kaitei Shinpan Kamakura*

Meishoki (Kamakura: Kamakura Shunjūsha, 1976), 1. Sawa also published a thirteen-volume series of documents on early modern Kamakura history under the title *Kamakura Kinsei Shiryō*. Hijikata Teiichi described the modern art museum in parallel ways when he explained in the pages of *The Kamakura Citizen* that he was mounting an exhibit on city planning that celebrated urban activists and public institutions, using an exhibit he had seen in Vienna as a model. Hijikata Teiichi, "'Warera no Wai-n' Ten no Koto," *Kamakura Shimin* 1, no. 4 (April 1960): 10–11.

72 See Masaki Chifuyu, "Koi yo, Dō ka Sodatte Okure," and "Kamakura Bungakukan o Tsukurō," Masaki, *Zuihitsu*, 71–72 and 86–89. The Kamakura Bungakukan is by far the most well attended of the modern attractions requiring an entry fee in Kamakura today. In 2014, 110,600 people visited, substantially higher than 96,000 in 2005 and 81,900 in 2002.http://www.city.kamakura.kanagawa.jp/kamakura-kankou/0803kankoukyakusuu.html (accessed March 11, 2016). In another project to preserve and celebrate modern urban local culture, Masaki also worked to turn the home and studio of artist Kaburagi Kiyokata into a museum after the artist's death in 1972. Masaki, "Kamakura to Geijutsuka no Uchi," Masaki, *Zuihitsu*, 90–92.

73 Kimura Eiichi, "Kokuritsu Toshokanron," in Ōuchi Hyōe Sensei, ed., *Sanrokushū*, 347–358.

74 Masaki, "Kenpō o Kurashi no naka ni" (Living under the Constitution), in Masaki, *Zuihitsu*, 53–56.

75 Masaki Chifuyu, "Kamakura Shi Heiwa Kinen Shūkai ni Attate," speech given at City Hall on August 15, 1971, in Masaki, *Zuihitsu*, 55–56.

76 Masaki Chifuyu, "Han Yasukuni Gyōshin e no messe-ji," in Masaki, *Zuihitsu*, 61–63, speech given on February 8, 1971.

77 Masaki, "Kamakura Shi Heiwa Kinen Shūkai ni attate," in Masaki, *Zuihitsu*, 53–56, 56.

78 Masaki, "Okinawa Henkyū ni tsuite—Okinawa Henkyū Cyaraban e no aisatsu," in Masaki, *Zuihitsu*, 64–67. David Tobaru Obermiller, "Senaga Kamejiro: Marxist, Resistance Leader, and an Overall 'A Pain in the Ass' Since 1927," paper given at Midwest Japan Seminar, St. Xavier University, Chicago, April 8, 2017.

79 Masaki, "Kenpō o Kurashi no naka ni," 53–56, and "Kamakura Kai no Heiwa ni Atari Betonamu Daihyō o mukaeru messe-ji," speech given on August 15, 1972, in Masaki, *Zuihitsu*, 66–67.

80 At that time there were progressive mayors in Yokosuka (Mr. Ito) and Fujisawa (confusingly named Mr. Hayama) as well as Yokohama, Tokyo, and Kyoto. See Tanabe and Miyazaki, "Ko Masaki Chifuyu-shi no Omoide o Kataru," 148, 165, in Masaki, *Masaki Chifuyu Nikki*. Also Wakimura and Masaki, "Nihon Keizai no 45 nen no Fūsetsu."

81 *Kamakura Shimin* 1, no. 1 (January 1960).

82 Nasu Ryōsuke in Hashizume, ed., *Kamakura Mikkakai Rokujū Shūnen Kinenki*, 89.

83   Interview, Tanabe Kōtarō and Amakawa Akira, Kamakura April 21, 2005. See also Kanagawa Ken Kōgai Taisaku Jimukyoku, ed., *Kanagawa no Kōgai: Genjō to taisaku no aramashi* (Yokohama: Kanagawa Ken Kōgai Taisaku Jimukyoku, 1971).

84   Takahashi Masao, *Watakushi no Zōhan* (Tokyo: Yomiuri Shinbunsha, 1970), 25–27, Shibata Tokue, "Yoron o Ugokashita Haigasu Kisei," part 5 of "Aru gakusha no tosei taiken ki," *Ekonomisuto* (October 21, 1980): 61.

85   Ōhashi, "The Study of Statistics in Japan," 53. Ōhashi also translated Samir Amin's 1977 work (in English, 1976 in French), *Imperialism and Unequal Development*. For his earlier writing on Ōuchi, see Ōhashi Ryūken, "Nihon no Tōkei Gakusha: Ōuchi Hyōe," *Nōrin Tōkei Chōsa* 13, nos. 7–9 (June to September 1963): 56–58, 42–45, 45–48.

86   Naitō Kunio interview of Suzuki Shun'ichi, "Jikan Hachinen Chiji Nannen," in *Suzuki Shun'ichi Chōsakushū*, vol. 6, 39.

87   Koizumi Chikataka interview, Kamakura, May 2009; Hara Minoru, "Shimin Rengō Hayari ni Suite," *Kamakura Shimin* 14, no. 3 (March 1974): 1.

88   Masaki was more supportive of labor unions than were many of his constituents. In 1972, he gave a May Day speech to mark the successful conclusion of the shuntō spring labor offensive, noting his pleasure that the unions had secured significant increases in wages and benefits. See "48 Nen Kamakura Me-De-no Aisatsu," Masaki, *Zuihitsu*, 68–70.

89   Interview, Tanabe Kōtarō and Amakawa Akira, Kamakura, April 21, 2005.

90   Sawada and Katō in Uchiyama Iwatarō, Yamamoto Shōichi, and Sawada Setsuzō, "Zadankai," *Kamakura Shimin* 1, no. 1 (January 1960): 3–6 and Uchiyama in Uchiyama Iwatarō, Yamamoto Shōichi, and Sawada Setsuzō, "Zadankai zoku," *Kamakura Shimin* 1, no. 2 (February 1960): 6. The pro-development mayor, Yamamoto Shōichi, sounded defensive when criticized on such grounds, as was prescient: his lack of enthusiasm for environmental and historical protection cost him the 1970 election to Masaki Chifuyu. His response to Uchiyama was, "I'm committed to protecting Kamakura so I'm careful about kinds of industry—things like whether it emits smoke or pollute the water. Now we have Mitsubishi Electric and Shiseido. They are both very *clean* factories. And we want more like that."

Conclusion

1   Koizumi debated Tsuru Shigeto in a set of 1952 essays, summarized in translation in "The Koizumi-Tsuru Debate on Peace," *Journal of Social and Political Ideas in Japan* 1, no. 1 (April 1963): 20–24.

2   Chalmers A. Johnson, *Blowback: The Costs and Consequences of American Empire* (New York: Metropolitan Books, 2000); Chalmers A. Johnson, *The Sorrows of*

Empire: Militarism, Secrecy, and the End of the Republic (New York: Metropolitan Books, 2004).

3   Lonny E. Carlile, *Divisions of Labor: Globality, Ideology, and War in the Shaping of the Japanese Labor Movement* (Honolulu: University of Hawai'i Press, 2005).

4   Masuda Hajimu, *Cold War Crucible: The Korean Conflict and the Postwar World* (Cambridge, MA: Harvard University Press, 2015), 237. See also Yui Daizaburō, *Mikan no Senryō kaikaku: Amerika Chishikijin to Suterareta Nihon minshuka kōsō*, 2nd edn (Tokyo: Tokyo Daigaku Shuppankai, 2016).

5   Kyoto resident Kōmoto Masahito's letter to the Prime Minister of January 5, 1951, at the National Diet Library, quoted in Hajimu Masuda, "Fear of World War III: Social Politics of Re-Armament and Peace Movements in Japan During the Korean War, 1950–53," *Journal of Contemporary History* 47, no. 3 (July 2012): 560.

6   Masumi Junnosuke, *Contemporary Politics in Japan*, transl. Lonnie E. Carlile (Berkeley: University of California Press, 1995), 3.

7   Masumi, *Contemporary Politics in Japan*, 6–7.

8   Iguchi Kazuki, Interview, Kyoto Prefectural Archive, November 19, 2011.

9   Ōta Hisayuki, *Minobe Tosei 12-nen-Seisakushitsu no Memo* (Tokyo: Mainichi Shinbunsha, 1979), 210–212.

10 They succumbed to the same factional infighting, dogmatism about abstract ideas, and, for a tiny but well-publicized minority, turn to self-defeating violence that marred allied movements in other parts of the world. Oguma Eiji, *1968 Wakamonotachi no hanran to sono haikei*, 2 vols. (Tokyo: Shin'yōsha, 2009) and Oguma Eiji, "Japan's 1968: A Collective Reaction to Rapid Economic Growth in an Age of Turmoil," *The Asia-Pacific Journal* 13, issue 11, no. 1 (March 23, 2015).

11 Simon Avenell, "Japan's Long Environmental Sixties and the Birth of a Green Leviathan," *Japan Studies* 32, no. 3 (December 2012): 425.

12 Tsurumi Yoshiyuki, "Beheiren," *Japan Quarterly* 16, no. 4 (October 1, 1969): 446, 448.

13 Marianne Hirsch, *Family Frames: Photography, Narrative, and Post-memory* (Cambridge, MA: Harvard University Press, 1997). She had dropped the hyphen in "postmemory" by 2008.

14 Honda Katsuichi, *The Nanjing Massacre: A Japanese Journalist Confronts Japan's National Shame* (Armonk, NY: M.E. Sharpe, 1999).

15 "'Kenshō—Sensō Sekinin' Sekinin to wa," *Yomiuri Shinbun*, September 29, 2005.

16 Ōuchi Hyōe, "Nihon wa hogokoku de yoi no ka—Shūgiin Anpō Tokubetsu Iinkai Kōtokukai ni okeru ichi kokumin no uttae," May 13, 1960, speech, reprinted in Ōuchi, *Ōuchi Hyōe Chosakushū* 7: 501–511. Orr, *The Victim as Hero* argues that such evasiveness is emblematic of the postwar peace movement.

17 Masaki Chifuyu, "Kin Hisei Shushō Kaikenki," 95–98, "Hada de Kanjita Chuche no Kuni," 99–110, "Heiwateki Sōitsu e no Kyoho," 111–115, all in Masaki, *Zuihitsu Kamakura Shichō*.

18 Arisawa Hiromi, "Kono goro omou koto," and "Bunkō no Kaimakushiki ni Yosete," in *Rekishi no naka ni ikiru*, vol. 2, ed. Arisawa Hiromi, Sensei no Shōwashi Henshū Iinkai Sewanin (Tokyo: Tokyo Daigaku Shuppankai, 1989), 291–293, 284–287.

19 Hiraiwa Gaishi, "'Rekishi ni Manabu' Kenten," in *Kaisō*, vol. 3 of *Arisawa Hiromi no Shōwa shi*, ed. Arisawa Hiromi Sensei no Shōwashi Henshū Iinkai Sewanin (Tokyo: Tokyo Daigaku Shuppankai, 1989), 105.

20 Yoshida says that the Chinese government changed its stance for two reasons: the reports on history textbooks in Japan and a perceived spiritual pollution in China. Takashi Yoshida, *From Cultures of War to Cultures of Peace: War and Peace Museums in Japan, China, and South Korea* (Portland, ME: Merwin Asia, 2014), 200–201.

21 On the other hand, Yoshida sees potential for reconciliation based on the fact that, unlike the permanent exhibit, a traveling show in 2008 depicted the devastation of Japan in 1945 and argued that the war experience was disastrous for both peoples. Yoshida, pp. 199–215.

22 For poverty statistics, Japanese Government, Ministry of Internal Affairs and Communications. Statistics Bureau. National Survey of Family Income and Expenditure. http://www.stat.go.jp/english/data/zensho/ See also Anne Allison, *Precarious Japan* (Raleigh, NC: Duke University Press, 2013). Takehiko Kariya identifies changed standards in 2002 as having triggered a steep decline in *Education Reform and Social Class in Japan: The Emerging Incentive Divide*. Routledge/University of Tokyo Series, 3. Trans. and ed. Michael Burtscher (London and New York: Routledge, 2013).

23 Takahashi Tetsuya, "What March 11 Means to Me: Nuclear Power and the Sacrificial System," *Asia Pacific Journal: Japan Focus* 12, issue 19, no. 1 (May 12, 2014). http://www.japanfocus.org/-Takahashi-Tetsuya/4114 (accessed August 7, 2014). Gavan McCormack, "Japan's Problematic Prefecture—Okinawa and the US-Japan Relationship," *Asia Pacific Journal: Japan Focus* 14, issue 17, no. 2 (September 1, 2016). http://apjjf.org/2016/17/McCormack.html

24 Jeff Kingston, ed., *Press Freedom in Contemporary Japan* (London: Taylor and Francis, 2017).

25 David McNeill and Justin McCurry, "Sink the Asahi! The 'Comfort Women' Controversy and the Neo-nationalist Attack," *The Asia-Pacific Journal* 13, Issue 5, no. 1 (February 2, 2015). http://apjjf.org/2015/13/5/Justin-McCurry/4264.html; Lawrence Repeta, "The silencing of an anti-U.S. base protester in Okinawa," *Japan Times*, January 4, 2017.

26 Casey Baseel, "Kamakura Library Offers Itself as Refuge for Emotionally Troubled Youths," *RocketNews24, Huffington News Japan*. http://en.rocketnews24.com/2015/08/28/japanese-library-offers-itself-and-its-manga-collection-as-refuge-for-emotionally-troubled-youths/ (accessed August 30, 2015)

Selected Bibliography

Archives used

Kamakura Central Public Library.
Kamakura and Hayama Museum of Modern Art Archive.
National Archives, RG 331, Supreme Command for Allied Powers.
National Diet Library.
Tokyo Bunka Zaidan Kenkyūjo (National Research Institute for Cultural Properties).
Tsuru Shigeto Archive, Institute for Economic Research, Hitotsubashi University.
Yokohama City Archive.
Yokohama National University, Carl Shoup Archive.

Interviews

Amakawa Akira and Tanabe Kōtarō. Kamakura, April 21, 2005.
Aoki Shigeru. Tokyo Bunka Zaidan Kenkyūjo (National Research Institute for Cultural Properties), Tokyo, April 27, 2016.
Hashizume Yukiome. Kamakura Central Public Library, August 17, 2015.
Hattori Hiroaki, Katō Shigeo, and Watanabe Akira. May 23, 2009. Kamakura Central Public Library.
Hijikata Yukue, Kamakura, February 27, 2009.
Hirata Emi. Kamakura Central Public Library, April 1, 2009.
Hori Takahiko. June 22, 2009. Kamakura Central Public Library.
Iguchi Kazuki. Kyoto Prefectural Archive, November 19, 2011.
Kagesato Tetsurō. April 3, 2009.
Koizumi Chikataka. Kamakura, May 2009.
Koizumi Chikataka, Kamibayashi Tokurō, and Kubo Takao. Institute for Public Policy in Kanagawa Prefecture, Yokohama, June 4, 2009.
Mizusawa Tsutomu. Associate Director (later director), Museum of Modern Art, Kamakura & Hayama, April 16, 2005.
Murakami Mitsuhiko. Kyoto, November 21, 2011.
Ōuchi Tsutomu. Tokyo, March 17, 2006.
Sakai Tadayasu. Setagaya Museum of Art, February 24, 2009.
Tanaka Atsushi. Tokyo Bunka Zaidan Kenkyūjo (National Research Institute for Cultural Properties), Tokyo, April 27, 2016.

Yamanouchi Shizuo. Director, Kamakura Bungakukan, November 11, 2001.

Yoshino Miyako. Kamakura, October 2011.

Published sources

Aguilar, Paloma. "Agents of Memory: Spanish Civil War Veterans and Disabled Soldiers." In Jay Winter and Emmanuel Sivan, eds., *War and Remembrance in the Twentieth Century*, 84–103. Cambridge: Cambridge University Press, 1999.

Allison, Anne. *Precarious Japan*. Raleigh: Duke University Press, 2013.

Amakawa Akira. "The Making of the Postwar Local Government System." In Robert E. Ward and Sakamoto Yoshikazu, eds., *Democratizing Japan: The Allied Occupation*, 253–283. Honolulu: University of Hawai'i Press, 1987.

Anderson, Ronald S. *Education in Japan: A Century of Modern Government*. Washington, DC: U.S. Government Printing Office, 1975.

Aoki Shigeru. "Sannin no Shūshōchi Seinen Gappi Oitachi to, Yonnin no Shibō Nengappi—Hijikata-san no Yakusho Issatsu, Yanase Nenpu sono 1–2." *Isshun*, nos. 59–60 (August, September 2014): 1–6.

Aoki Shigeru. "Wasurenu Uchi ni—Hijikata Teiichi Nenpu." *Isshun*, no. 56 (November 2013): 1–6.

Aoki Shigeru. "Yanase Masamu Nenpu III Hijikata Teiichi No Yakusho." *Isshun*, no. 61 (March 2015): 1–6.

Arisawa Hiromi. "Arisawa Hiromi Bunko no Kaimakushiki ni Yosete." In *Rekishi no naka ni ikiru*, vol. 2 of Arisawa Hiromi, *Arisawa Hiromi no Shōwa shi*. Tokyo: Arisawa Hiromi no Shōwashi Hensen Iinkai, 284–287.

Arisawa Hiromi. "Kono goro omou koto." In *Rekishi no naka ni ikiru* (A life within history), vol. 2 of Arisawa, *Arisawa Hiromi no Shōwa shi*, 284–297. Tokyo: Arisawa Hiromi no Shōwashi Hensan Iinkai.

Arisawa Hiromi. "Nihon Sensō Keizai no Hōkai ni tsuite." In Amerika Gasshūkoku Senryaku Bakugeki Chōsadan, *Nihon Sensō Keizai no Hōkai—Senryaku Bakugeki no Nihon Sensō Keizai ni Oyobaseru Sho Kōka*, 1–3. Tokyo: Nihon Hyōronsha, 1950.

Arisawa Hiromi. *Sangyō Dōin Keikaku*. Tokyo: Kaizōsha, 1934.

Arisawa Hiromi. *Waimaaru Kyōwakoku Monogatari*. Vols. 1, 2. Tokyo: Tokyo Daigaku Shuppankai, 1978.

Arisawa Hiromi. *Waimaaru Kyōwakoku Monogatari Yowa*. Tokyo: Tokyo Daigaku Shuppankai, 1984.

Arisawa Hiromi, Miyazaki Toshiyoshi, and Wakimura Yoshitarō. "Eiga wa Tanoshi." *Fujin Kōron* (1953): 166–171.

Arisawa Hiromi and Morita Yuzō. "Intabyu." In Arisawa Hiromi and Nihon Tōkei Gakkai, *Nihon no Tōkeigaku 50 Nen*, 3–65. Tokyo: Tokyo Daigaku Shuppankai, 1983.

Arisawa Hiromi and Takahashi Masao. "21 seiki o mae ni shite." In Takahashi Masao Sensei Seibi Kinen Kankōkai, ed. *21 Seiki no Gunzō: Takahashi Masao Sensei no Shōgen*, 195–237. Tokyo: Daiichi Shorin, 1989.

Asahi Gurafu Ni Miru Shōwa No Sesō. Asahi Shinbunsha. Vol. 9. Tokyo: Asahi Shinbunsha, 1976.

Asahi Shinbunsha. "Kamera No Tabi: Kamakura to Kaigansen." In *Asahi Gurafu*. Tokyo: Asahi Shinbunsha, July 26, 1950.

Asahi Shinbunsha. "Kanagawa Kenritsu Kindai Bijutsukan." In *Nihon Yōga to Kanagawa Kenritsu Kindai Bijutsukan*, 125–135. Tokyo: Asahi Shinbunsha, 1983.

Asano, Toru and Masahiro Koike. *Kishida Ryūsei Ten: Botsugo 50-nen*. Tokyo: Asahi Shinbunsha, 1979.

Atkins, E. Taylor. *Primitive Selves: Koreana in the Japanese Colonial Gaze, 1910–1945*. Berkeley: University of California Press, 2010.

Avenell, Simon Andrew. "Japan's Long Environmental Sixties and the Birth of a Green Leviathan." *Japan Studies* 32, no. 3 (December 2012): 423–444.

Avenell, Simon Andrew. *Making Japanese Citizens: Civil Society and the Mythology of the Shimin in Postwar Japan*. Berkeley: University of California Press, 2010.

Awaki Kōjirō. "Teatoru-Kukura Sono Hoka." In Hijikata Teiichi Tsuitō Kankōkai, *Hijikata Teiichi Tsuisō*, 44–46. Tokyo: Heibonsha Kyōiku Sangyō Sentaa, 1981.

Baelz, Erwin, *Awakening Japan: The Diary of a German Doctor: Erwin Baelz*. Edited by Toku Baelz. New York: The Viking Press, 1931.

Barclay, Paul. "Peddling Postcards and Selling Empire: Image-Making in Taiwan under Japanese Colonial Rule." *Japanese Studies* 30, no. 1 (May 2010): 81–110.

Barshay, Andrew. *The Gods Left First: The Captivity and Repatriation of Japanese POWs in Northeast Asia, 1945–1956*. Berkeley: University of California Press, 2013.

Barshay, Andrew. *The Social Sciences in Modern Japan: The Marxist and Modernist Traditions*. Berkeley: University of California Press, 2004.

Baseel, Casey. "Kamakura Library Offers Itself as Refuge for Emotionally Troubled Youths." *RocketNews24, Huffington News Japan*, August 28, 2015. http://en.rocketnews24.com/2015/08/28/japanese-library-offers-itself-and-its-manga-collection-as-refuge-for-emotionally-troubled-youths/.

Bennett, Tony. *The Birth of the Museum: History, Theory, Politics*. Culture: Policies and Politics. London; New York: Routledge, 1995.

Bourdaghs, Michael. *The Dawn That Never Comes*. New York: Columbia University Press, 2010.

Bourdieu, Pierre. *Distinction: A Social Critique of the Judgement of Taste*. Trans. Richard Nice. Cambridge, MA: Harvard University Press, 1984.

Breen, John and Mark Teeuwen. *A New History of Shintō*. Chichester: Wiley-Blackwell, 2010.

Brodey, Inger Sigrun and Sammy I. Tsunematsu. *Rediscovering Natsume Sōseki: Celebrating the Centenary of Sōseki's Arrival in England 1900–1902*. Folkestone: Global Oriental, 2000.

Brook, Timothy. "Collaboration in War and Memory in East Asia: A Symposium." *Asia-Pacific Journal-Japan Focus* 6, no. 7 (July 2, 2008). http://apjjf.org/-Timothy-Brook/2802/article.html

Brownlee, W. Elliot, Eisaku Ide, and Yasunori Fukagai, eds. *The Political Economy of Transnational Tax Reform: The Shoup Mission to Japan in Historical Context.* Cambridge: Cambridge University Press, 2013.

Brumann, Christoph and Rupert Cox. *Making Japanese Heritage.* Routledge, 2010.

Carlile, Lonny E. *Divisions of Labor: Globality, Ideology, and War in the Shaping of the Japanese Labor Movement.* Honolulu, University of Hawai'i Press, 2005.

Chita Kenzō. "Hijikata Sensei o Shinobu." In Hijikata Teiichi Tsuitō Kankōkai, *Hijikata Teiichi Tsuisō,* 68–69. Tokyo: Heibonsha Kyōiku Sangyō Sentaa, 1981.

Clinton, Maggie. *Revolutionary Nativism: Fascism and Culture in China, 1925–1937.* Durham and London: Duke University Press, 2017.

Cohen, Warren I. *East Asian Art and American Culture: A Study in International Relations.* New York: Columbia University Press, 1992.

Conant, Ellen P. "Introduction: A Historiographical Overview." In Ellen P. Conant, ed., *Challenging Past and Present: The Metamorphosis of Nineteenth-Century Japanese Art,* 1–30. Honolulu: University of Hawai'i Press, 2003.

Culver, Annika. *Glorify the Empire: Japanese Avant-Garde Propaganda in Manchukuo.* Vancouver: University of British Columbia Press, 2013.

Dickinson, Frederick R. *World War I and the Triumph of a New Japan, 1919–1930.* Cambridge: Cambridge University Press, 2013.

Doak, Kevin. "Under the Banner of the New Science: History, Science, and the Problem of Particularity in Early Twentieth-Century Japan." *Philosophy East and West* 42, no. 2 (April 1998): 232–256.

Dodd, Stephen. *Writing Home: Representations of the Native Place in Modern Japanese Literature.* Harvard East Asian Monographs 240. Cambridge, MA: Harvard University Asia Center, Distributed by Harvard University Press, 2004.

Dower, John W. *Embracing Defeat: Japan in the Wake of World War II.* New York: W.W. Norton, 1999.

Dower, John W. "Japan's Beautiful Modern Wars." In John W. Dower, *Ways of Forgetting, Ways of Remembering: Japan in the Modern World.* New York: The New Press, 2012.

Dower, John W. "Yoshida in the Scales of History." In *Japan in War and Peace.* New York: The New Press, 1993.

Duara, Prasenjit. "Local Worlds: The Poetics and Politics of the Native Place in Modern China." *South Atlantic Quarterly* 99, no. 1 (Winter 2000): 13–45.

Duara, Prasenjit. *Rescuing History from the Nation: Questioning Narratives of Modern China.* Chicago, IL: University of Chicago Press, 1997.

Emmerich, Michael. *The Tale of Genji: Translation, Canonization, and World Literature.* New York, NY: Columbia University Press, 2013.

Enders, Siegfried R. C. T. and Niels Gutschow, eds. *Hozon: Architectural and Urban Conservation in Japan.* Stuttgart, London: Edition Axel Menges, 1998.

Etō Jun. *Tozasareta Gengo Akima—Senryōgun No Kenetsu to Sengo Nihon.* Bungei Shunjūsha, 1989.

Faison, Elyssa. *Managing Women, Disciplining Labor in Modern Japan.* Berkeley: University of California Press, 2007.

Florida, Richard. *Rise of the Creative Class and How It's Transforming Work, Leisure, and Everyday Life*. New York: Basic Books, 2002.

Frühstück, Sabine. *Colonizing Sex: Sexology and Social Control in Modern Japan*. Berkeley: University of California Press, 2003.

Fu, Poshek. *Between Shanghai and Hong Kong*. Stanford, CA: Stanford University Press, 2003.

Fujita Sada, "Hijikata Teiichi-kun to Senji." In Hijikata Teiichi Tsuitō Kankōkai, ed., *Hijikata Teiichi Tsuisō*, 84–86. Tokyo: Heibonsha Kyōiku Sangyō Sentaa, 1981.

Fukuda Kazusuke. "'Kurama Tenjin to Hitoraa-Yuugendo." *Shūkan Shinchō* (August 24, 2006): 140–141.

Fukushima Masao. *Kaisō no Tokyo Teidai Setsurumento*. Tokyo: Nihon Hyōronsha, 1984.

Fukushima Masao and Kawashima Takeyoshi, eds. *Hozumi Suehirō Sensei to Setsurumento*. Tokyo: Tokyo Daigaku Setsurumento hōritsu sōdanbu, 1963.

Furukawa Takumi. *Season of the Sun (Taiyō no Kisetsu)*. Nikkatsu, 1956.

Garon, Sheldon. *Molding Japanese Minds: The State in Everyday Life*. Princeton, NJ: Princeton University Press, 1997.

Germer, Andrea. "Visual Propaganda in Wartime East Asia—The Case of Natori Yōnosuke." *The Asia-Pacific Journal* 20, no. 3 (2011). http://apjjf.org/2011/9/20/Andrea-Germer/3530/article.html

Gordon, Andrew. *Labor and Imperial Democracy in Prewar Japan*. Berkeley: University of California Press, 1991.

Guichard-Anguis, Sylvie and Okpyo Moon. "Introduction." In Sylvie Guichard-Anguis and Okpyo Moon, eds. *Japan Tourism Travel and Culture*. London; New York: Routledge, 2009.

Hall, Robert King. *Education for a New Japan*. New Haven, CT: Yale University Press, 1949.

Hama Masanari. "Ōuchi Sensei to Shinshū," in Ōuchi Hyōe Sensei Kiju Kinen Zuisō Shūshutsuban Sewaijini Daihyō and Arisawa Hiromi, *Sanrokushū*, 208–214. Privately published, 1965.

Hara Minoru. "Kamakura Mikkakai No Ugoki." *Kamakura Shimin* 1, no. 2 (February 1960): 17.

Hara Minoru. "Kamakura Mikkakai to wa." *Kamakura Shimin* 1, no. 4 (April 1960): 17.

Hara Minoru. *Rekishiteki Fūdo no Hozon: 'Kamakura shimin' no hibi*. Odawara: Akansasu Kenchiku Kobō, 1989.

Hara Minoru. "Shimin Rengō Hayari ni Suite." *Kamakura Shimin* 14, no. 3 (March 1974): 1.

Harootunian, Harry. "Time, Everydayness and the Specter of Fascism." In Christopher Goto-Jones, ed., *Re-politicizing the Kyoto School as Philosophy*, 96–112. London: Routledge, 2008.

Hashimoto, Akiko. *The Long Defeat: Cultural Trauma, Memory, and Identity in Japan*. Oxford: Oxford University Press, 2015.

Hashizume Yukiome. "Kaihō Daiji No Nazo." *Mikkakai Kaihō*, December 1992, 23.

Hashizume Yukiome, ed. "Kamakura Mikkakai no Gojūnen: Kamakura Mikkakai Kaihō to Sono Jidai: Sokugō 50 Shūnen kinen (1)," 2001, manuscript deposited at the Kamakura Central Public Library.

Hashizume Yukiome. "Kamakura Mikkakai o Hajimatta Jidai to Hitobito." In Hashizume Yukiome, ed., *Kamakura Mikkakai Rokujū Shūnen Kinenki*, 62. Kamakura: Kamakura Mikkakai, 2010.

Hashizume Yukiome, ed. *Kamakura Mikkakai Rokujū Shūnen Kinenki*. Kamakura: Kamakura Mikkakai, 2010.

"Hashizume Yukiome." http://www.kcn-net.org/my_kamakura/my_kama40/mykama_40.html (accessed August 17, 2015).

Hatenaka Shigeo. "Bringing the Liberals to Heel." In Haruko Taya Cook and Theodore Cook, eds., *Japan at War*, 64–68. New York: The New Press, 1992.

Hatta Motō. "Masaki Chifuyu no Koto—kōyū 50 nen." In Masaki Chifuyu, ed., *Zuihitsu Kamakura Shichō*, 187–189. Tokyo: Chūō Kōronsha, 1983.

Hattori Shisō. "Kindai Nihon No Naritachi." In *Meiji Isshin No Hanashi, Kindai Nihon No Naritachi*. Tokyo: Aoki Shoten, 1990 (1948).

Havel, Vaclav. "New Year's Address to the Nation," speech, Czechoslovakia, January 1, 1990, Czech Republic Presidential Website Speeches. http://old.hrad.cz/president/Havel/speeches/index_uk.html

Havens, Thomas R. H. *Parkscapes: Green Spaces in Modern Japan*. Honolulu: University of Hawai'i Press, 2011.

Hayes, Peter. *Why? Explaining the Holocaust*. New York: W.W. Norton, 2016.

Hein, Carola. "Machi: Neighborhood and Small Town. The Foundation for Urban Transformation in Japan." *Journal of Urban History* 35, no. 1 (November 2008): 75–107.

Hein, Laura. "The Art of Bourgeois Culture in Kamakura." In Christopher Gerteis and Timothy George, eds., *Japan from 1945: From Postwar to Post-Bubble*. London: Continuum Books, 2013.

Hein, Laura. "Modern Art Patronage and Democratic Citizenship in Japan." *Journal of Asian Studies* 69, no. 3 (August 2010): 821–841.

Hein, Laura. *Reasonable Men, Powerful Words: Political Culture and Expertise in Twentieth-Century Japan*. Berkeley: University of California Press, 2004.

Hein, Laura. "Reckoning with War in the Museum: Hijikata Teiichi at the Kamakura Museum of Modern Art." *Critical Asian Studies* 43, no. 1 (March 2011): 93–110.

Hein, Laura. "Takahashi Masao: Flexible Marxist." In Anne Walthall, ed., *The Human Tradition in Japan*, 175–194. Wilmington, DE: Scholarly Resources Press, 2001.

Henry, Todd. *Assimilating Seoul: Japanese Rule and the Politics of Public Space in Colonial Korea, 1910–1945*. Berkeley: University of California Press, 2014.

Herf, Jeffrey. *Reactionary Modernism: Technology, Culture, and Politics in Weimar and the Third Reich*. Cambridge: Cambridge University Press, 1984.

Hijikata Teiichi. "Amusuterudamu No Kindai Bijutsukan to Gendai Oranda Bijutsu." *Mizue*, no. 567 (November 1952): 50–55.

Hijikata Teiichi. "Atogaki." In *Hijikata Teiichi Chosakushū*, 7: 429–436. Tokyo: Heibonsha, 1976.

Hijikata Teiichi. "Chūgoku No Kikoku." *Hijikata Teiichi Chosakushū* 11 (1977): 373–392.

Hijikata Teiichi. *Gendai Bijutsu: Kindai Bijutsu to Rearizumu*. Tokyo: Azuma Shobō, 1948.

Hijikata Teiichi. "Ishoku Bunka to Shite no Yōga: 'Pari no Shutten' Ron no Konkyo". In Hijikata Teiichi, ed., *Hijikata Teiichi: Bijutsu Hihyō, 1946-1980*, 26–31. Tokyo: Keibunsha, 1992 [1947].

Hijikata Teiichi. "Kakurete Iru Meisaku." *Asahi Jyaanaru* 6 (1966): 26–27.

Hijikata Teiichi. "Kanagawa Kenritsu Bijutsukan." *Atorie* 303 (February 1952).

Hijikata Teiichi. "Kindai Bijutsukan Sōseiki." *Geijutsu Shinchō* 2, no. 7 (July 1951): 56–69.

Hijikata Teiichi. *Kuree*. Tokyo: Misuzu Shobō, 1955.

Hijikata Teiichi. "Maegaki." In Kanagawaken Bijutsu—Bakumatsu Meiji Shoki, ed., *Kanagawa ken Bijutsu Fūdōki*, ix–xiv. Kamakura: Kanagawa Kenritsu Kindai Bijutsukan, 1970.

Hijikata Teiichi. *Mekishiko Kaiga*. Tokyo: Misuzu, 1955.

Hijikata Teiichi. "Nittenhyō—Kore wa Hitotsu no Jōzetsu Saidan." *Bijutsu*, April 1946.

Hijikata Teiichi. *Takahashi Yūichi Gashū*. Tokyo: Kōdansha, 1972.

Hijikata Teiichi. "'Warera no Wai-n' Ten no Koto." *Kamakura Shimin* 1, no. 4 (April 1960): 10–11.

Hijikata Teiichi Tsuitō Kankōkai. *Hijikata Teiichi Tsuisō*. Tokyo: Heibonsha Kyōiku Sangyō Sentaa, 1981.

Hiraiwa Gaishi. "Rekishi ni Manabu Kenten." In Arisawa Hiromi Sensei no Shōwashi Henshū Iinkai Sewanin, ed., *Kaisō*, vol. 3 of *Arisawa Hiromi no Shōwa shi*, 103–105, Tokyo: Tokyo Daigaku Shuppankai, 1989.

Hirase Reita. "War and Bronze Sculpture." In Asato Ikeda, Aya Louisa McDonald, and Ming Tiampo, eds., *Art and War in Japan and Its Empire, 1931–1960*, 229–240. Leiden: Brill, 2013.

Hirata Emi and Kamakura-shi Kyōiku Iinkai. *Kamakura Kindaishi Shiryō Daijūnishū: Seishun Kamakura Akademia*. Kamakura: Kamakurashi Chūō Toshokan, 1997.

Hirayama Ikuo. "Kindai Nihonga No 150 Nenten, 'Minzokuteki Kosei to Dentō.'" In *Mizue*, 1967.

Hirosawa Ei. *Waga Seishun No Kamakura Akademia*. Tokyo: Iwanami Shoten, 1996.

Hirsch, Marianne. *Family Frames: Photography, Narrative, and Post-memory*. Cambridge, MA: Harvard University Press, 1997.

Hobsbawn, Eric and Terence Ranger, eds. *The Invention of Tradition*. Cambridge: Cambridge University Press, 1983.

Hockney, Allen. "Felix Beato's Japan: An Album by the Pioneer Photographer in Yokohama 'Places.'" *Visualizing Cultures*. http://ocw.mit.edu/ans7870/21f/21f.027/ beato_places/fb1_visnav01.html (accessed January 29, 2016).

Hofmann, Reto. *The Fascist Effect: Japan and Italy, 1915–1952*. Ithaca, NY; and London: Cornell University Press, 2015.

Honda Katsuichi. *The Nanjing Massacre: A Japanese Journalist Confronts Japan's National Shame*. Armonk, NY: M.E. Sharpe, 1999.

Hornle, Edwin. *Puroretaria Kyōiku No Konpon Mondai*. Translated by Yai Sai'ichi [Hijikata Teiichi]. Tokyo: Sekaisha, 1930.

Hughes, David W. *Traditional Folk Song in Modern Japan: Sources, Sentiment and Society*. Folkestone, UK: Global Oriental, 2008.

Hunter, Janet. "Earthquakes in Japan," *Modern Asian Studies* 50, no. 1 (January 2016): 415–435.

Hutchinson, Rachel. "Introduction: Negotiating Censorship in Modern Japan." In Rachel Hutchinson, ed., *Negotiating Censorship in Modern Japan*, 1–12. London: Routledge, 2013.

Ichinohe Yoshiyuki. "Masu Rao-tachi no michinori." In Kaneko Tsutomu, ed., *Kamakura Mikkakai 60 Shūnen Kinenshi*, 12–23. Kamakura Mikkakai, 2010.

Ienaga Saburō. *Japan's Past, Japan's Future: One Historian's Odyssey*. Translated by Richard H. Minear. Lanham, MD: Rowman & Littlefield, 2001.

Ienaga Saburō. *The Pacific War, 1931–1945: A Critical Perspective on Japan's Role in World War II*. New York: Pantheon Books, 1978.

Igarashi, Takeshi. "Peace-Making and Party Politics: The Formation of the Domestic Foreign-Policy System in Postwar Japan." *Journal of Japanese Studies* 11, no. 2 (1985): 323–356.

Ikeda Katsumi. "Kindai Bijutsukan Ni Tsuite." *Mizue*, no. 566 (October 1952).

Ikegami, Eiko. *Bonds of Civility: Aesthetic Networks and Political Origins of Japanese Culture*. Cambridge: Cambridge University Press, 2005.

Inoue Fusao. "Kamakura ni Kansuru Chihō Shiteki Kenkyū no Dōko." *Kamakura Shimin* 1, no. 2 (February 1960): 15–16.

Inoue, Kota. "Uneven Space of Everyday Modernity: The Colonial Logic of the Suburb in Tanizaki Jun'ichiro's *A Fool's Love*." *Japan Forum* 27, no. 2 (June 2015): 189–212.

Isaki Masakaki. "Hitokoto-Omoidasu koto nado." In Kamakura Kenritsu Kindai Bijutsukan, *Chiisa na Hako: Kamakura Kindai Bijutsukan no 50 Nen, 1951–2000*, 81–84, 100. Tokyo: Kyūryūdō, 2001.

Ishihara Shintarō. *The Japan that Can Say No: Why Japan Will Be First among Equals*. New York: Simon & Schuster, 1991.

Ishihara Shintarō. *Season of Violence: The Punishment Room, the Yacht and the Boy*. Transl. John G. Mills, Toshie Takahama, and Ken Tremayne. Rutland, VT: Charles E. Tuttle Co, 1966.

Iwakura Hiroshi. *Aru Senjika no Teikō-Tetsugakusha Tosaka Jun to "Yuiken" no Nakamatachi*. Tokyo: Kadensha, 2015.

Iwata, Oh and Takashi Oguchi. "Factors Affecting Late Twentieth Century Land Use Patterns in Kamakura City, Japan." *Geographical Research* 47, no. 2 (June 2009): 175–191.

Japan Travel Bureau. *Pocket Guide to Japan*. Tokyo: Japan Travel Bureau, 1953.

Johnson, Chalmers A. *Blowback: The Costs and Consequences of American Empire*. New York: Metropolitan Books, 2000.

Johnson, Chalmers A. *MITI and the Japanese Miracle: The Growth of Industrial Policy*. Stanford, CA: Stanford University Press, 1982.

Johnson, Chalmers A. *The Sorrows of Empire: Militarism, Secrecy, and the End of the Republic*. New York: Metropolitan Books, 2004.

Judt, Tony. *Postwar: A History of Europe since 1945*. New York: Penguin, 2005.

Kadota, Isao. "Kamakura Zakkan." In Asahi Shinbunsha, ed., *Kamakura Shito Sanpo*. Tokyo: Asahi Shinbunsha, 1966.

Kage, Rieko. *Civic Engagement in Postwar Japan: The Revival of a Defeated Society*. Cambridge: Cambridge University Press, 2010.

Kamakura, photos by Nagano Shigeichi. Tokyo: Iwanami Shashin Bunkō, 1950.

Kamakura Mikkakai. "Mikkakai to Wa." *Kamakura Shimin* 1, no. 1 (January 1960): 3.

Kamakura Mikkakai. "Shisei memo." *Kamakura Shimin*, 1, no. 8 (August 1960): 14–15.

Kamakura Mikkakai kōhōbu. "Zeikin no hanbun ijō o kū—Kamakura shi jinkenki no Jittai." *Kamakura Shimin* 1, no. 9 (September 1960): 14.

Kamakura-shi Shishi Hensan Iinkai. *Kamakura Shishi–Kindai Tsūshi*, 7 vols. Vol. 7. Tokyo: Yoshikawa Kōbunkan, 1994.

Kami Shōichirō and Ōmori Toshio. *Tokyo Teikoku daigaku setsurumento jūninenshi*. Tokyo: Kyūzansha, 1998.

Kamiya Michinori. *Fukaku Aruku—Kamakura Shiseki Sansaku*. Vols. 1 & 2. Kamakura: Kamakura Shunshūsha, 2008.

Kanagawaken Bijutsu—Bakumatsu Meiji Shoki hen. *Kanagawaken Bijutsu—Bakumatsu Meiji Shoki*. Kamakura: Kanagawa Kenritsu Kindai Bijutsukan, 1970.

Kanagawa Ken Kōgai Taisaku Jimukyoku, ed. *Kanagawa no Kōgai: Genjō to Taisaku no Aramashi*. Yokohama: Kanagawa Ken Kōgai Taisaku Jimukyoku, 1971.

Kanagawa Kenritsu Kindai Bijutsukan/The Museum of Modern Art, Kamakura & Hayama. *Sensō/Bijutsu: 1940–1950: Modanisumu to Rensa to Henyō*. Kamakura: Kanagawa Kenritsu Kindai Bijitsukan, 2013.

Kaneko, Maki. *Mirroring the Japanese Empire: The Male Figure in Yōga Painting, 1930–1950*. Japanese Visual Culture, volume 14. Leiden; Boston, MA: Brill, 2015.

Kaneko, Maki. "New Art Collectives in the Service of the War: The Formation of Art Organizations During the Asia-Pacific War." *positions: east asia cultures critique* 21, no. 2 (Spring 2013): 309–350.

Kariya, Takehiko. *Education Reform and Social Class in Japan: The Emerging Incentive Divide*. Routledge/University of Tokyo Series, 3. Translated and edited by Michael Burtscher. London and New York: Routledge, 2013.

Karlin, Jason G. *Gender and Nation in Meiji Japan: Modernity, Loss, and the Doing of History*. Honolulu: University of Hawai'i Press, 2014.

Katagi Atsushi, Fujitani Yōetsu, and Kadono Yukihiro, eds. *Kindai Nihon No Kōgai Jūtakuchi*. Tokyo: Kajima Shuppankai, 2006.

Katō Atsuko. "Shuppan bunka to wakamono." In Shōnan no Tanjō Kenkyūkai, ed. *Shōnan no Tanjō*, 222–239. Fujisawa: Fujisawa Kyōiku Kenkyūkai, 2005.

Katō, Osamu. *Koto Kamakura Annai*. Tokyo: Yōsensha, 2002.

Katō, Shūichi. *A Sheep's Song: A Writer's Reminiscences of Japan and the World*. Berkeley: University of California Press, 1999.

Katō, Tetsurō. *Waimaaruki Berurin No Nihonjin: Yōkō Chishikijin No Hantei Nettowaaku*. Tokyo: Iwanami, 2008.

Kawashima, Ken C., Fabian Schafer, and Robert Stolz, eds. *Tosaka Jun: A Critical Reader*. Honolulu: University of Hawai'i Press, 2013.

Keene, Donald. *So Lovely a Country Will Never Perish*. New York: Columbia University Press, 2010.

"'Kenshō-Sensō Sekinin' Sekinin to wa." *Yomiuri Shinbun*, September 29, 2005.

Kimura Eiichi. "Kokuritsu Toshokanron." In Ōuchi Hyōe Sensei Kiju Kinen Zuisō Shūshutsuban Sewaijini Daihyō and Arisawa Hiromi, ed., *Sanrokushū*, 347–358. Privately Published, 1965.

Kimura Hikosaburō. "Danjurō-Haruo San." In *Kamakura Kiokuchō*. Kamakura: Kamakura Kyōdōshi, 1986.

Kimura Hikosaburō. *Hase Kannon Yukari no Bungakusha*. Kamakura: Hasedera, 1956.

Kimura Hikosaburō. *Me de Miru Kamakura-Zushi no 100 Nen*. Shizuoka: Furusato Shuppansha, 1992.

Kingston, Jeff, ed. *Press Freedom in Contemporary Japan*. London: Taylor and Francis, 2017.

Kitada Hirōyuki. "Postwar Reconstruction of Statistical System in Japan." *Forty-Year History of the Statistics Council* (1995): 67–119. Revised 2002 version posted at http://www.soumu.go.jp/main_content/000327474.pdf (accessed August 17, 2015).

Kleeman, Faye Yuan. *Under an Imperial Sun: Japanese Colonial Literature of Taiwan and the South*. Honolulu: University of Hawai'i Press, 2003.

Kobayashi, Victor N. *John Dewey in Japanese Educational Thought*. Ann Arbor, MI: The University of Michigan School of Education, 1964.

Koikari, Mire. *Pedagogy of Democracy: Feminism and the Cold War in the U.S. Occupation of Japan*. Philadelphia, PA: Temple University Press, 2008.

Koizumi Shinzō and Tsuru Shigeto. "The Koizumi-Tsuru Debate on Peace." *Journal of Social and Political Ideas in Japan* 1, no. 1 (April 1963): 20–24.

Kokaze Hidemasa. "Shōnan No Tanjō." In Shōnan no Tanjō Kenkyūkai, ed., *Shōnan No Tanjō*, 86–110. Fujisawa: Fujisawa Kyōiku Kenkyūkai, 2005.

Kokaze Hidemasa. "Yokohama Kyoryūchi to Enoshima." In Shōnan no Tanjō Kenkyūkai, ed., *Shōnan No Tanjō*, 6–26. Fujisawa: Fujisawa Kyōiku Kenkyūkai, 2005.

Kokita, Kiyohito. "Majority of Tokyo Urbanites Crave Escape to Coastal Kanagawa Area." *Asahi Shinbun*, January 9, 2016.

Kon Hidemi. "Hihyōka Hijikata Teiichi No Tōjo." In Kon Hidemi, Kagesato Tetsurō and Sakai Tadayasu, eds., *Hijikata Teiichi: Bijutsu Hihyō, 1946–1980*, 2–9. Tokyo: Keibunsha, 1992.

Kosai Yoshishige. "Haisen no Hi." In Murayama Tomoyoshi, ed., *Hachi Jūgo Haisen Zengo*, 95–112, 290–293, 279–289. Kyoto: Sekibunsha, 1975.

Koschmann, J. Victor. *Revolution and Subjectivity in Postwar Japan*. Chicago, IL: University of Chicago Press, 1996.

Kramer, Hans Martin. "The Prewar Roots of 'Equality of Opportunity': Japanese Educational Ideals in the Twentieth Century." *Monumenta Nipponica* 61, no. 4 (Winter 2006): 521–549.

Kubota Jun. *Kamakura Shimin Akademia: Mō Hitotsu No Seishun Gakushū.* Tokyo: Gendai Keikakushitsu, 1991.

Kume Masao. *Aozora Shōnen.* Tokyo: Shōnan Shobō, 1948.

Kume Masao. "Tiger." Translation in Donald Keene, ed., *Modern Japanese Literature,* 288–299. New York: Grove Press, 1956.

Kusumoto, Katsuji. *Kamakura Naruhodo Jiten.* Tokyo: Jitsugyō no Nihonsha, 2002.

Lucken, Michael. *Imitation and Creativity in Japanese Arts from Kishida Ryūsei to Miyazaki Hayao.* Translated by Francesca Simkin. New York: Columbia University Press, 2016.

Mack, Edward. *Manufacturing Modern Japanese Literature: Publishing, Prizes, and the Ascription of Literary Value.* Durham: Duke University Press, 2010.

Maekawa Kiyoharu. *Kamakura Akademia: Saigusa Hiroto to Wakakikamometachi.* Tokyo: Simul Shuppankai, 1994.

Maekawa Kiyoharu. *Saigusa Hiroto to Kamakura Akademia: Gakumon to Kyōiku No Risō o Motomete.* Tokyo: Chūō Kōronsha, 1966.

Mann, Michael. *Fascists.* Cambridge: Cambridge University Press, 2004.

Mark, Ethan. "The People in the War; Translator's Introduction." In Yoshimi Yoshiaki, ed., *Grass Roots Fascism.* New York: Columbia University Press, 2015.

Marshall, Byron K. *Academic Freedom and the Japanese Imperial University, 1868–1939.* Berkeley: University of California Press, 1992.

Martin, Charles E. "Report of the United States Cultural Science Mission to Japan," to Supreme Commander for the Allied Powers: Civil Information and Education Section. Published by University of Washington, Institute of International Affairs. January 1949.

Maruyama, Masao. "Author's Introduction to the English Edition." In Ivan Morris, ed., *Thought and Behavior in Modern Japanese Politics,* xii. Oxford: Oxford University Press, 1963.

Masaki Chifuyu. "Honsho no yakushutsu ni tsuite." In Amerika Gasshūkoku Senryaku Bakugeki Chōsadan, *Nihon Sensō Keizai no Hōkai—Senryaku Bakugeki no Nihon Sensō Keizai ni Oyobaseru Sho Kōka,* 1–5. Tokyo: Nihon Hyōronsha, 1950.

Masaki Chifuyu. *Masaki Chifuyu Nikki.* Tanabe Kōtarō and Miyazaki Masayasu, eds. Tokyo: Chiiki Kenkyūkai, 2003.

Masaki Chifuyu. *Zuihitsu Kamakura Shichō.* Tokyo: Chūō Kōronsha, 1983.

Masaki Harue. "Sazanbara No Saku Koro: Masaki Haruesan Ni Kiku Chifuyu to Seishun." Manuscript in National Diet Library,1998.

Mashita Shin'ichi. "Ichi Tetsugakusha No Kaisō." In Murayama Tomoyoshi, ed., *Hachi Jūgo Haisen Zengo.* Kyoto: Sekibunsha, 1975.

Masuda Hajimu. *Cold War Crucible: The Korean Conflict and the Postwar World.* Cambridge, MA: Harvard University Press, 2015.

 Selected Bibliography

Masuda Hajimu. "Fear of World War III: Social Politics of Re-armament and Peace Movements in Japan During the Korean War, 1950–53," *Journal of Contemporary History* 47, no. 3 (July 2012): 551–571.

Masumi Junnosuke. *Contemporary Politics in Japan*. Translated by Lonnie E. Carlile. Berkeley: University of California Press, 1995.

Mazower, Mark. *Dark Continent: Europe's Twentieth Century*. New York: Vintage Books, 1998.

McClelland, Mark. *Love, Sex, and Democracy in Japan during the American Occupation*. New York City and Basingstoke: Palgrave Macmillan, 2012.

McCormack, Gavin. "'All Japan' versus 'All Okinawa'–Abe Shinzo's Military Firstism." *The Asia-Pacific Journal* 13, no. 10 (March 16, 2015). http://apjjf.org/2015/13/10/Gavan-McCormack/4299.html

McCormack, Gavin. "Japan's Problematic Prefecture—Okinawa and the US-Japan Relationship." *Asia Pacific Journal: Japan Focus* 14, issue 17, no. 2 (September 1, 2016). http://apjjf.org/2016/17/McCormack.html

McNeill, David and Justin McCurry. "Sink the Asahi! The 'Comfort Women' Controversy and the Neo-nationalist Attack." *The Asia-Pacific Journal* 13, Issue 5, no. 1 (February 2, 2015). http://apjjf.org/2015/13/5/Justin-McCurry/4264.html

Mehring, Franz. *Die Lessing-Legende. Resshingu Densetsu*. Translated by Hijikata Teiichi and Asō Shuei. Tokyo: Mokuseisha Shoin, 1929.

Mehring, Franz. *The Lessing Legend*. New York: Critics Group Press, 1938.

Mimura, Janis. *Planning for Empire: Reform Bureaucrats and the Japanese Wartime State*. Ithaca: Cornell University Press, 2011.

Minobe, Ryōkichi. "Watakushi no Kakushin Toseiron–Ninenme no Kadai ni Mukatte." *Sekai*, no. 272 (July 1968): 47–59.

Mitchell, Timothy. *Rule of Experts: Egypt, Techno-Politics, Modernity*. Berkeley: University of California Press, 2002.

Mitsuda Yuri. "'*Bijutsu Hihyō*' (1952–1957) Shi to Sono Jidai—'*Gendai Bijutsu*' to '*Gendai Bijutsu Hihyō*' No Seiritsu." *Fuji Xerox Art Bulletin* 2 (2006): 1–52.

Miyamoto Kenichi. "Kōgai Kenkyū Iinkai to Tsuru Shigeto Kyōju," special issue, "Tsuru Shigeto o Yomu: Sono Hito to Shisō to Miryaku," *Shisō no Kagaku*, no. 126 (March 1990): 38–39.

Mizuno, Hiromi. *Science for the Empire: Scientific Nationalism in Modern Japan*. Redwood City, CA: Stanford University Press, 2008.

Moore, Aaron Stephen. *Constructing East Asia: Technology, Ideology, and Empire in Japan's Wartime Era 1931–1945*. Stanford, CA: Stanford University Press, 2013.

Morito Tatsuo. "Education Reform and Its Problems in Postwar Japan." *International Review of Education* 1 (1955): 338–351.

Morris-Suzuki, Tessa. "Freedom of Hate Speech; Abe Shinzo and Japan's Public Sphere." *The Asia-Pacific Journal* 11, issue 8, no. 1 (February 25, 2015). http://apjjf.org/2013/11/8/Tessa-Morris-Suzuki/3902/article.html

Morton, Leith. "Self-Censorship: The Case of Wartime Japanese Poetry." In Rachel Hutchinson, ed., *Negotiating Censorship In Modern Japan*, 112–132. London: Routledge, 2013.

Mosse, George L. *Fallen Soldiers: Reshaping the Memories of the World Wars*. New York: Oxford University Press, 1990.

Mosse, George L. *The Image of Man: The Creation of Modern Masculinity*. New York: Oxford University Press, 1996.

Motomiya Ichirō. "Gōrakuchi Shōnan No Kakuritsu–Taishūka no Hinten to 'Kankō' chi." In Shōnan no Tanjō Kenkyūkai, ed. *Shōnan No Tanjō*, 176–199. Fujisawa: Fujisawa Kyōiku Kenkyūkai, 2005.

Murakami Mitsuhiko. "Fukkatsu: Kamakura Kaanibaru." *Misuzu*, no. 486 (September 2001): 89–93.

Murata Ryōsaku. "Kamakura Kindai Bijutsukan—1-nen No Seiseki." *Geijutsu Shinchō*, 4, no. 1 (January 1953): 165–167.

Murayama Tomoyoshi. 'Chōsen de No Haisen' and 'Kaisetsu: 8.15 no Ishiki.' In Murayama Tomoyoshi, ed., *Hachi Jūgo Haisen Zengo*, 95–112, 290–293. Vol. 5 of *Gendaishi no Shōgen*. Tokyo: Sekibunsha, 1975.

Murayama Tomoyoshi. *Engeki Nyūmon Tadashii Shibai No Yarikata-Mikata*. Kumiai Raiburari. Tokyo: Rōdō Kyōiku Kyōkai, 1949.

Murayama Tomoyoshi. "Georuge-Gurotsusu." *Atorie* 3, no. 1 (January 1926): 87–133.

Murayama Tomoyoshi. *Murayama Tomoyoshi: Bijutsu Hihyō to Handō*. Edited by Takizawa Kiyo'uji. Tokyo: Yumani Shobō, 2013.

Murayama Tomoyoshi. *Murayama Tomoyoshi: Gurafikku No Shigoto*. Tokyo: Hon no Izumisha, 2001.

Murayama Tomoyoshi. *Seitan 100 Nen Murayama Tomoyoshi "Shōzōga" Ten*. Tokyo: Daichi Seimei Hoken Kabushiki Kaisha, 2001.

Mutsu Ito. *Kamakura Fact & Legend*. Tokyo: Maruzen, 1918.

Nagai Ryūo. "Chō." In Sawa Jurō, ed., *Tsurezure no Kamakura, Kaitei Shinpan Kamakura Meishoki*. Kamakura: Kamakura Shunjūsha, 1976.

Nagai Tatsuo. *Shirarezaru Kamakura*. Tokyo: Yomiuri Shinbunsha, 1978.

Nagasu Kazuji. "Chōji." In Hijikata Teiichi Tsuitō Kankōkai, *Hijikata Teiichi Tsuisō*, 3–4. Tokyo: Heibonsha Kyōiku Sangyō Sentaa, 1981.

Naitō Kunio and Suzuki Shun'ichi. "Jikan Hachinen Chiji Nannen." In *Suzuki Shun'ichi Chōsakushū*, vol. 6. Tokyo: Ryōshofukyūkai, 2001 [1979], 37–58.

Nakahira Ko. *Crazed Fruit*. Released in United States: Criterion Collection: Home Vision Entertainment, DVD, 2005. (*Kurutta Kajitsu*, Nikkatsu, 1956.)

Nakamura, Masako. "'Miss Atom Bomb' Contests in Nagasaki and Nevada: The Politics of Beauty, Memory, and the Cold War." *Japan-U.S. Women's Journal* 37 (2009): 3–29.

Narumi Masayasu. "Matsushita Keiichi no 'Jijitai Kaikaku Toshi Seisakuron' no Genryū." *Jiji Ken Kanagawa Geppō*, no. 160 (August 2016): 11–19.

"National Survey of Family Income and Expenditure." Japanese Government, Ministry of Internal Affairs and Communications. Statistics Bureau, n.d. http://www.stat. go.jp/english/data/zensho/

Natsume Soseki. *Kokoro*. Translated by Edwin McClellan. South Bend, IN: Gateway editions, 1957.

Natsume Soseki. "Mangan tokoro dokoro." (1909) In Inger Sigrun Brodey and Sammy I. Tsunematsu, eds., *Rediscovering Natsume Sōseki: Celebrating the Centenary of Sōseki's Arrival in England 1900–1902*. Folkestone: Global Oriental, 2000.

Nishimura Takaaki. *Bijutsukan Sanpō in Kanagawa*. Yokohama: Kanagawa Shinbunsha, 1993.

Nozaki, Yoshiko. *War Memory, Nationalism, and Education in Post-War Japan, 1945–2007: The Japanese History Textbook Controversy and Ienaga Saburo's Court Challenges*. London: Routledge, 2008.

Obermiller, David Tobaru. "Senaga Kamejiro: Marxist, Resistance Leader, and an Overall 'A Pain in the Ass' Since 1927." Paper given at Midwest Japan Seminar, St. Xavier University, Chicago, April 8, 2017.

Ogawa, Manako. "'Hull-House' in Downtown Tokyo: The Transplantation of a Settlement House from the United States into Japan and the North American Missionary Women, 1919–1945." *Journal of World History* 15, no. 3 (2004): 359–387.

Oguma Eiji. *1968 Wakamonotachi no hanran to sono haikei*, 2 vols. Tōkyō: Shin'yōsha, 2009.

Oguma Eiji. *A Genealogy of Japanese Self-Images*. Melbourne: Trans Pacific Press, 2002.

Oguma Eiji. "Japan's 1968: A Collective Reaction to Rapid Economic Growth in an Age of Turmoil." *The Asia-Pacific Journal* 13, issue 11, no. 1 (March 23, 2015). http://apjjf. org/2015/13/11/Oguma-Eiji/4300.html

Ōhashi Ryūken. "Nihon no Tōkei Gakusha: Ōuchi Hyōe." *Nōrin Tōkei Chōsa* 13, nos. 7–9 (June–September 1963): 56–58, 42–45, 45–48.

Ōhashi Ryūken. "The Study of Statistics in Japan: Its Development, Present State and Future Task." *Kyoto University Economic Review* 29, no. 2 (1959): 40–77.

Oka Isaburō, ed. *Kishida Ryūsei Zenshū*, 10 vols. Iwanami, 1979.

Ōkochi Kikuo. "Chūgoku Kanren No Tenkan." In Kamakura Kenritsu Kindai Bijutsukan, *Chiisa na Hako: Kamakura Kindai Bijutsukan no 50 Nen, 1951–2000*, 81–84. Tokyo: Kyūryūdō, 2001.

Ōmori Yoshitarō. "Antantaru Nihon Keizai No Tenbō." *Kaizō* 19, no. 9 (September 1937): 2–19.

Omuka, Toshiharu. "Tada=Dada (Devotedly Dada) for the Stage: The Japanese Dada Movement 1920–1925." In Gerald Janecek and Stephen C. Foster, eds., *The Eastern Dada Orbit: Russia, Georgia, Ukraine, Central Europe and Japan, Crisis and the Arts: The History of Dada*, 223–310. New York and London: G.K. Hall & Co. and Prentice Hall International, 1998.

Orr, James. *The Victim as Hero: Ideologies of Peace and National Identity in Postwar Japan*. Honolulu: University of Hawai'i Press, 2001.

Osaragi Jirō. "Jo." In Uchiyama Iwatarō, ed., *Hankotsu 77 Nen*. Yokohama: Kanagawa Shinbunsha, 1968.

Osaragi Jirō, ed. *Kamakura Rekishi Sanpō*. Tokyo: Kawade Shobō Shinsha, 1961.

Osaragi Jirō. *Kikyō*. Tokyo: Shinchōsha, 1948. Translated by Brewster Horwitz as *Homecoming*. Rutland, VT: Tuttle, 1956.

Osaragi Jirō. *Ōkami Shōnen: Shin Kanazukaiban*. Tokyo: Shōnan Shobō, 1947.

Osaragi Jirō. *Osaragi Jirō Zenshū*. Vol. 3. Tokyo: Asahi Shinbunsha, 1974.

Osaragi Jirō. "Saisho No Chihō Bijutsukan." *Mainichi News*, November 21, 1951.

Osaragi Jirō. *Suishōyama No Shōnen*. Tokyo: Shōnan Shobō, 1948.

Osaragi Jirō. *Tabiji*. Kadokawa Shoten, 1954. Translated by Ivan Morris as *The Journey*. New York: Knopf, 1960.

Ōta Hisayuki. *Minobe Tosei 12-nen-Seisakushitsu no Memo*. Tokyo: Mainichi Shinbunsha, 1979.

Ōuchi Hyōe. "Nihon wa hogokoku de yoi no ka–Shūgiin Anpō Tokubetsu Iinkai Kōtokukai ni okeru ichi kokumin no uttae." May 13, 1960, speech, reprinted in Ōuchi, *Ōuchi Hyōe Chosakushū*. Vol. 7, 501–511.

Ōuchi Hyōe. "Watakushi no Shinjō," *Sekai*, no. 64 (April 1951). Reprinted in *Ōuchi Hyōe Chosakushū*, Tokyo: Iwanami Shoten, 1975, vol. 12, 3–8.

Ōuchi Hyōe, Arisawa Hiromi, Wakimura Yoshitarō, Takahashi Masao, and Minobe Ryōkichi. "20 Nen Mae." *Sekai*, no. 148 (March 1958): 114–128.

Ōuchi Hyōe and Arisawa Hiromi. Nihon Keizai wa Dō Naru ka: Zoku Nihon Infureshyon no Kenkyū. Tokyo: Ōdōsha, 1946.

Ōuchi Hyōe, Itō Takeo, and Chiiki Keizai Kenkyūjo, eds. *Nihon Sangyō Zusetsu*, vol. 9 of *Zusetsu Zenshū*. Tokyo: Iwasaki Shoten, 1956.

Ōuchi Hyōe and Naito Masaru. *Nihon Zaisei Zusetsu*. Tokyo: Iwanami Shinsho, no. 564, 1965.

Oya Ayumi. "Enoden No Kaihatsu." In Shōnan no Tanjō Kenkyūkai, eds., *Shōnan No Tanjō*, 70–85. Fujisawa: Fujisawa Kyōiku Kenkyūkai, 2005.

Ozu Yasujirō. *Tokyo Chorus*. Shōchiku Kinema, 1931. Released in Criterion Collection, 2008.

Pai, Hyung Il. *Heritage Management in Korea and Japan: The Politics of Antiquity and Identity*. Korean Studies of the Henry M. Jackson School of International Studies. Seattle, WA: University of Washington Press, 2013.

"Paris Exhibiting Nippon Ceramics." *Nippon Times*, December 18, 1950.

Peterson, Ad. *Sandberg: Designer and Director of the Stedelijk*. Rotterdam: 010 Publishers, 2004.

Pincus, Leslie. "A Salon for the Soul: Nakai Masakazu and the Hiroshima Culture Movement." *positions: east asia cultures critique* 10, no. 1 (Spring 2002): 173–194.

Polkinghorn, Frank A. "Diary and Memiors of Two Years with the Occupation in Japan." Verona, NJ, 1969. Claremont College Digital Library. http://ccdl.libraries. claremont.edu/cdm/search/collection/khp/searchterm/Polkinghorn/order/nosort

Ramus, Pierre. *Militarisms Kommunismus und Antimilitarismus*. Translated by Hijikata Teiichi. Austria: Klosterneuburg, 1921.

Repeta, Lawrence. "The Silencing of an Anti-U.S. Base Protester in Okinawa." *Japan Times*, January 4, 2017.

Richie, Donald. *Ozu*. Berkeley: University of California Press, 1974.

Roberts, Glenda. "Shifting Contours of Class and Status." In *A Companion to the Anthropology of Japan*, 2nd ed., 104–124. London: Blackwell Publishing, 2008.

Roberts, Lisa C. *From Knowledge to Narrative: Educators and the Changing Museum*. Washington, DC: Smithsonian Institution Press, 1997.

Roden, Donald. *Schooldays in Imperial Japan: A Study in the Culture of a Student Elite*. Berkeley: University of California Press, 1980.

Rogaski, Ruth. *Hygienic Modernity: Meanings of Health and Disease in Treaty-Port China*. Berkeley: University of California Press, 2004.

Rohlen, Thomas P. "Education in Japanese Society." In Daniel I. Okimoto and Thomas P. Rohlen, eds., *Inside the Japanese System: Readings on Contemporary Society and Political Economy*. Stanford, CA: Stanford University Press, 1988.

Rubin, Jay. "From Wholesomeness to Decadence: The Censorship of Literature under the Allied Occupation." *Journal of Japanese Studies* 11, no. 1 (1985): 71–103.

Ruoff, Kenneth. *Imperial Japan at Its Zenith: The Wartime Celebration of the Empire's 2,600th Anniversary*. Ithaca, NY; and London: Cornell University Press, 2010.

Saida Moriuji. *Shito Kamakura*. Kamakura: Tsurugaoka Hachimangu Shamusho, 1946.

Saigusa Hiroto. "Fūhyō Daigaku O Tsubusu." *Chūō Kōron*, no. 744 (February 1951): 141–150.

Sakai, Naoki. "Imperial Nationalism and the Comparative Perspective." *positions: east asia cultures critique* 17, no. 1 (Spring 2009): 159–205.

Sakai Tadayasu. "Kaisō No Bijutsukan Funtōki." In Kamakura Kenritsu Kindai Bijutsukan, *Chiisa na Hako: Kamakura Kindai Bijutsukan no 50 Nen, 1951–2000*. Tokyo: Kyūryūdō, 2001.

Sakai Tadayasu. *Sono Toshi mo Mata: Kamakura Kindai Bijitsukan o Meguru Hitobito*. Kamakura: Kamakura Shunjūsha, 2004.

"Sakai Tadayasu Speech at Museum." In *Bijutsukan Sanpō in Kanagawa*, 13–15. Yokohama: Kanagawa Shinbunsha, 1993.

Sakakura Junzō. "Kamakura No Gendai Bijutsukan." *Geijutsu Shinchō* 2, no. 3 (March 1951): 90–93.

Sand, Jordan. *House and Home in Modern Japan: Architecture, Domestic Space, and Bourgeois Culture, 1880–1930*. Harvard University Asian Center of Harvard University Press, 2003.

Sasaki Kōzō. "Hijikata Ikka." In Hijikata Teiichi Tsuitō Kankōkai, ed., *Hijikata Teiichi Tsuisō*, 48–49. Tokyo: Heibonsha Kyōiku Sangyō Sentaa, 1981.

Sasaki Seiichi. "Kamakura Kinbi Bijutsukan No Shuppatsu." In *Kanagawa Kenritsu Kindai Bijutsukan 30-nen No Ayumi: Shiryō-Tenrankai Sōmokuroku, 1951–1981*, 12–16. Kamakura: Kanagawa Kenritsu Kindai Bijutsukan, 1982.

Satō Kaori. "GHQ No Bijutsu Gyōsei: CIE Bijutsu Kinen Bukka Ni Yoru 'Bijutsu No Minshūka' to Yashiro Yukio." *Kindai Gasetsu* 12 (2003): 80–95.

Saunavaara, Juha. *In Search of Suitable Political Leadership: Japanese Conservatives in Occupation Plans and Policies 1942–1947*. Acta Universitatis Ouluensis. B, Humaniora 93. Oulu: University of Oulu, 2010.

Sawa Hiroshi. *Kanagawa Picturesque*. Yokohama: Tourist Section, Kanagawa Prefecture, 1953.

Sawa Jurō. *Tsurezure No Kamakura*. Kamakura: Kamakura Shunjūsha, 1976.

Sawaji, Osamu. "Carving Out a Balance in Kamakura." *Highlighing Japan*, no. 108 (April 2017): 30–31.

Sawatari, Kiyoko. "Innovational Adaptations: Contacts between Japanese and Western Artists in Yokohama, 1859–1899." In Ellen P. Conant, ed., *Challenging Past and Present: The Metamorphosis of Nineteenth-Century Japanese Art*, 83–113. Honolulu: University of Hawai'i Press, 2006.

Saxon, Antonia Brooks. "Random Notes from Shōnan: A Translation of Tokutomi Roka's 'Shonan Zappitsu.'" MA thesis, Cornell University, Ithaca NY, 1998.

Schencking, J. Charles. "The Great Kanto Earthquake and the Culture of Catastrophe and Reconstruction in 1920s Japan." *Journal of Japanese Studies* 34, no. 2 (Summer 2008): 295–331.

Scott, James C. *Seeing Like a State: How Certain Schemes to Improve the Human Condition Have Failed*. New Haven, CT: Yale University Press, 2008.

Seaton, Philip. "The Nationalist Assault on Japan's Local Peace Museums: The Conversion of Peace Osaka." *The Asia-Pacific Journal* 13, issue 30, no. 2 (July 27, 2015). http://apjjf.org/2015/13/30/Philip-Seaton/4348.html

Seaton, Philip and Takayoshi Yamamura. "Japanese Popular Culture and Contents Tourism-Introduction." *Japan Forum* 27, no. 1 (December 13, 2014): 1–11.

Shirai Eiji, ed., *Kamakura Jiten*. Tokyo: Tokyodō Shuppan, 1976.

Sherif, Ann. "The Aesthetics of Speed and the Illogicality of Politics: Ishihara Shintarō's Literary Debut." *Japan Forum* 17, no. 2 (2005): 185–211.

Sherif, Ann. "The Politics of Loss: On Etō Jun." *positions: east asia cultures critique* 10, no. 1 (Spring 2002): 111–139.

Shibata Tokue. "Yoron o Ugokashita Haigasu Kisei," part 5 of "Aru Gakusha no Tosei Taiken Ki." *Ekonomisuto*, October 21, 1980.

Shimamoto Chiyo. "Bessochi No Bunka." In *Shōnan No Tanjō*, 136–151. Fujisawa: Fujisawa Kyōiku Kenkyūkai, 2005.

Shimamoto Chiyo. "Shōnan No Bessō Chika–Kugenuma Chiku o Chūshin Ni Shite–." In Shōnan no Tanjō Kenkyūkai, ed., *Shōnan No Tanjō*, 48–69. Fujisawa: Fujisawa Kyōiku Kenkyūkai, 2005.

Shimizu, Yoshiaki. "Japan in American Museums—But Which Japan?" *Art Bulletin* 83, no. 1 (March 2001): 123–134.

Shiota Masashi and Hasegawa Masahiro, eds. *Kankōgaku*. Tokyo: Dōbunkan, 1994.

Shōnan no Tanjō Kenkyūkai. *Shōnan No Tanjō*. Fujisawa: Fujisawa Kyōiku Kenkyūkai, 2005.

Shoup, Carl. *Federal Finances in the Coming Decade: Some Cumulative Possibilities, 1941–1951*. New York: Columbia University Press, 1941.

Siegenthaler, Peter. "Architecture, Folklore Studies, and Cultural Democracy: Nagakura Saburō and Hida Minzoku-Mura." In Rupert Cox and Christoph Brumann, eds., *Making Japanese Heritage*. London: Routledge, 2010.

Siegenthaler, Peter. "Looking to the Past, Looking to the Future: The Localization of Japanese Historic Preservation, 1950–1975" (Ph.D. diss., University of Texas, Austin, 2004).

Snyder, Harold E. and Margretta S. Austin, eds. "Educational Progress in Japan and the Ryukyus; a Report of a Conference of Major American Non-Governmental Agencies." Washington, DC: American Council on Education, May 25, 1950.

Sodei, Rinjirō. *Were We the Enemy?: American Survivors of Hiroshima*. Boulder, CO: Westview Press, 1998.

Soja, Edward W. "Writing the City Spatially." *City* 7, no. 3 (November 2003): 269–280.

Sontag, Susan. "Fascinating Fascism." In *Under the Sign of Saturn*. New York: Vintage Books, 1972.

Sorensen, André. *The Making of Urban Japan: Cities and Planning from Edo to the Twenty-First Century*. The Nissan Institute/Routledge Japanese Studies Series. London: Routledge, 2003.

Staaveren, Jacob van. "The Growth of Parent-Teacher Associations in Japan (A Prefectural View)." *Peabody Journal of Education* 27, no. 3 (November 1949): 162–166.

Sugao, Tamotsu. "Conservation of Russian-born Ballerina's Memorabilia at Issue in Kamakura." *Asahi Shinbun*, May 15, 2014.

Sugita, Yoneyuki. "Universal Health Insurance: The Unfinished Reform of Japan's Healthcare System." In Mark E. Caprio and Yoneyuki Sugita, eds., *Democracy in Occupied Japan: The U.S. Occupation and Japanese Politics and Society*. London and New York: Routledge, 2007.

Sugiura Minpei. "Kuraiya no Jidai no Fureai." In Hijikata Teiichi Tsuitō Kankōkai, ed., *Hijikata Teiichi Tsuisō*, 54–55. Tokyo: Heibonsha Kyōiku Sangyō Sentaa, 1981.

Sugiura Yasuhei. *Shōnan no Gojūnen: Shōnan o Tsukiageta Senkushatachi*. Tokyo: Bara Shuppan, 1977.

Sullivan, Michael. *Art and Artists of Twentieth-Century China*. Berkeley: University of California Press, 1996.

Supreme Commander for the Allied Powers. *Senryōki Todō Fuken Gunsei Shiryō*, vol. 41. Tokyo- Kanagawa-ken (3) in National Diet Library.

Supreme Commander for the Allied Powers. Civil Information and Education Section, Education Division. *Education in the New Japan*. Vol. 1. Tokyo: Tokyo, General Headquarters, Supreme Commander for the Allied Powers, Civil Information and Education Section, Education Division, May 1948.

Suzuki Ichirō. "Kamakura Mikkakai No Gojūnen: Kamakura Mikkakai Kaihō to Sono Jidai: Sokugō 50 Shūnen Kinen (1)," 2001. Kamakura Central Public Library.

Suzuki Shun'ichi. "Minshushugi to Jihō Jiji," Discussion with Matsuyama Yukio. In *Suzuki Shun'ichi Chosakushū*, vol. 6, 107–120. Tokyo: Ryōsho Fukyūkai, 2001.

Suzuki Takashi. *Gakuen to Kankō No Kamakura*. Kamakura: Shimamura Shoten, 1955.

Takahashi Hideo. *Kamakura Bunko to Bungei Zasshi "Ningen."* Tokyo: Ōzorasha, 1993.

Takahashi Hiroto. *Sengo Kyōiku Kaikaku to Shidō Shuji Seido*. Tokyo: Kazama Shobō, 1995.

Takahashi Masao. *Happō Yabure—Watakushi No Shakaishugi*. Tokyo: TBS-Buritanika, 1980.

Takahashi Masao. *Tenkeiki no Seiji to Keizai*. Tokyo: Ōdōsha, 1947.

Takahashi Masao. *Watakushi no Zōhan*. Tokyo: Yomiuri Shinbunsha, 1970.

Takahashi Masao and Arisawa Hiromi. "21 Seiki o Mae Ni Shite." In Takahashi Masao Sensei Seibi Kinen Kankōkai, ed., *21 Seiki No Gunzō: Takahashi Masao Sensei No Shōgen*, 195–237. Tokyo: Daiichi Shorin, 1989.

Takahashi, Tetsuya. "What March 11 Means to Me: Nuclear Power and the Sacrificial System." *Asia-Pacific Journal-Japan Focus* 12, no. 19 (May 12, 2014). http://www.japanfocus.org/-Takahashi-Tetsuya/4114.

Takami Jun. *Haisen Nikki*. Tokyo: Chūō Kōronsha, 2005 [1959].

Takase Yoshio. *Kamakura Akademia Danshō: Nōzan No Daigaku*. Tokyo: Mainichi Shinbunsha, 1980.

Takayanagi Hidemaru. "Kamakura Kaanibaru." *Shōnan Bungaku* 14 (Spring 2001): 141–147.

Takeda Naoko. "Ubeshi Ni Okeru Chōkoku Setsubi Jigyō no Kaisho." *The Japanese Institute of Landscape Architecture* 65, no. 3 (2002): 259–267.

Takemae, Eiji. "C.G. Tilton and the Occupation of Japan." *Tokyo Keidai Gakkai Shi* 146 (1986): 545–580.

Takemae, Eiji. *Inside GHQ: The Allied Occupation of Japan and Its Legacy*. Translated by Robert Ricketts and Sebastian Swann. London: Continuum, 2002.

Takeuchi Yō. *Gakureki Kizoku no Eiko to Zasetsu*. Tokyo: Chūō Kōron Shinsha, 1999.

Takeuchi Yō and Inose Naoki. "Kyōyōshugi to iu 'kabe.'" *Geppō* (1999): 4 insert to Takeuchi Yō and Itō Takashi, *Nihon no Kindai*. Vol. 12, Tokyo: Chūō Kōronsha, 1999.

Takizawa Kiyouji, ed., *Murayama Tomoyoshi: Bijutsu Hihyō to Handō*. Tokyo: Yumani Shobō, 2013.

Tanabe Kotarō. "Kakushin Kanryō No Senzen to Sengo—Masaki Chifuyu Nikki Ni Miru Sengo Kaikaku." *Kinki Daigaku Tandai Ronshū* 35, no. 2 (March 2003): 43–54.

Tanabe Kotarō. "Kamakura No Midori to Masaki Chifuyu." *Nihon Rekishi*, no. 687 (August 2005): 86–88.

Tanabe Kotarō and Miyazaki Masayasu. "Ko Masaki Chifuyu-shi no Omoide o Kataru: Masaki Harue Intaabyū." In Tanabe Kōtarō and Miyazaki Masayasu, eds., *Masaki Chifuyu Nikki*. Tokyo: Chiiki Kenkyūkai, 2003.

Tanaka, Hikōjūrō. "Kamakura Arinomama." *Kamakura Shimin* 1, no. 2 (1960): 14–15.

Tang, Xiaobing. *Origins of the Chinese Avant-Garde: The Modern Woodcut Movement*. Berkeley: University of California Press, 2008.

Tange Kenzō. "Kokuritsu Kindai Bijutsu ni Tō." *Geijutsu Shinchō* 4, no. 1 (January 1953): 32–35.

Tansman, Alan. "Introduction." In Alan Tansman, ed., *The Culture of Japanese Fascism*, 1–29. Durham, NC and London: Duke University Press, 2009.

Thurston, Donald R. *Teachers and Politics in Japan*. Princeton, NJ: Princeton University Press, 1973.

Tipton, Elise. *The Japanese Police State: Tokko in Interwar Japan*. London: Bloomsbury, 2012.

Tokyo Daigaku Keizaigakubu. *Tokyo Daigaku Keizaigakubu 50-nen Shi*. Tokyo: Tokyo Daigaku Shuppankai, 1976.

Tokyo Shisei Chōsakai. *Kamakurashi No Kankō Jittai Chōsa Hōkokusho*. Tokyo: Tokyo Shisei Chōsakai, 1955.

Tsuchikane, Yasuko. "Picasso as Other—Koyama Fujio and the Polemics of Postwar Japanese Ceramics."*Review of Japanese Culture and Society* 26 (December 2014): 33–49.

Tsurisuto Gaidobukkusu Meibundō Henshūbu. *Kamakura*. Tokyo: Meibunshō, 1955.

Tsurumi, Yoshiyuki. "Beheiren," *Japan Quarterly* 16, no. 4 (October 1, 1969): 444–448.

Tsuruta Heihachirō. "Kanagawa Kenritsu Kindai Bijutsukan." In Asahi Shinbunsha, ed., *Nihon Yōga to Kanagawa Kenritsu Kindai Bijutsukan*, 125–135. Tokyo: Asahi Shinbunsha, 1983.

Tucker, David. "Learning from Dairen, Learning from Shinkyō: Japanese Colonial City Planning and Postwar Reconstruction." In Carola Hein, ed., *Rebuilding Urban Japan after 1945*, 156–187. London: Palgrave, 2003.

Uchiyama Iwatarō. *Hankotsu 77 Nen*. Yokohama: Kanagawa Shinbunsha, 1968.

Uchiyama Iwatarō, Yamamoto Shōichi, and Sawada Setsuzō. "Zadankai." *Kamakura Shimin* 1, no. 1 (January 1960): 4–6.

Uchiyama Iwatarō, Yamamoto Shōichi, and Sawada Setsuzō. "Zadankai zoku." *Kamakura Shimin* 1, no. 2 (1960): 5–6.

Ueno Junko and Masahisa Sonobe. "Urban Sustainability: A Case Study of Environmental Movements in Kamakura." In Tamagawa Hidenori, ed., *Sustainable Cities: Japanese Perspectives on Physical and Social Structures*, 205–232. Tokyo: United Nations University Press, 2006.

Volk, Alicia. "Review: Gennifer Weisenfeld, *Imaging Disaster: Tokyo and the Visual Culture of Japan's Great Earthquake of 1923*; John W. Dower et al., *The Brittle Decade: Visualizing Japan in the 1930s*; Asato Ikeda, Aya Louisa McDonald, and Ming Tiampo, *Art and War in Japan and Its Empire, 1931–1960*." *Art Bulletin* 45, no. 4 (December 2015): 457–461.

Wakimura Yoshitarō. "Kaisō no Senchū-Sengo-Sensō to Gakusha." Interview by Mitani Taichirō. *Chūō Kōron*, nos. 1332–1333 (November–December 1995): 129–209, 160–175.

Wakimura Yoshitarō. "*Sekai* No 50-nen to Watakushi-'Sekai No Ushio' Shuppatsu No Koro." *Sekai* 617 (January 1997): 121–123.

Wakimura Yoshitarō, ed., *Wakimura Yoshitarō Taidanshū: Sangyō to Bijutsu to*. Tokyo: Nihon Keieishi Kenkyūjo, 1990.

Wakimura Yoshitarō and Masaki Chifuyu. "Nihon Keizai no 45 nen no Fūsetsu: '*Ekonomisuto*' no ayunda jidai," *Ekonomisuto* 46, no. 13 (April 2, 1968): 116–124.

Wakimura Yoshitarō and Minobe Ryōkichi. "Danatsu No Arashi." In Andō Yoshiō, ed., *Shōwa Keizai Shi e no Shōgen*, 146–176. Tokyo: Tokyo Mainichi Shinbunsha, 1966.

Watanabe Nobuyuki, "Kamakura Akademia Sokuritsu 70 Shūnen." *Asahi Shinbun* Digital edition. http://www.asahi.com/area/kanagawa/articles/ MTW201605301502800001.html. May 16, 2016.

Weisenfeld, Gennifer. *MAVO: Japanese Artists and the Avant-Garde, 1905–1931*. Berkeley: University of California Press, 2002.

Welcome Society, Tokyo. *A Short Guide-book for Tourists in Japan*. Tokyo: Tokyo Printing Company, 1905.

Williams, Junko Ikezu. "Visions and Narratives: Modernism in the Prose Works of Yoshiyuki Eisuke, Murayama Tomoyoshi, Yumeno Kyūsaku, and Okamoto Kaneko" (Ph.D. diss., Ohio State University, Columbus, OH, 1998).

Winter, Jay and Emmanuel Sivan. "Setting the Framework." In Jay Winter and Emmanuel Sivan, eds., *War and Remembrance in the Twentieth Century*, 6–39. Cambridge: Cambridge University Press, 1999.

Winther-Tamaki, Bert. *Art in the Encounter of Nations: Japanese and American Artists in the Early Postwar Years*. Honolulu: University of Hawai'i Press, 2001.

Winther-Tamaki, Bert. "'The Mexico Boom' in the Japanese Art World." Paper given at *Japanese Art Since 1945: The First PONJA GenKon Symposium*, April 2005. http:// www.yale.edu/macmillan/ceas/japanartabstracts.pdf.

Witkovsky, Matthew S., Carol S. Eliel, and Karole P. B.Vail, eds. *Moholy-Nagy: Future Present*. New Haven: Yale University Press, 2016.

Yagyū Fujio. "1950 Nendai No Omoide." In *Kanagawa Kenritsu Kindai Bijutsukan 30-nen No Ayumi: Shiryō-Tenrankai Sōmokuroku, 1951–1981*, 17–20. Kamakura: Kanagawa Kenritsu Kindai Bijutsukan, 1982.

Yagyū Fujio. "Wasurenagusa." In Kamakura Kenritsu Kindai Bijutsukan, *Chiisa na Hako: Kamakura Kindai Bijutsukan no 50 Nen, 1951–2000*, 68–70. Tokyo: Kyūryūdō, 2001.

Yamanaka Shirō. "Tōkei Kondankai Izen no." In Nihon Tōkei Kenkyūjo, ed., *Nihon Tōkei Seido Saiken Shi—Tōkei Iinkai Shi*, Vols. 1–4. Tokyo: Nihon Tōkei Kenkyūjo, 1963 [1946].

Yamazaki, Masako. *Kyoto Jinbun Gakuen: Seiritsu o Meguru Senchū Sengo no Bunka Undō*. Tokyo: Kazama Shobō, 2002.

Yasuda, Saburō, Nagai Michiko, and Yamada Kimio. *Kamakura Rekishi Sansaku*. Osaka: Hoikusha, Kara Bukkusu, 1976.

Yiu, Angela. "Atarashikimura: The Intellectual and Literary Contexts of a Taisho Utopian Village." *Japan Review*, no. 20 (January 1, 2008): 203–230.

Yiu, Angela. "'Beautiful Town': The Discovery of the Suburbs and the Vision of the Garden City in Late Meiji and Taishō Literature." *Japan Forum* 18, no. 3 (December 2006): 315–338.

Yonekura Mamoru. "Tokujiku Nohahikae—Wakimura Yoshitarō." part 19 "Hasegawa Jin: Garō, Gaka, Shūshūka" no. 345, *E* (November 1992): 16–19.

Yoshida, Takashi. *From Cultures of War to Cultures of Peace: War and Peace Museums in Japan, China, and South Korea*. Portland, ME: Merwin Asia, 2014.

Yoshimi Shunya. *Posuto Sengo Shakai*. Tokyo: Iwanami, 2001.

Yoshimi, Yoshiaki. *Grass Roots Fascism*. New York: Columbia University Press, 2015.

Young, Louise. *Beyond the Metropolis: Second Cities and Modern Life in Interwar Japan*. Berkeley: University of California Press, 2013.

Young, Louise. *Japan's Total Empire, Manchuria and the Culture of Wartime Imperialism*. Berkeley: University of California Press, 1998.

Yui Daizaburō. *Mikan No Senryō Kaikaku: Amerika Chishikijin to Suterareta Nihon Minshuka Kōsō*. 2nd ed. Tokyo: Tokyo Daigaku Shuppankai, 2016.

"Zaimokuza Kaidan," *Kamakura Shimin* 1, no. 1 (January 1960): 8–9.

Studies of the Weatherhead East Asian Institute

Columbia University

Selected Titles

(Complete list at: http://weai.columbia.edu/publications/studies-weai/)

Resurrecting Nagasaki: Reconstruction and the Formation of Atomic Narratives, by Chad Diehl. Cornell University Press, 2018.

Making Time: Astronomical Time Measurement in Tokugawa Japan, by Yulia Frumer. University of Chicago Press, 2018.

Promiscuous Media: Film and Visual Culture in Imperial Japan, 1926–1945, by Hikari Hori. Cornell University Press, 2018.

The End of Japanese Cinema: Industrial Genres, National Times, and Media Ecologies, by Alexander Zahlten. Duke University Press, 2017.

The Chinese Typewriter: A History, by Thomas S. Mullaney. The MIT Press, 2017.

Forgotten Disease: Illnesses Transformed in Chinese Medicine, by Hilary A. Smith. Stanford University Press, 2017.

Aesthetic Life: Beauty and Art in Modern Japan, by Miya Mizuta Lippit. Harvard University Asia Center, 2017.

Youth for Nation: Culture and Protest in Cold War South Korea, by Charles R. Kim. University of Hawaii Press, 2017.

Socialist Cosmopolitanism: The Chinese Literary Universe, 1945–1965, by Nicolai Volland. Columbia University Press, 2017.

The Social Life of Inkstones: Artisans and Scholars in Early Qing China, by Dorothy Ko. University of Washington Press, 2017.

Darwin, Dharma, and the Divine: Evolutionary Theory and Religion in Modern Japan, by G. Clinton Godart. University of Hawaii Press, 2017.

Dictators and Their Secret Police: Coercive Institutions and State Violence, by Sheena Chestnut Greitens. Cambridge University Press, 2016.

The Cultural Revolution on Trial: Mao and the Gang of Four, by Alexander C. Cook. Cambridge University Press, 2016.

Inheritance of Loss: China, Japan, and the Political Economy of Redemption After Empire, by Yukiko Koga. University of Chicago Press, 2016.

Homecomings: The Belated Return of Japan's Lost Soldiers, by Yoshikuni Igarashi. Columbia University Press, 2016.

Samurai to Soldier: Remaking Military Service in Nineteenth-Century Japan, by D. Colin Jaundrill. Cornell University Press, 2016.

The Red Guard Generation and Political Activism in China, by Guobin Yang. Columbia University Press, 2016.

Accidental Activists: Victim Movements and Government Accountability in Japan and South Korea, by Celeste L. Arrington. Cornell University Press, 2016.

Ming China and Vietnam: Negotiating Borders in Early Modern Asia, by Kathlene Baldanza. Cambridge University Press, 2016.

Ethnic Conflict and Protest in Tibet and Xinjiang: Unrest in China's West, coedited by Ben Hillman and Gray Tuttle. Columbia University Press, 2016.

One Hundred Million Philosophers: Science of Thought and the Culture of Democracy in Postwar Japan, by Adam Bronson. University of Hawaii Press, 2016.

Conflict and Commerce in Maritime East Asia: The Zheng Family and the Shaping of the Modern World, c. 1620–1720, by Xing Hang. Cambridge University Press, 2016.

Chinese Law in Imperial Eyes: Sovereignty, Justice, and Transcultural Politics, by Li Chen. Columbia University Press, 2016.

Imperial Genus: The Formation and Limits of the Human in Modern Korea and Japan, by Travis Workman. University of California Press, 2015.

Yasukuni Shrine: History, Memory, and Japan's Unending Postwar, by Akiko Takenaka. University of Hawaii Press, 2015.

The Age of Irreverence: A New History of Laughter in China, by Christopher Rea. University of California Press, 2015.

The Knowledge of Nature and the Nature of Knowledge in Early Modern Japan, by Federico Marcon. University of Chicago Press, 2015.

The Fascist Effect: Japan and Italy, 1915–1952, by Reto Hofmann. Cornell University Press, 2015.

The International Minimum: Creativity and Contradiction in Japan's Global Engagement, 1933–1964, by Jessamyn R. Abel. University of Hawaii Press, 2015.

Empires of Coal: Fueling China's Entry into the Modern World Order, 1860–1920, by Shellen Xiao Wu. Stanford University Press, 2015.

Index

www.ingramcontent.com/pod-product-compliance
Lightning Source LLC
LaVergne TN
LVHW011250150725
816074LV00006B/62